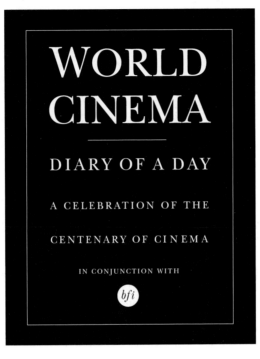

WORLD CINEMA

DIARY OF A DAY

A CELEBRATION OF THE

CENTENARY OF CINEMA

IN CONJUNCTION WITH

bfi

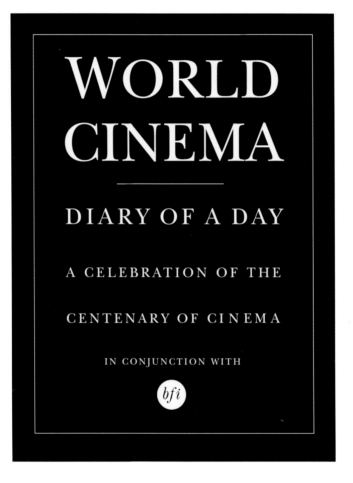

WORLD CINEMA

DIARY OF A DAY

A CELEBRATION OF THE

CENTENARY OF CINEMA

IN CONJUNCTION WITH

THE OVERLOOK PRESS

WOODSTOCK · NEW YORK

First published in the United States in 1995
by The Overlook Press
Lewis Hollow Road
Woodstock, New York 12498

Library of Congress Cataloging-in-Publication Data

World Cinema: diary of a day / edited by Peter Cowie:
1. Motion Pictures. I. Cowie, Peter.
PN1994.W668 1995 791.43–dc20 94-28116 CIP
ISBN: 0-87951-573-2
Printed in the United Kingdom
246897531

Contents

INTRODUCTION

The "centenary" of the cinema is exploding about our ears. Arguments rage over exactly when and where the first film was made, screened, or even thought of. Was it in the United States, where Muybridge photographed animals in motion, Edison invented the Kinetoscope, and his contemporaries devised the first projectors? Or was it in France, first via Étienne Jules Marey and then the Lumière brothers, whose pioneer screenings took place in Paris on December 28, 1895? Over the past century the cinema has raced through all manner of changes and technical improvements; as both art and industry, it is now practised in all parts of the world. Hollywood predominates, as it almost always has, but as a medium for personal expression film continues everywhere to attract some of the brightest minds of each new generation. So this "snapshot" of world cinema, this mosaic of activities, ideas and opinions, demonstrates the extraordinary degree of commitment that the cinema commands. Not just from the high and the mighty, the great and the good, the rich and the famous; but also from those who toil at every level to ensure that the ultimate experience of going to the movies is a rewarding one.

The British Film Institute, one of the world's major institutions for the understanding and appreciation of cinema, was naturally eager to mark the Centenary itself in a suitable and yet unconventional manner. In particular, the Institute wanted to signal the international importance of cinema. Despite being the British Film Institute, its concern remains with cinema throughout the world.

The aim of the BFI's project, One Day in the Life of World Cinema, was to emphasise that, despite the fascination and appeal of Hollywood in every country of the world, cinema takes a number of different forms, fulfils a variety of roles within different societies and has different models of its social function. We were also determined to reflect not just what happens when a film is being made (which is what we usually hear and read about), but to report on all stages of the production cycle, and what happens afterwards as well.

Film-makers all over the world were invited to write a diary about the work they were doing on one day. The day of Thursday, June 10th, 1993, was selected almost at random. We did, however, avoid the traditional climaxes of the film-making year: the Cannes Festival, the Academy Awards in Hollywood, or any big opening nights. More than a thousand individuals kept a diary for the BFI's project. Their names are listed at the end of this book, as testimony to their collective celebration of the world's most popular art. Of these, we have found space for around 420. Some entries ran (prior to abridgement) to ten closely-typed pages; others to a mere four lines. Some, like a great pass in soccer, have exactly the right weight, length, and forward drive. Some remain factual and chronological to a fault; some forget the circumstances of the day altogether and dart off into the undergrowth of personal obsession and philosophy. Some are extraordinarily candid and intimate; others use the occasion to speculate on the nature of cinema and the tensions and responsibilities it involves.

For some, the day begins in an airport, or a gym, or in a foreign land. Many rise at dawn, others work into the small hours. While most diary entries express the enthusiasm associated with teamwork in film-making, several lament the lack of an assignment, or ruminate on the gulf between the artifice of the cinema and the realities of everyday life. A majority of the correspondents, however, is united by an abiding commitment to cinema as a medium for expression, as a team effort in the face of technical and financial challenges. People somehow survive the day as such, bobbing and weaving while the phones ring, the faxes unfurl, and the weather deteriorates on some distant location.

Most of the books published for the Centenary will reflect, inevitably, on film history. It seems vital to the Institute, at a time when the cinema is under economic pressure from other media, to celebrate the strength and resilience of contemporary cinema, to show what a wealth of talent and dedication exists, and, by implication at least, to point towards the future.

This book goes behind the scenes of numerous movies that, by the time you read these lines,

will have been released. Directors, screenwriters, actors, producers, cinematographers, editors, composers, production designers, costume designers, sound engineers, makeup experts – all these may be found among the contributors. But we have made room also for diaries from those individuals who help to get a film on the screen – distributors, exhibitors, press agents, festival programmers, projectionists – as well as journalists, film students, and teachers. In short, here are the thoughts and deeds of hundreds of people who are in some way wedded to the cinema.

The framework I have devised for the book allows the reader either to dip into the diaries at random, or to track the development of the film-making process from start to finish, from the moment of conception in the mind of the screenwriter to the premiere and distribution of a picture.

The second part of World Cinema includes diaries from the people who make it all happen, from the financiers to the archivists, as well as the more contemplative responses. Certain events and occasions are viewed through the words of several diarists – the East West Producers' Conference in the Czech Republic, the funeral of Kazuko Shibata in Japan, the EAVE Conference in Denmark, the previews of *Jurassic Park* in the United States.

Personal concerns, love affairs terminated or revived, arguments with colleagues, births and deaths sprinkle these diaries too, although I have, pace the ghost of Samuel Pepys, eliminated scores of opening and closing sentences along the lines of "Awoke at 6.15 AM and fed the cat" or "Crashed out beside my long-suffering wife."

The sign [. . .] means that a passage has been omitted from the author's original diary.

We are indebted to all our contributors, whether published or unpublished. It is little short of miraculous that so many people took time off on the same day, whether in the midst of shooting or post-production, or travelling, to keep a diary and send it to us in London. We are also grateful beyond measure to those diarists who sent in photographs to accompany their text, giving the book that visual dimension so indispensable to any work about the cinema.

The names of everyone who wrote a diary for *World Cinema: Diary of a Day* are listed on pages 414-415 as testimony to their collective celebration of the world's most popular art.

On a personal level I would like to thank my colleagues at *Variety* and the *International Film Guide*, who sacrificed many hours in rounding up the diaries from their various territories; and to the industrious translators of at least twenty languages.

Perhaps the warmest applause of all should go to Tana Wollen and Janet Willis at the British Film Institute, whose diligent research and cross-checking ensured that we harvested the maximum number of diaries (and illustrations) in the minimum space of time. Their thoroughness and attention to detail are matched only by their enthusiasm and refusal to be discouraged by deadlines or missing entries!

I am grateful also to Jeremy Thomas, Chairman of the British Film Institute, who led from the front; to his predecessor Lord Attenborough, for serving as Chairman of the project; to all the Honorary Patrons who found time to contribute a diary; to Ed Buscombe, Head of Book Publishing at the BFI, whose dream has, I hope, been fulfilled; and above all to my wife, Françoise, who gave me the love, strength and peace to finish the project.

Peter Cowie, Editor

Acknowledgements

The British Film Institute is indebted to the honorary patrons of "One Day in the Life of World Cinema", Lord Attenborough, Bille August, John Boorman, Youssef Chahine, Paul Cox, David Cronenberg, Chen Kaige, Nagisa Oshima, Sembene Ousmane, Euzhan Palcy, Francesco Rosi, Martin Scorsese, Mrinal Sen, Fernando Solanas, Penelope Spheeris, István Szabó, Bertrand Tavernier, Wim Wenders.

Special thanks are due to Kathleen Luckey, Anita Miller and Elvis Da Costa and his team at the British Film Institute, who handled enormous amounts of data and international communication with enviable efficiency and tolerance.

The British Film Institute gratefully acknowledges financial assistance from BSkyB and the support given by Jane Reed of News International.

Sincere thanks are due to the following people all around the world, without whose help and enthusiasm "One Day in the Life of World Cinema" would never have been realised. Mark Adams, Martin Amstell, Dace Andzane, Matti Apunen, Sue d'Arcy, Rafik Atassi, David Aukin, Patrick Barratt, Hercules Bellville, Peter Besas, Peter Biskind, Martin Botha, Paul Brett, Gerard Browne, Henning Camre, Dennis Carrigan, Peggy Chiao, Michel Ciment, Lorenzo Codelli, Vaune Craig-Raymond (PCR), Uma da Cunha, Willie Currie, Rashmi Doraiswamy, Suzanne Dormer, Atilla Dorsay, Wayne Drew, Bobbi Dunn (PCR), Ignacio Durán, Giselle Dye, Hans Ehrmann, Derek Elley, Barrie Ellis-Jones, Andi Engel, Dan Fainaru, James Ferman, Stan Fishman, Bengt Forslund, Justina Franco Bastos, Voula Georgakakou, Behroze Ghandy, John Gillett, June Givanni, Julian Graffy, Trevor Green, Alan Gregory, Aijaz Gul, Marwan Haddad, Sabrey Hafez, Stuart Hall, Eric Hansen, Romaine Hart, Tony Hearn, Chris Hedges, Sue Henny, Michael Henry, Jim Higgins, John Hogarth, Gilly Hutchinson-Houa, Japan Actors' Union, Amarnath Jayatilaka, Clyde Jeavons, Jeon Yang-June, Tim Johnson, Munni Kabir, Hayashi Kanako, Jimmy Katz, Kim He Beom, Barry Kimm, John King, Maj-Britt Kirchner, Sarah Kirk, Tom Lasica, Baharudin Latif, Stefan Laudyn, Mary Lee, Yves Legaré, Peter van Lierop, Melanie Lindsell, Julian Low, Fei I Lu, John Mahony, Michael Malek, Ian McGarry, David Meeker, Dennis Michael, Sunil Mihindukula, Phil Mottram, Michael Myers, Kim Newman, Mike Nicolaidi, Sue Oake, Jamal Omid, Mahmut Tali Öngören, Andrew Patrick, Mr and Mrs Peng, Wenlan Peng, Simon Perry, Gerald Pratley, Susanna Pyrker, Tony Rayns, Ian Riches, Ken Rive, Esther Ronay, Jaan Ruus, Rakesh Sanghvi, Markku Salmi, Libby Shearon, Keith Shiri, Ana da Skalon, Nick Smedley, Fawzi Soliman, Agustin Sotto, Angela Spindler-Brown, Kate Stables, David Stratton, Judit Sugár, Marselli Sumarno, Tricia Sumner, Alberto Tabbia, Catherine Tait, Jeremy Thomas, Katalin Vajda, Tise Vahimagi, Raja Weeratna, Wanda Wertenstein, Mike Wheeler, Sheila Whitaker, Paul Willemen, Bob Wittenbach, Wong Ain-Ling, John Woodward, Liz Wrenn, Eva Zaoralová.

Translators of letters and diaries written for the project were Hanifa Dobson and M Fawzi (Arabic), Mr J.P. Gupta (Bengali), Wenlan Peng and Wai Hsai Peng (Chinese), Angela Spindler-Brown (Czech), Anne Born (Danish), Mrs S Bloch (Dutch), Lynn Johnson (Dutch and Russian), Eve-Külli Kala (Estonian), Jamal Omid (Farsi), Aline Cook and Françoise Cowie (French), Barrie Ellis-Jones (German), Maria Margaronis (Greek), Mradula Sedani (Gujerati), Eva Abrahams (Hebrew), Ashish Rajadhyaksha (Hindi), Esther Ronay (Hungarian), Mr Hanafi (Indonesian), Anna Muzzarelli and Geoffrey Nowell-Smith (Italian), Takako Imai (Japanese), Kim He-Beom (Korean), Clyde Jeavons (Norwegian), Roman Lachowicz and Ania Witowska (Polish), Nighat Farood (Punjabi), Tom Lasica (Russian), Christina Baum and Roberto Mader (Portuguese), Priyath Liyanage (Sinhala), John King and Tamy Zúpan (Spanish), Eivor Martinus and Shirley Herasingh (Swedish), Rajes Balasubramian (Tamil), Mehmet Koyunc and Shirley Herasingh (Turkish), Aijaz Gul (Urdu).

1. Hollywood Marks the Day AS ALL ROADS ONCE LED TO ROME, NOW FOR ANYONE IN THE FILM WORLD THEY LEAD TO LOS ANGELES, WHERE THE STUDIOS AND INDEPENDENT PRODUCTION COMPANIES HAVE LONG AGO SPREAD OUT BEYOND THE RATHER SCRUFFY, NONDESCRIPT BOUNDARIES OF HOLLYWOOD ITSELF. IN A YEAR WHEN TWO AMERICAN FILMS (*JURASSIC PARK* AND *SCHINDLER'S LIST*) BY THE SAME DIRECTOR, STEVEN SPIELBERG, IMPRESSED ON THE ONE HAND WORLDWIDE AUDIENCES AND ON THE OTHER THE MOST CYNICAL OF CRITICS, IT IS PERHAPS ONLY RIGHT THAT WE SHOULD BEGIN OUR DAY IN HOLLYWOOD.

EPY 5018

Michael Tolkin achieved that rare distinction for a movie screenwriter – fame – when Robert Altman directed his splendid original, *The Player*, in 1992. Now he is editing his own picture, *The New Age*:

"Meeting at Nick Wechsler's to talk about the completion schedule for *The New Age*. Oliver Stone is executive producer and he's making a

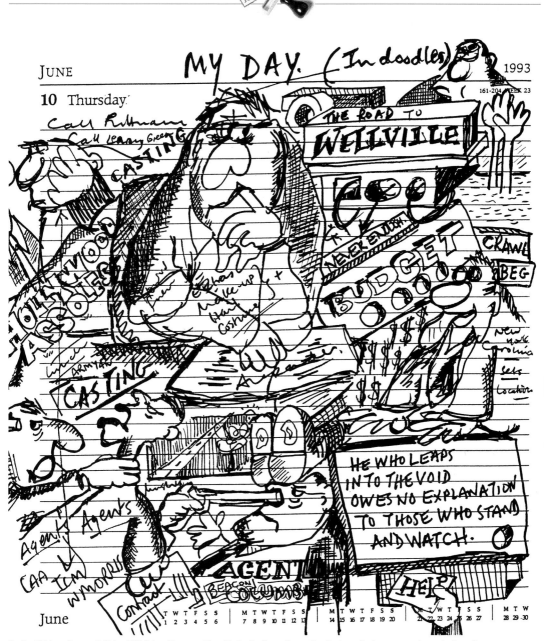

Left: *Writer-director Michael Tolkin.* Above: *Alan Parker's diary shows that he is as lively a cartoonist as he is a director*

movie now, and there's no locked film until he can see it. We had hoped, originally, to be ready for the fall, but it might be better to wait. There's nothing gained from rushing to release and the fall is already crowded with interesting movies.

Watched a new version of the beginning of *The New Age* with Suzanne Fenn, the editor. Suzanne cut *The Rapture* and she's a true friend. Last year, using the AVID System, she edited *Younger and Younger* for Percy Adlon. Now she's cutting *The New Age* on the AVID, and it's the best thing since sliced bread. The film has been digitized, with time code. Using two monitors, a keyboard, a mouse, and a hundred thousand dollars' worth of hard drives, we're cutting the film in two-thirds the time it used to take, with only one assistant in charge of equipment. The only drawback to the system is that I have never seen my

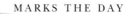

movie on film, only on video, since the cost of printing on film and then conforming the reels would add too much to our budget. The loss is significant, but in a few years every director, except those with the fattest deals, will be editing this way, particularly as the price of the system drops. I can imagine a $15,000 version of this in a few years, something to pack in a few suitcases and take anywhere in the world.

The issue today was to see how the title sequence worked in a version we'd just thought of last week. The script called for opening the film with Peter Weller in a clothing store, shopping with his father, played by Adam West. Then we went to his office, and then we met Judy Davis, at her job. We had already juggled some scenes, but still we were missing something. We had three scenes before the real action began. Those scenes set up character and context. We dropped one, and then took the other two and intercut them with the titles. The titles are over black, and we cut from the scene to the titles. It seems to work nicely. As the image drops away, we hear the actors' voices and somehow this draws us into the movie. *We have invented radio!* **99**

Penelope Spheeris, one of the few top women directors in Hollywood since her runaway box-office hit, *Wayne's World*, rises early as usual to start work:

66 5.30 A.M. Coffee and a script – only eight more to go before the weekend. I arrive at Twentieth Century Fox at 8.30 A.M. Call Gersh Agency in N.Y. to pass on the script I've just read.

9 A.M. meeting with editors re. *The Beverly Hillbillies*. We have to show the film to Fox on June 28th and we are all preparing for a video screening for ourselves this afternoon. I decided to cut the film electronically on the Rightworks System because it's much more efficient than film cutting. After some last-minute instructions to the editors, I meet with the music supervisor and the music editor. We are in the throes of deciding what music to put in the film. It's gotta be country-oriented, reminiscent of the TV series and yet

Penelope Spheeris on the set of The Beverly Hillbillies

please the current audience – a tough assignment.

My assistant Rhonda brings in an article re. *The Beverly Hillbillies* that will appear in the Sunday edition of *The Los Angeles Times* – great article – but I come off as a 'bitch on wheels.' Oh well, I promise to be nicer on my next movie.

3 P.M. The editors, Rhonda, my sister Linda, set decorator George, sit down and watch the cut of the movie. The film's funny – the laughs are all in the places I thought they'd be – but at almost two hours it needs a hell of a lot of work. I realise I have to call the studio and tell them I need more time before showing it to them. I meet with the sound effects editors; I'm going for those exaggerated sounds – more laughs, I tell them.

I talk to my agent re. doing *The Little Rascals* at Universal for Steven Spielberg. My assistant calls Amblin (Spielberg's company) to arrange a meeting with Spielberg to discuss it further. **99**

Left: *River Phoenix, who died suddenly during the production of* Dark Blood. *Above:* Michael Apted, *who was cutting* Blink *on June 10th*

A Pole who has found recognition abroad, Agnieszka Holland (*Europa Europa, Olivier Olivier*, and many screenplays for Wajda), spends June 10th in Los Angeles. Her day includes a poignant encounter with River Phoenix, just before his death:

66 Awfully busy day. Los Angeles. Hot. There was the final working screening of *The Secret Garden* (my new film) for Warner Bros. Final mix and a working print. It was very well received. Distribution suddenly woke up and demanded a copy so as immediately to show the movie to the press. Rush, panic, everybody screams. For the last time I exploded with anger to studio executives because of an awful song they wanted to put at the tail-end credits as if the movie could not be promoted by a good song which has something in common with it as well as with Zbyszek Preisner's score.

Then a loose evening with my sister and friends; we came back to the hotel at 1 A.M. (already June 10th). I knew that River [Phoenix] was late for his plane and that he arrived after 10 P.M. I thought he would be asleep (in Florida, where he came from, it was already 4 A.M.) but a receptionist gave me a bunch of messages from him and I am told that he's still awake. I called him; he demands to meet me immediately. He

was sweating, drunk, tired, very beautiful. I suspected that he had just read *Jack and Jill*, a screenplay by Robbie Baitz which is supposed to be my next movie. He very much wants to play Adam. He played Adam for an hour. He achieved what he wanted; I escaped from his room, I was dying of fatigue, but I was sure that none of the other wonderful actors I had met for this role would have such truthfulness, would have such courage and self-awareness of auto-destruction as River [Phoenix] does. **99**

English-born director Michael Apted (*The Coal Miner's Daughter, Gorillas in the Mist, Thunderheart*) flies across America and prepares for the ordeal of a first screening:

66 My day begins as the day begins. It's just past midnight somewhere over Kansas on a delayed last flight from N.Y. to L.A. I've just had three gruelling days shooting a commercial and I'm wondering why I put up with it. Agency and client in your face thrusting crummy ideas at you. Sometimes it can be fun, sometimes you learn stuff, but basically it's the money, to keep you afloat as the movies and documentaries get harder to find and harder to set up.

Ten hours later I'm in the cutting room, looking at assembly scenes of *Blink*, a movie I finished shooting a month ago for New Line Cinema. I've yet to face the ordeal of the first screening – when all the euphoria of actually getting through the shoot is abruptly replaced by the cold reality of how much work has to be done to make what you thought might be quite good even presentable. However good the rushes might seem, you know that nothing means anything until you see the first cut – then you see if the film has motion and energy, whether the performances make sense, whether the story is worth telling. I don't know how other directors work, but I like to get the scenes in fairly decent shape before I submit myself to the whole movie. I can shake out the obvious shortcomings, remove chunks of flab and push the narrative on. But there comes a point when this has to stop, so in five days I'll bite the bullet and watch the film.

So today there's a feeling of unreality as we nervously tinker with a couple of scenes not even knowing if these will ever make it into the final cut. But reality comes bounding in in the form of decisions to be made about special effects and music. There are more visual effects in *Blink* than in anything I've done, which makes me wary and defensive. You hand the raw material over to other people to do their complicated and unfathomable work, and with it you hand over control of a crucial part of the film. You then have to wait and see if they come up with anything remotely like you imagined. It's also a very expensive process and by Hollywood standards this is a modestly-priced film – $11.5 million. New Line doesn't throw money around, which is why they've survived so long and it's been a struggle to do a classy film with two stars, Madeleine Stowe and Aidan Quinn, in 45 days and know there's very little room for error. This makes these special effects decisions even more crucial because we'd better get it right first time. It's frustrating.

I also have to make a decision about a composer. My usual collaborator James Horner isn't available so I have to find a new best friend. I listen to tapes, meet people, check things out with other directors and pray that I choose well. When

it comes to final decisions on a movie, everybody and their dog becomes an expert on the music, so not only do you need someone of vision and talent to lift your pedestrian work and make it soar, but also you need a man/woman of steel to resist all the inane notes from producers, studio execu-

tives and their families. I feel vulnerable without James – he's so expert at taking my musical platitudes and turning them into something coherent and fresh. But I need to get someone working soon, so I take home tapes and CD's to see if anything takes flight. It's a busy day, but kind of

Michael Apted on the set of Blink, *working with actress Madeleine Stowe*

nerve-wracking. I'm sitting on important decisions and, at this stage, wrong moves could cost me dearly. **99**

The versatile Val Guest: still nurturing projects

Another British director, Val Guest, whose versatile talent embraced musicals, horror films, and science fiction among other genres (*The Quatermass Experiment, Casino Royale, When Dinosaurs Ruled the Earth, Expresso Bongo*), still relishes the prospect of making a new picture in Hollywood:

“ Beautiful Palm Springs morning and all's well with the world. After months of labour pains the screenplay (for the Fox remake of my film, *The Day the Earth Caught Fire*) completed and delivered yesterday. It was exciting enough the night this picture won a British Academy Award [1961], but to have it remade all these years later is an undreamed-of bonus. Dived into the pool and out again for a London call from my agent, Dennis Selinger, to say the company who plans to remake one of my later films, *Expresso Bongo*, have agreed to the contract terms. Two remakes in one year? Wow! My wife, Yolande, went out to test drive a new Mercedes. What can go wrong on such a day? Plenty. And it does, around noon.

A call from someone at Fox. 'Thought you'd like to know the new boss has read the script and had a brilliant idea. What if the male lead, the hard-drinking, self-destructive reporter, was a woman? Keep up with the times.' Are they serious? Very. 'Of course,' he goes on, 'this means the leading lady will now have to be a man.'

Shades of the *The Crying Game*. After the first shock I come back with my brilliant idea. Why does the leading lady have to be a man? Why isn't the hard-drinking, self-destructive woman reporter in love with another woman? Keep up with the times. Fox calls hasty conference.

Lunch. Had a Cobb salad with my friends Mike and Bob Pollock, writer-producers of the popular 'Dynasty' series. 'What,' I asked them, 'if Aaron Spelling had suddenly suggested Joan Collins's Alexis should be a man?'

'We'd take a month's cruise to see if it could work out,' said Mike. However, I don't think Fox would stand for my cruise.

In the evening I barbeque with another neighbourhood chum, author Harold Robbins.

'What do you suggest I tell them?' I ask Harold. 'I'll tell you exactly what to tell them,' he said and proceeded to do so. But somehow I don't think Fox will like to do that either. Which only goes to show that in a writer's life there's no such thing as a perfect day. **99**

Executive producer of the worldwide hit, *Fried Green Tomatoes at the Whistle Stop Cafe*, Sara Duvall continues to forge ahead as an independent force in Hollywood:

66 7.30 A.M. My partner arrives [at our office in Culver City] and we have our usual morning tea and strategy session. This morning's heated discussion concerns whether to pull exclusivity from a star actress who has had one of our

scripts for five months while verbally agreeing to do the film in October of this year. Yesterday her agency (one of the big two) announced that she would not be available until June of 1994. The discussion centres on whether and how much she and the agency are jerking us around, given that we have set the financing for October and that this is the third time we have raised the financing for this project.

Following the strategy session, I make calls to the East Coast, London and Brazil before the Hollywood day gets rolling.

9 A.M. Partners' meeting. We decide to seek out another director and actress for our October financed film script. We strategise over the phone

Sara Duvall (right), with partners Shannon Silverman (centre) and Anne-Marie Gillen

JUNE 10th

with the rival agency about which 'A' names are available. The writer (prolific, Academy Award winner, powerful) is not pleased at our decision to pull exclusivity, but will co-operate with our efforts to achieve our October start date. He hopes we are not doing irreparable damage to our relationship with the star and the director. I call and break the news to the president of the actress's agency and the agent tracking this project. They are polite, but we all know the fat is in the fire.

Percy Adlon, one of the few German directors to establish himself as a force to be reckoned with in North America (*Bagdad Cafe, Rosalie Goes Shopping, Salmonberries*) writes from the warmth of Pacific Palisades:

❝ The delivery of the German dubbed version of *Younger and Younger* is weighing on me. The film is finished and now the work starts. [. . .] Donald Sutherland won't agree the interna-

German director Percy Adlon, photographed in his garden by his son, Felix

a Django Reinhardt film. Script, direction, co-production. Our German company, maybe the Bavarian Film Fund, would be ideal for it. Django? Daniel Day-Lewis? Andy Garcia? Yes, very attractive! It was my childhood, after all. When Django died I was eighteen, in 1953. Bohemian, anarchist, untamed, childlike, genius, sensualist, sensitivity, hot temper, his burnt hand, and the girls. In those days people danced up close. Lots of sensuality and the sweet, sweet music. Grapelli's seductive violin. $10 million budget . But only if I can squeeze a good story out of it. It can't be a bio-pic. If I am going to make that, and then *Herschel* with Jennifer Jason Leigh and Anthony Hopkins, and after that *Louis with a Star*, that's the next six-years gone. I'll be 64 then. Cheers! And I only want to make little films, really, with no name actors; discover young people, discover old people, Indians, Mongols, Haitian women. Just as long as they're not bloody boring whites time after time! I want to make films again like I used to, like my documentaries, like my *Walser* and *Celeste*. **99**

21 ≪

Kilian Kerwin, of Venice, California, has a tranquil day, even by Hollywood standards:

66 More or less routine. My partner Jim Skotchdopole and I spent the day in our trailer at Twentieth Century Fox devising a production strategy for a feature we are producing, tentatively entitled *The Ten Commandments*. (You'd know the trailer by the 'Beverly Hillbillies Wardrobe' placard out front.)

The project is an original idea which we have set up at Fox. It involves ten different 8-10 minute segments, each driven by a different comedy force, each thematically concerned with one of the Ten Commandments. We are dealing, therefore, with the equivalent of producing ten different movies. Each must take into consideration a different set of factors vis-à-vis availability, location, crew, etc. Yet as the pieces fit together to construct a feature-length theatrical release, a realistic overview must be designed to accommodate production needs and budgetary concerns.

Jim and I more or less spent the day on this as we were meeting our Fox executives the next day. We also spent time discussing appropriate writer/

tional distribution poster as it is; the textless backgrounds are much more expensive than budgeted; the insurance won't pay up for the motorbike accident that had already been agreed; the U.S. contracts are shuttling between the damned lawyers and so on and so forth.

Lunch with Jean-Luc Ornières, who offers me

Jack Nicholson starred in the 1966 Monte Hellman film, Ride in the Whirlwind

director choices for individual *Commandment* segments with our Executive Producer, Lynda Obst. Frank Oz, who is helming one of the segments, called to talk about a writer he'd like to use.

Unfortunately, as the project is at the beginning of its developmental stages, nothing too exciting happened. We did, however, assemble a respectable production blueprint to prepare us for our meeting with Fox. 99

Monte Hellman, a legend for his offbeat films of the 1960s such as *The Shooting* and *Ride in the Whirlwind*, continues to immerse himself happily in the film-making process:

66 8 A.M. Conference call with Barry Cooper, my partner, and Katherine Wilson (who brought the Ken Kesey story, *Last Go 'Round* to us) re. my talking to Jonathan Demme about his becoming Executive Producer on *Last Go 'Round* – for me to direct.

10 A.M. Checked with Tony Safford, acquisitions executive at Miramax, to see if he had read *Nothing More than Murder* (script from the Jim Thompson novel, for me to direct). He hadn't.

10.30 A.M. Checked with Carol Thompson (acquisitions executive at Live Entertainment), to see if she had read *Strange Girls*, a Michael Laughlin script for him to direct. She said she just got a positive reader's report and would read it herself this weekend.

11 A.M. Talked to Jonathan Demme re. *Last Go 'Round.* He said he wanted to cut back on executive producing in order to spend more time with his kids, but was intrigued by the project because of subject matter and me. He said he would consider it, and asked to see existing script by Kesey and others, even though it was to be totally rewritten by Charles Eastman.

Lunch meeting at Al Gelato, with Barry, Michael Laughlin, and Howard Salen (Michael's creative and business partner) re. strategy for *Strange Girls.*

4 P.M. Long conversation with Carlos Goodman (attorney for *Reservoir Dogs*) re. discussion with Live over *Reservoir* profit participation.

We went over the numbers, and I faxed him my notes and figures. We arranged to meet over the weekend to go over everything in more detail prior to sending a letter to Live.

This was a typical non-production day in my current career as a hyphenate [director-producer-writer-editor], and the first time in my life during which I have been developing several projects at one time.

Alfred Molina has made an impact in films like *Looking for Brezhnev* and on British television. His diary pinpoints the love-hate relationship many Europeans have with Hollywood in their creative work:

In his book *Money into Light*, John Boorman tells of the 'pilgrimage,' the journey film-makers almost inevitably have to make to Hollywood in order to raise money or get a job. My day consisted precisely of that. Each time I make this trip I'm filled with excitement and dread in equal measure. Am I wasting my time? Will they know who I am? Will I survive this madness?

The dread is the English in me. The Italian blood my mother gave me starts to warm up as I land in Tinseltown. This, after all, is the place where dreams and hopes come to life.

Contradiction is typical of the place itself. No-one returns your calls but they do get movies made. They have some of the best restaurants in the world, but you can't get a decent cup of tea. I love being here but I'm terrified of forgetting my way back.

Today I have to learn some lines from a script in order to play a scene or two in a meeting at Disney. This is to show them that I can do an American accent. Nowhere along the line has anyone inquired whether I can act, so can I safely assume they believe I can? I still don't relax, for fear that they may change their minds.

None of my jokes – all tried and tested to death – went down well. This town is too serious for that. The new Disney building, or 'Mouseleum' as it is known, is amazing. At the front are huge pillars held up by the seven dwarves. I pass the time trying to remember all their names. What a way to earn a living!

23 ◀◀

Alfred Molina: "None of my jokes [. . .] went down well."

King Hu captivated audiences at Cannes and throughout the west in the mid-1970s with his brilliant historical action picture, *A Touch of Zen*. Now this Hong Kong director makes his home in Pasadena, California:

" 10 A.M. Working on *Editorial Cartoons*, hope to have them syndicated. That's one of my dreams which I've cherished for years. At noon, Eva drives me to Santa Monica to attend a meeting with [producer] Sarah Pillsbury. She said that she had a very fruitful conversation with the Mayfair Entertainment people in London about [my project] *I Go Ono*.

Eva and I attend the opening of the American Film Institute Film Festival, hosted by my old friend Ken Wlaschin. A reporter from Taipei

Still from Hong Kong director King Hu's acclaimed film A Touch of Zen

came to L.A. to cover the opening of *Jurassic Park*. She insisted that I should have my photo taken with Charlton Heston prior to a screening of *El Cid*, the version restored by Martin Scorsese, and sponsored by Miramax. Magnificent! "

Another outsider, Kay Tong Lim, an actor from Singapore, seems more attuned to the rhythm of life in L.A.:

" I jog up in the hills. Coming up Runyon Canyon Park, you can see the towers of downtown on a clear day. There's a shroud draped over the buildings today. Further ahead are obscured views of the Valley and Universal City. After heading back down into Hollywood, I pick up *Daily Variety* and *The Hollywood Reporter*. Wind down back in my apartment with Tai Chi, and that completes the routine for the day. The rest is taken moment by moment.

Nancy Kwan calls [and] suggests working on a couple of projects – a possible love letters tour of Asia and a screenplay she has written. I have offered to show her script around in Singapore. Interest is picking up slowly there and now is the time to seek funding for movies.

The customary Californian rays begin to slant through the blinds and the courtyard is bathed in sunlight. Time to work on a script by Terrence Malick. He hasn't done anything since *Days of Heaven* in the 1970s. Malick has adapted his play (for that's what it is) from a Japanese story.

I wonder why I spend part of my life here in L.A. It most certainly isn't a city of angels. The place is divided, factionalised, segregated and often tense. Perhaps the weather, the sprawl and the food make up for the negatives. And getting to read a story by Terrence Malick. And the movies. This city has a remarkably large number of art houses. Together with the weekly openings of commercial studio product, filmgoing here is an experience in diversity.

I collect Nancy's screenplay from my agent. Thumbing through it I can see its potential as an independently-made movie. Must try to get this off the ground. Before dinner, I drop in at the Beverly Hills Library to browse. Need material on medieval Japan concerning the Malick script. "

Leah Tunkara has worked in TV (*Fame*, for example) and film, and catches the mood of many of those living on the edge of Hollywood life:

" Driving down Sunset in my Caribbean gold-painted car, feeling a little misplaced, determined to really find the G spot in life, I asked myself, 'Well, what the hell do you really want to do?' Something told me to drive to the American Film Institute.

On the way there I thought about my screenplay (*The African American Princess*). Am I really ever going to find a sensuous (one who can exhibit great vulnerability) British mulatto actor to play the love interest or am I just dreaming?

When I reached A.F.I. a graduation party was in progress. I recognised an actor I had worked with on *Fame*. While I said hello to him, I reflected for a moment on those years [. . .] then someone screamed 'Leah Tunkara!' Scared half to death I turned around to find a director, Andrea. She thanked me for working with her on her film and assured me I would have a credit as an assistant editor. I know it's a small thing (my first technical credit), but this moment felt better than being kissed on the cheek by Marvin Gaye or massaging Stevie Wonder's hands or that time in Paris when Roman Polanski meekly wrote down his address for me. "

Jürgen Vsych, a would-be feature director, has survived in Hollywood the hard way, sometimes even by housecleaning, but she has retained an engaging sense of irony:

" 4 A.M. Wake up in a sweat after terrible nightmare. John Sayles and I were having a fistfight to the death to see who would get $5 million from Sean Connery. Sayles was beating me to a pulp and I kept crying, 'But he's a 6' 4" man and I'm a 5' 4" woman!' And Connery said, 'You wanted equality, lassie!'

Can't get back to sleep, so I storyboard a feature I've written and will direct, some day, called *Curl Up and Dye*. I don't know why I bother. If I'm lucky enough to get someone like Freddie Fields, he won't even look at it. But it will help me.

I've spent the last two years in Scotland making short films. I had hoped to return 'a star' (or even a small planet), but everyone I knew has either left the industry or forgotten me. Need money to pay entry fees for film festivals, for my short, *Pay Your Rent, Beethoven*.

Drive through West Hollywood. I almost ran over John Malkovich a few weeks ago. He dashed out in front of me just like a real New Yorker. I slammed on the brakes, he nonchalantly waved 'thanks' and disappeared. Boy, that was exciting.

5 P.M. Home. Message on the machine from Gale Ann Hurd's assistant (!) saying how much she liked *Pay Your Rent, Beethoven*. As I dance on the kitchen table, she goes on to say, however, that she doesn't want to read any of my screenplays, because they don't want comedies. If I were to write a big-budget action script, they would be interested. I've never even considered doing an action picture. I'm trying to break in as a writer-director, and they'd never give one of those to a 'first-time director' (I've only done 27 short films). "

25 ◀◀

Leslie Bohem, a screenwriter living on Griffith Park Blvd, experiences the lethargy to which so many succumb in Hollywood:

" I have a deal to write a period murder mystery for Interscope and I should be working on that script, but this is down time [. . .] not enough time to get started, too much time to kill.

Another producer has sent me a book. I am halfway through it and I decide to finish it up. It is a Wright Morris novel called *Love Among the Cannibals*. It's set in L.A. and Acapulco during the 1950s. It's an inspired piece of writing, but the producer has told me he wants to do it contemporary, change the 41-year-old songwriting narrator to a younger, rock 'n' roll writing hero. I'm 41. I like 41-year-old narrators. I don't know if I feel like ruining Wright Morris today.

I'm late [for my appointment with a producer on another project], but I'm still there first. She arrives. I give her my notes. I try to feign enthusiasm and I nod appreciatively when she tells me they 'blew away' Taylor Hackford because his approach was too dark. [. . .] She makes a directors' list. 'Scorsese'. I don't think this is the sort of thing Marty would do. "

Above: *Still from* The Cronos Device, *co-produced by Arthur Gorson*

David Saperstein lives in New Rochelle, in New York state, but slips easily into the Hollywood pitching mode during his frequent trips to the West Coast:

66 This is the last day of a meet and greet/pitching trip to Los Angeles [. . .] I have spent the past ten days in more than thirty meetings on eight different projects. I do this two or three times a year – this was my Spring line.

I breakfast with Jennifer Alward of Hearst Entertainment. She is a first-class producer who optioned a treatment of mine last year for a MOW (Movie of the Week). She got Meredith Baxter attached to it and I came out last fall to pitch CBS. [. . .] It involved music and CBS said they weren't interested in MOW's with music. 'Too soft' – how often I hear that. I wonder how many people are sorry they told me that when I brought *Cocoon* around. I am partners with Mike

Another still from The Cronos Device

Hertzberg (*Blazing Saddles, Silent Movie, Memories of Me,* etc.) on this project. We have now given it a country spin, and Jennifer is interested once again. We discuss two other TV projects I have under option. She will read them and hopes we can do business.

My next and last L.A. meeting is with Hutch Parker, Vice President of HBO Films. He is gracious and takes the time to explain what kind of projects HBO is interested in. We discuss the changing marketplace and distribution channels, i.e. the 'baby boomers' are going to be the dominant audience – older and affluent. Cable, pay per view and fibre-optics are the future of distribution. I explain that when it comes to original material I no longer pitch ideas or treatments. I write the script. That way I get a yes or no without casual input. We discuss one original screen-play of mine, *Joshua's Golden Band,* and a book I have just optioned, *Fighting Back.* He is interested in both projects. I promise to send him the script and the book. I sense it was a good meeting. I like him and would like to work with him. Off to the airport and back to New York **"**

Arthur Gorson's entry illustrates the waiting, wondering, and hoping that constitute so much deal-making in the international movie community:

" It's a hot day in L.A. Seems like a hot day for deal-making too. It starts with an early fax from New York. A deal is on the table today, from a strong independent, for U.S. theatrical distribution for our film *Cronos Device* [a co-production between my company Ventana Films and Mexico's Producciones Iguana, and directed by Guillermo del Toro]. They saw it at Cannes and want it. The offer is good for 48 hours. Many phone/fax communications between here, our agent at I.C.M., Robert Newman, our lawyer, Bob Kaplan, and our Mexican partners. The advance is a bit lower than we would have liked, but our participation is high. Guaranteed release in at least 30 major markets including L.A. and N.Y. We have put in well over a year on this project at great cost, and are under heavy pressure to see some rapid financial return. Must stay cool. Hoping to get all points up a bit so we can say yes.

[Later] I get a call from close friend and screenwriter Michael Thomas from his home in the English countryside in Wiltshire. He has been contacted by a funding source about our film *Fire on the Mountain.* We have been in development on this project for more years than we care to remember and it is now at a major studio. This is a strange project – nothing will happen for a long time then suddenly everyone wants it again. I remind Michael that there is almost one million dollars in it in development [money] and it's not easy to move. Call on the other line also from England. It's photographer/director David Bailey who we are interested in doing a project with.

Bob Kaplan calls with more information regarding the *Cronos* deal. Now they want sequel and remake rights, but things seem to be getting closer on other points. **"**

2. From Pens To Pc's: The Writing Stage

WRITING SCREENPLAYS OFFERS EVEN THE AMATEUR AUTHOR ONE OF THE MOST SEDUCTIVE PROSPECTS IN THE MODERN WORLD. LOS ANGELES IS PACKED TO THE RAFTERS WITH WANNABEE SCREENWRITERS, WHO BUY LARGE QUANTITIES OF TEXTBOOKS AND ATTEND COURSES ON THEIR CRAFT. THE EUROPEAN SCRIPT FUND IN LONDON RECEIVES THOUSANDS OF APPLICATIONS EACH YEAR; SO DOES EVERY FILM COMPANY, PRODUCER, AND AGENT AROUND THE WORLD. YET, AS THESE ENTRIES REVEAL, SCREEN-WRITING IS A LONELY, OFTEN FRUSTRATING OCCU-PATION AS ONE WAITS FOR IDEAS TO MAKE THEIR SPORADIC APPEARANCE ON THE HORIZON . . .

Most films begin in the mind of the writer or writer-director, the auteur in European parlance. Louis Malle at sixty has behind him a string of rich and beguiling films (*The Lovers, Le Feu follet, Atlantic City, Au revoir les enfants*, and *Damage*):

" I got up early and had breakfast at the Café de Flore, where a friend came to bring me the keys of his country house near Paris. It was very warm, very thundery this morning and when I arrived at my friend's house in a village in the Seine & Marne district, it had begun to rain.

Louis Malle: writing and eating, hand in hand . . .

I had just settled down before a large desk, and got out the manuscript of the first scenes of my future film, which is provisionally entitled *L'été 44* (or *Creole Love Call* in English), and was preparing to write when I realised that I was incredibly hungry – and I could hardly write on an empty stomach.

Here I am in the village restaurant, with the rain still falling. By chance, I happen to know the proprietor, so we chatter on, and the meal stretches out longer than I intended. The restaurant is a restored mill on an offshoot of the Loing. I take advantage of a bright interval to walk along the river. The nature is magnificent, and the actual scenery fires my imagination. The road bends sharply and crosses the river over a bridge in bad repair, a bridge that recalls the landscape of my childhood, at the other end of France. Without looking for them, I conjure up images, images that come together to form a scene for my film. It's an ambush, with the Resistance trying to destroy a retreating German convoy, which they have managed to immobilise near the bridge. It is very hot, with thousands of butterflies. The scene is observed by a child. We are in August 1944.

I hurry back to write the scene – it will be my only work of the day but on reading over what I wrote I am rather pleased. Exhausted by this effort, I take a siesta, and awake to a deafening concert of birdsong. Night is falling; I have no desire to go home, but a very boring dinner awaits me in Paris, alas. **"**

Censorship anxieties colour the diary of Li Shaohong, one of the emerging Chinese directors of the so-called Fifth Generation:

" Holding my script under my arm, I enter the film censorship offices. I've spent the past two years preparing *Red Powder* and today I've come to hear their decision on whether or not I can make the film.

I know these people. In fact, I understand them. All day long, they wait in positions assigned to them by the government, from which they rule and are ruled. Their jobs are strenuous yet simple – holding the yardstick of artistic and literary policy. Their salary is generally quite low, although they're well educated; for days on end, they breathe the turbid air and inky smells of the office and their faces are gloomy. The large majority of them are honest and sincere people. They do their work cautiously and conscientiously. Each year they must approve over a thousand scripts and more than a hundred films.

But they've rejected my script. The comments they raise are earnest and assured, but completely at odds with my artistic concept. According to them, my script does not indicate if the central character, a prostitute, has been completely rehabilitated. They believe an artistic work should distinguish clearly between good and evil and depict the struggle between those forces, with good winning. But I have treated this historical period in

the 1950s when China closed down all her brothels and rehabilitated prostitutes from an individualistic point of view and it lacks social significance. What can be the point of making a film like that?

I sit there, tears trickling down my face. I know full well there can be no common link between us. They cannot control my generation's views on history or art or life. But they have decided the fate of my art. I respect their integrity and am aware of the political responsibility that they must shoulder in doing their kind of work. In a certain sense, I realise they cannot express their own views.

Faced with this situation, I ask them only not to be hasty in writing, 'Not To Be Filmed' on my script and to let me think how I can amend it so that both of us will be satisfied.

As I leave, some of those with whom I'm familiar throw me a complicated look mingled with sympathy. I give a thin smile.

June this year has been scorchingly hot. I shade my eyes from the sun and walk along the bustling street, my mind a blank. **"**

Bernardino Zapponi is another major figure in European screenwriting, having written for the late Federico Fellini (*Satyricon*, *The Clowns*, *Casanova*, *Roma* etc.), Dino Risi, Ettore Scola, Luigi Comencini and others:

" I work very well in the early morning: everybody is asleep, the sirens of police cars and ambulances alert me that life is beginning again, the smell of frying stockfish from the rotisserie assures me that people will eat today as well. I sit at my AEG Olympia typewriter and write a treatment I care about very much. It is the story of a 16-year-old boy who falls in love with his 55-year-old grandmother, a still beautiful widow, sweet and naughty; the couple will live out a brief and stormy love affair. Then I write a piece I'm going to deliver on radio tomorrow. It's an introduction for a film to be shown on TV, Hitchcock's *North by Northwest*. I chose this because it's one of my cult movies, along with Ford's *Stagecoach* and Dreyer's *Vampyr*.

Later a young director, Cristina Comencini, to whom we had offered the chance to direct one of my screenplays, phoned me; she said she liked the story a lot but the characters are too bad and

Still from Fellini's Satyricon, *co-scripted by Bernardino Zapponi*

she doesn't feel able to work with this material. Naturally I don't agree that those characters are nasty, but it's difficult to convince a director with such fixed ideas. Never mind, some other time.

[Later] I meet Silvio Clementelli who is producing my current film. We talk about Cristina Comencini's refusal; we need to find another director and Clementelli has prepared a list of possible names and reads it to me. To each name we give a mark, as at school. It's amusing. The preparation phase for a film is the best one. We talk, we imagine what the film will be like, like a son about to be born. We fantasise about it and project it in our minds; we discuss it as though it already existed. Cinema is fantasy art, it stimulates the imagination. That's why I love to invent stories; they are as yet pure and unreal. **99**

Some veterans continue passionately to carve and chisel their screenplays. Suso Cecchi d'Amico has a distinguished career behind her, having written for De Sica (*Bicycle Thieves*), Visconti, Antonioni and Rosi among others:

66 The producers have chosen this novel [*Di buona famiglia*] because it has sold very well in Italy; I have been chosen because my name is a guarantee for the foreign financiers sought by the producers to set up this co-production, as much as the name of [the director] Franco Giraldi is a guarantee for Italian television. Long gone is the time when a producer would get excited about an idea or theme we enthusiastically brought to him, and would press on without either the slightest concern about costs or the opportunity to secure well-known actors. **99**

Also in his seventies, Dino Risi knows how to poach black comedy from the seedy texture of everyday reality:

66 Hot day. Sunshine. Traffic noise. The city is dirty. Opposite my windows, the cages of the zoo. Three old eagles attempt a short, laborious flight. I go back to my old typewriter. I'm writing a script. I write one a day. Then I wonder, whom will I send it to? Film producers have disappeared. Every day a [movie] theatre closes

down. There is only one good film in Rome these days, Campion's *The Piano*. I saw it in Cannes. Beautiful. Cinemas in Rome are ugly, dirty. Television is full of films, films shown two or three times already. Seen them all. I went to the cinema. An American film, in Dolby stereo. I was sitting under a speaker that produced just the noises. I could hear only the sound of footsteps, crockery and cutlery, then cars and gunshots. The script I'm writing is about a man in a hotel room, in a city he doesn't know. He has decided to kill himself. Suddenly he hears voices and shouts coming from the street. He leans out of the window. A few minutes earlier a man was watering the flowers on his balcony in the house in front. Now the man, in a yellow shirt, lies on the pavement, dead. The man had been quicker than him. Our hero gets out, goes into the first cinema he finds. Falls asleep. **99**

A younger Italian satirist, Daniele Luchetti, reveals the essential curiosity of the writer during that same hot June day on the streets of Rome:

66 At 4.30 P.M. I have a meeting with the screenwriters Rulli and Petraglia. I get there half an hour early, and I can see from the street that the shutters of Petraglia's flat are shut to keep the sun out. Perhaps he wants to rest until 4.29. So I go round the block three times walking very slowly. I'm walking in the shade, like the Indians in the Grand Canyon. Very near Petraglia's front door there's a cine-club. It's the 'Azzurro Scipioni.' Today's programme is Orson Welles' *Othello*. The first show starts in ten minutes, but nobody is waiting outside the cinema. The projection booth, which can be seen from the street, is deserted. I peer inside the hall, no one at the box-office either. Perhaps this is an automatic cinema that doesn't need a projectionist? Or perhaps there's an electronic box-office where one can pay with credit cards? Perhaps it's a self-contained cinema, which needs neither a film nor an audience?

[. . .] When I was little I lived in cinemas. In summer the ceiling would open. I could see the stars and the cigarette smoke diappearing in the sky; it was like being in an interstellar spaceship. On the screen, Totò. First memory of the day.

An hour later I am with Rulli and Petraglia in the cool shade of a big house, working on a **"** new film project, my fifth . . .

And who wrote those legendary comedies starring Totò? None other than Age (the professional pseudonym for Agenore Incrocci), who for decades has graced the credits of innumerable Italian films:

"We must finish the proposal today, or tomorrow at the latest. Franco Bernini, my son Adriano and myself were already working on this idea last year, and have recently dug it out again. The title is *Terque Quaterque*. The story takes place in Thrace, in the forests around the river Danube in 330 A.D. 'The Fourth Century is amazingly similar to the Twentieth Century,' an Italian art critic, Ranuccio Bianchi Bandinelli, once wrote. Populations are on the move and mixing, various ethnic groups are in conflict, the old boundaries cease to exist, old rules no longer have value, and new ones are being born with great difficulty. In short, a 'philosophical' film, filtered through the revisitation of the classic war and adventure genre: the Roman legions on one side, the barbarians – Gepids and Visigoths – on

the other. But there's also a sense of irony, or at least we're trying. We have two portable computers, but we only work on one (mine). We take turns at the keyboard, shifting from one file to another. We already have a few written pages of a previous draft. We alter some factual **"** details, insert some new scenes . . .

Jiří Menzel, who won an Academy Award for Czechoslovakia with *Closely Observed Trains* in 1967, continues to maintain a strenuous pace as writer and director:

"I listened to the news at 6 A.M. and when I learnt that the Balkan war had not yet reached Prague and that all the world's catastrophes were still occurring at a safe distance from my city, I turned over and slept until 8 A.M. I had breakfast in bed. Until lunch I worked on a film script which I have been developing for some time. In the afternoon I went to Milovice where the set for our next film is being built. Shooting will begin at the end of June. The story is based on Vladimir Vojnovic's novel, *The Life and Extraordinary Adventures of Private Chonkin*. It takes place in a Russian village, and we are **"** having one built near Prague.

Still from The Life and Extraordinary Adventures of Private Chonkin, *for which Jiří Menzel wrote the screenplay*

For Asghar Abdollahi, a screenwriter in Tehran, the moment of writing remains the most precious commodity in an industry depleted by recession:

“ It has become a habit with me to get up early on Thursdays and to busy myself with a script I have entitled *Hedda Gabler's Lost Dress*. This has been going on for the past six years, and I have forgotten the original circumstances under which it occurred to me to write a script about an actress who performed Hedda Gabler on stage in Abadan forty years ago. Many years later the elderly actress, who is now residing in London, fancies having the dress she wore in the play, and writes to the oil company authorities who run the theatre, asking them to send her the dress. But it cannot be found in the theatre's stockroom, and a detective is commissioned to find it.

On June 10, I pick the script off the shelf and gaze at its yellowed pages. I drink a cup of tea, light a cigarette and think of the detective who chains his Indian-made bicycle to a post in front of the teashop in the middle of the dates plantation, and hurries to question the old theatre concierge. There my imagination stalls.

I leaf through the 32-page script, and thank God that screenwriting in our country has not really become a professional job. I can put aside or abandon the screenplay without a qualm. We don't work according to the Hollywood formula, and I am not under a contract to finish this script.

So I put it away on the shelf. I stroll to the window and look at the kittens playing in our backyard. [...]

Nowadays the industry is facing a recession. Nobody is making any films, and nobody wants a script. And thank God we don't have to shut ourselves up in a room and finish scripts on deadline as they do in Hollywood. Our scripts are conceived in tiny rooms, and take shape through the sweat of the soul. But whether or not they are one day filmed does not matter. We have become used to thinking only of the moment of writing, never caring if it will ever be filmed. ”

Still from The Life and Extraordinary Adventures of Private Chonkin

British producer and writer Allan Scott spends the day drafting and revising

Charlie Harris, a British writer, devotes himself to various projects simultaneously. On June 10, he hears some reactions:

The more I write, the more I value the time I spend before writing. Yesterday I had a phone call from a friend who asked me to help write a low-budget film for him. We talked over his story some months ago, but things went quiet his end, as often happens. Now he says he can offer me money, not a lot, as long as he can have a synopsis to show people very soon. I try to explain to him that the work is not in proportion to the length. A synopsis has to be a synopsis of something. A dazzling two pages can be harder to write than sixty. We agree to meet next week to see how to proceed.

The story [of my thriller script] so far is a ragbag of potentially exciting scenes, set at somewhere like Cannes, with a vaguely horror/thriller/comedy feel to it. I am determined to keep the budget low, because there is so little money in Britain at the moment. I tend to be attracted to stories with explosive tensions under the surface, usually sex

and violence rear their ugly heads, and this is no exception. I'm hoping I'll offend a few people, or it won't be worth doing.

Allan Scott, also a British writer and producer, works with companies in both L.A. and London, drafting and redrafting:

The first draft of *The Last Spy* (Paramount, producer Mace Neufeld) sits on my desk waiting to be shortened and tightened before I send it out. Dan Rissner already sent Mace the first eighty pages. I hate that happening. On the other hand there is a good side to the practice, since Jeff Katzenberg [at Disney] sent Meg Ryan the first 87 pages of *Lilah* and I heard last night that she loves it.

A call from Anthea [Sylbert] with tiny revisions to four pages. I faxed them this morning. Barely worth the paper but this draft is now Katzenberg-ready. Curiously, I've enjoyed the process of writing a script with an executive committee on my tail. Firstly because the quality of comment and input is very high. Secondly because every executive at every level recognises that the writer does something unique – he actually writes. The process also has some of the fun of puzzle-solving. I probably wouldn't think so if the script had turned out badly.

This afternoon I began the second draft of *Morgan's Passing*. I've been nursing Sydney Pollack's notes for several months. They're very sharp. His theme is to reduce the eccentricity of the main character so as to keep him in the real world. No disagreement with the objective, but we all have a different view of what is real and what is eccentric. Especially those of us who live out of L.A., where I plan to take the revisions in mid-July – the week in which *The Firm* opens. **99**

Spanish writer-director D. Gonzalo Suarez (*Epilogo, Rowing with the Wind*, etc.), exemplifies the solitary nature of the quest for ideas and images:

66 I have spent the day in my house in Lledías (Asturias), rewriting a sequence of *The Detective and Death*, and the characters of the film swirl around me. They are, as yet, spirits without flesh, ungraspable and fluctuating. They remain in the air, waiting for the actors to give them body and the camera to give them reflection. I have faith in their existence, but only the cinema will provide them with an outward appearance. It will make them phantoms who are as real, in the

Still from Spanish writer-director D. Gonzalo Suarez's film Epilogo

EPY 5018

7   7A

Left and above: *Stills from Michael Verhoeven's Academy Award-winning film* The Nasty Girl

memory, as real people, who, through death or absence, are now no longer with us. No difference, in the memory. Because to imagine is to remember what never took place and to make cinema is to make what has been imagined take place. Without any need to describe it or detail it. Playing the game of gestures, lights and shadows. For that reason today, when I try to recount what is happening to me, at the moment that it is happening I must resign myself to consign to this diary just what I perceive, before it has completely happened. An old man who 'has cold skin like a lizard's' is going to die. A mature and beautiful woman, nicknamed the Duchess – 'time has slept with her, but has not managed to fuck her.' A gunman, named 'the obscure man,' a perverse

young woman, an innocent young woman, a detective, a blue house, a city at night, a child crying in a garret, are things that are happening to me, while I press the keys of the old Olivetti and the fly continues to buzz against the window. **99**

Michael Verhoeven (Germany) earned an Academy Award nomination for Best Foreign Film with *The Nasty Girl* in 1992. Accompanied by his wife, Senta Berger, he works in Manhattan on a new project:

66 I am sitting at a desk which is much too small and revising the scenes in my script in which 'Mary' jumps from the roof. I have to change *every-thing*. I still have not found a point of view for it.

Above: *German director Michael Verhoeven.* Right: *Youssef Chahine, the most celebrated of Egyptian film-makers, whose diary is characteristically laconic*

The producer, Patti Zohn, calls up from L.A. and asks me how far I have got. I say I need another two weeks of intensive work, not like now, where I write every now and then for a few hours.

I do not want to omit the scurrilous sub-strands from the film version. There is nothing left of Barbara Gowdy's overheated petit-bourgeois satire if it is told in a linear way.

I make another attempt, which simply falls apart after two hours. In spite of my temporary utter despair I take my manuscript with me into the Plaza Diner on Second Avenue, but do not open it. I have them warm the Budweiser beer and have the iced glass replaced by one that is not iced, which prompts the waiter to ask if I come from Europe. **99**

For some, the day is divided, or rather sliced, methodically, into segments. Here is the diary kept by Egyptian director Youssef Chahine, who has enjoyed a long and distinguished career since 1950:

66 4.00 A.M: Wake-up. Prepare tea and convince myself to sit at my writing table.

4.30 A.M: Start writing or rewriting script or storyboard.

7.30 A.M: Sleep again.

8.30 A.M: Shower, go to office to (a) scan

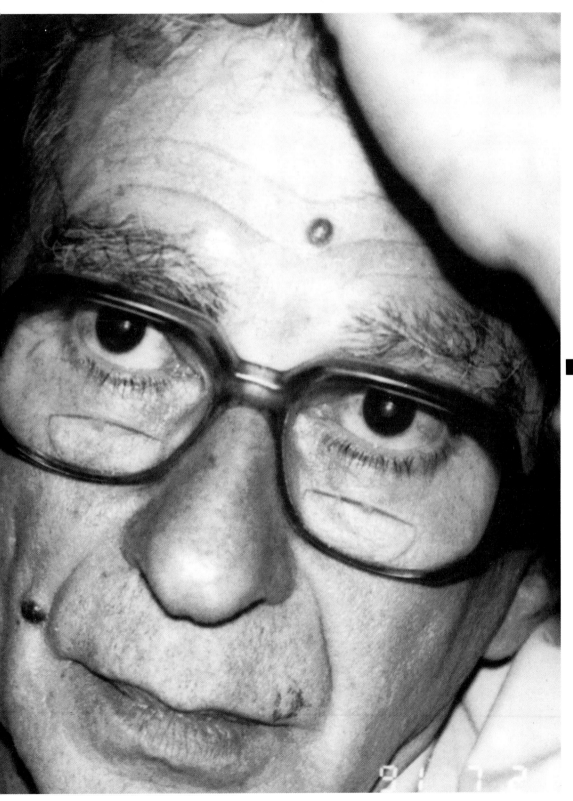

newspaper headlines, (b) check schedule according to priorities, (c) check with set designers, wardrobe, accessories in short meetings with all heads of departments, (d) make all international calls, to co-producers, festivals etc.

10.30 A.M: Waste time talking bullshit to local officials.

11.30 A.M: Break to get over headache caused by officials' imbecilities.

1.00 P.M: Work on the script.

2.30 P.M: Lunch.

3.30 P.M: Afternoon siesta and shower.

4.30 P.M: Back to office. Check casting, meetings with actors.

8.30 P.M: Readings.

9.00 P.M: Dinner.

10.00 P.M: TV5 French news, Super Channel news in English which puts me in a bad mood.

11.00 P.M: Daily haggle with wife which puts me in an even worse mood.

11.30 P.M: Go to bed for meetings with nightmares.

The exasperation that accompanies the screenwriting process emerges from Lawrence Matthews' entry:

❝ *Anna Mae's Cafe* is the screenplay that Fred, Terry, Shelby, Roc and I wrote more than sixteen months ago. We have gone through a multitude of emotions since we first sat down to put Fred's idea on paper. We have been rewriting the script forever, it seems, and at age forty it's very frustrating working through this. The longer it takes to get the script in shape, the longer it will be before it can become reality. [. . .] The idea for this movie came from Fred while we drove back and forth from Sacramento to San Francisco when we worked as extras on the now defunct *Midnight Caller* series on NBC. [. . .] This is a first-time project for all of us and I know lack of experience is the leading cause of a number of problems. Obtaining financing, getting the actors you want, getting a crew together, are some of the things I reflect upon constantly. I learn through my Black Filmmaker Newsletter that Spike [Lee] is accepting outside scripts, and maybe Quincy Jones would be interested.

Finding the time to concentrate on creative writing proves harder the more involved a director is in his society's changing landscape. Krzysztof Zanussi, with Kieslowski the most celebrated Polish film-maker since Wajda, spends a hot June 10th at his house outside Warsaw, entertaining a theatre group from Estonia, and then making a TV appearance:

❝ Late evening. When everyone is asleep I start to work on [the Clara Schumann story commissioned by my French producer]. How to restructure the whole thing? My message goes entirely against the trend – Clara refuses to marry Brahms after Schumann's death because she loves Brahms and understands that this marriage may ruin his genius. Is anybody going to believe that a denial may be an expression of ultimate love? My other project, a Polish one, will be unpopular as well – I want to describe freedom as something difficult and painful. Everybody today thinks the opposite in this country.

Later. Kieslowski calls. I want to listen to his advice concerning my problems but for the time being I am co-producing his film, *Three Colours: Blue*. It's going smoothly, but I find that Kieslowski sounds profoundly exhausted. ❞

George Sluizer, like Rademakers, a Dutchman with a cosmopolitan flair, reached a sudden and wholly deserved place in the sun with *The Vanishing* (1988). This year he was in the midst of shooting *Dark Blood* when River Phoenix, one of the principal stars, collapsed and died outside a Los Angeles nightclub on October 31st. The film had to be shut down and abandoned. This entry was of course written before the disaster:

❝ Jetlag. Just flown in [to New York] from Amsterdam for pre-production on *Dark Blood*. 10 A.M. I am called regarding the wish to alter or amend my already signed contract, so that there can be a sexy, sexier, sexiest version of the movie depending on national and censorship rules. It makes me feel like a pimp selling sex, instead of filming according to emotion.

Krzysztof Zanussi, Polish director, producer, and polymath

11 A.M. Have a cup of tea with Lisa Eichhorn who played a small part in [the U.S. remake of] *The Vanishing*. We talk about serial killers, Jeroen Krabbé, and the collaboration between actor and director. Wow! [...]

Lunch with Daniel Stern (the writer) and Bruce Weiss. We discuss the treatment of *The Tenants* based on Bernard Malamud, with a screenplay by Daniel. I like it. Talk a lot about modern-day tensions between blacks and Jews and reflect on the artist's problem when *writing* about love and life instead of *living* life. [. . .]

6 P.M. Long phone conversation with Judy Davis about her profession in *Dark Blood*, and some of her character's motivations. Talked a lot about breast implants! In retrospect – this is after hanging up – I was irritated by our partly frivolous talk. Some of us make movies because we are unable to communicate. With a bit of exaggeration, I might add that I like filming in order to avoid the telephone!

Despite all that, I started, two days ago, to work on a new scenario I had put off for some time. The film relates to all the widespread massacres in the world – and the Middle East has been their most fertile ground . . . **"**

In 1987, Fons Rademakers crowned an energetic and audacious career with his Academy Award for *The Assault*. A Dutchman who worked with De Sica and Bergman, he now lives in Rome:

" A very hot day in Rome. A little breeze in Fregene might help. It does. 'Sogno del Mare,' a large, well-kept beach, with few people

around on this Thursday, is ideal for the purpose. At 7 P.M., coming home, a call from Los Angeles. Gary Salt of my agency Paul Kohner Inc., tells me that he likes the script a lot. He intends to give me news about production possibilities within a couple of weeks. I gave him the script, which had quite difficult birth-pangs, in Cannes. It is entitled *Whites*, based on stories by Norman Rush (National Book Award-winning author of *Mating*). The stories are set in Botswana.

The problem was, as always, to find the right structure. Jan Blokker, a Dutch columnist and screenwriter, discovered an excellent solution. So I dared send a copy to the author . . .

Spanish director Rosa Verges (centre) directing Futoshi Kasagawa and Emma Suarez in Souvenir

On the morning of June 11th I heard Norman Rush's voice on my answering machine: 'Nobody could have done a better job! Congratulations!'

So, a great day for me and – if we succeed in finding finance – a good day for world cinema as well. **99**

Not all writers commence their labours at dawn. Sameer Zekra (Syria), whose *The Half Metre Incident* was screened at festivals in 1983, has been immersed in a TV serial for some time and now wants to return to the cinema:

66 I usually start writing at ten o'clock in the morning. With the coffee, I start listening to a piece of classical music, which I choose to suit the work mood and to help me concentrate and begin to write. For some years now, they have been cutting off the electricity supply in the morning. So, no music except those silly radio melodies. The present administration is even more ignorant: they stopped the making of my film *The Dinghy* after they accepted the story and the screenplay I had produced. I began to look for locations in preparation for filming . . . Now, they discover that 40% of the film must be filmed in Moscow, according to the film's events. They no longer understand anything about Moscow! Not the price of the dollar or who they should be dealing with. The project was lost between **99** Damascus and Moscow.

Rosa Verges is a Spanish woman director who has been trying to set up a new film, *Souvenir*, for almost three years:

66 Last night I got back from Bulgaria after a brief visit to some film studios. I went through a splendid set for a luxury hotel. In silence, for a moment, I felt I was part of the crew while they were filming. The magic of the cinema invaded me once again. I felt nostalgic. It's three years since I finished my first film, *Boom, Boom*. A new journey, a new project is beginning now. I am dedicated to a dream which can only be fulfilled if one fights passionately for it. [. . .]

I meet Jordi Belfran, my co-scriptwriter, my ideal partner in fiction. I tell him about my experiences in Bulgaria where I felt like my character, cut off by language, an anonymous tourist. I've experienced the impact of a different culture. As

45

Still from Rosa Verges's Souvenir

meets him, her kind father, the opposite to her own brutal husband. He untangles her from the torn fishing-net, shows her how to mend it, just like when she was a child, the two of them together, it's her life she is mending . . . What does it look like down there? Just dark?

12.30 P.M. 'That depends on where you are,' says my husband, a fanatical sports-diver, when I tell him my new angle on the scene. He talks about the light, colours, rock formations, shoals of fish, seaweed floating like a forest . . . THAT'S IT . . . Elsa's fishing net drifting into the distance, where to, death or?

12.45 P.M. I'm writing, full of joy, as the scene now makes sense. It ties Elsa's past with the future, and the father is the link, the love and kindness he implanted in his daughter give her the strength to make her decision. Ahhhhhh . . . I like it! **"**

Pat Murphy, an Irish director, prepares a presentation to the Irish Film Board of his feature film project, *Nora*:

" Tiernan MacBride and I discuss *Nora* over breakfast, last minute details about co-ordinating our proposal. I am trying to juggle a synopsis, treatment and screenplay. Each of them seems to be a document about a particular kind of writing, different languages stalking the same film. I want to make some changes. Tiernan feels that I do this as a way of avoiding proper consultation.

Nora is a feature film, the love story of Nora Barnacle and James Joyce. Tiernan is producing it, and I will direct. I talk to my sister, Deirdre, on the phone. She is reading the Brenda Maddox biography and what she says sticks in my mind: 'It's as if they should never have got together, but if they didn't, then nothing would have happened.' She's right. Their chance meeting on a Dublin street and the immediate intensity of their love affair profoundly affected Twentieth Century thinking and the ways in which women were written about. The core of the film is the deep connection between Nora and Joyce, which survives the constant changes in their relationship.

Nearly every film I've seen which deals with sexual obsession seems to end with death. It's as if cinema can only deal with sexuality in an operatic

---

so many times before, we turn over the script. We keep discovering new things. Luckily, we don't have the personal computer organiser with us. It makes writing so much easier, but it is also very dangerous. The infinite possibilities of erasing, changing, or 'undoing' writing has taken one away, at times, from the meaning of words. And now I press down with my pen, forming letters once again with black ink. **"**

Laila Rakvaag, based in Vatne in Norway, works on a scene from her next film:

" 10 A.M. An entire wall is covered with brown wrapping-paper, dotted with small yellow notes: EXT, BEACH, DAY, ACTION, INTENTION . I drink my coffee, arrange my papers, find the scene, the difficult scene: the apparent suicide of my heroine, Elsa, in my feature film script, *Spring Offer*. Elsa, in desperation, decides to end a life of degradation, violence, religious suppression. Her longing for her dead father leads her to the sea. She slowly whirls down . . . down . . . my fingers start running. She

way – an intense experience which is suddenly cut off, leaving the audience with nowhere to go, emotionally. But Nora brings Joyce through a kind of tunnel, into a space where life can be lived again. I really want to make that work in terms of the film, to show that their obsession with each other is one part of the journey and not all of it. I am reminded of something Lynda Myles said when she was here producing *The Commitments*, and we were discussing *Nora* and the problem of portraying sexuality in the cinema. 'All these films – and nothing seems as alive or as vibrant as *L'Atalante*.' We talked about how Vigo created a kind of charged, erotic essence which modern cinema can't quite grasp. **"**

Peter Rowe, a Canadian screenwriter, thrives on the practical obligations of his craft:

" I basically spent the day trying to finish a script I was commissioned to write for the series, *African Skies*, entitled *Extinct Is Forever*.

I had finished the first draft the previous week, and had devoted three days of this week to rewriting. I thought I could finish the rewrites today, so bicycled in to the office by 9 A.M. There was a fax waiting for me which had arrived from Africa overnight regarding my work permit (I am directing six episodes this summer).

By 1 P.M. I have the script finished and after proof-reading it several times I fax it off to the series' creator, Phil Savath, in Vancouver. I turn my attention to an offer I am writing for a book I'd like to make into a TV movie, but within twenty minutes the phone rings – it is Savath, who to my amazement has read the script already, and gives his approval and some notes for some further changes. After an hour on the phone I've heard them all and agree, since he is heading off for the Banff TV Festival, to make these changes rather than his doing them.

I eat a sandwich at the desk, then talk to the Atlantis lawyer Ted Kelterborn about my contract for the script (like many film contracts, it will not be completed until after the work has been done). Having enough of film, I walk down the street to the water [Lake Ontario], and at the ship's chandlery buy some boat rigging hardware.

Returning, I hit the computer and get all the changes done by 7 P.M., and fax the new script back to Phil. **"**

Financial pressures add to the professional scriptwriter's burden, even in enlightened film industries. Olof Rhodin is an independent film-maker in Stockholm:

" I am sitting at my computer as usual. The script I'm writing must be ready by Monday. I realise that I'm not going to be able to finish it. So I phone the producer at the Swedish Film Institute and get a new deadline. I won't get any money until the script is ready.

Decided to take a long walk. Sometimes I wonder why I work in film, it's like banging your head against a wall. Only when it's ready and after the premiere does it seem worth it. I'm probably a masochist. Met an old friend in the street, an independent film-maker, in roughly the same situation as me, without money. Always money. He's just been made bankrupt. He borrowed 500 crowns from me; I know I won't get it back.

Got a new idea for the script when I was out walking. I started sketching in my thoughts, got annoyed with myself. [. . .] The idea was about a married couple who have written a will, each with different beneficiaries. The couple die in an accident and it has to be decided who died last. Everything develops according to the saying, 'When God comes with death, Satan comes with heirs.'

I left the idea and sat down in an open-air cafeteria and had a beer. It's really hot now, and that's why it's hard to go back to any work-room. If I could afford it I'd buy a laptop and sit outside and write. [. . .]

[Back home] I sit down by the computer again and try to penetrate my writing. It took a while, then it went fine. Sometimes I lose contact with my characters, they grow alien to me . . . The script I'm writing is about the problems of kindness, the inability to say no that leads to complete self-destruction. It's about me. I think I'm a kind person, but I'm alone in that.

It's late evening. I've written five scenes that I'll have to rework. My writing is moving like a syncopated tango. I hope it rains tomorrow, then it'll be easier to stay in and write. **"**

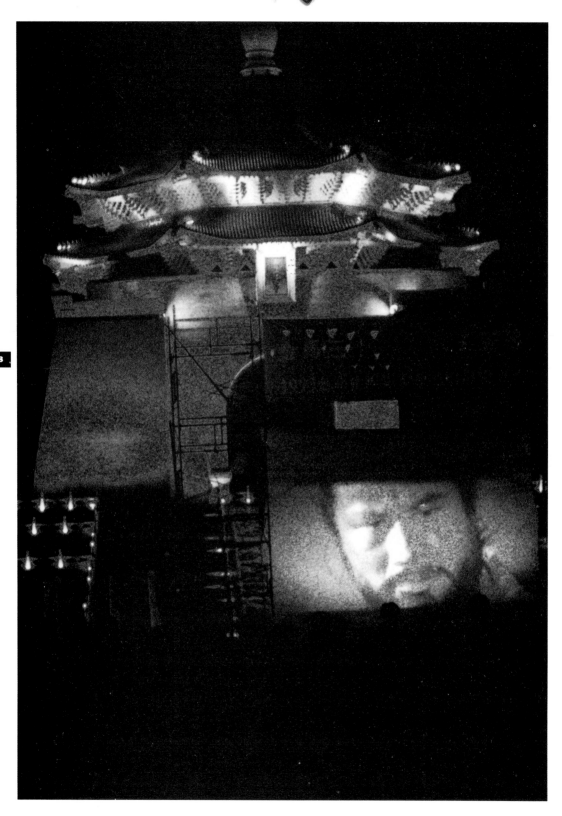

Left: *Screening of* Autumn Execution *in Taipei*. Above: *Lee Hsing accepting an award*

Portmanteau films, with each episode helmed by a different director, have been around since the 1940s. But Taiwanese director Lee Hsing, with over fifty features to his credit, now plans an ambitious and more subtle collaboration with colleagues bound by language rather than nationality:

" Lee Han-hsiang left Taiwan 22 years ago after directing Shih Ying at the China Film Studios. Now he's back in Taipei to audition Lee Hsiang-lan for the female lead in his new film, *Star in a World of Chaos.*

This afternoon, after much discussion, both of us finally decided to get together with mainland Chinese director Xie Jin and direct a film collaboratively. For the time being, we are calling the film *Mother*. Each of us will direct a third, depicting the 'mother' that we have in our mind's eye.

The idea of bringing together three directors from Taiwan, Hongkong and Mainland China was first mentioned during a seminar with Hongkong directors at the First Mainland China-Taiwan Film Exhibition in mid-January, 1992. We'd agreed then that we would start planning and preparing for the project. But it's been about

49 ◀◀

a year and a half since then, and still no results.

Xie Jin is presently directing *An Old Man and His Dog* on the Mainland, to be followed by *Under the Eaves of Old Shanghai*, on which I'll be acting as consultant. Han-hsiang's working on *Star in a World of Chaos*, and he starts shooting this year. Right now, I am busy organising the 30th Golden Horse Awards. So our plans for *Mother* will inevitably be put off until 1994.

The collaboration between us is not merely to make this particular film, but to combine our strength while we're still active to do something positive for Chinese film – that's our ulti- mate wish and goal. **99**

In India, the world's most prolific film nation, Buddhadeb Dasgupta in Calcutta tries to concentrate on a new project:

66 I have rambled through the pages of my new script that I finished a couple of months back. I thought of adding one more sequence at the end, but have simply corrected a few spellings. A strange idleness has crept into my system. I make a long-distance call to my camera- man Venu to discuss with him how to light a par- ticular shot in a sequence in the new script. His wife tells me that he has gone out for a long booze session and is not likely to come back before tomorrow morning. I dial my editor's number. No reply. Then my actress. Her maid picks up the receiver to inform me that she cannot take calls now. I heard my actress's voice shouting at some- body. Then I call my actor, who tells me candid- ly that he is terribly busy with his girlfriend and will see me next morning to discuss more about his role. The last call I make is to my producer and this is really shocking. He tells me about his son who has run away from the school hostel and has been missing for three days. No way does he want to talk about cinema right now. And if the boy is not found there is a chance he may cancel the project. Suddenly I start feeling cold. I think about the boy who I have never seen and how so much depends on him. I flick on the TV remote in order not to think any more about cinema today – it's so depressing! President Clinton dissolves on the screen, **99** smiling. I return his smile.

Edgardo Cozarinsky emigrated from Argentina to Paris during the 1970s and has served the cinema well with various analytical documentaries and essays:

66 8.30 A.M. To the typewriter. Not yet a word processor, no longer the purely mechanical device, but a compromise – Brother EP 44. Work on the screenplay for *Rothschild's Violin*, a film less about than around the opera by Benjamin Fleischmann (a student of Shostakovich, killed early in the Second World War, his unfinished only work to be orchestrated by his professor). [. . .]

[Lunch]. Bernard Eisenschitz is helping me search for Stalinist films I want to quote from in *Rothschild's Violin*. We discuss Ermler's *The Great Citizen* (1939) with music by Shostakovich – a hagiographic biopic of the Leningrad party boss, Kirov, whose assassination 'by a terrorist' Stalin engineered in order to launch his campaign **99** of terror in the 1930s.

Néjia Ben Mabrouk is an African film- maker living in Belgium, and contriving to combine the search for inspiration with life as a mother and wife in the big city:

66 Brussels. My day started on June 10th at midnight. I am in the last phase of writing the script for my second full-length feature. A dif- ficult stage, which consists of tightening a text that is far too long. I quite like the one and a half hour length because it forces me to stick to it. Today's agenda consists in re-studying a scene that takes place in a supermarket. I feel that it is not power- ful enough and breaks the rhythm which has been harmonious up to now. I still do not know where the problem lies because we need it for the pro- gression of the story. However, my first experi- ence with a full-length film has taught me that this type of problem can be solved only if I give free rein to my nocturnal wanderings, especially between two and three in the morning.

I am not sleepy but I have palpitations. I go out on the terrace to breathe the fresh air for ten

Still from African director Néjia Ben Mabrouk's film, La Trace

minutes. There are only a very few stars in the sky. The building opposite is black and quiet. Just one week ago, a woman on the top floor committed suicide. I was just going out for ten minutes to take the fresh air when I saw the ambulance people take her body out. My husband asked the policemen who were guarding the building for an explanation. They said something about its being a 'professional secret' and 'not very nice to see'. The sudden and violent death reminds me of the human condition that we see in its crudeness, every night at eight o'clock on television, with its rosary of injustices, of cowardice, abuse of power, of sufferings . . . I ask myself questions about my commitment to cinema, about the necessity of my subject-matter, about its effectiveness. And also about the cost of production that is always out of proportion, however modest it may be, compared to the standard of living of millions of Africans . . . I come back to my sequence 'Interior/night/supermarket.' I feel tired. I can clearly hear the purring of my cat. That was his way of reminding me gently of his mealtime when I would go on working too long. In fact, my cat died six months ago, a sudden stroke . . . Such hours always stimulate me to make a supernatural film. Probably my third movie.

I have slept the prescribed seven hours that enable me to sustain this marathon to the end without collapsing.

11 A.M. I ring my lawyer. My production company, the No Money Company, being a co-operative, causes me problems in the face of German legislation. The payment owed by the satellite-channel ARTE for the broadcast of *La Trace* (my first feature) is thus delayed. There is no co-operative left in the Federal Republic since the wall came down. I find myself obliged to provide a dossier to prove the legality of my firm in Belgium and the validity of my exercise as secretary. I seem to be losing a priceless amount of time with only one desire: to complete my script. Bureaucracy gives me headaches.

The telephone rings again. A cinema in Marseilles urgently requires a copy of *La Trace* for the opening of their cycle on Mediterranean

Another still from the film La Trace, *directed by the Néjia Ben Mabrouk*

Néjia Ben Mabrouk at work on her latest screenplay

cinema. I postpone a reply and leave the flat with the conviction that the telephone sabotages my decision to stay outside the world while writing.

At 1 P.M., I am in my office, without a telephone. I read an article on Dizzy Gillespie that I re-located after a long search. Among other things, he explains the meaning of *A Night in Tunisia* that I have listened to quite often while writing my script. From this article stems an emotion that gives me the desire to create something beautiful with my ten fingers.

I wrote until 6 P.M. After only three hours devoted to my son and to my husband, I wrote again until 3 A.M. the following morning. My five year old son has promised to stage a hold-up so that I don't have to write until three in the morning. My husband, being more realistic, types what I have corrected the day before to enable me to make progress.

Valentin Kuik, from Tallinn in Estonia, gives us his observations on the importance of the synopsis as a form:

“ Writing a screenplay is a long-term voluntary imprisonment. After finishing a script entitled *And in Your Hands Is the Fire of Hell*, about a man who was called Jack the Old Heathen, and who yearned to be blessed and failed [. . .], I came to the conclusion that my chances of turning this into a film are very slim. Why?

The key words of our modern film industry are freedom and money. After gaining freedom we discover that we are very poor and that money and freedom are notions that exclude each other because, with the coming of the new freedom, the old sources of finance were lost. It turned out that the keys to the safe were in the censor's pocket.

Fortunately, there is nothing absolute in this

world, including the shortage of money. Every film-maker knows that there's a lot of money in America, quite a lot in Western Europe, and much less but (compared to Estonia) quite a bit in Finland. One should not count money that's not one's own, but the mere knowledge of its being there is nice. [. . .]

That is how I and many of my colleagues learned how to write summaries of films not yet born. The synopsis, as this kind of summary is called, is a special genre of literature. Its form is canonical, meaning that you must blend the most

Still from Nëjia Ben Mabrouk's La Trace

thrilling film possible with the human pathos it contains, and your own mental anguish and that of your heroes, on a single page at most, because who would care to read a script coming from God knows where in our busy times? So you write a single page – the synopsis.

A synopsis is a love letter to a wealthy stranger in which it is suggested that the sender has the most beautiful legs and sexiest bottom, the loveliest face and most fabulous eyes. But as everyone, and a rich person is no exception, is apart from all else a spiritual being, one should not forget to add that the exceptional external specifications and irresistible sex appeal are combined with outstanding spirituality.

A synopsis is a simultaneous appeal to somebody's feelings and purse. Faxed over the ocean or the Gulf of Finland, it is waiting for its moment like a bride, longing for attention and a noble contract of international co-operation to be set in motion no matter by whose money (preferably with American film stock and equipment and cheap Estonian labour).

A synopsis is a crystal reflecting intricate human destinies and fascinating characters. A crystal containing both the author's religious and philosophical convictions, as well as powerful erotic vibrations and a coy promise to enrich all those who would help to turn this compressed description into a film. **99**

Kaspar Rostrup, whose film *Waltzing Regitze* was nominated for an Academy Award in 1990, reflects on the vocation:

66 Scriptwriting is at once the most wonderful and terrible thing. In total concentration you are lost to the world around you in order to devote yourself to your imagination and your feelings, and at the same time you are turned into a hermit, a mole, whose hypersensitivity, sensibility, doubt and paranoia can unleash severe depression. Considering that this mood can change in the space of seconds into hysterical outbursts of joy when something succeeds, and that in the end you are more your characters than you are yourself, it's not hard to understand that gradually you become ill-suited to associate **99** with normal people.

3. Art of the Pitch: Getting a Project Off the

Ground ONCE THE SCREENPLAY HAS TAKEN SHAPE,

WRITERS MUST SELL THEIR IDEAS. SO TOO MUST

THE PRODUCERS, DIRECTORS AND ANY NUMBER OF

ASSORTED MIDDLE-MEN. PATIENCE, PERSISTENCE,

AND A FLAIR FOR WHAT IS TERMED "THE PITCH" TO

STUDIOS AND FINANCIERS ALIKE, MAY DECIDE THE

FATE OF EVEN THE MOST FINELY-TUNED SCRIPT.

Terry Gilliam, whose audacious vision has given us *Brazil*, *Time Bandits*, and *The Fisher King* among other films, remains Britain's most maverick director. His diary reflects the constant shifting between creative and financial concerns that makes up the independent's day:

66 For the last seven months I have been writing and preparing a film called *The Defective Detective*. The whole process is slow and frustrating and has been turning me more and more into a hermit . . . and a crab. It has been almost three years since I have been behind a camera. I'm not happy and I leave the house less and less. My contact with the outside world is primarily via the telephone and the fax. Richard Lagravanese, my co-writer, is in New York. Margery Simkin, my co-producer, is in Los Angeles. [. . .]

However, this morning as I climb the stairs to start my ritual of making cups of cappuccino and staring at bits of paper, Jonathan Pryce drops in for a chat. Fresh from a series of successful commercials and talk shows in the US of A, he is try-

Above: *Terry Gilliam's forehead contains vital info.* Right: *His storyboard for* The Defective Detective

ing to decide between two conflicting film offers – on the one hand, an offer to play the villain in a big budget Hollywood film, on the other, a part in

— WHIP THRU —

Defective Detective
Storyboard —
10-6-93

a smallish three-hander alongside Judy Davis and River Phoenix [this film, *Dark Blood*, was abandoned in November 1993 after the death of Phoenix]. So the choice is once again the old favourite . . . do you go for the money and exposure or go for the more interesting and challenging . . . a chance to work with great artists – letting the quality of the work dictate your career rather than having your career dictate the quality of the work. 'Stick to art', say I. [. . .]

With the bulk of the morning now gone and no work done on the script, I attack the telephone. First call: Joyce Herlihy re. preparing a budget for *The Defective Detective*. Next I get my wife, Maggie, to run down to ProntoPrint to make more copies of the script so that they can be sent to Joyce and the accountant.

[. . .] I pick up a book at random: *Barcelona*, by Robert Hughes. The first page I turn to is about Catalan ironsmiths. Suddenly I'm back in the world of Vulcan, a world I thought I had spent sufficient time in during *The Adventures of Baron Munchausen*. These chance meetings always amaze me. They are invariably a result of the mess that surrounds me in my studio. I am always bumping into information that can be useful in jolting me out of whatever creative block I currently find myself trapped in . . . or providing me with surprising new paths down which I can ramble to avoid the task at hand. I use these occasional moments of serendipity as justification for my innate sloppiness.

[After lunch] I turn my attention to a script called *Bayswater* that has been sent to me with the hope that I might direct it in the autumn. Although it's nicely written, it doesn't manage to excite me, so I call the producer, Brian Eastman, and talk myself out of another chance to make a film.

10 P.M. At last the world is dark and still, the pigeons [on my roof], the house, and all in it are asleep. I can finally concentrate on drawing my storyboards. The sequence I am working on involves complicated special effects and needs to be laid out in careful detail. With each stroke of the pen the film begins to come alive . . . a flying bed transports the detective and a mysterious boy into a child's glorious fantasy world. I don't refer to the script. I just let the pictures come. The characters begin to breathe . . . the world

becomes real. The bed soars over a mountainous castle and dives down to a mirror sea. The sunset glows amber as they sweep along their reflection in the still surface of the sea and begin to climb towards the colossal tree in the clouds . . . 🙶

Keeping two or three projects in the air belongs to the art of the professional screenwriter in today's multimedia world, as Adrian Hodges of London implies:

🙶 After the usual prevarication I face the computer at about 10 o'clock. I'm working on a series called *Hopeless Romantics* – three

Willem Dafoe and Miranda Richardson in a scene from Tom & Viv, *written by Adrian Hodges*

episodes for Carlton TV. I'm on the second, but progress so far has been slow and unhappy, partly because this is my first attempt at a long running series and partly because I'm distracted by the news that *Tom & Viv*, a film I wrote three years ago, has finally received its production go-ahead. It's adapted from the play by Michael Hastings about T.S. Eliot's unhappy first marriage. Miranda Richardson and Willem Dafoe have agreed to star. A friend rings up to tell me that the upper echelons of Fabers (the publishing house where Eliot worked for the latter part of his life) are deeply unhappy about the film, still more so about Dafoe as Eliot. I imagine they are wonder-

ing how a man last seen having hot wax poured over his genitals by Madonna [in *Body of Evidence*] will adapt to playing the great poet in English of the century. Personally I'm delighted by the casting – Dafoe is a serious and intelligent actor, and by all accounts a nice guy. I give way to creeping paranoia for a few moments as I brood over changes made to the script by the director, Brian Gilbert, which I am very uneasy about. [. . .]

The phone rings again – it is the producer of another of my films, *Tell Me You Love Me,* an

American adaptation of my BBC-TV film. She tells me that everyone in L.A. 'loves' the script, though not yet enough to actually make it. We wonder whether the absence of a gimmick – a mad nanny/secretary/milkman/orang-utang – is the real problem. Following Neil Jordan's success with *The Crying Game* I offer to make my hero a transvestite. The producer regards this with suspicion and reminds me not to be ironic when I go to Hollywood in July. **99**

Jerry Schatzberg belongs to that distinguished brethren of New York-based directors whose work has been applauded around the world (*The Seduction of Joe Tynan, Scarecrow, Reunion*) yet rarely in Hollywood:

66 10 A.M. I am reviewing my notes of the last five months relating to a film project, working title *Birds of Passage* (it will certainly change).

The film will be loosely based on a book, *1492*, by Jacques Atali, documenting the events in Europe at the time. I was brought into the project when the producer, Jacques Kirsner, heard I was coming to Europe to do a documentary on David Ben-Gurion. It is one of a hundred being done by one hundred directors, on famous people who changed the world. *Birds* attracted my curiosity; 1492 was a year of upheaval in politics, art, medicine, man's inhumanity to man, anti-Semitism (the Spanish Inquisition and the expulsion of Jews from Spain). I would like to keep the focus on one family of Conversos (Jews converted to Christianity), living in Spain and influential in the court of Ferdinand and Isabella [and how their life becomes a nightmare when confronted with the reality of the Inquisition].

The contracts were finalised on Saturday, June 5, and at 2 P.M. today I am having my first meeting with Ira Lewis, a playwright. We will spend the next week or two discussing a concept.

Meryl Streep and Alan Alda in Jerry Schatzberg's The Seduction of Joe Tynan

After that we will go to Paris to consult with Atali and Kirsner and then start the first draft. [. . .]

1.15 P.M. Ira called; he is stuck at the studio and has to cancel our meeting. He's doing dialogue for Al Pacino on *Carlito's Way*. Ira has done that for Pacino on his last three films. Al will be finishing filming in July and I will have Ira full time. We did discuss the film a little on the telephone. There are great similarities in the events of the Fifteenth Century and those of the Twentieth. We will explore this.

At the very heart of the power-play sustaining Hollywood stand the agents. Arnold Rifkin, Worldwide Head of the Motion Picture Division at William Morris, one of the oldest and most respected firms in the business, handles such prestigious clients as Bruce Willis and Robert Duvall. His tightly-constructed day symbolises the need for constant activity in Tinseltown:

5.15 A.M. Normal wake-up time. Twenty-five minute aerobic workout followed by weight work in the gym.

6 A.M. Review outstanding paperwork for the office. [. . .] Read today's trades – *Daily Variety* and *The Hollywood Reporter*. [. . .]

8.45 A.M. Arrive at office and begin returning outstanding calls from prior three days which were spent in the New York office.

10 A.M. Agent/lawyer conversations regarding potential meeting with actor/star to change representation. Set meeting for Monday with lawyers and star to discuss same. Met internally with staff.

11 A.M. Internal meeting with senior board members of William Morris Agency re. fee structure for presentation to large entertainment client with whom I am engaged in closing a deal for representation.

Noon. Meeting with Oscar-winning client together with associate, Nicole David, to review the week of lawyer meetings the client took regarding her decision to take on legal representation.

1 P.M. Grabbed sandwich in office with talent staff to review all current deals, and with business affairs regarding current agent deals.

2 P.M. General phone activity.

3.30 P.M. Learned that final decision to replace director on a William Morris-packaged movie had been made, and that final negotiations for new director were in play. [. . .]

4.30 P.M. Meeting with potential client – young male actor starring in a movie in release in the U.S.

5 P.M. External meeting with people regarding negotiations to finance new film being put together with client Blake Edwards to rewrite and direct.

5.45 P.M. Return outstanding phone calls from the day.

6.15 P.M. Meeting with key executives re. department head dinner next week. Have preliminary conversations regarding motion picture department retreat in October.

7 P.M. Leave office to visit location of *Color of Night*, starring Bruce Willis.

7.30 P.M. On set.

8.45 P.M. Leave set. Make final phone calls from car.

9.15 P.M. Arrive home. Read script for client consideration that requires immediate response.

Hugh Hudson has spent the last several years coming to terms with Hollywood, and still wrestles with the legacy of the late David Lean – a screen version of Joseph Conrad's *Nostromo* – among other things:

7 A.M. Los Angeles Four Seasons Hotel. Summer. But I'll be here in Autumn, Winter and Spring as usual. Seasons come and go as the highs and lows of a film director's career pass by. Twelve years ago, *Chariots of Fire* was the talk of Hollywood and the sweet taste of success was in my mouth. An intoxicating substance but very dangerous. It affects the equilibrium. You lose your place in the world and start to believe the myths that are printed about you without even noticing it. It may be a long, hard grind to the top but it's a swift descent to the bottom if you've had your head turned by your good fortune. In the end, though, these low periods of one's life turn out to be more valuable than the high times. You find yourself a human being again back in touch with people and their lives and naturally that is where the interesting stories are.

EPY 5018

2A 3

Hugh Hudson: intent on setting up Nostromo, *a project initiated by and slated for the late David Lean*

Breakfast meeting. The Hollywood institution. Irish oatmeal for me. Good for the bowels although a successful movie would be even better. My attorney, who only drinks black coffee, and I discuss the progress of a contract with TriStar. Half an hour to strike the deal and six months to wait until the draft is ready to sign! [. . .]

Nostromo, the movie I'm setting up at the moment, is based on the novel by Joseph Conrad. A tale of greed and corruption. It's centred around a silver mine in a fictitious country in South America. A European film but, with a large budget, we could do with some American dollars, so we need an American star. Now the

problems start. The studio naturally want someone they feel will justify their investment and I want somebody I can believe in. The compromises begin. How far can I stray from the original idea of *Nostromo*? Should I agree to anyone, to get the film made? I can't do that even if I wanted to. I need to be convinced that the actor is the part. If I start the film without that magic then I'm lost.

[. . .] The intense relationship that I have with the French producer [of *Nostromo*], Serge Silberman, intrudes into my daily life. I've experienced negligent producers, selfish producers and greedy producers but never one with such a compulsion to articulate every single aspect of the progress of the film as it lurches from one stage to the next. [. . .] He's a stimulating man with a passion to make the film and producers with his generosity of spirit are hard to come by. [. . .]

Evening. The first night of the AFI Festival. It opens with the epic *El Cid* (re-mastered version running at 3½ hours) starring Charlton Heston and immediately after that screening, Steven Spielberg's *Jurassic Park* is shown. The dinosaur of epics followed by an epic of dinosaurs!

I go back to my room at the Four Seasons. It's so late I can reach Serge in his office in Paris. We talk at length about actors and budgets and schedules etc., and I eventually go to bed. Another day of wheeling and dealing in L.A. has ended. Tonight I dream. Tomorrow I dream . . . 99

Another British director whose work has charmed American audiences finds himself waking in Los Angeles too. Charles Sturridge (*Brideshead Revisited, A Handful of Dust, Where Angels Fear to Tread*) works on TV commercials to pay the rent, and continues to battle for funding on projects close to his heart:

Anthony Andrews and Jeremy Irons in Brideshead Revisited

66 I am in Los Angeles because *A Foreign Field*, a film that I made last year for the BBC with Lauren Bacall, Geraldine Chaplin, Alec Guinness, Leo McKern, Jeanne Moreau, Ed Herrmann, and John Randolph is being screened at the Los Angeles Film Festival. I am also trying to find a way of financing the script for a new film: *Buffalo Soldiers*, based on the brilliant novel by Robert O'Connor. Set on a U.S. Army Base in Germany, it's the story of a love affair between the battalion drugs dealer and the young daughter of the sergeant who is out to destroy him. [. . .]

Susan Arnold and Donna Roth at MGM have just produced *Benny & Joon*, which I haven't seen. It's perceived as 'difficult material' and so is *Buffalo Soldiers* (i.e. no part for Schwarzenegger). [. . .] In fact they are both very nice, and I launch into my crablike introduction as to why I want to make the film, and they smile encouragingly and say they will read the book. I leave for the car park in a panic because I have forgotten the number of the space I parked in. One of the puzzling factors of this process is that I do not really expect

to finance the development of the script out of Los Angeles; however, I have to demonstrate some interest here in order to persuade any European money to invest. It's a pity I'm not on commission from Knopf, the American publishers of *Buffalo Soldiers*.

11 A.M. Culver City for a 'general meeting' with Laura Ziskin, producer among other things of *Accidental Hero*, therefore deemed to have an interest in English directors. TriStar is being completely rebuilt and, after some rather skilful (I think) Los Angeles navigation, I arrive at the half-completed white gates. [. . .] Laura Ziskin is brisk and efficient and we have a straightforward conversation, and at the end she promises to read the book, and to try to come to the screening of my film.

12.30 P.M. Speedy lunch with Cary Woods in the Sony Pictures Executive dining-room, which is satisfyingly full of Japanese executives. Woods introduces himself as the 'agent who set up *Drugstore Cowboy*' (spot the connection). He has been encouraged to meet me by a young producer, Randy Poster, who I had met a couple of days earlier and who also loves the book. Woods is now a successful producer, but he thinks like an agent: 'Is there a part for Gary Oldman?' 'Well, no, not really.' 'Pity, never mind . . . what shall we eat?'

3 P.M. Cappella is a relatively new company, whose finance is German-based and as much of the expenditure of the project will be in Germany where the story [of *Buffalo Soldiers*] is set, this might seem to be a more likely home for the film. David Korda has already read the book, and 'passed' because he does not feel it is mainstream enough. However, he has agreed to listen to me talk about the film. Each time I tell the story, it takes on a more precise life as I experiment with slightly different methods and try out different emphases. Slowly it begins to put down roots and grow inside of me. The meeting is a good one, and I feel they have got a clearer picture, literally, of what I want to do. David Korda likes the ideas, but is still uncertain if the film will attract a big enough audience and therefore make money. However, he'll send the book to his chairman in Germany and if he is drawn to the material then they would seriously consider development. **"**

64

Adapting to offers and counter-offers is all part of the texture of most directors' daily lives. Nick Holland is an Australian based in Surrey Hills, New South Wales:

" This wintry Thursday was mostly taken up in a long meeting with my producer/partner, Richard Fricker. He returned from Japan two days ago, after yet another reconnaissance mission to find possible co-producers for our first feature film.

I was hopeful that our Japanese contacts would be more responsive to our new treatment, entitled *Hamaki*, than others we've presented in the past.

Richard is now a veteran of these 'knock, knock, look who's here again' trips and happily reported that they were indeed more enthused: apparently all we need to do is to take the story out of its WWII setting and place it sometime in the dark future! [. . .] It's now clear that they are finally regarding Richard as a trustworthy business person. So much so, that Hero Communications in Tokyo have more or less handed us the rights to an historical drama epic all about Genghis Khan, and free rein to distrib-

ute the thing however we choose throughout Australia and New Zealand.

[. . .] So, we'll have to quickly learn a thing or two about finding a market for Mongolian epics. We appreciate Australia is a very multi-cultural society but this will undoubtedly be something of a challenge.

In any case, we both agree that learning a few things about how exhibitors operate will be extremely useful when the time comes for them to handle our feature!

Also, after both having been in the business for fifteen years or so, we realise that opportunity does not necessarily appear as one might have imagined: I leapt from a long acting career to directing career without any training and now five years later, as an established 'drama' director, find another chasm with a little signpost: 'Feature Film Success Ahead.'

However, as I look down I see thousands of lost souls piled up in the valley below, clutching treatments, scripts, contracts or just a battered Filofax. I suppose if we wait long enough, eventually we'll be able to simply walk over the bodies to the other side! **"**

Gail Singer is an independent writer/ director from Toronto, and talks of the compulsive, neurotic nature of productive work in film:

" I have two feature films in pre-development: one is based on the real-life alleged theft of intellectual property – a cookie recipe; the other is set in a train that crosses the great expanse of Canada and involves a formerly ordinary woman who has broken out of her humdrum life by committing an unlikely act. Disguised as a railway detective, she is pursed by a railway detective disguised as an Australian soundman.

I am also struggling with a documentary which I will start shooting in the fall, on an arcane aspect of violence against women. [. . .]

I spent the morning on the phone. The producer I am to meet at 11.30 has her secretary call to ask if I could possibly postpone the meeting until 11.30! Of course, I say graciously, arriving fifteen minutes late. [. . .] The producer and I talk for a few minutes, then she says she hopes I won't mind but she will have to take a long-distance call very shortly. [. . .] We proceed with our discussion, which is about two really great ideas I have had, one for a TV drama series and another for an animated series. I want to [have] a creative producer role. Suddenly I realise I am pitching these ideas which was not my intention. These ideas feel too good to be reduced to a pitch, or am I kidding myself? Or am I tainting 'pitching' with my own neurotic defence system? Later, I have to say to myself, how else do these things happen but for the telling of them to people who can participate in making them happen!

Miriam Gallagher, an Irish screenwriter, sports that persistence of vision so indispensable to surviving in the film world, and to keeping a deal alive:

❝ As Domino, our black and white cat, has no food, I must slip out to the shops before starting my morning's work on my second full-length feature screenplay, *Making Waves*. [. . .] This is based on my novel of the same title. I struggle with a tricky scene in the first 'Act' and bring it off. Success! Of such little unrecognised moments (actually one hour) are my satisfactions

Scene from Gypsies, *scripted and directed by Miriam Gallagher*

as a writer made. Now I relish every hill walked, every word that works, and *give myself* feedback rather than waiting for the world – bless it – who has taught me that writing – especially for the movies – is sheer folly. But I will persist. I like the way *Making Waves* (the tale of a photographer who 'mislays' his beautiful wife) is shaping up. [. . .]

At lunchtime I meet John Lynch, producer/ director of *Girls in Silk Kimonos*, which I tell him was featured in the New York Daily News. [. . .] He has no joyful news on the production front. This screenplay was written with my heart's blood. I got an Arts Council award for it, went to Cannes, London and New York, promoting the idea of it. Everyone loves it. Why is there no move on it? Financial reasons. Together we applied and got a European Script Fund award for this celebration of the Gore Booth sisters, passionate dreamers who dared to make their dreams come true. The film is romantic, adventurous and, I am told, 'expertly put together.' Will I be 100 when it is screened? [. . .]

I attack my storyboard for *Gypsies*. This lovely little piece of work concerns a child's dramatic encounter with gypsies at the seaside. It is based on my own live meeting as a child in Tramore

Still from Miriam Gallagher's Gypsies, *shot on location in Ireland*

Sketch for Gypsies *by Gerhardt Gallagher*

(Co. Waterford) with 'Tinkers' who roped me in to collect money for them along the length of Tramore strand, to my delight and thirst for adventure and to the horror of my parents. [. . .] I'm happy with the crew and actors and the composer. All we need is money! I am determined to make this film and know it will happen – even if I have to busk on the streets! I decide to spend a session on the budget and to apply to all sources of funding again and again!

One of Iran's most gifted and established directors, Dariush Mehrjui (*The Cow, The Postman, The Cycle*) continues to work in a kind of limbo between assignments:

Because of the trip to Bushehr (a southern port), I came back late last night. [. . .] I have a knot in my heart, a bit depressed seeing Bushehr so changed. All the old houses on the shore have vanished, perhaps been destroyed. The piers are fenced with thick walls, impossible to reach the sea. No more hurly-burly on the pier as in the past. And so now I must look for another port, maybe Bandar-Abbas or Bandar-Lengeh . . . until I find the proper setting for *Akbarou*, which takes place 25 years ago.

Akbarou is a tragedy I've been working on in the past year, after the temporary failure of *Inspector Yahya* – two years spent looking for a producer, and now in limbo. Still hopeful that it might get going, but for now I stick to *Akbarou*. These are the two projects I am now involved with and I have no idea which one will get started. It still seems like the first film I'm trying to get done. Same difficulties as a first-timer. The difficulties of feasibility and the constantly changing economic and cultural situation have made filmmaking akin to the ascent of the Himalayas: laborious, exhausting, and dream-like. Can I? Will I?

The best and easiest thing to do is to stay put and dive into day-dreaming. So I have projects by the dozens. For cinema, for TV, and for video. The first two are tough ones; they take a lot of force and energy. Video is easy, but it has not yet been legally established [in Iran]. So it has no economic definition yet, and since it is cheap to produce, the assumption is that it does not produce worthy returns.

Bimal Majumder's diary from Howrah in India projects the screenwriter as reluctant businessman:

June 10, 1993 was the day I completed the second draft of the script of my next film, *Time Immemorial*. At this moment I am considering this draft as final. It will be my first feature film.

I have sent a letter to a film production company in Bombay, requesting them for financial assistance for making the picture. I have also decided to submit this script to the National Film Development Corporation, an Indian government organisation. I am approaching Doordarshan (TV) for finance too.

Dulal da (Dulal Dutta, the film editor with whom Satayajit Ray worked during his career) is also contacted today. I expressed my idea of reading the full script to him because he is the only

person with whom I have discussed the development of my concept from time to time. We will sit down together during the week ahead. I decide that Dulal da will edit the film also, as he did my earlier short, *Rupashi Sahar*. [. . .]

I spent most of the rest of the day either doing sketches for the script or engrossing myself in thinking about prospective actors/actresses – old faces and new faces, child actors/actresses, locations, frame composition, colour, and so on – for my next film, *Aabahamankal*. But sometimes during the day I felt very depressed because I know that for a new young film-maker to get a **"** producer for his film is extremely difficult.

Aparna Sen made her name as an actress in Indian films for Satyajit Ray and others. Now, as a director and journalist also, she is playing the "pitching" game too:

" 6.35 A.M. Arrived in London en route to the U.S. A dismal rainy morning, soggy enough to dampen my already considerably low spirits! The only reason I'm stopping in London is so that I can meet Farrukh Dhondy of Channel 4 in the hope that he can provide funding (either full or partial) for my next film/films.

Actually, I'm planning to leave three ideas with him. One is about Calcutta – a serialised docu-feature for television about the city. [. . .] So many films have been made on our much-maligned city – each worse than the next! It needs a Calcuttan with all the love and hate and disgust and tenderness that she feels for her city to make such a film ring true. [. . .]

The other two ideas are for feature films. One (like all my other films) written entirely by me is, on the surface, about a marriage that is coming apart. Two people in their forties who live in different cities for work reasons, like so many modern urban couples, decide to go back to the little fishing village where they had come seventeen years earlier for their honeymoon, to try and put their marriage together again. [. . .] The third idea is from a story by one of our best Bengali authors. It is called *Motilal Padre* and is about an old padre who lives among some tribals in India.

Actress, director, and journalist Aparna Sen behind the camera

A young tribal woman gives birth to an obviously illegitimate child in Motilal Padre's church and the old priest interprets this as the Second Coming! The film deals with his faults and his doubts and his relationship with the tribals, and ultimately celebrates his faith in humanity, which rises above all institutionalised religious beliefs. Will Farrukh like the ideas? How difficult it is to sell oneself.

10 A.M. Phoned Farrukh Dhondy's place of work and, bad news, he is in Wales! They've just announced on television that parts of Wales are flooded! Damn! Supposing Farrukh can't get back to London before I have to leave? I tried so hard to call him from Calcutta to make an appointment before I actually arrived. I must have talked to his answering machine at least a dozen times!

[. . .] Funding is such a problem for our kind of cinema that I wonder if management of funds is what film direction is all about! It exhausts you completely, saps your energy and makes it very nearly impossible to sustain the inspiration that made you want to make the film in the first place. That we film-makers often manage to do so speaks volumes about our fanatical passion for cinema!

11 P.M. Just talked to F.D.'s answering machine again. It sounded sleepy, or did I imagine **"** that? I'll try again tomorrow morning . . .

In many countries, the film-maker must be a Jack or Jill of all trades, juggling domestic commitments with the constant search for artistic funding and solutions, as Åsa Sjöström reports from Tullinge in Sweden:

" After five years cramped in a small flat with two sons playing at acrobatics, drums, electric guitars and general swashbuckling, I have had enough of trying to put films together somewhere between the Kitchen Sink and the Deep Blue Sea, and with cutting films on a Steenbeck stuck awkwardly in the hall by the front door [. . .] and of myself struggling to retain some measure of sanity in my multi-role as Producer /Director/Animator/In-Betweener/Charlady and Artist, the Artist refusing any knowledge of Anything and Anybody outside the privileges of her Ivory Towers, and especially any Awareness

Vilgot Sjöman's I Am Curious – Yellow *was until recently the most commercially successful foreign film released in the U.S.*

whatsoever of the Producer's difficult task, trying to keep to Some-kind-of-plan (i.e. Budget). [. . .]

I have only a few days to finish painting and plastering the house, as I must start on the next job, for which I am getting some development money from the [Swedish] Film Institute. It is a short film with an environmental message, and I have the basic concept in my head, but need to make a detailed storyboard in order to estimate a budget and the technical requirements. One big problem has been the tax office's delaying of the money to be paid out, because I don't have the right forms and classification, so that although the money is ready to be paid out, I can't have it as yet, at least not without numerous phone calls and personal visits to the tax office. But this is the usual story, the same every time I receive a production grant. It is to be expected. Would life be the same if the tax people were human?

Vilgot Sjöman was, until *The Crying Game* came along, responsible for the most commercially successful foreign film released in the United States: *I Am Curious – Yellow* (1967). Now in his late sixties, he hopes to direct a massive biopic about Alfred Nobel:

❝ I'm in church with my wife. Our youngest son is finishing school, 'forever' he says. He doesn't want to carry his graduation cap. The headmaster talks flirtatiously to all the classes.

The organ plays. I'm not here, I'm in Cambodia. I just came back.

I'm staring at an old woman's face. She is protecting herself against the feverish sun. It's somewhere between Phnom Penh and Takeo. She earns two dollars a month by hammering larger stones into smaller pieces. She has a sweet old face. I don't know what to do with that face. She won't be back when I return. *If I ever return.* I've been doing research for a new documentary. Three weeks in the company of Michael Vickery, author of the best book on the Pol Pot period. What will the decision makers say? When I told them I wanted to do a documentary in the Smokey Mountains in the Philippines, they said no. Anyhow, the film was made. I ended up in TV-INPUT. *Innocence and Garbage* was bought by the BBC. When was it shown? Last December? I got two fan letters.

Tomorrow is a meeting. I will go to a Saturday-Sunday meeting in Waxholm. Katinka [Faragó, the producer] wants me to meet a Danish production designer. We shall spend two days going through my script. It's the first time I've ever been commissioned to do a script. It's on the life of Alfred Nobel. Biographical films are boring. But something happened to me when I looked into his life. *That man was a self-torturer.* I'm fond of self-torturers. I wrote the script twice, as I always do. The Sandrews [film company] people liked it. They have accepted it. They have even told me what the budget should be: 34 million Swedish crowns [approx. $4.6 million]. Now we should check if the script fits into the budget! I've a feeling the meeting will be decisive.

There is another idea, close to my heart. It's out of my own fantasy. A brother-and-sister story. No, they are not going to have a baby together. It's not another *My Sister, My Love* [made by Sjöman in 1966]. This time the brother is suicidal, so the sister brings him back to their childhood home. Memories keep popping up. But they don't *talk* about their dead parents. Film isn't talking. They start to imitate them, first for fun, then for real. And there is a change of sex. The girl imitates the father, the boy the mother. People who have read the first draft say: this can be done on the stage, not on film. Nonsense, I say. So Per Lysander, the newly-appointed pro-

duction consultant at the Swedish Film Institute, has given me money to prove my point. In a few days from now I will shoot a pilot film with Maria Lundquist and Kjell Bergqvist.

The organ stops playing. I'm filled with anger and hatred. There are too many obstacles around the corners: I could murder anyone who stands in my way.

Outside is the mild Swedish summer. My guy is walking away to get the final results of his thirteen years in school. He isn't smiling, either. **99**

David McGillivray, a film buff whose encyclopedic knowledge has enriched the pages of *Film Review* for more than twenty years, finds it hard to set up his own projects:

66 Mark Forstater [the producer] phoned. He likes my treatment for a film of my book, *Doing Rude Things: The History of the British Sex Film 1957-1981*, but says it's too expensive. He can only raise enough money for maybe two days in a studio. Didn't like the sound of this. Nor did my publisher Anthony Blampied when I told him. We want a week on location. Phoned Mark back and told him I could shoot it dirt cheap with minimal crew. He was vague about how much dosh was available. I said I'd find the rest. He said he'd ring me back. [. . .]

Went round to see production manager Simon Kennedy about *Afterdeath*, a horror film I plan to shoot on Guernsey. He says I'm nuts to use my own money and that he can find backing. He wants to budget the script but I can't bring myself to show it to him in case he thinks it's crap. Obviously I'll have to pull myself together in the not too distant future. **99**

From the chaos of the former Yugoslavia, Milan Ljubic sends a journal full of good cheer, reinforcing Slovenia's resolve to make films into the future:

66 It is midnight. We are sitting in director Bostjan Hladnik's residence, drinking some fine French Pernod – on the rocks, of course. Outside is a warm spring night. We are all gathered round a table: Bostjan Hladnik, a renowned Slovene avant-garde film-maker, Peter Zobec

and I, Hladnik's former assistants and Irena Felicijan, a costume designer who began her career as a scriptgirl together with us under Hladnik's guidance. Exactly thirty years have passed since then. An hour ago I was invited to drink a toast to the great news that the film *Adagio* (with Peter Zobec as scriptwriter and director, and me as producer) was approved by the government. The Slovene Ministry of Culture required nine months to give its okay.

In the afternoon I tackled my correspondence [and] prepared a draft for a drama feature entitled *E-94*, a kind of road movie dealing with the first few days of the war of Slovene independence, and the initial military operations within Slovenia which moved from here to neighbouring Croatia and beyond to Bosnia, where the bloody climax of the Yugoslav tragedy is unfolding . . . The budget isn't high – 1.5 million Deutschmarks . . .

9 P.M. I read the latest version of the script for *Adagio* that Peter Zobec handed me. This version is much better. I write some comments and, despite the late hour, call him to point out the bits he should pay particular attention to. **"**

73 «

After *Hear My Song*, British director Peter Chelsom might be regarded as a surefire bet. But, as his diary reveals, nothing can be taken for granted:

" If I were ten years younger [he is 37] I would be celebrating the fact that we look to be financed for *Sam and the Sergeant*, the film I have turned everything else down to do this year. Caution tells me to stand by for a long road still to come on this one. Our cast to date is Sam Neill, Cybill Shepherd, Martin Landau, Oliver Reed as Major Disaster and Lionel Jeffries as 'the Sergeant'. Sam Neill has a lot to bring to the film at the moment, not just because he is going to be excellent in the lead, but because *Jurassic Park* is opening in two days' time in the U.S. and promises to be everything you want it to be. Should put him in the top drawer. I'm still hoping that some of the other possible investors may come off the fence if it does. All this aside,

Peter Chelsom, still smiling after the success of Hear My Song

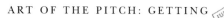

our film is still perceived as a massive risk.

Spoke to Adrian Dunbar (co-writer on *Sam* and long-time friend) and told him that I had learnt that Guy East of Majestic Films still has a problem with the film because he 'has always run a mile from any kind of mental illness.' Have we written a book about mental illness? Or rather, do we want someone selling the film as the one about mental illness? The next *Cuckoo's Nest*? It's one way of seeing it, I suppose. [. . .]

Encouraged that Sam Neill returned my call from Washington where he was attending the Presidential screening of *Jurassic Park*. My insecurity has me looking out for signs that Sam wants to do something else first and doesn't know how to tell me. I think that if having him on our film has not made any real difference in four weeks' time, it never will and I will have to move on to something else. [. . .]

Have been budgeting *Sam and the Sergeant* properly here [in London] and L.A., which means really thinking things through, which in turn starts to feel like it is going to happen, the actual doing of it, rather than the endless pitching, talking, hoping, and wondering where I will be in six months – the Matterhorn with Oliver Reed starting an avalanche (in character, of course) or getting another orange to roll and stop next to the pack in a juice commercial. **"**

The "off-on" nature of much film-making outside the mainstream induces feelings of uncertainty, even fear, in Viktor Aristov, a director based in St. Petersburg. Sadly, Aristov died in January, 1994:

" I've been making my latest film *Rains in the Ocean* for well over two years now and I sense that I will not finish it. Shooting started in November 1991, continued in July 1992 and now I am preparing myself for a third shoot. This time I have only got enough money for two episodes – the restaurant and the lavish interior of the main character's cabin. She by the way has just had her 18th birthday. When we started she hadn't even turned 16.

The late Viktor Aristov, working on his last film, Rains in the Ocean

At first I got production money from Lenfilm who were no doubt 'softened' by the Silver Bear I had been awarded at the Berlin Film Festival for my film, *Satan*. After only six months, Lenfilm realised that my film would be too expensive for their budget and so I found myself alone with my idea, my actors, and film crew. This is now the third year that I have been unable to find any money either in Russia or abroad.

I spent the first half of today with a headache, trying to think how I could rewrite the script and make it as cheap as possible without losing my artistic concept. [. . .]

At 6 P.M. I chose the people to be included in the crowd during the restaurant scene. I wandered among hundred of agitated, pleading eyes that were trained on me in the hope of being selected. To some you say yes, to others no. And in one way or another you solve something by doing this but somewhere deep in you a fear is growing that a new era has begun and that this era does not consider you interesting enough. You have missed the train and you are left standing on a platform which is crowded with strange people who are talking in a different language, which you cannot understand, and these people live by an alien set of laws and morals.

Thomas Constantinides, an American writer-director, touches upon the chaos, prevarication and duplicity encountered by many an independent film-maker:

Day 830 of attempting to secure funding for my next film [*Pale Love*]. I am filled with anxiety, dread, anticipation and depression. For the past three months the Canadian half of the money has been making excuses. Vincent continues to promise and partially completes his due diligence. His pattern has been just at the moment of closing some other factor arises that must be fulfilled and sidetracks the deal. I believe he is standing for some unexplained reasons other than he doesn't really have the money.

Six days earlier, I finally took complete control and informed my partner about Vincent's

Another still of Russian director Viktor Aristov, who died in January 1994

business pattern. Hesitant, she agreed. [. . .]

Today is Vincent's deadline. He has to deliver a banking official to verify that his money is in place. Everyone is nervous. The broker, Bernard, attempted to save his position. He proposed to Vincent that his attorney and the Canadian banker talk to verify the production funds. Vincent agreed. It is the last date he has to play with the rights to my project.

End of day, June 10, 1993. Vincent did not comply with his own promise. The banker's name was never secured by anyone. For over three months he played a cat and mouse game, but when pressed could not deliver.

The second half of the money remains in place awaiting the first half. There are two other entities, both viable distribution companies willing to put up advances for this film if the casting requirements are met.

June 10, 1993, ended without production funds being put into place. With all the other feelings inside me running rampant, I still have a small glimmer of hope that my film will be financed sooner or later.

Henning Carlsen, the Danish director of *Hunger*, one of the best films of the 1960s, has decided to return to the Norwegian author of *Hunger*, Knut Hamsun; this time he has opted for *Pan*:

Went to Kastrup airport to pick up my old friend Erik Borge from Oslo. We are going to work together as we did in 1965/66 when he was the manager of ABC-Film, my Norwegian co-production partner on *Hunger*. [. . .] Now he runs Northern Lights A/S with Axel Helgeland. Our new project is also a Hamsun story, namely *Pan*, for which Northern Lights and my company Dagmar Film Production bought the rights earlier this year.

I briefed [Erik, Helge, and Peter Aalbæk Jensen of Zentropa Entertainment] on my progressing work with the first draft of the screenplay which I expect to finish towards the end of this month. We had a short talk about the schedule and took into consideration the different datelines for the European Script Fund and the Nordic Film & TV Fund. I used Zentropa's Mac to print out the first forty pages of the screenplay which I had on a floppy, and gave them to Axel with all my reservations.

We agreed to create a consortium between our three companies as the production body for *Pan*, with Northern Lights as the executive producer. Axel will set up a draft agreement. The consortium may seek co-production deals with other companies in Sweden and/or Germany. **99**

Taylor Hewstan, a screenwriter from British Columbia, writes about her own frustrations and the elusiveness of the "deal" even in well-endowed Canada:

66 Yesterday had lunch with friends who are still somewhat influenced by the Canadian propaganda that waxes poetic in regard to our (with sarcasm) ever so vast film industry. What a laugh! I've been looking around for independent financing for a feature that I want to direct since I returned from L.A. in March and according to those in the know, I might as well pack it up and move to the North Pole. [. . .] As soon as the government gets involved you know you're going to run into bureaucratic bullshit. If you can jump through hoops to their satisfaction you might just be able to get them to put a fraction of the funding required toward the making of your film. The bad news is, one of their requirements for funding is that you must have a Canadian distributor, which is to say no distribution at all. Catch 22. Not exactly the most beneficial trade-off. Feature film-making here has two chances of making any headway – fat and slim. The rules set up to protect our non-existent national identity only serve to keep Canada reinventing the wheel rather than using the progress already made by those who have used it as a jumping-off point. Canada is a country of documentarists. We like to watch. That way there's a guarantee of remaining uninvolved and no chance of making anything that's too financially successful. Hollywood North. What a joke. The only people who call Canada Hollywood North are those who don't know that Canada is viewed as Mexico North by the industry in L.A. [. . .]

Now if only CAA [agency] would call me back and say that they'd love to represent me.

They've had two of my scripts since February. How long should one wait, I wonder? I suppose, considering the fact that this is my agency of choice, I should be happy to wait for their decision . . . and wait . . . and wait. [. . .] Oh horrors! I'll be old and grey before I get a response. **99**

"Development" dictates the working pattern of most producers for longer than they anticipate. Australian writer and producer Ross Dimsey lives in Brisbane:

66 *Long Tan* [is] a planned feature film which tells the story of a bunch of young Australian blokes facing battle for the first time in Vietnam. Film Queensland has supplied the government element of the development funds to date.

This project presents a dilemma. It's going to be difficult to do it justice for less than A\$10 million, yet, even with the help of our Australian Film Finance Corporation, this budget will be hard to raise without international elements.

It is becoming increasingly clear that, like the boys in the battle, we are in no-man's land. Either incorporate more market-friendly elements, risk being untrue to the story and further increase the budget, or go cheaper and risk shortchanging the effectiveness (and thus the real horror) of the battle scenes. To be able to make a judgement I need to do some alternate budget analyses against script variations, and of course this will cost money. [. . .]

My instinct is to pare the budget down from A\$10 to about A\$7 million and attempt to finance the picture at that level. It doesn't sound like much on a world scale but it is difficult with such an Australian subject. The trick is convincing distributors that it deals with universal themes and will appeal to the international market. **99**

Another Australian writer/producer, Des Power, uses the day to conclude a deal for a controversial documentary:

66 Last night, I had dinner with Tran Hoa and Luu Xuan Thu of Seco Film, Hanoi. It's nice to start a day knowing that the prospect of shooting a film in Vietnam is now a reality. For months, we have been negotiating to make the

Australian writer and producer Ross Dimsey

official film to commemorate the 50th anniversary of the formation of the Republic of Vietnam. I made *Celebration of a Nation* with director Dick Marks – the official film for the Australian bicentenary in 1988. It was persuasive in our talks with Seco.

Thu is a veteran of thirty years in the film industry. He tells me he has worked on several French films including the movie *Dien Bien Phu*, and that he made a large number of documentaries during the course of the Vietnam War. Hoa speaks excellent English which he learned in Russia; he's Seco's production manager.

They flew from Hanoi straight to Cairns in North Queensland where Jim McElroy is shooting *Traps* – a co-production with Seco. They arrived in Brisbane yesterday. Early this morning my fellow producer Michael Swan at Provisible took them to the Movie World/Warner Roadshow studios on the Gold Coast where *Penal Colony* is currently in production – the biggest feature ever to be made here. Around A$25 million.

This afternoon wrapped up the finer points of the deal with Seco; production costs in Vietnam are attractive, but we have to fund the film totally. **99**

The British Film Institute Production Unit has supported several excellent films over the past fifteen years. Ben Gibson, who manages the Unit, recognises the advantages and disadvantages of funding without close supervision of budgets and schedules:

66 Working on a paper to go to our Production Unit's Away Day about low-budget films. For two years we've been running a propaganda campaign about how there can be lots, and should be lots of kinds of British film from £300,000 to £10 million. This is more likely to make British film authentically British. Even when you're spending public money, and television licence fees, there is such a thing as 'market value' and actually audiences know it – either they want to see a bonfire of banknotes up on the screen or some wily character doing a lot with a little. They're smart enough to spot a compromise.

[. . .] There have been two low-budget documentaries this year and Derek Jarman's astounding feat on *Wittgenstein*, shot for under £300,000 in twelve days, but just generally not enough. We've decided to ask the board not to invest in any of the funded films with a total cost of over £450,000. [. . .]

2 P.M.: A meeting with a woman I met in Cannes, a young film-maker who has been trying to launch some features and documentaries, mainly with Iranian stories and a London connection. We had the meeting because she came up to me in a coffee bar at the Cannes Festival, where I was sitting reading the daily trades in a back street. I immediately recognised her and sort of wondered what kind of deals she might be doing in Cannes. It had been a very emotional week, as it often is for film-makers hoping to make connections in that insane environment,

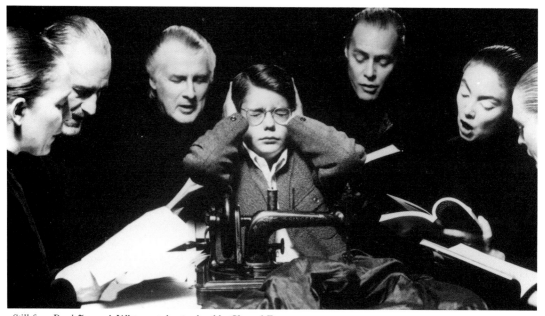

Still from Derek Jarman's Wittgenstein, *produced by Channel Four*

and seeing me triggered off a powerful sensation that she was trying to talk about films in a world of deals. She asked if I had really looked at her material over the last few years, and whether I didn't want to talk about what she was trying to do there and then. It was all much too emotional and I suggested meeting when we were back home. Her pictures are OK, and she might do a 'New Directors' film [for the BFI]. **"**

Fred Roos has been the producer on many of Francis Ford Coppola's greatest films, as well as a tenacious independent who always has several projects on the boil:

"Talked by phone to agent in New York regarding the availability of directors Michael Ockrent and Michael Blakemore for a movie I am producing for George Lucas's company, *Radioland Murders*.

Talked to director Lewis Teague about possible writers for a thriller we are developing. [. . .]

Talked to agent Robert Stein (UTA) re. his client Mel Smith as a possible director for *Radioland Murders*. Sent him a script.

Received fax from my *Radioland* co-producer Rick McCallum which might require me to go to New York next week to begin casting for *Radioland Murders*. Talked to my New York casting director Rosalie Joseph about this.

Received call from James Edward Olmos about a book I had sent him, *The Brave*. We talked about his possibly directing a movie based on this book.

Talked to *Sports Illustrated* writer Kenny Moore in Eugene, Oregon, about the 1996 Olympic Games in Atlanta, of which I hope to produce the official film. I want Moore to be the main writer.

Sent screenplay, *Gunfighter's Moon*, to a company in N.Y., Arrow Entertainment, as a possible financing source.

Went to the William Morris agency for a meeting with agent Ron Mardigian re. his client Neil Leifer possibly directing *The Brave*. [. . .]

Script meeting with writer Michael Umble and my Head of Story Development Meredith Stiehm re. a project he is writing for us entitled *Imaginus*. Talked about a whole new approach to the story. [. . .]

Phone conversation at home with Linda

Ronstadt re. her possibly doing an end-titles song for our film, *The Secret Garden*. She's willing to try it. [. . .]

At home, screen tape of the Mel Smith-directed movie *The Tall Guy*, to see his directing abilities.

This was a rather typical day for me and I did not view it as particularly successful or unsuccessful. Just another day in which a little bit of progress was made on several different films. **"**

Harley Cokeliss, a British director, calls his entry, "Another Day in Development Hell." It exemplifies the exasperation of those who want to work on interesting projects that still have a chance of being accepted:

" 9.30 A.M. Went up to the office and turned on the computer. Called Peter Milligan to discuss revisions to the third draft of our desert thriller, *Pilgrim*. Among the many changes, decided to relocate the opening scene from the Joshua Tree area to the dry salt lake just north of town, which is called Mystic Lake. 'Mystic Lake' – great title we thought until we considered possible confusion with the film, *Mystic Pizza*. [. . .] Left Pete to get on with the revision. We want to get the new draft to actors by July. We have a foreign sales company committed, and even American distributors interested, but they all ask that one question: 'Who is in it?' When we can answer that we will have a movie . . . [. . .]

2.30 P.M. Up to the office again. Stared at my notes for the latest revision to *Balefire*, an adaptation of an American novel that I have been working on for almost two years. Two writers and four drafts later, I am still addressing the essential contradiction of trying to reconcile what intrigued my investors enough to want to adapt the book in the first place, and constructing a viable screenplay. The book takes an almost mosaic approach, considering all the characters of equal value (it's not surprising that the author is a forensic scientist), until more than halfway through the book the hero emerges. This has the effect of making the villain the central character, certainly for the first half of the book. This would be fine if the story was about him, like in *Henry, Portrait of a Serial Killer* or *Day of the Jackal*, but it's not.

[. . .] 6 P.M. Went into the West End for

81

meeting with Peter Briggs. We rendezvous at William Morris Agency, where Pete was meeting with his agent. Ended up, as usual, at Pete's favourite bar. We discussed the slow progress of acquiring the rights to the 2000AD character *Rogue Trooper*. I had the rights four years ago, but made the mistake of getting into business with a major studio and a major producer. Three years later, the studio executive in charge of my project was replaced and the new man swept his desk clean. Never liked the corporate approach to script development. One time we had six executives in a meeting who each had their own, mutually contradictory notes. Who do you listen to? It's easy to get lost, and we did.

Pete and I have a new storyline, and a potential producer, but since I last acquired the rights, the publishers have made a lot of money on another of their characters and have gotten greedy. We now need to find $25,000 to $30,000 just for the right to begin. Ouch! 🙶

▶▶ 82

Not all agents dwell in Hollywood. Englishwoman Jenne Casarotto's diary illustrates the often mundane round of a typical day in the life of an agent:

🙶 To the office for early morning contracts and silence. Jim Ballard's contract for *Running Wild* is OK at last after months of negotiation and because I've finally given way on 'theme park rights' – given the nature of this dark moral tale it's hardly likely [to appear] next to Mickey Mouse! [. . .]

11 A.M. Meeting at Working Title with producer Eric Fellner and writer Anita Bronson. Unusually, the writer herself has acquired film rights in a book and is writing the screenplay, but as Eric knows the book well, she would like 'support.' Eric is laid back, charming, and will read the screenplay. Anita's high on her new ITV series as she's found a smashing director – tough when he has to commit 18 months of his life.

In the office again I am back to chasing the deals for U.S. theatrical rights and the BBC re. Stephen Frears's *The Snapper*. After Cannes everything was incredibly urgent – now everyone has gone quiet, classic for the movie business. I discuss with writer Don Macpherson the prickly

Hungarian director María Sós (right) watches while her cameraman sorts out a shot on the film Tandem

problem of two excellent U.S. producers asking him to write a screenplay of the same public domain subject. He would like to write it but must end up an unpopular fellow with one of them. Still, it is a flattering problem and he is busy for now. [. . .]

At last Scala [Productions] have got *Dark Blood* fully financed – I believe! Jim Barton, the screenwriter, is in Australia and George Sluizer, the director, is in Amsterdam or else we would cele-

brate – it's over three years since we first took on the script to sell. [. . .]

Los Angeles calls start. I'm trying to convince Bonni Lee at Geffen that Robert Bierman's perfect to direct *Mavis Keates*. How do we persuade Michelle Pfeiffer? I talk to writer/client in L.A. about his meetings so far this week. I talk to TriStar Business Affairs re. a producer's deal. We still can't agree. [. . .] Sally Willcox at CAA calls re. David Leland's deal to write and direct *Running Wild*. This particular deal has taken me 2½ years to pull off – I'm dead chuffed. Actually this is what makes it worthwhile! **99**

María Sós, who directed the Hungarian film *The Unhappy Hat* in 1981 and *Tandem* in 1985, is seeking the go-ahead for a new feature, *Climax*:

66 I started to watch the 'Morning' programme on Channel 1 of Hungarian TV. This programme is something new, and an exacting enterprise, but besides I have personal reasons too. The permanent chief cameraman is my friend. We have a strange inter-personal relationship. We can have a talk, even if we are not side by side. One day he told me: 'The invisible film

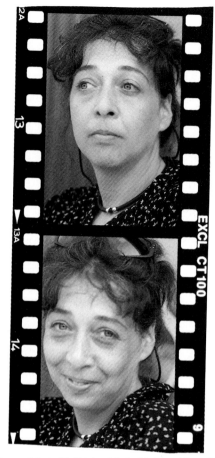

Above: *Maria Sós*. Right: *Maria Sós (second from right) during production of her film*, Tandem

exists. You make it on paper, because of the money . . . but it is a film too.' I do not believe it, or rather I do not want to believe it, although I am in this situation. I have been ready for many years to make my new feature film, but the advisory board of the Hungarian Motion Picture Foundation has awarded me only half of the amount required. Well, my invisible film is being made. [. . .]

Europe. My film would be European. It WILL be.

[In the afternoon] I arranged my phone calls to Paris and Munich. I am looking for some foreign financial support for my film. I decided that I was going to head to Europe with my screenplay.

I went to the TV station. I had to cut a very nice 15-minute documentary. I am glad that sometimes I can stand close to the camera. I think that without it I would be seized with cramp. 99

Siraj Zaidi, an actor and producer, works out of Dublin, and seems confident that his film, *Honey and Saffron*, will see the light of day:

" Around 9.45 A.M. I settled down with lots of paper and tried my best to make some sense out of what my corporate financier had illustrated to me regarding the tax-based film financing under the current Irish finance legislation.

It's a big relief to know that they can provide up to 60% of the budget (with only 12% of the actual risk money), on condition that I can produce: (i) the balance of the budget, i.e. 40%, (ii) completion bond or guarantee in place, and (iii) adequate pre-sales to underpin the investment.

They expect me to provide all this without any development finance – which obviously they can't furnish because it's 'high risk' money.

My new film, *Honey and Saffron*, will be the first Irish feature film to be produced under the auspices of the film and TV co-production treaty between Ireland and Canada.

3.15 P.M. Telephoned Brian Lenehan, M.P., who had signed this co-production treaty in 1987. He promised me to find some details from the Department of Foreign Affairs and issue a certificate to this film project.

The film has already established a co-production with a Toronto company, Bar Harbour Films Inc., who in turn are dealing with Alliance Entertainment for adequate pre-sales. They have projected their financing plan for meeting 50% of the budget, i.e. £1 million, and the task of raising the remainder of the production finance – a further £1 million – lies ahead of me. "

A more depressing note is struck by Dimitry Svetozarski, a Russian director based in St. Petersburg:

" From nine o'clock in the morning until noon, I am on the phone to my producer sorting out two things: firstly, a sponsor, investing private money into the film we are shooting, has quite clearly become embroiled in some

Siraj Zaidi, actor and producer, preparing his Irish feature,
Honey and Saffron

financial difficulties and has consequently disappeared – together with the money for the film; secondly, the composer is accusing the studio of breaching a number of laws and although his accusations are quite ridiculous and legally unsound, he is threatening to take court action against the studio.

From noon onwards I am at Lenfilm studios. They are letting us use a series of their administrative areas for filming. Unfortunately, they have no idea that we have no money to pay for this.

I soon find that today's shooting is under threat of being discontinued; the company making the costumes is refusing to hand them over until we have paid in cash which of course we cannot do.

Things are not much better with the filming equipment. The firm providing us with video cameras has left us on the black list, which in simple terms means we cannot get anything from them. We desperately search for someone who can give us a camera on credit. Of course such people do exist, but they demand cash. [. . .]

Four o'clock in the afternoon and the critical moment has arrived. The producer informs me that he has no other choice but to close the film down. I try to convince him that to do that now would mean losing all the money we have spent thus far. Eventually, we decide to get the money on credit so that we can continue making the film for a few more days and then . . .

Seven o'clock in the evening. Filming goes ahead although we are drastically behind schedule, sixteen hours behind, but filming at least begins. The main female character, the heroine and *prima* of the Kierov ballet company, flies into hysterics, threatening to tear up her contract and for us this would be an utter catastrophe. [. . .] It is the last straw. My nerves snap! I rant about this not being the Kierov theatre and that there a poor devil applies his own rules and what would she know about the real state of our affairs anyway.

My ranting and raving has the effect of shocking her into silence. Filming continues . . .

At midnight, I go home and phone the producer. The news is so-so. A sponsor has been found. In other words, a madman has been located who is prepared to lend us money. [. . .]

Is this a typical day? Events today were possibly more dramatic than usual but I am quite convinced that if you were to water it down by 50% you would get a typical day in contemporary Russian cinema. **99**

In Beijing, Chinese director Xia Gang faces problems with the censors on his new film, *Recollections of the Past*:

66 Judging by their reaction to *The Story of Art* and *Farewell My Concubine* [both starring Gong Li], the authorities seem to have a morbid fear of politics and sex – particularly the latter.

During the last few days, while I was in Xuzhou, [Meng Zhu] had finished correcting the script of *Recollections of the Past* and reading the proofs. The printed copy would be ready for collection today. Meng Zhu had been involved in a few of my films and now she'd become my indispensable assistant and collaborator. This versatile and capable wife of mine is a person of many talents. Scriptwriter, producer, stage manager, public relations officer and housewife all in one, and outstanding in each role!

We'd just collected the script and got into the cab, when it started raining. We were soaked through, but with a copy each in our hands, we immediately began proof-reading and correcting: one copy would be sent to the head of the [Beijing] film studios for his approval, the other to the investor so that he could start getting the finance together.

After dinner I went with Meng Zhu to see Cheng Zhigu, head of the film studios. [. . .] We gave him *Recollections* and described the storyline. [. . .] He was ecstatic and said immediately that if he could get the financing for it, he wouldn't bother with any approval formalities. But the studio would charge around $70,000 as an administrative fee. On the surface, *Recollections* looks increasingly hopeful. All that remains are specific contractual discussions. But both of us persisted in asking Mr. Cheng to read the script thoroughly, because we sensed he might **99** change his mind any time

Director Xia Gang faced similar censorship problems from the Chinese authorities on his film Recollections of the Past *as did the highly successful* Farewell My Concubine *(left).*

Above: *Pakistani screenwriter Ejaz Ahmad Bhatti.* Right:
Ejaz Ahmad Bhatti (right) in discussion with a distributor

**The Pakistani cinema has not achieved
much international acclaim in recent
decades. Screenwriter Ejaz Ahmad Bhatti
[alias Ejaz Arman] keeps several projects
in the air on June 10th, an extremely hot
day in Lahore:**

❝At the studios I visited the editing rooms
and checked the progress of my film *God
Forbidden*, which is in its final stages and due for
release in September 1993. I saw some rushes
and as a screenwriter I discussed changes in certain scenes with my director.

After lunch I went to another director to discuss a new subject which will be lensed in London
in May 1994. Then I visited a distribution office
where we discussed the satellite and cable TV, as
well as the video, invasion of the cinema business.
Some cinemas in Pakistan have been turned into
shopping malls in the face of this onslaught. But it
is my belief that the big screen caters for a
different taste and time will come when the
video-viewer in turn visits the cinema to see a
movie on the big screen. It was agreed that we
should work hard and produce quality films on

Above: *Ejaz Ahmad Bhatti (left) discussing new projects.* Right: *At the editing table*

an international level and present extraordinary subjects which attract moviegoers. [. . .]

In the evening I visited two film producers and presented new projects. They objected that in Pakistan these subjects could not enjoy any success at the box-office because our people would be unable to follow the approach. I explained that our subjects had been prepared with the new cinema world in mind and that unless we give people new thoughts, and teach them new ways and show them advanced ideas, they could not emerge from the old system. It was our bad luck that the majority of our people still believe in fundamentalism. I explained that my projects were based on human rights and not on fundamentalism. Moreover, being Muslim our religion clearly teaches us human rights. But I am sorry to come to the conclusion that in Pakistan the percentage of literacy is only 10%; so we will not be able to present new thoughts unless we expand the education of our people.

Our film industry, which has recently been recognised by the government as an 'industry,' cannot develop until the Film Censor Code is revised and educated producers and directors enter the business. **99**

The talent agent plays a pivotal role in "getting the backing" for clients, as Tim Stone writes from his office in Hollywood:

66 Every day brings a multitude of small episodes for an agent. Always pieces of a whole that sometimes never happens, but rarely happens as fast as (a) one would like and (b) one would hope.

Here are some of the pertinent involvements today:

Staff meeting. We discuss as many clients as time permits and what problems we have with them, and the possible jobs they may be offered, or be trying, or wanting to get – and the merits of those jobs.

The breakdowns. I suggest actors in writing for upcoming projects. I have sometimes read the scripts. For feature films always. For TV, sometimes.

A client who has campaigned, as have I, to be part of *Wyatt Earp*, starring Kevin Costner, directed by Larry Kasdan, is finally offered a small role. He is devastated because he wanted more. We tell him this is the most important feature project this year. [. . .]

I tell a New York actor client he will not be auditioning for a Ron Howard movie he has heard about. It involves agent politics.

I tell anybody I can that Anthony Crivello (a client) won a Tony Award for *Kiss of the Spider Woman*.

I look at four hopeful actor tapes and decide not to represent them. [. . .]

I play cool to a casting director who wants an important client for a less than important rate on a Meryl Streep movie.

I hustle more jobs. Ad infinitum, but not ad nauseam. I love it. 〞

4. Cast Away: In Pre-Production BEFORE SHOOT-

ING CAN BEGIN ON ANY MAJOR PICTURE, THOSE

INVOLVED MUST IMMERSE THEMSELVES IN THE BUSI-

NESS OF CASTING ACTORS AND ACTRESSES, BRINGING

TALENTED TECHNICIANS TOGETHER, AND COPING

WITH EVERYTHING FROM BUDGETS TO INSURANCE.

THE CASTING STAGE CAN MAKE OR BREAK A FILM

IN PRE-PRODUCTION.

Any odd moments were taken up with discussing how to overcome the usual problem of the quality of actor we wanted against the shortage of money available for them.

4.30 P.M. Rushed back to the office to start calls to Neil Jordan and Steve Woolley in Los Angeles about who to cast in *Interview with a Vampire*. Home at 6 P.M. and calls from L.A. agents re. both films.

Susie Figgis is a British casting director who is working on two major new features:

Gavin Millar, a British director known for his TV drama and his sensitive work with children, heads north to Newcastle upon Tyne to cast his new film, *The Dwelling Place*, a 3-hour telefilm adaptation of Catherine Cookson's novel:

❝ Having organised my youngest daughter and got my eldest daughter to school I grabbed a taxi to the Royal Society of Arts for the final day of casting children for *The Browning Version*, to be directed by Mike Figgis. We saw boys every 30 minutes with no lunch break until 4 P.M. Mike and I were pretty much in agreement as to who were the best. I slightly prefer one boy, he another. We decided to sleep on it overnight.

❝ It's raining in Newcastle and bitingly cold. This is a summer picture. We're casting children at Dave Holly's opposite the station. I note that he shares the floor with a business called HeMan Contracts. Is this reassuring, I wonder? [...]

The talented middle-class [children] can't do even a hint of a Geordie accent. The talented

Left: *Susie Figgis, with Mike Figgis, her cousin.* Above: *Gavin Millar (centre) on location in Newcastle upon Tyne*

Gavin Millar (top left) directing his cast of youngsters on The Dwelling Place, *which also stars James Fox (bottom left)*

working-class ones are barely comprehensible to me, even though I've worked with Jimmy Nail, watched an episode of *Spender* and spoken to a Newcastle taxi-driver.

Liz, our casting assistant, is a serious professional chain-smoker and it's a small room. I open a window from time to time which involves bringing down the Venetian blinds in an inextricable cascade. The kids love this. But when fresh air leaks in, so does the roar of traffic and I can't hear the kids even if I could understand them. But I smile and nod a lot, and ask what their parents do for a living and pretend to write things down. [. . .]

The first girl thinks she's doing A level and scares the daylights out of me. She reckons Catherine Cookson is a bit repetitive (she is if you've read all 86 of them) and that the book's too much about rich and poor. I reckon that's quite an accurate reflection of the world but I keep mum. [. . .]

The next boy pretends to be fourteen but it's clear that he's married with kids. Then in comes Joe – tiny, with jug-ears – well Joe at six anyway (they all have to age three years – a nightmare). It's funny when you instantly know somebody's right. I want to hear what this one says so I shut the window. But soon I've lost sight of him in the fog and I can't breathe. Maybe he can't either, I reflect, and we'll never know. But good lad, he pipes up from out of the murk, still cheerful, and I know we're on to a winner. Liz is **99** wreathed in smiles, I think.

Pascal Verdosci with Alex Martin, co-writers on a project called The Incredible Harry Wind

Pascal Verdosci, a Swiss writer and development producer, spent his day in Ebeltoft (Denmark), where the European Film College held a working session for producers, poised on the fragile cusp between the planning and the realisation of a project:

❝ On top of the hill overlooking the bay of Ebeltoft, over fifty producers and writers from more than a dozen countries from Europe were discussing and planning their projects, ranging from TV series and feature films to documentaries, at the invitation of EAVE [a MEDIA initiative of the European Union].

Coming myself from Switzerland, I felt at ease in this small country. This was the day my project was to be discussed, *The Incredible Harry Wind*, a feature film, 110 minutes, based on a novel by Swiss author Walter M. Diggelmann. You rarely get the chance as a newcomer to be torn apart by such experienced film-makers as EAVE provides.

Script analysts Martin Daniel (from Minneapolis), and Pascal Lonhay (Brussels), were very nice to me but didn't hide the fact that my treatment did not work. In less than an hour I was back at square one – after working with my co-writer Alex Martin for more than six months. Writing is rewriting, as they say. And they are right. A script is never finished. You always find new scenes, more characters to explore to finally get your theme across on screen. [. . .]

So I left the script doctors to be torn apart next in my Group Work. Group leader Lise Lense-Møller, an independent producer from Copenhagen, was also very nice to me, but also didn't hide the fact that my production and financing strategy were useless. It really was my day. Had it not been for her (and the script doctors') good ideas as to how to change the project, I might have felt desperate and not continued my work. But this is what you want from them. Deep analysis and good advice for your project. At the end of the day, a very long day, I knew how to proceed and I'm sure that one day *The Incredible Harry Wind* will reach the screen. [. . .]

After long discussions about scripts, films, contracts, completion bonds, money in general and the weather, we were actually very tired. But the days are long in summer in Denmark. Sun sets at almost midnight. So we sat on top of the

Jim McBride, with his Flemish "masterpiece" in the background

hill, overlooking the water, drinking beer. After some bottles, our feelings about this day were growing, we almost felt as though we were the new breed of European film-makers. After some more beers, our feelings changed: we were already worrying about the next day. What more struggles would we have to go through to fulfil our dreams? **99**

Jim McBride, who has fought his way through years of fringe and independent film-making (*David Holzman's Diary, My Girlfriend's Wedding, The Big Easy*), gets to grips with the nerve-shredding process of pre-production in Barcelona:

❝ The day starts at 1 A.M., when we go to bed in the sublet apartment we've just occupied. We don't sleep. There's a dripping sound that can't be located and won't go away. And cathedral bells next door that ring on the quarter hour.

At 9 A.M., we move into new production offices in a refurbished old factory building. The phones don't work, but the computers do. There are five of them for only about ten people in the office. Mine is the only Mac, so my version of the script is differently formatted than everyone else's.

The financiers didn't send the money for next week's cash flow, as they had promised. This is the second time this has happened. We discuss this for an hour.

I finally meet someone I would like to hire as my assistant, but she doesn't want to start for ten days. I need someone now.

We saved a lot of money in the budget by hiring relatively unknown actors. And some more from a devaluation of the peseta (we get our money in dollars). Now, the financiers want all that money back, rather than let us spend it on the movie. We discuss this for an hour.

After a search that took several weeks and led down many false tracks, we hire a painter to create the fifteenth-century Flemish 'masterpiece' that is at the centre of our movie [provisionally entitled *The Flemish Board*]. We need to delay the start of shooting for a week to allow time for the creation of this. But the producer is afraid to tell the financiers, so we're making believe we're on schedule, even though this will eventually cost more money and more time. We discuss this for another hour.

We have lunch with the guy who comes from Madrid to sign the cheques every week. But there's no money today, so he eats and goes back.

I discuss the Flemish 'masterpiece' with the new Production designer. (The old one just up and left one day, without a word of explanation, presumably overwhelmed by the task of creating the picture.)

We hire a guy to find fair, Flemish-looking models to pose for the 'masterpiece.' He has a daunting job in this city of dark-skinned, dark-haired, dark-eyed Latins.

I discuss the clothes for the figures in the picture with the costume designer, my wife.

I work on the script with the co-writer/co-line producer/assistant director. It still has an artificial ring to it, because we don't know Barcelona and its people as well as we ought to yet. [. . .]

It hasn't been a particularly productive or successful day. But, by the time anyone reads this, we will have made the movie. It will be either good or bad, and nothing that happened today will matter in the least. **99**

Marion Hansel is a Belgian producer and director whose work has cruised the festival circuit in recent years. She writes of "a normal day, a mixture of joy and burden. Creative and productive work."

66 A few days before June 10th, we (Man's Films) and the director Dominique Guerrier had taken the big decision to postpone the shooting of his first feature film, from this July to Spring 1994. Our leading actress being pregnant, and the insurance companies refusing to cover her in these circumstances, it is safer for everybody to halt pre-production and wait until the baby is born.

I spent most of the 10th calling the crew and announcing the changes. It wasn't really funny, as there is very little work at present in Belgium and everybody was hoping for a nice shoot during this summer.

The rest of the day, I was busy with several calls, mainly political contacts concerning a project for a new cinema complex, five screens in the heart of Brussels. Explaining and trying to convince people of the importance of having a different type of exhibition, less linked to just the big American commercial hits in the **99** 'capital' of Europe.

Yvonne Mackay, a film and TV director for the Gibson Group in New Zealand, spends her day nourishing and massaging various projects:

66 Re-read the readers' reports of our next feature film, *Clare*, in preparation for a fourth draft meeting with writer Fiona Kidman.

Discussed with producer Dave Gibson and production accountant Jeannie Buxton the possibility of my having to fly to London etc. to shoot the various establishing shots around the world for *Typhon's People* [a four-hour TV mini-series]. Trying to get such shots from film librarians was proving unsatisfactory. I suggested combining this trip with an initial visit re. casting some English actors in *Clare*, with casting agent Lucy Boulting in London. [. . .]

Re-read the last act of *Clare*. This movie is based on the true story of Clare Matheson who took on the power of the establishment at the biggest teaching hospital in the Southern Hemisphere – National Women's Hospital in Auckland, N.Z. After she finds out she has unknowingly been part of an unfortunate experiment and now has cervical cancer, she causes a public inquiry to be held – and wins. This third act has been giving us problems dramatically because it's been hard to sift through mountains of research from a nine-month inquiry and so far it has proved difficult to depart from the real inquiry timetable to get *our* dramatic structure right. [. . .]

Tried to jack up a meeting with Executive Producer Dorothee Pinfold and Dave Gibson re. the overseas money for *Clare*. It's not easy or even particularly desirable to fully fund a New Zealand feature from within the country. Dorothee **99** not back from Cannes until the weekend.

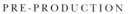

Norwegian cinema languished for many years in the shadow of its Swedish counterpart. Anja Breien, with *Wives, Games of Love and Loneliness*, and *Witchhunt*, led a new wave of directors towards international recognition. This diary is especially poignant because soon afterwards Ms. Breien resigned from the production, and her friend and colleague Erik Borge took over the director's chair:

❝ We are in the final stage of pre-production for my new film *Second Sight*. We, Northern Lights Film Production, the producers Hilde Berg and Erik Borge, an excellent unit of people and myself, are working long days to be able to start shooting on June 28th.

The film takes place around the year 1350 and it is the story of an eight-year-old girl who is the only survivor in a remote valley on the Norwegian coast ravaged by the Black Death, the most serious plague that has ever threatened the population of Europe. It is a story about survival and about growing up, based on my own screenplay.

8 A.M. I met with the actor Bjørn Sundquist in the costumes department. I have been a bit nervous about talking to him. He is a great actor and has been offered a very small part. But he was obviously happy about it and he looked very good in the costume. [. . .]

9 A.M. The actress Liv Osa, the makeup artist Barbo Haugen and I met with Dr. Holck, who is a specialist in medieval illnesses. We asked numerous questions and showed him makeup samples of extravasation and boils.

11 A.M. Rehearsal with Liv Osa and Bjørn Wilberg Andersen, mother and father in the film. We went through the scenes that they have together. We also met with a specialist on the dialect of Justedalen (the remote valley). Both actors are from the West coast, and they had no problems with the language. But we must moderate it somewhat. Otherwise we will have to subtitle the film in Norway. THAT we must avoid.

2 P.M. My exciting leading actress Julia (8), who plays the little girl Maren, arrives. She does not take part in regular rehearsals, but has to be prepared in a different way. We go to the cos-

tumes department. I make some stills of them, and find that they look very credible as a family. But something is wrong. The material for the costumes is too heavy, and we decide to make them from lighter wool.

4 P.M. Meeting about props. Some I get to see, others I see in photos, as they have already been sent to Justedalen. We also study seventeen pictures of a sheep dog. One is selected. It looks good and must be tested.

6 P.M. I am about to panic because of the pressure. One important actor is yet to be found. I have a disagreement with the sound man, I give the production secretary five different instructions at the same time and leave her in total confusion. I discuss the problems with my two producers. We agree on a strategy . . . and that helps.

[. . .] In two weeks I will be in Justedalen where we have a remarkable setting. We are building a medieval farm just below a huge glacier, and surrounded by mountains. I am about to make a film on a theme which has occupied me for years. It is four years since my last production, and this is definitely my most important film. May the gods support me. ❞

A Swedish woman director, and a close contemporary of Anja Breien, is also preparing for a new film. Marianne Ahrne's work has focused on the outsiders in society (*Near and Far Away, The Roots of Grief*):

❝ The day started with a rotting corpse of a kind too horrible to be put in a film. The nose and half the mouth were gone already – the man in white trying to open what was left of it while explaining to us the benefits of living in a country like Sweden, where excellent dental records are available from childhood.

'Very useful for identification in cases like this,' he said, looking with a glint in his eye at three young ladies trying to shield themselves from the stench behind the long hair of a fourth. It made them look like beauties entangled by an octopus. The expression in their eyes did not contradict the image.

'Worms,' said one of them with disgust. 'There are WORMS!'

'Oh, yes,' answered the pathologist lightly,

'but not very many this time. Sometimes, when I open these doors in the morning, the worms come crawling out like a little white river. Very good for angling, actually. Maggots. Ever heard of them?'

One of the boys weakly raised his hand. I glanced at Anna, my twenty-four-year-old actress. Still on her feet, stronger than she looked.

The two of us had spent almost a month now as 'extra' pupils at the Swedish Police School, and today we were visiting the morgue to take a look at different kinds of bodies: a man who had just hanged himself, a victim of a traffic accident three days earlier, and this unfortunate fellow, found in his apartment after weeks of disintegration. [. . .]

In the film we are preparing [*Kimsalabim*], Anna will play the part of a police cadet, partly in school, partly on her first real-life training, so before writing the script we try to get acquainted with as many aspects as possible of the life of these future police officers. [. . .] The film of course has a story of its own – but we want to make the background and the secondary characters as authentic as possible.

One of the most active film-makers in Sri Lanka, Amarnath Jayatilaka, begins and ends his day with meditation:

It has been a ritual with me throughout my life to light an oil lamp before the statue of the Buddha as soon as I get up, mostly around 5 or 5.30 A.M. Then to practice yoga and meditation. As usual during the last few years my mind is very preoccupied with my proposed film on the life of Buddha entitled *Buddha: The Enlightened One*, which I am planning to do in English for worldwide release.

Amarnath Jayatilaka (right) at his office in Colombo, with Michael Subasinghe

A sketch by Norman Garwood for the assassin's fortress in Smoke and Mirrors

Around noon I revised the final draft of the treatment which the screenwriter prepared from the existing script of *Buddha: The Enlightened One*, which I need for mailing to Cinemart in Rotterdam [fund for films from developing countries].

In the afternoon I received a fax message from my partners in Los Angeles re. the proposed project of Lankafilm to set up a state-of-the-art film production facility in Sri Lanka to produce American movies on location here.

Towards evening I contemplated the adaptation and restructuring of the screenplay based on the bestseller, *A Drop in the Reign of Terror*, the next Sinhala film I am planning to do. [. . .]

As usual the day ended with the meditation on Metta: The Loving Kindness, and the reading of a book on Buddhist philosophy. It is the next subject I am involved with as it is my aim to use cinema as a means of communication to put across the teachings of Buddhism.

In Kensal Green, London, writer-director Phil O'Shea juggles a number of projects:

8.50 A.M. Down to my desk to resume the final, final polish of a feature film screenplay commissioned by an American producer. A biopic, 120 pages of crackling, real-life action set in every continent of the world. One hell of a movie, but will it get made? Being an American project must help the odds.

9.20 A.M. Mike Kelk, the producer on my English feature *Wonder World*, rings. The film, which I wrote and hope to direct this year, was developed by the British Film Institute, and Mike and I are busily trying to raise finance anywhere else we can find it. Mike needs a copy of the original contract I made with the B.F.I., just to check that we can defer the development money invested in the project by the Institute (i.e. my fee for writing it) until after the picture is made. Low

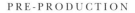

budget is the buzz in the U.K. industry at the moment, and we're waiting on three of the four usual ports of call who have expressed an interest in the project. Waiting, waiting . . .

[. . .] 12.50 P.M. Mike Kelk rings again. He has had a call from our casting director. Our first choice for one of the leads in *Wonder World*, Charlotte Gainsbourg, has read it, and loves it. She'll be in London tomorrow, and can we fix up a meeting? This piece of good news leaves me speechless for a moment. Writing, then meetings. Thus the second stage of film-making begins.

2 P.M. Still rewriting the U.S. feature. I kill off a character and chop a few speeches. The danger with rewrites is that you go so far that you forget what the original intention of the screenplay was. I wrote it down somewhere six months ago. That original intention . . . Now where was it?

Presenting a budget and shooting schedule is a fine art in itself. Norman Garwood, a British production designer, has been at work on *Smoke and Mirrors*, set in Paris and Algeria during the mid-Nineteenth Century, and directed by Frank Marshall:

8 A.M. Breakfast with Pat Carr, the production manager on my new project, *Smoke and Mirrors*. We discussed the day ahead, which was a visual presentation of locations in Morocco and Spain followed by a budget and schedule meeting. This is to be held at Paramount Studios in the offices of the Kennedy/Marshall Company. We leave the hotel at 9 A.M., and arrive at Paramount where I set up my visual presentation comprised of photographs, reference pictures, and my sketches. [. . .]

The presentation went very well and I felt a very positive mood in the meeting about all the locations and design concepts. We have one major location where I must build an assassin's fortress in what would be an almost inaccessible location visually. This is a difficult design problem as it will have to be created probably using opticals, models, as well as construction to create the final visual illusion. [. . .] Two hours later we progress to the shooting schedule for all the location work.

After lunch I have discussions with Ricky Jay, the 'magic' consultant, about some of the major magic and illusions he is to create in a palace in Spain. We decide to recreate the palace courtyard at Pinewood Studios outside London, where we will have more control and we can avoid night shooting in Spain.

Uma da Cunha of Medius (India) Services has considerable experience in casting and arranging locations for both fellow Indian directors and for visiting productions such as *Octopussy*, *Sea Wolves*, and *Staying On*.

It was not a usual day. I was casting for Dev Benegal's film, *English August*. He called me early to say he would like to shoot the pre-title sequence to the film a month in advance – on June 21st! I had to line up an American (middle-aged and yet young), a young German, a thirtyish Frenchman and an avante-garde Indian. My morning and afternoon were spent calling up people, in the midst of other things, to line up an audition for the coming Sunday. By evening I was reasonably certain that at least three of the people would be okay for the roles. [. . .]

More calls in the evening, this time to look for places where babies could be found and filmed who were under a year old. [. . .]

I was happy when Dev Benegal asked me to be Casting Director on *English August*. That was a year ago. Now the shooting is about to begin. I've loved working with Dev and his unit. He is exacting and particular about his requirements – both qualities that I respect. When he and I finally agree on an actor – it is an achievement for both of us – and a good feeling.

As the days dwindle prior to commencement of principal photography on a film, production managers tend to become more agitated – especially if, like Lynne Motijoane, they are working in the townships of South Africa:

Woke up late, reluctant to rush off to the production office and the freezing cold school classrooms we have converted into a production company. Thought about the film [*The Line*, a Channel 4 TV drama series] and dreadful feelings of nervousness crept in – two weeks left

Lead actor Jerry Mojokeng (centre) harassed by two South African policemen while filming The Line

before we shoot – where did the other five weeks of pre-production disappear to? Have we achieved enough? Have I achieved enough? [. . .]

We are only due to film in Soweto in six weeks' time – will there be trouble [at ANC official rallies], will it be safe for the crew and cast? I know I will be expected to answer this question to at least four people today. My response remains the same daily: 'We will have alternate locations BUT this movie is set in Soweto, we will shoot there – relax! – we will decide the day before depending on the events of that day! We can't predict the politics, we cannot plan negatively, we need to think positively!' [. . .]

The day at work begins as expected. I'm confronted by the assistant directors, the locations manager, and unit manager – 'Taxi wars have broken out in Soweto . . . we need to find somewhere else to shoot, we need to postpone the recce!' The debate rages for thirty minutes, the recce is postponed but everyone agrees to take more seriously the idea of looking for 'Plan B' locations in another township – just in case.

At last I can go into my own office and try again to begin the day. [. . .] Telephone messages to answer, crew looking for jobs, suppliers wanting to finalise their quotes. I shoved most of the messages aside, dealt with others. In the middle of

Road-block scene from The Line, *set up in a Soweto street*

a serious negotiation with a sound equipment supplier, the electricity in the building failed – my call was cut off, the co-ordinator lost a computerised letter, the producer storms in angry!

All of a sudden it's lunchtime. What have I done? Half a deal on sound equipment, employed and interviewed briefly a set-dresser, had a meeting with the director and a stunt co-ordinator, organised a quote, signed all the salary cheques for pay day tomorrow, and spoken to half a dozen others about locations, catering, extras, *and* called an electrician to come in urgently!

Research occupies many hours for even the most detached of film-makers. Livia Gyarmathy, whose documentaries make her the prime exponent in Hungary of that special genre, finds this aspect of pre-production both intriguing and exasperating:

❝ I decide that today I will continue with my research on SF.

SF was a strange, contradictory man whose life provoked a kind of bizarre hysteria. I am collecting material about him which I want to use in the script of my next feature film. At 8 A.M. I make some phone calls. A few people agree to let me record interviews with them.

I go to the Cultural Institute in Etele Street. I meet SF's last but one boss before his death. I learn that SF's chief characteristic was an exaggerated desire to fit in. As a personality he was excitable, agitated and tirelessly hard-working. He never talked about certain periods of his life. Everyone noticed this fact. His boss tells me that SF used to be a major in the army but for some reason was discharged. After that he was a manual labourer somewhere and in the 1980s had become influential again in the cultural sphere. He could not adapt to the huge transformation of Eastern Europe in 1990. When he arrived to work for his latest boss, he gave up. He died there and then.

11.45 A.M. I go to a meeting with the representative of a transport company. I am hoping that this rich company will put up some money for my film-making activities. They are not reassuring. They support sick people, not cultural activities.

12.30 P.M. I call SF's wife from a phone box. We meet. She avoids every significant question. She doesn't know why her husband was kicked out of the army nor what he did after that nor if anyone helped him to get an influential post again in the 1980s. Her husband always dodged her questions. Maybe she didn't really know him. He was modest and not a spendthrift. He loved her. He was the victim of the upheaval that took place here [in Hungary] as a result of the political changes in Eastern Europe. [. . .]

I arrive thirty minutes late for my appointment with SF's last boss. This man has visibly come down in the world and I can see from his puffy face that he is a heavy drinker. He has a job fetching and carrying in a suburban library. He was just about to leave for home when I arrived and he makes me feel guilty that I am late. He asks me to switch off the cassette recorder. He says that SF always set himself goals that he was incapable of reaching. He was ambitious, and that's why he 'bent with the wind.' As his boss, he often told SF not to be so pompous and to be a respectable person. During this meeting I learn

Livia Gyarmathy, the Hungarian documentarist

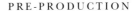

that SF was discharged from the army for embezzlement. Apparently he had lost at cards and had too many debts. He used to live in grand style, threw his money around, and I should speak to JJ about all this because JJ kicked him out of the army and knew a lot about him. It was no accident either that after the scandal SF was open to blackmail and later on became a regular police informer. [. . .]

11.30 P.M. I go to bed, and start thinking I should make a comedy about SF, whose most characteristic trait would be that he wants to please and satisfy everyone. **"**

Another woman film-maker, Willeke van Ammelrooy, better known during the 1960s and 1970s in the Netherlands as an actress, prepares to tackle her first feature, *The Butterfly Lifts Up the Cat*:

" Today, I feel ready for anything. I am busy working on a film and during each day of production there have been problems. [. . .] I decide to go to Amsterdam to buy a viewfinder at Holland Equipment. My cameraman, Eduard van der Ende, is an old bird in the profession and I am still not fluent in the technical language he uses for lenses and video-editing even though as a director I should be. [. . .] Eddy is mad. Our 35mm lens has been hired out to another Dutch production team which is having problems with out-of-focus material. Consequently we have an emergency but it is wonderful when someone else gets angry about something which is of benefit to your film only. As I awkwardly get Eddy to take a look at the most expensive viewfinder, it seems that even this one is not good enough. 'Have your name clearly marked on it because it's an extremely popular piece of equipment!' says Eddy, disconcerted by the experience.

I drive with my first assistant, Marc van der Bijl, to a rehearsal room rented out to us in an old gas factory. Today, rehearsals begin with the four most important actors and actresses in my film. [. . .] We still have nineteen days before the first day of filming. I have to cast the rest of the roles.

Debut director Willeke van Ammelrooy (right) on set in the Netherlands for The Butterfly Lifts Up the Cat

On location in Holland (see Willeke van Ammelrooy's entry)

[. . .] At the door we collect a brand new wheelchair while my main actor, Arjan Kindermans, arrives. He is playing a multiple sclerosis patient and for the first hour we work together on the movements of somebody in the various stages of MS which will be shown in the film. [. . .]

In the weeks prior to today I have been spared very little. My original cameraman left six weeks before the start of the project. My original main actor, who I had had in mind for six years, left a week ago. Now that I am working with Arjan, who is much younger and has very little experience in films, and now that I am working with Eddy and Cor, who are much older and have much more background in the cinema, I cannot believe my luck at how things are going. Setbacks are inevitable, I know, but I am a fighter who successfully follows her intuition, otherwise I would have fallen to pieces by now.

An exuberant Gordon Seaman returns to his native Toronto one week before production begins on *Just for Fun*:

After the most excellent, non-stop homosexual action at the AIDS conference in Berlin, I arrive home seven days before shooting begins on a half-hour drama about queer-bashing. I'm the producer and I'm thrilled that the crew hasn't strapped on their platforms and pulled a Nancy Sinatra in my absence. It's my first time and they tell me they'll be gentle. But I like it rough. That's why I fell in love in Berlin.

A driving hailstorm knocks out my phone service for the day. Set up in a phone booth, I learn of an impending revolt. Some residents around a park in the east end [of Toronto] don't like the idea of our shooting a queer-bashing scene all night long in their park. This is nasty, WASP Toronto in full gear. They have good children and pay their taxes. They are also over-tanned, over-fed and want us out of their park. Lots of calls from my tiny new office and the film office finally decides in the production's favour. The film permit is issued. Imagine my queer pride a week later when my feminist, skinhead, dyke friend marches into the park at dusk and strikes her pose as the continuity chick. I should have gone in drag.

Next it's a crash course in writing contracts. Recognising it as a good cause, the lawyer provides the lesson free. But who needs a meeting with a lawyer when they're jet-lagged and already longing for Berlin's backrooms?

With the Gay Pride Swim Meet looming, I drag my ass to practice. It is a sleepy, relaxed swim. I think about taking German lessons, pray for good weather for the outdoor locations, and wonder who the fuck will fund my next project.

Gordon Seaman beside a Canadian poster protecting gay rights

Herbert Achternbusch is a Bavarian director involved in new film *Off to Tibet!*, which promises to pursue his derisory vision of the modern world. Author of several books, screenwriter (for Herzog's *Heart of Glass*), and social commentator, Achternbusch laments the current state of Germany:

" On June 10th, that dreadful Ascension Day, and even more ghastly Fathers' Day. I drove back to Munich from Waldviertel [. . .] which lies in an Austria scarcely more than a quarter of what it was. I drove back into a whole Germany, which is being split apart by a despicable minority that imagines it has the supportive, silent majority behind it, simply because the ruling politicians do not make use of the stern objectivity of democracy

This has relevance for my film, *Off to Tibet!*, the second part of which we have already shot in the Himalayas. It is not until I'm in Windviertel, that I get some distance from the demanding production work. On the way back I call in on my Polish cameraman Adam Olech, who lives in an old castle. We discuss the first part of the film, which is set in Munich. How we are to avoid the dreary glossiness of current films. Woody Allen tries to do it in *Husbands and Wives* with quick pans from person to person during the dialogue. And *Arizona Dream* succeeds in making you forget the gloss thanks to Jerry Lewis. [. . .]

In the car I was listening to classical Indian music. It is all too pleasant to drive past Linz, and even more so Salzburg, listening to this Indian music. It is going to be my next film score, for *Off to Tibet!* Tibetan Buddhism is just like any other

Still from Before the Rain, *produced by Judy Counihan*

Indian Buddhism. I remember the three basic tenets, to care what one thinks, what one says, and what one does. That should come through in my film, though with a light touch. Well, so I speed down the *autobahn*, into the white of the west, which was being thoroughly oppressed by the black. So let's do the dream sequence in **99** black-and-white, Adam. OK?

Dealing with insurance is one of the hazards confronting every producer trying to firm up a project, as Judy Counihan reports from London:

66 Woke up with a start with that familiar feeling of anxiety mixed with excitement, and a million and one lists of 'things to do' for the day tumbled in my head. Rush to the office in

Soho for the first meeting of the day with our insurer for the film [*Before the Rain*]. The wonderful Kevin O'Shea, Sam and I sit and answer a myriad of questions about the production and its schedule. Yes, we're filming in Macedonia this summer, and no, there is no war going on there . . . yet. Yes, the U.N. are there in force and might actually loan us some guns. Eventually we decide that live guns might not be such a good idea on the set of a film about the Bosnian crisis. Models will be used instead. Yes, there are animals involved, and the director has 'ordered' two lambs to be 'born' in the scene with Dr. Saso. The director's cousin is a vet who artificially inseminates sheep so we can film the birth of the lambs outside the **99** 'lambing season'. This business is *crazy*!

5. Scouting Locations EVER SINCE THE FRENCH NEW WAVE DIRECTORS TOOK THEIR CAMERAS INTO THE STREETS AND ATTICS OF PARIS IN THE LATE 1950S AND EARLY 1960S, THE SCIENCE OF LOCATION SCOUTING HAS ACQUIRED CONSIDERABLE SIGNIFICANCE IN THE PRODUCTION OF ALL MOVIES.

Alice M. Allen works as a Park Ranger for the National Park Service in California, where numerous films have been shot:

Take person from our Regional office in San Francisco to Paramount Ranch to show her the *Dr. Quinn, Medicine Woman* [TV series for CBS] operation. It is important that I bring people here to see what is happening. It is important that they understand why it is appropriate for Santa Monica Mountains National Recreation Area to encourage, and even solicit filming at Paramount Ranch, when the policy of the National Park service is to be responsive to requests.

Paramount Ranch has a history of over 65 years as a filming location. The National Park Service is responsible for preserving the history of the United States in the Twentieth Century, and film and television production is certainly a major part of popular culture. We are seeing movie ranches disappear all around Los Angeles. We may not have the oldest, biggest, or best equipped movie ranch, but we have a good example, and we will manage it in a way that balances preservation of the past with uses today, and into the future. [...]

Meet with the director, location manager, production manager, FX technician and Fire Department to discuss the upcoming episode of *Dr. Quinn*. Since we are now into the fire season, we want to discuss all the parameters for the three fire effects described in the script. I noticed several valley oak seedlings around the location of one of the fires. I will talk to the art department and see if we can put set dressings near them to keep people from damaging them. During the scout, we also started discussing the possibility of a future episode with snow. What will we need to do for environmental review and approval for the substances that will be needed?

The Paramount Ranch, constructed in the Santa Monica Mountains National Recreation Area

Huang Jianzhong on a location recce in the Gobi Desert

Huang Jianzhong, winner of two Golden Flowers Awards for Best Film (1979 and 1990), visits the Gobi Desert prior to his new film, *The Great Wilderness*:

❝ 2.20 A.M. Our plane lands at Beijing airport. I've just come back from a two-week location recce in the desert.

It's hard to believe quite how many ancient forts fill the Gobi. Twelve hundred years ago, these were flourishing cities. Together, they formed ancient China's passage to the West – the old Silk Route. Our Land-Rover raced more than 300 km every day through the dust-clouds of the deserted road. Those broken walls and ancient coins that you can sometimes pick up in the sands, fragments of earthenware, shapeless objects which can be dimly recognised as cooking stoves, random piles of bones belonging to oxen, horses and camels, boulders left from ancient battles, beacon towers . . . It wasn't difficult to imagine the magnificence and excitement of those

days. But history has no pity. Nature has swallowed all these cities and abandoned them to the desert.[. . .]

It was here that I was searching for the theme of my new film and somewhere to place my main character. Pushed out of the city by the current economic boom and also by personal tragedy (he's lost his wife), he comes to live in solitude in these cities of yore. But in the ancient, empty forts, he finds the simplest means of communication. He gains the love of a young woman and discovers human warmth.

The film's five characters live in this arid desert, but their emotions are full of hope and colour.

We travelled over 4,000 km in two weeks. On the last day, I got a deep gash in my head from a piece of wire. I bled profusely and had seven stitches at the Xining No. 1 Hospital, a souvenir from my journey across the Gobi. **99**

Academy Award-winning production designer Dean Tavoularis has contributed significantly to the look of films such as Coppola's *Godfather* trilogy and *Apocalypse Now*:

66 The clock strikes midnight and June 10th begins. I am in the famous Pump Room in Chicago having a nightcap. A large black woman stands at the bar leafing through some sheet music. As she starts moving towards the piano she looks at me and asks if I would like to hear something. Cole Porter, I reply. She sits and begins to play 'Night and Day' and then she sings. I didn't expect her to sing. It's beautiful. I notice a woman, alone, at a small table. She is attractive. She sways a little with the song and she mouths the words and plays with her drink.

I better get out of here. I live upstairs in this hotel and tomorrow is another day of location scouting. That's why I'm in Chicago – working on a film called *I Love Trouble*. We arrived on Sunday from Los Angeles [and] started by scouting the airport we landed in, O'Hare, and then two others on the way to the hotel. Today we'll visit the railway station. We need the station and

Robert Duvall in Apocalypse Now, *designed by Dean Tavoularis*

the train platforms for several days of filming. Shooting begins on October 4th. After that, we look at three rooftops for another sequence. Very interesting. Then a tour, for research purposes only, of the *Chicago Tribune*. Very interesting again.

The story of the film involves two competing newspaper reporters. Nick Nolte is the journeyman who has seen it all and works for the 'Great Chicago Newspaper' and Julia Roberts is the upstart with the faltering tabloid.

Six weeks before the start of shooting on David Puttnam's production, *The War of the Buttons*, location manager Liz Kerry set up shop in West Cork:

Called Mrs. Lannin, Headmistress of Goleen National School, to check if permission had yet been sought from the Local Schools' Inspector and Governor to use the school as a location. She confirmed that she would be speaking to both of these people during the day and would call back with an answer during the evening. I explained that in the event of a positive response the director, production designer, and myself would like to recce the school next Monday.

Called Avis Rent-a-Car re. their letter quoting rental rates for minibuses. Asked for an improvement on the rate.

Called Ritchie Brown, manager of local fishing co-operative to ask which weather forecasting centre the trawlermen used. We had a friendly chat and he gave me the number for the West Cork region. [. . .]

Meeting at our office with local police officer, Sgt. McCarty, to explain our activities in general terms, to ask his advice on security and on possible availability of retired officers for night security at construction/props base. He offered to contact four recently retired officers on my behalf. [. . .]

Left office to drive fifteen minutes to Castle Freke for meeting with representatives from local council and National Parks & Wildlife from Dublin. Concern was expressed about using these particular dunes as a film location since they are shortly to be designated a conservation area. For our purposes this location must provide a 'battlefield' for children and a herd of cattle so clearly these dunes are unsuitable. However, the

Location recce picture for The War of the Buttons, *taken by Liz Kerry*

National Parks & Wildlife Officer was extremely helpful in describing and recommending alternative areas of sandy, as opposed to grassy, dunes in the area of Tralee. This meeting was an excellent example of how valuable co-operation and interest from local specialist bodies can be. [. . .]

rvin near skibbereen

Met local estate owner [. . .] to discuss clearing dense undergrowth and building rough track to facilitate a site where we propose to build a derelict boathouse. After much tramping through undergrowth we settled on the most suitable route bearing in mind that not only building materials but subsequently crew and equipment will use the track. Agreed a deadline for completion and rate for the job to start immediately. **"**

Sally Hibbin, a film critic's daughter who has proved one of Britain's brightest producers, spent her Thursday scouting locations in Latin America:

" We were in Nicaragua establishing the possibilities for filming [*Greysuits*] there. Paul Laverty, a Glaswegian who has worked on human rights there, has written a script about the

Nicaraguan village where Ken Loach was planning to shoot Greysuits

romance between a Glaswegian bus driver and a Nicaraguan refugee and their journey back to Nicaragua during the contra war. The script has been developed with the assistance of the Scottish Film Production Fund and the European Script Fund. Paul, Ken Loach (the director), and I were touring the country looking for locations and contacts to see how we might make the film and how much it would cost.

The day started in a small country hotel north of Matagalpa, leaving us with a major logistical headache. The main action of the film takes place in the north – where most of the fighting was – but it was becoming obvious that filming here would be hard. Filming in Nicaragua would be difficult at the best of times as there is no infra-

structure for film-making but one of the essentials was a decent hotel where our crew could be moderately comfortable for the four weeks of filming.

The Selva Negra above Matagalpa was reputedly the best hotel in the north but despite its beautiful location and the welcome coolness of the mountains it was impossible as a base. The water is not good and the rooms are literally hopping with insects. [. . .] We drove to Esteli, a Sandinista stronghold, still in the north [. . .] The majestic beauty of the mountains, the warmth and experiences of the local people, the comparative coolness of the climate, the co-operation of the local council and through them the army and – above all – the new, modern hotel convinced us that we could indeed film in the north. **99**

Sally Hibbin, on location in Nicaragua

The late Mai Zetterling, already a Swedish star in her teens thanks to her leading role in Alf Sjöberg's and Ingmar Bergman's *Frenzy*, and in later years recognised as a courageous writer/director, finds that scouting locations in France can be hazardous:

" Every time I have completed a film I say never again, and I mean it. [. . .] Why? Chasing after money in Europe, finding the right producer, co-producer, TV links in different countries, government funds, script funds, meetings being postponed all over the place, too many people saying 'No, thank you, it's not for us.' Depression lurks around every corner, yet here I am again, preparing to make another film, the third script accepted by the Dutch. I'm now doing the recce in the French Cevennes.

Nora, my assistant, and I are on our way [. . .]to see some revoltingly fascinating plastic rubbish heaps which [Nora] found by accident. [So] we decide to take a small detour on the way to Lozère.

We go through an underclass world which is hard to believe exists in southern France, with families living in partly ruined houses overlooking closed mine-shafts or huge blackened offices with every window smashed. It is deeply depressing to see the poverty, peopled by Algerians, Moroccans, and old French pensioners. [. . .]

We leave the main road and turn into a sad-looking wood, the air is rank and sodden all at once and the sun has gone into hiding as we reach the first plastic pyramid which is vivid blue, bound together with red rope that seems to be twisted and knotted in a painful fashion.

Indeed it is interesting, just as Nora had said, but what is not interesting is finding three teenage boys with motorbikes in this smelly environment. They glare at us and start making comments and catcalls. Let's turn round, I don't like the look of those boys, I say. Nora manages to turn in a small space while the boys now call out rudely after us. 'Damn it,' says Nora, 'I so wanted you to see the black and white pyramids, they're fantastic . . . Typical, women just can't go to places like this on their own, it's pathetic. In London I take for granted being restricted in my movements. I had forgotten that one has to think about it everywhere. Restricted, always restricted,' she fumes, and of course I fume with her.

From the main road we spot a strange looking house in the hills, behind the road we have just taken. We decide to find it and when we think we have finally located the right road, it turns from macadam into a dirt track. One old house lies forlorn in the landscape with two cars outside, one of which is a wreck. The road is full of potholes and mud and narrows suddenly. I don't like the feeling this road gives me, it's sinister and gets darker as the trees mark a dark tunnel of leaves above us.

Then the road stops for no reason, and I can't believe what I see – the same three boys with their motorbikes stand staring at us in an unfriendly fashion, then laugh and jeer. Some fifty metres behind them is a clearing which is obviously used as a kind of trial ground for

Mai Zetterling in Frenzy, *her first starring role, scripted by Ingmar Bergman*

motorbikes. [. . .] Nearby stands a ramshackle car with four youths chain-smoking. What on earth are they doing in such a depressing place, on a balmy summer's day? As if she'd heard my thoughts, Nora whispers, 'Drugs.'

There is nowhere for us to turn, so I say, 'Reverse as fast as you can, I don't like this much.' 'Lock the door!' she shouts, as she reverses back down the narrow, muddy lane. My heart is beating faster as I see the boys scrambling into their car, which squirts up mud as they turn around.

The boys on their motorbikes are revving their engines. I now realise that we are on the other side of the rubbish dump as I can see a white plastic pyramid sticking up through dead trees. We manage to reach the house with the two cars and turn on two wheels in the mud. We drive toward the main road being chased by the motorbikes and the car. We finally make the main road and manage to lose the boys with some clever, tricky driving from Nora. We are shaken by the ordeal and discuss the nasty situation. **99**

Zhou Xiaowen, a Chinese director (known in particular for _Desperation and Obsession_), although not encountering the same dangers as Mai Zetterling, still has some serious if jovial doubts about his location:

66 Had an accident. But we were lucky. No one was hurt and the car can still move. The location's no good. But the building's fine – made of bricks stolen by peasant farmers from the Great Wall. The whole village is full of houses like this – the Great Wall must have gaping holes.

Too many trees, and spread all over the place. Even if they weren't so untidy, it'd still be no good. The very trees destroy the image.

Liu Jing said: 'The shape of the mountains is no good either. The peaks are too sharp. They don't look like the mountains of northern Shaanxi – worn smooth. That's what tells you their age.'

I suddenly discover that Liu Jing, my assistant director, is doing a job that doesn't match his talents. He can identify certain problems more clearly than I can.

The props in the village are quite good. They say this used to be an army camp in the old days. That explains the stone posts for tying horses to. Could they be used in the film?

The beacon towers on the mountain-tops are quite interesting and could be used in the background from time to time. But will that look too affected and give people the impression that we're deliberately trying to emphasise a feeling of history or civilisation? Must watch out for that.

Met a young woman in the village, who's very much like the Ermo I have in mind [for the film]. Tried speaking to her, but her face showed fear. I thought I spoke very gently. Why was she scared of me? I think she resembles a tiger, but I can't say why exactly. A very beautiful tiger.

She can't speak in complete sentences, just a few single words – nouns and verbs. Then it struck me that the dialogue in our script isn't right. Peasant folk don't talk like that. Especially long, complex sentences can't be used. The dialogue will have to be rewritten. Must get Ermo to say single words. Actors are more difficult to find than locations.

Is the location more important than the actors? It's always the same question. Must have thought about this a thousand times, but never found an answer. What came first, the chicken or the egg? Tomorrow I must get the car fixed. 99

Andrew G. Munro, from Toronto (Canada), scouts locations for the CBC, a profession requiring infinite negotiating tact:

66 My day began at the Canadian Broadcasting Corporation Broadcast Centre in Toronto. I assist in selecting and maintaining locations for the Canadian television drama, _Street Legal_. The locations for the upcoming Episode #5 were 'locked in,' or so we thought. One location that was going to serve as an office in the script became a problem. The agreement to use this location was made with a person who failed to inform us that they had a partner who was unaware of the arrangement. When this new partner found out, he demanded renegotiation of the contract for double the original amount. After trying to discuss this with the second partner, it was clear that he was not interested in compromise.

Time was running short, since the producer, director, art director, gaffer and other crew members needed to have a definite location so that they could make their plans. Since the original location was now beyond budgetary constraints, an alternative was needed quickly. After several phone calls and meetings with local business people, a new contract was negotiated with an office four doors down the street. The shoot was a great success, and we intend to make the new location a part of our regular locations to visit in Toronto while filming _Street Legal_. 99

Ate de Jong, a Dutch director now resident in Los Angeles, has his car stolen on a visit to Budapest in search of locations:

66 Our project is based on a novel by Simone de Beauvoir, _All Men Are Mortal_. The story is set in Paris in the late 1940s, but shooting in Paris is difficult. Budapest has a similar architecture and we're told that one can still persuade people, against a fee, of course, to remove their cars.

[. . .] The previous day I finished a film in Munich, the first 'Movie of the Week' for RTL [German broadcaster]. I got the gig via my Los

123 «

Angeles manager and was very hesitant to accept it. But being in Europe has its advantages, for instance to push the *All Men Are Mortal* project forward. [. . .]

As I came from Munich to Budapest with a car from the RTL production, I feel very responsible [for the theft]. At the hotel they assure me that at least four foreign cars a week disappear from the parking lot. Within a few hours they end up in Yugoslavia, Poland, or Russia. Not a great selling point for shooting in Hungary. [. . .]

We visit a film set of a French feature. The production manager is a friend of ours. He smiles at our question whether or not it's cheaper to shoot in Hungary compared to France. He explains: in France you have four gaffers [senior electricians], in Hungary they cost half as much but you're obliged to hire eight.

Fifteen minutes before we want to leave we get a call from a Hungarian producer. The police had found his business card in our car, which has now been retrieved in a small village thirty miles outside the city. **"**

Above: *Dimitri Dolinin.* Right: *Actors in his screen version of Chekhov's* In the Ravine

Dimitri Dolinin of St. Petersburg prepares a screen version, entitled *The Road to Sakhalin,* of the Chekhov short story, *In the Ravine*:

" The action takes place in a Russian village at the end of the Nineteenth Century and it concerns a relatively well-to-do merchant's family. The production budget is tight and so it was decided not to build a good exterior of a provincial house but to find one. We will need it for about twenty minutes of screen time.

Together with the director of photography and the art director we toured a number of Russian provinces but without any luck. [. . .] In the end, on the advice of a painter friend we travelled to the province of Pskov where in the village of Velê we were told that a remarkable merchant's house was still standing and was now in use as a school. [. . .] We travelled there by coach, a journey that took eight hours. The temperature in the hotel room was as cold as it was outside in the open air. The only thing dribbling out of the tap was cold water.

The school is a one-story building with plastered walls that have been painted white. A number of old barns still stand in the large yard. We walked around the buildings looking for suitable shooting points and counted up what the cost of the building work would be likely to reach. However, little by little everyone began to feel that the style and size of the house was not right. [. . .] The following day we again wandered round the buildings and tried to come to some form of compromise, to talk ourselves into it, because basically there was no more time to carry on looking for locations.

As we were returning to the hotel, we had travelled no more than 200 metres when the director of photogaphy told the driver to stop. And then we saw the house. A remarkably well-preserved building, with an absolutely fantastic courtyard, surrounded by barns and all standing in a square. We had driven past it so many times without noticing it. And it was just hiding from us behind some high, densely-leaved trees.

And all this happened on June 10th, 1993. Just as if it had been commissioned. Or maybe it was Divine Providence. **"**

6. Action! The Shooting Phase WITH TIME AND FINANCIAL PRESSURES AT THEIR PEAK, THE SHOOTING PHASE OF ANY FILM IS THE MOST TESTING FOR DIRECTOR, PRODUCER, AND TECHNICIANS ALIKE. IF ONE IS ON LOCATION, THE WEATHER MAY PLAY A CRUCIAL ROLE; IN THE MUFFLED CALM OF THE STUDIO SET, ONE STRUGGLES TO ACHIEVE AN

AUTHENTICITY OF IMAGE AND PERFORMANCE.

Gabriele Salvatores, the Italian director who won an Academy Award for _Mediterraneo_, is shooting his new film, _South_, on location in the southernmost tip of Italy:

" 1 P.M. I wake up with a start: the alarm clock had gone off, but I must have fallen asleep again. We went to bed at six this morning, having worked all night. I only have an hour to get ready and reach the set. Tonight we shoot the famous scene 106! We have been rehearsing it for days – a single, four-minute tracking shot to be achieved with a Steadicam, in which all the characters of the film are reunited in a square crowded with _carabinieri_, photographers, ambulances, and military vehicles. It's the last scene in the film, where all the characters' personal stories come to an end. Hence the idea of putting them together in the same scene, but there's another reason: the feeling of working collectively I would like to convey to the crew (probably the best I've had in recent years) and the demonstration that together we can accomplish the most difficult tasks.

[. . .] Driving the road to the set is agreeable: four km skirting the sea among agaves and prickly-pears. I go over the scene I have to shoot while I'm driving. The sound engineer and the cameraman will have the heaviest work since they will have to follow the action from every angle of the square.

On the square the set-designers are spreading a thin layer of sand. The _carabinieri_ have already arrived; the actors are mentally walking through their movements. Now we have to rehearse with everybody . . .

Left: *Gabriele Salvatores*. Above: *The final sequence from Salvatores'* South

7.45 P.M. The sun is going down. We have finished rehearsing and at 8 P.M. there's an hour's break until it is dark enough to start shooting. [. . .] At 9 P.M. we do a final run-through with the Steadicam and, magically, everything works to perfection: everybody is in place at the right time, the movements of the extras are perfect, there are no problems with the sound, the lights, or even the camera; we decide to shoot . . .

The first take is good. There is only a moment's hesitation due to an ambulance's coming late into the scene, but it's an easily soluble problem. During the second take the camera signals a shutter fault. We have to stop shooting and replace the camera with a heavier one, more difficult for the cameraman to operate. We have to strip the camera of all but the most vital parts. This takes over an hour. The crew relaxes, the actors wander around the square, the extras gather in little groups . . .

When we start shooting again everything works well technically, but the earlier creative tension is lost. At this juncture I decide to change the scene in such a way that the special layout of the location has to be almost completely rethought. I can read the dismay on everybody's face. [. . .] A crew is sometimes like an army or a football team up against it; it has to feel the danger and find the strength to overcome it through its unity as a group.

Under the worried eyes of the producer we begin rehearsing again, tightening up time and action. In less than two hours the set is ready, but we have just an hour left before dawn. There is just the right concentration and tension when I call 'action!' The first two takes are perfect; we shoot a third for good measure which is even better. When I say 'stop!' the cameraman shouts with joy and applause erupts in the square. The technicians, the extras, the actors, the *carabinieri*, the production team are all clapping frantically. In less than half an hour the sun will rise; we can all go to the beach for a game of volleyball. "

Philippe Rousselot has joined the distinguished ranks of those European cinematographers who find work and acclaim in Hollywood. His work on *A River Runs Through It* earned him an Academy Award. Here he reports from the set of *La Reine Margot*:

The day begins with traffic jams. It's already too hot, and the buildings that lie wholesale on the horizon are almost swallowed up in a sky that's like liquid chalk. In the unusual light, the outskirts of Paris are transformed into the suburbs of some Third World city: the same thickness in the air, the same honking, the same din.

The journey to the set is already like another world, a strange land. I imagine tents along the road, the lepers who bang on the windows of the car in Bombay. The trip towards the Sixteenth Century passes, today, via India.

June 10th, 22nd day of shooting on *La Reine Margot*, the third day devoted to the death of Charles IX.

The studio is a large metallic cube which increases the heat from outside and promotes dust. The decor in the Louvre is austere, all sombre woodwork that no spotlight seems able to free from the shadows. In the middle of a room a large black bed with wreathed columns is being covered with linen sheets soaked in blood.

Shooting advances with nerve-wracking slowness, in a silence troubled by calls for silence and the buzz of the red light. I light without thinking, from instinct or sheer economy, by the red of the candle-flames and the red of the blood. The Chinese lanterns that I use as lights give the set an atmosphere of a botched party.

Charles IX oozes fake blood and soaks the sheets in red liquid. He whispers or groans his lines in muffled silence and suffocating heat. Everyone saves his breath and his speech, for the day will be long, very long, a day without incident and without harshness, the same as the one before but just a little hotter, just a little longer.

Things grind to a halt with the repetition of commands and the monotony of whisperings. Between each shot I escape from this scarlet and black cavern towards the light and a telephone in order to call the hospital.

Jean-Hugues Anglade in La Reine Margot

A distraction anyhow, in the form of a visit (rare) to the set by the producer. He talks to everyone, threatens and reassures, blames and compliments, and each of his sentences contradicts the previous one. He leaves very quickly without obtaining anything because in fact he doesn't ask for anything, and his presence will only barely disturb the surface like a leaf falling on water.

The day ends with no hope of rain and coolness, with more traffic jams, and scarlet and black rushes, with death and blood.

A hundred kilometres away, in a hospital room and in broad daylight, my father lies in agony trying to breathe and I'm pinned down at the bedside of a dying man who isn't even related to me and who's faking it. There are days when I loathe the cinema.

Michel Deville has directed an uninterrupted stream of good-natured, inquiring films (*Le Dossier 51*, *Péril en la demeure*, *La Lectrice*, etc.) since the early 1960s, when he burst on the French scene with *Ce soir ou jamais*:

Thursday June 10th. Got up at 5.30 A.M. 33rd shooting day on my new film. Place: a small cemetery in the French Vexin region. 8 A.M. Preparations for shooting. 9.15 A.M. The first shot is done. The weather is grey, ideal.

But soon, big black clouds roll across the sky. I think of Prévert's verses : 'In Arles, where rolls the river Rhone . . .' That is the wrong film, Arles was in *La Lectrice*.

My four women, Anémone, Nicole Garcia,

Michèle Laroque and Hanna Schygulla are on the set. And a new one, Denise Bonal, who is starting with us today. She is over there, so small at the other end of the cemetery. I communicate with her through a megaphone. Not very intimate.

The wind is getting stronger and stronger. My women's hair becomes animated. It is beautiful. Scrupulously, before each take, the two hairdressers come and touch up their hair style. The wind detroys everything the moment they turn their back. The hairdresser today is the wind.

'Are you writing your memoirs?' the cameraman asks me.

'Yes,' I answer, and I found the title for them: 'Memoirs from Beyond the Grave.'

10.30 A.M. Rain. Oilskins, boots, rainhats are taken out. The team resembles a lost congregation of Breton fishermen. To cheer us up, sandwiches are being distributed.

Brief lulls. We manage two shots. Then disaster, the skies are breaking up, the sun reappears: that does not work anymore. Fortunately, big clouds return in force. For one hour, rain and sunshine alternate. We shoot in between.

Already midday. Time that goes by, weather that goes wrong: these are the two major obsessions that plague a director when shooting outdoors.

Lunch in our mobile restaurant. The production team has invited the mayor. I am, of course, placed next to him . . .

French director Michel Deville

Anthony Hopkins and Debra Winger in Richard Attenborough's Shadowlands

From 1 P.M. until nightfall, the rain does not stop. No way we can make the two shots that I need. The team, heroic, is waiting in the rain, for the sky to clear up. In vain.

5 P.M. We decide to give up. Pow-wow with the production team. We will come back later for these two poor shots.

7 P.M. I go back home. Exhausted, I lie down, close my eyes. Only to re-open them at midnight. I get up . . . But already, June 10th is over, end of the diary. Title of the film: *Aux Petits Bonheurs*. It is a comedy. **"**

Lord [Richard] Attenborough continues to shrug aside commercial disappointment (*Chaplin*) and to fling himself into projects that move him personally; all this in a life otherwise packed with voluntary activity, and the occasional return to screen acting (*Jurassic Park*, no less):

" [This] was the 37th day of shooting on *Shadowlands* – the unit call was 8 A.M. I got up as usual at 6.15, leaving home and picking up my partner Diana Hawkins on the way to arrive at Shepperton Studios at 7.50 A.M.

Anthony Hopkins, Debra Winger and Peter Firth were on call. We were shooting sequences in a hospital office and X-ray room. Tony plays the part of C.S. Lewis; Debra, Joy Gresham to whom he is married, and Peter plays the specialist concerned with her illness.

We had at this juncture completed approximately one and a half hours' screen time, having shot some 183,400 ft of film of which some 110,000 had been printed. We averaged approximately two and a half minutes per day as a result of some ten or eleven set-ups. The work went very well. Tony and Debra are remarkable artists, totally professional and always word perfect.

We saw dailies at lunchtime and the unit wrapped at 6.20 P.M. We had a production meeting to complete discussions for the next few days' work until about 7 P.M. and I arrived home at around 7.45 P.M., not a little tired but very happy. "

Shooting in Iran represents the triumph of ingenuity over lack of sophisticated equipment. Behruz Afkhami is a young director who insists on pressing ahead:

" Today I have been shooting one of the final scenes of a picture entitled *Day of the Angel*, about a man who dies – or imagines that he has died – for eleven hours. Actually the scene pertains to the middle section of the story where the man, or rather his ghost, sees his will being read by his family and relatives whom he has disinherited. The ghost dances with pleasure when he sees his family become mad with rage.

To shoot the scene, we had to add special equipment to the crane which allowed us to mount the camera and the actor on the crane, and to present the actor 'hovering' in the air. The whole set-up had to be placed inside a rather small hall and presented some technical difficulties. But I think the result was on the whole satisfactory. At any event I am making a film which the circumstances permit. At the same time I keep thinking of John Ford's remark, 'I never could make the films that I wanted to make.' When a great director says this of his film career, I feel that I should have no complaints. "

The actor "hovering" in the air, and suffering – from Behruz Afkhami's Day of the Angel

Ramses Marzouk, an experienced Egyptian director of photography, describes a somewhat hazardous shot on *The Immigrant*:

66 Despite the fact that Youssef Chahine's *The Immigrant* was scheduled to be shot in November 1993, we had to film one scene ahead of schedule, involving a wheat-field on fire. This is because the wheat harvesting season in Egypt ends in June, so we had to shoot that scene before the end of the month.

At first light we started preparing the field which was to be set ablaze. Afterwards we studied the wind direction, placed our cameras in a position that would protect them from the flames and made the necessary tests before the shoot – all this while the fire was raging – and moments before the cameras started rolling, the wind, to our surprise, changed direction. This seemed sure to send the flames in the direction of the cameras and technicians. So we had to find a quick solution. We erected glass panels in front of the cameras as well as the technicians to protect them from the heat. The scene turned out a great success. 99

Left: *Still from Youssef Chahine's* The Immigrant.
Above: *Ramses Marzouk*

Nigel Stafford-Clark, a producer with Zenith in London, describes an incident that recalls the famous scene with the cat in Truffaut's *Day for Night*:

" I'm standing in the kitchen of a large house in East Molesey, and wondering what I've ever done to Glenn Chandler that he should do this to me. The thought is provoked by a ginger cat which stands on the other side of the kitchen, with a tea-towel on its head and a smirk on its face. The cat owes its existence in the script of *Deadly Advice* to Glenn, who wrote it. It's supposed to flee in terror when Imelda Staunton throws a tea-towel at it. Instead it stands there looking like an advertisement for a rakish style of feline headgear. Tempers are beginning to fray. The cat has been on set now for two days and has yet to do anything it's supposed to.

The weather is sultry, and for several days now we have been starting at midday and finishing late at night. It's a good way of covering scenes set at dusk, but the crew find it hard to sleep late and everyone is tired. [. . .] During a break for re-lighting, Mandie Fletcher, the director, and I exchange animal horror stories. My favourite is the cow that escaped from the studio during a commercials shoot and thundered up Wardour Street pursued by hapless production assistants. "

José L. Cuerda sends a concise and cheerful account from the set of his latest film in Madrid:

" Twelfth day of filming *Crisis*, my second urban comedy. Final meeting between 'Andrés' and 'Fulgencio.' They haven't seen each other for a while. 'Andrés' has stopped going to 'Gina's' club where he used to be a regular. 'Fulgencio', who almost never went before, is now a good client. With women you have to go in for

Edward Woodward, Hywell Bennett, John Mills and Billie Whitelaw in Deadly Advice, *produced by Nigel Stafford-Clark*

Above: *Still from Bogdan-Christian Dragan's Romanian feature,* East Side Story. Below right: *Bogdan-Christian Dragan*

methodical doubt. Make them desperate. And I'm just talking A.B.C. here. I'm not sure if even the Marquis de Sade could go through the whole alphabet.

A good day's shooting. Every day has been good. The improvisations complement the script and improve it. Everything is inventive and fertile. The characters deceive each other as much as they want. There is no language in which one cannot lie. The characters deceive themselves at the same rate. The light does not cure the blindness. Comedy gives us such a great kick in the guts. Hi there, Mister Wilder! **99**

Film production in Romania has not recovered as swiftly as had been hoped in the wake of Ceausescu's demise. However, Bogdan-Christian Dragan tries to make *East Side Story*, "a metaphor for totalitarianism":

66 On June 10th I had to shoot one of the most difficult parts of my film: the scene where a beautiful woman gives birth to a monster.

At 8 A.M. the actors were on hand: three beautiful girls and one man. We began to rehearse. It was hard enough because the girls

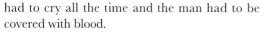
had to cry all the time and the man had to be covered with blood.

At 9 A.M. we began rehearsing while listening to music – a German song, 'The Monster Born Is a Skinhead.'

At 10 A.M. the other members of the crew arrived. Unfortunately there was not enough light so there was a delay of two hours until our first take. There was also not enough artificial blood.

At 1 P.M. my 'monster' was so exhausted that he had to rest for an hour. The props man had a problem at home, and left the set. I was alone, thinking what a great scene I had missed.

At 4 P.M. I shot some small, detailed shots. I was also very tired.

At 5 P.M. the production manager declared that we'd had enough for the day. I told him that I had scarcely shot anything. He looked at me, smiling: 'Well, young man, you must realise that in Romania, a film director must first of all learn to wait, secondly to wait, and lastly to wait! **99**

>> 136

Wu Ziniu, a member of the "Fifth Generation" or new wave of Chinese film-makers, describes the frustrations of shooting on a tiny island when others have the same idea:

66 4.50 A.M. A dawn full of hope. Between the sea and the sky there appears a streak of red. All is calm. We take a small boat to a lighthouse on a tiny island in the sea so that we can set up our camera before the sun bursts forth in all its radiance.

Once I step onshore, I suddenly discover that two other camera crews have arrived before me. One is from Hongkong; they want to take a shot of an ancient warrior fighting with a sea monster against the background of a red sun. The other is from a video production company, who also want to use the red sun as a backdrop to film a woman singing a woeful love melody. And I want the same red sun for the opening shot of my new film, a young man in a small boat, floating in the sea in the light of the sun, going in search of his vagrant brother. I've come to this lighthouse three times now just to capture this shot of the red sun.

The lighthouse is very small, like a droplet of

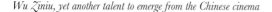
Wu Ziniu, yet another talent to emerge from the Chinese cinema

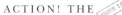

John Bloomfield fitting one of his costumes on the set of Rapa Nui, *made on location at Easter Island*

water in the sea, unable to bear the weight of three cameras. After I wish the other two cameramen good morning, I realise I'll not be able to do anything today. Today's sun is theirs. I'm very disheartened. I'll have to wait until tomorrow. [. . .]

I cannot bear to watch that stirring moment when the red sun leaps out of the surface of the sea. Instead, I get into the boat and head back. But that woman's alluringly plaintive voice makes me turn round, just in time to witness the ancient warrior brandishing his sword to strike the sea monster. For me, another morning's filming has gone by. **99**

Most films involve a greater or lesser degree of shooting on location, whether it be Toronto or Los Angeles doubling for New York City, or in remote and exotic landscapes such as Easter Island, where costume designer John Bloomfield found himself on June 10th, 1993:

66 5.30 A.M. out of bed and by 5.40 in my jeep driving to location. The secret of this life is to lay your clothes out at night so that you can slide straight into them – gives you fifteen minutes extra in bed.

I am a British costume designer working on Kevin Reynolds' film *Rapa Nui* which we are shooting on Easter Island (the Rapa Nui of the title). A dot on the map in the South Pacific, the most remote inhabited place on earth. I have been here for seven months.

The drive takes thirty minutes, mostly in four-wheel drive. There is a speed limit of 20 kph and anyway it's impossible to go much faster. Even so I am surprised at the amount of dust I create considering there was a torrential storm at the weekend – some two inches of rain on Sunday morning. Can you measure the depth of rainfall when it travels sideways? This island is unnervingly quiet, but when the wind blows, it really blows.

Having to write this diary makes me look again at a now familiar route. The bright moonlight brings out the cinder cones and volcanic hills in sharp relief – beautiful and powerful. The whole island is a volcano. They tell me it has been inactive in historical time, but do I believe them? It is so easy to imagine the lava flowing.

Today we are shooting on the crater of Rano Raraku, the original quarry for the statues for which the island is famous. We have built a false rock section in the side of the mountain and will be moving out our own sixteen-metre high statue and walking it down the hill. Even our imitation weighs three tonnes – how did the ancients do it? Watch our film and find out.

The base camp for this location is a collection of large Chilean army tents. We have two to store the wardrobe and dress the extras plus a container truck for the actors' costumes and small army tents as dressing-rooms for the actors. No Hollywood luxury here!

At 6.30 A.M. the extras start to arrive in trucks and old buses. Two hundred assorted Easter Islanders who will be playing the labour gang pulling and levering the Moai (Rapa Nui name for the statues). They get channelled past the coffee and hot soup already bubbling on the log fires into wardrobe and makeup. It's like a time warp production line, they enter as moderns complete with watches and headsets, and exit as Stone Age workers – slaves to the obsessions of ancient gods.

It's now starting to get light, and also starting to rain. If it is dry this job is easy, if it's wet it's a nightmare. Today I am lucky and the squall passes. The good part is that it is followed by the most magnificent full-arc double rainbow of such intensity it looks painted.

By 9 A.M., all actors and extras are ready and we move to the set. I am surprised to see Jason Scott Lee, our lead actor, arrive. He was scheduled for a day off but has been called in to do a swimming sequence with the second unit. Not fun anymore. This may be the South Pacific, but the last couple of weeks have definitely turned wintry, and those waves are big!

The set is a bizarre mixture of ancient and modern as well as quite a blend of cultures and languages – Rapa Nui of course plus Americans, Chileans, Australians, New Zealanders, Mexicans, Spanish, English, French, and even a Belgian.

By 10 A.M., everybody is in position – knows which rope to pull, which lever to push, which stone to carry, and we are ready to shoot. **"**

Pupi Avati has recently begun to achieve recognition outside his native Italy, with films like *Bix* and *Magnificat* in competition at Cannes. His diary finds him at work on *Childhood Friend*, shot, like much of *Bix*, on location in Iowa:

" We are in the second week of shooting in the U.S. and my biological clock is still set to Italian time. But my unusual disquiet is not so much due to this confusion; this is the third film I have made in the States, and for my brother Antonio and I, Davenport [in Iowa] has become a second home.

The anxiety I feel is caused by the story in my film. It's the story of a friendship brought to its most extreme and having tragic consequences. The story of a bond between two boys that was once very strong and has now become a sort of psychopathy that is splitting them apart. The story of an atrocious vendetta. If I look back at my past, I realise that the vendetta theme is present in everything I do, as if my relationship with 'them' – the people and events in my past – were not completely resolved, and required further continual and painful scrutiny.

1 P.M. The lunch break is over. We've shot the scene where Arnold, the main character, star

of the *Chicago News*, is trying to find out what has become of Eddie Greenberg, his childhood friend and the man he fears is blackmailing him. These are scenes 72/76/77.

6.30 P.M. During the afternoon we have shot other scenes in Arnold's flat, scenes that concentrate on Arnold's growing certainty that the criminal threatening him is in fact his boyhood pal.

Although the production is perfect and the crew splendid, both professionally and as people, I am behind schedule. Perhaps I have piled up too many interiors which require lots of cuts to give the right rhythm to the story. This is the first time I have shot a film based on a script of 260 sequences.

I've had a touch of flu for a few days, with shivers and a feeling of sickness which normally disappears on the set, but returns later in the car as I'm driving back to the hotel. **99**

>>140

Menahem Golan, along with his cousin Yoram Globus, enjoyed some years of glory in Hollywood during the late 1970s and early 1980s, when he chaired the temporarily immense Cannon corporation. As an Israeli director, however, he has remained loyal to his first love, making films, good, bad, and indifferent. Here is an extract from his excellent, detailed diary:

66 June 10th, 1993, was one of those wonderful summer days [in Tel-Aviv]. My involvement in the films I make is total. I think up the ideas, I write them, I produce them, and sometimes I direct them too. I am also involved in putting them together, financing and dealing with their international sale and distribution. Being fully involved in the creation and making of a motion picture is what gives me the utmost feeling of fulfilment.

6 A.M. Yael my daughter and my line producer on the film I'm currently directing, *Deadly Heroes*, picks me up and drives me to the location – Ben Gurion Airport.

Breakfast on the set. I speak with some of the Heads of Department like Avner my first A.D. [Assistant Director] and with Hilik Neeman, my Director of Photography, about the fact that I'd like to cover the first scene of the morning with three cameras. I tell him the lenses I'd like him to use, and the mood I think he should create in his lighting. [. . .] Rachel Zaltzman – my costume designer – comes to warn me that she prepared only two doubles of the shirts for our star Michael Pare who gets wounded in the scene.

7 A.M. My Art Director, Avi Avivi, brings me in to the set. A Greek duty-free shop and a passenger waiting-room. It looks very authentic . . . The special effects guy, 'Polak', shows me exactly where the bullet effects will be displayed, among the Greek ornaments in the shop. I place my actors in safe positions.

7.30 A.M. Rehearsals with my cast, Michael Pare, Jan Michael Vincent, and Billy Drago. A few changes are necessary for safety reasons. Head of the airport's security tells me that the cameras are not allowed to photograph a certain building seen outside the window (security – Israel is still in a state of war with terrorism and on the roof of that building secret snipers have their post). We move one camera position, and change the choreography, and of course the lighting. We lose 15 minutes. I am worried, we have the location only for one day. This is of course one of the limitations of low-budget movies. [. . .]

8.30 A.M. The first set-up is ready. I rehearse the dialogue with Michael Pare and Jan Michael Vincent and the local Israeli actors Alon Aboutboul and Juliano Mer. I check the shot once again, last check-up of the guns, last touch of makeup. We shoot. It looks good on all three cameras.

9 A.M. I begin to prepare my second set-up. We go for close-ups, extreme close-ups and inserts of our special effects. By lunchtime I have devoured at least eight cups of water. It's over 30 degrees Celsius. The humidity is heavy, but the shooting goes well and that is what counts. [. . .]

7 P.M. Watching dailies in the screening room at Herzelia United Studios, choosing the good takes that should go into the film. My editor is with me, so is my Director of Photography. It's good seeing your scenes come to life on the big screen for the first time, an experience that can't be matched. [. . .]

8.40 P.M. My editor for [my other new film] *Crime and Punishment* is on the line. She has just completed the rough-cut of the eleventh reel. She

Colin Nutley (centre) shooting The Last Dance *on location in Blackpool*

has a question: should she transfer it to video so she could ship it to Tel-Aviv for me to see and give my comments, before she moves on to reel twelve? Of course send it to me immediately, I'm so eager to see it . . . and put my thoughts in, and supervise the editing process. [. . .]

11 P.M. Rachel my wife throws me into the shower, then – to bed, well my wife needs some attention too. Then she asks me if I'll accept the invitation to see a new Israeli movie this coming weekend. A day off? Of course I'll go to see a new movie.

After the success of his Swedish comedy, *House of Angels*, the expatriate British director Colin Nutley alights once more in his own country for shooting on *The Last Dance*:

❝ I wake up at 3 P.M. I'm in bed in a hotel in Blackpool. We've been filming nights for the past four days on my fourth Swedish feature film. The first six weeks in Stockholm were fairly calm – normal filming days – but Blackpool has been a bastard. A dead body under the pier – on paper easy to write – the reality of filming not quite so simple. The tide, the light, the rain, the wind, tons of cable, a massive crane, tractors and Range Rovers plus a Swedish crew – fantastic but not used to tides – and I wrote the script so I can complain only to myself!

Next week it's the West Indies for two weeks but last night it was Yorkshire pudding and bread and butter pudding. Today another night on the pier and fish and chips. We will film a scene with Ewa Fröling and Helena Bergström – a fight which leads up to the death of Eva's character. The girls are dressed and made up, the lighting fixed . . . It takes four hours and the weather is great. The rig is fixed and we rehearse, the weather still holds. The pier is full of old-age pensioners going to the 'end of the pier show.' They find us and the actresses (dressed in ballroom costume) odd. We have our fish and chips from Harry Ramsden's (a name wasted on my Swedish crew), we have Marmite sandwiches (an English delicacy wasted on my Swedish crew!). We go back on to the pier and the wind is up and the evening sky is turning black with rain clouds.

Frames from Jan Svankmajer's extraordinary Faust

Jan Svankmajer eludes easy classification as a director. A brilliant inventor of animated forms, this Czech has been gracing festivals and TV screens for more than thirty years with his compelling, entrancing, and often bizarre short films:

66 This is the 131st day of filming *Faust Teaching Us a Lesson*. Today's sequence is a parody of Charles Gounod's opera. We are filming dancers in tutu. They look as though they are straight from *Swan Lake* but they come rushing on the set carrying wooden rakes. The set is a puppet theatre which has been built in a real, sun-lit meadow. But instead of a backdrop we have real wooded hills with clear blue skies. While the chorus is singing about the morning that calls them back to work in the fields (played on the playback) the dancers are gathering hay into haystacks. The heat is unbearable. There is no shade to be found. Everybody is irritable. It took the whole morning to build the set and now the wind is getting stronger and is starting to lift the striplights. We have to shoot as fast as possible before the weather changes. So we skip lunch. Sour milk provided by a local farmer is our refreshment. The 99 dancers are attractive despite the rakes.

Abbas Kiarostami has established himself at the forefront of Iranian directors, with films like *Where Is the Friend's Home?*, *And Life Goes On . . .* and *Close Up*:

66 We set up the camera and waited for a cloudless sunset. This is perhaps the fifteenth day on which we have prepared for the last shot of my film *Under the Olive Trees*, a scene in which the actors walk away from the camera and disappear among the trees as the sun sets. There was a brief shower yesterday. And then after two weeks a golden afternoon sunlight appeared over the olive tree tops.

Sound, camera, action. The actors started moving away from the camera towards the horizon. 20, 30, 40, 60 seconds passed. Everything was going so well that I couldn't believe my eyes. I was anxious that something might happen. I turned away so as not to look. Then somebody shouted, 'Who are they?' I turned around and

Now we're on the run. Will we get the scene – yes – no – let's try for it – it rains – it stops – we start – the lights blow – they're fixed – we start again – so does the rain – we get the master [shot] – it's good – we go for the close-ups – the lights blow again – they're fixed once more – the rain starts – we stop and start and stop until 3.30 in the morning. The crew and actors are exhausted; as the [electricians] pull in the tons of cable, my first [assistant director] asks me why we do this as a job. I'm too tired to answer and I dream of the West 99 Indies. Let's hope it doesn't name.

saw three boys running towards the camera. We all started shouting at the top of our voices: 'Go back! Go back!'

But they kept coming forward, and finally the cameraman cried: 'They're in the frame. What shall I do?' I said, 'Cut.' There was silence. The actors were still walking away, while the boys ran towards us. It took them ten minutes to run up the hill on which the camera had been set up with such difficulty. I waited for the boys to approach. Their innocent faces were covered with sweat and beaming with joy. I tried to pour all my anger into my question: 'Why did you come?' 'We wanted to watch a film being made.' 'But you've spoilt our work,' I replied. They laughed and did not believe me. But when they found out what they had done they sat on the grass shamefacedly.

So we have set up the camera again today, and we're waiting for the weather to clear up. Our young friends are with us again, and now whenever other children try to approach us, the youngsters shout at them not to spoil the shot. 99

Robin Crichton has worked for three decades as a documentarist in Scotland. Now he is involved with full-blown feature work – _Moonacre_, a Scottish-Welsh-Slovenian-Czech co-production!:

66 We did not start shooting until lunchtime as we were scheduled for a partial night shoot. The location was Predjama in Slovenia, one of the most extraordinary castles in the whole of Europe. The region has more caves per square mile than anywhere else and the original castle was a cave fortress, halfway up a cliff face. [. . .]

Backed by eleven European partners, _Moonacre_ is probably Scotland's most ambitious co-production to date. [. . .] The cast includes Jean Anderson, Iain Cuthbertson, Phillip Madoc, Miriam Margolyes, and Graham Stark from the U.K., Polona Vetrich from Slovenia, and Allanah O'Sullivan and John Cairney from New Zealand. The Director of Photography, Pete Warrilow, is an expatriate Scot now resident in Hollywood.

The screenplay by William Corlette is based on the classic novel _The Little White Horse_, by Elizabeth Goudge. A young girl, Maria, and her brother are orphaned and sent, with their governess, to live with their uncle in the back of beyond. Maria quickly discovers that for generations her new home has been cursed by a feud with a neighbouring valley and that she alone has an opportunity to solve the mystery and resolve the dispute. It is part ghost story, part detective story, and part adventure fantasy.

The scenes we were shooting involved the rescue and escape of Maria from the castle where she was being held hostage. During the day the clouds built up and the night shoot started with a spectacular thunderstorm and sheet lightning which turned night into day. This was a bonus, as two nights earlier we had rented every light in Slovenia to shoot the castle exterior at night, with two generators running red-hot and spitting out bits of molten metal. The scissor arcs which we had brought in from Zagreb really hadn't managed to create the lightning effects that we had

Abbas Kiarostami (left) on location

Scene from Robin Crichton's Moonacre, *set in Slovenia*

hoped for, so the storm allowed us to pick up the effects for real. [. . .]

Yes, June 10th, 1993, was a memorable day. At midnight we were still trying to shoot dialogue in between the thunder-claps that cracked open the Slovenian sky. **99**

Arguably the most gifted Indian director since Satyajit Ray, Shyam Benegal has veered between keenly-felt features (such as *The Churning* and *The Ascent*) and full-length documentaries (the huge TV series on Nehru, for example, as well as small-screen conversations with Ray):

66 Guntur, Andhra Pradesh. Arrived here last night from Bombay, 850 km. away. [. . .] We are about to leave for the location of the film, a temple town called Amravati. I am making a short film of 25 minutes as part of a TV series. The film is based on a vignette entitled *Sweet Basil* written by a well-known author, S. Sankaramanchi. The story I am doing describes a priest of a small shrine near a very large temple who finds it difficult to make a living from the donations made by

devotees at his shrine. It deals with one day in his life. I am shooting the film over four days.

The location is wonderful, with a fourteenth century temple dedicated to Lord Shiva on the banks of the river Krishna. A small lane with a row of tiny houses behind the temple make up the township. This was originally a Buddhist community about 2,000 years ago.

I have two main actors. A young man, Sri Vallabh Vyas from the desert city of Jaisalmer and a young woman, Sashi Sahai. Neither is familiar with this environment or the language or dialect spoken here, but both are very good actors. I have been rehearsing them in the dialect they must use. Sri Vallabh has to learn (in addition to the dialect) several Sanskrit verses. He pronounces them well. His diction is excellent, perhaps because he comes from a Brahmin family. His natural gestures and body language are perfect for the part – the reason why I chose him for this role. Both are getting into their costumes and makeup.

I am at the river-bank for my first shot. The producer tells me that the crane has not arrived. Neither has the rain machine. I am mad at him. I

suggest he sends for the fire brigade. That will take an hour or more. [. . .] The script calls for rain. [. . .] I cannot do this without the rain machine, and I'll now have to change my script.

10.30 A.M. A pig wandered into the frame. So did a couple of stray dogs. That was good. The fire brigade has turned up. Not very satisfactory but still possible to get some of the shots I need.

Noon. It has actually started to rain. Quite useless for me as it stopped before we could set up a shot. I will now have to shoot when it is not raining and create my own, otherwise I will have problems matching the rain. [. . .]

1.45 P.M. Lunch. I am working on the revised script. The crane has arrived, after being delayed by a traffic accident on the highway. The weather is dreadful. Hot and steamy. But the landscape is lovely, evenly lit with a very grey sky. [. . .]

5.30 P.M. It has suddenly turned dark. There is a heavy downpour. We have moved inside the temple. I was to shoot the interiors tomorrow. I decide to do them now.

7 P.M. The rain has ceased. It is the magic hour. I've asked my cameraman for a couple of shots of the river for the title sequence. Then we pack up for the day.

Shyam Benegal (right) prepares a scene for his short film, Sweet Basil, *starring Vallabh Vyas (left)*

Simon Relph is a British producer who has frequently collaborated with other countries (*Damage* is a recent example), and writes here of the anxieties of keeping to schedule when actors have other commitments ahead:

" Sadly, June 10th turned out to be one of the worst days on our film *Camilla* which has been shooting in Toronto and Georgia for nearly eight weeks now. We completed in Savannah, Georgia, the night before and moved to Jekyll Island two hours to the south early on the Thursday morning. My partner Christina Jennings and I stayed behind in Savannah to settle a lot of bills and sign cheques which were

urgently required in Toronto. Because of the late finish the night before we had to change our schedule to permit Bridget Fonda and Jessica Tandy a twelve-hour turnaround between the finish of call one day and the start of work the next. So a scene that had been scheduled for the latter part of Thursday was brought forward to the morning.

It was extremely important that this scene should be completed by lunchtime because the other scheduled scene involved Graham Greene (*Dances with Wolves*), who had flown in specially for the day to complete the part he had begun in Toronto. I telephoned our assistant director mid-morning to try and impress upon him the urgency

Jessica Tandy and Bridget Fonda meet Graham Greene on the set of Camilla, *co-produced by diarist Simon Relph*

of getting through the scene he was on, only to find that all sorts of problems had arisen on arrival, because there were no four-wheel drive vehicles to get the unit and equipment to the point at which they want to shoot. [. . .]

By the time Christina and I arrived it was apparent that the scene would not be complete until mid-afternoon which would only leave us three or four hours to get through the scene with Graham Greene. Well, of course we failed; he was due to fly to Santa Fe the following morning and had to leave us no later than 10 A.M. With four shots left to complete and again the twelve-hour turnaround problem, that looked impossible. Sunset came at about 8.30 P.M. as it always does and we were left with four shots to do between 9 and 10 the following morning when our average was closer to one per hour. We rushed around the actors' trailers negotiating and by 9 o'clock there was at least a plan by which Graham Greene could catch his plane the following morning. It was not until 9.30 P.M. that we had time to settle into our extremely comfortable surroundings at the Jekyll Island Club. [. . .] My wife and I dined with Graham Greene and his wife Hilary and all the agonies of the day subsided.

P.S. The four shots were completed by 10 A.M. and Graham Greene caught his plane to Santa Fe. All's well that ends well. 🙶

Deep in the jungles of Venezuela, Carlos Caridad comments on the nightmares of location-shooting with a sardonic eye:

🙶 We climbed up. Rosana the director, Laura the stills photographer, and I, the cameraman. Six hours by mule into the sierra. The Yukpa are used to the white man. They greet us, however, with suspicion: we whites have taken so many lands away from them. A group of Colombian guerrillas are in the area. [Later.] The water's finished. We have to drink from a spring. There's no alternative. We are three hours away from the nearest village, in the middle of the jungle. The Yukpas are attacked by a sort of unknown hepatitis, which is fatal to whites. Rosana and Laura drink unconcerned. I pee against a tree and give a start. The urine's changed colour. Hepatitis for sure. Hypochondria. [. . .]

Laura is fair-haired, white and has one green and one blue eye. The Yukpa children touch her arms curiously. They call her 'Wafia' (white woman). Rosana is cinnamon and red. The children call her 'Chubíri' (short-haired woman). My back is sunburnt and the children draw landscapes and war tattoos on the singed flesh. They don't give me any name in particular. [. . .]

The filming has been no problem. I just think about going back. I haven't had a steady job ever since I returned to Venezuela. 🙶

Gholamreza Moosavi, an Iranian producer, notes the dangers of staging a fire scene in certain locations:

🙶 On June 10th we had to shoot a fire scene on board one of the largest oil-tankers for the film, *War of the Oil-Tankers*. To give an idea of the immense difficulties, I only have to point out that smoking is prohibited on board tankers. For the past few days the director, Mohammad Reza Bozorgnia, the director of photography, Hassan Gholizadeh, the special effects man and myself have been planning for the scene in consultation with the anxious captain of the tanker. We are working in 40 degree Centigrade weather, and higher temperatures have been forecast for the coming days.

By 10 A.M. everything is ready. Bozorgnia cried, 'Action!' For the next several, tense hours I stood beside the captain, assuring him that all precautions had been taken. Everything went off like clockwork, and by 1 P.M. all the necessary shots had been taken. A modest party awaited the cast and crew in the ship's dining hall in which the tanker's crew also participated.

When after this exhausting ordeal I returned to my tiny cabin [. . .] I started thinking of my first encounter with the magic of motion pictures. I was five years old. We were staying with some relatives. After supper the host's son took my brother and me to the movies. We crossed several rooftops in the neighbourhood, and settled on the roof of a house adjacent to an open-air movie theatre, and watched. The pleasure of the first view of the moving images was perhaps intensified by the beating I received later from my father. I wonder if I will ever be able to live without cinema. 🙶

147

Ingmar Bergman began his career as a "scriptgirl" on Alf Sjöberg's *Frenzy*. Today, the term is "script supervisor" and Claire Best, at work on *Barcelona*, admits that she is "everybody's dogsbody and everybody's master in the same breath and [her] responsibilities cross with nearly everybody's department, informing them of anything they might need to know or have overlooked in the script and responding to anything they might have to change":

❝ Call time: noon. Day 38 of shooting on location in Barcelona as part of a truly international cast and crew: Americans, Canadians, British and Spanish. Whit [Stillman, the director] and I are the most fluent in Spanish among the Anglo-American contingent and used to do a lot of the interpreting for the others, but now the predominant language on set seems to be Spanish and even the British and American cast are having Spanish lessons every day on set to help the communication. [. . .]

Today has been a typical day with no real complications, only the pressure to hurry up and finish our interiors as soon as possible as we are about to lose the location. As well as being the director, Whit also wrote the script, so every little detail and suggested nuance is much more crucial on this film than it might be on someone else's. As my position on set is sitting or standing between him and John Thomas [director of photography] all day, I get to hear his thoughts on performance, framing, costume, makeup, art direction or anything else. [. . .]

My first job of the day is to start filling in my daily production report with the call time and the time that we got the first shot off. I also have to calculate (using judgement and my stopwatch) how much in minutes and seconds of what we have filmed each day will end up on the screen; how many set-ups we do; how many scripted pages we complete and how many scenes. All of this information helps the producer keep track of the film's progress.

[Once we are ready to shoot] I tell the

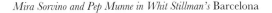

Mira Sorvino and Pep Munne in Whit Stillman's Barcelona

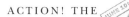

assistant camera-person (or clapperloader) and the sound recordist what number to give the slate (to identify the shot to the lab and the editor). In turn they tell me what camera and sound rolls they are up to, what lens is being used, what aperture and filters (if any). I catalogue this information on a special form along with a brief description of the shot. Then I time each take and write down whether it is complete, a good or a bad take, and any other information that might help the director and editor decide at a later date whether to print a take that was not selected at the time of shooting. These notes might include focus problems, sound interferences from noises off the set such as a siren or telephone ringing, dialogue changes or fluffs, costume discrep-**"** ancies, posture and gesture changes.

Short films made on location can require the same attention to detail, and provoke the same hassles, as the most lavish features. Jacalyn "Jackie" Hyman is a British production designer involved in _One Night Stand_:

" Well, it's gone midnight now, so I guess that June 10th has already started. As for me and Al, the construction manager, June 9th hasn't finished yet! We are still working, putting up a false hallway outside the room we've been filming in today in this fabulous apartment in Holland Park [London]. Bill Britten, the director, couldn't use what already existed so we've created a new hallway and front door for him. Only trouble is, it couldn't be there during the last shot, and it must be up for the first set-up tomorrow, so here we are on a hot and sticky night, slaving away.

[. . .] By 3 A.M. we've got the structure up and papered and painted so we can finally go home and get some sleep . . . Only to be back here at 7.30 A.M. I am such a tyrant that I dragged the lads back in before the call time to rehearse a tricky bit of rigging that we'll have to do mid-morning. This apartment is on the ground floor, but it's supposed to be on the third floor with a tree outside the window. We have a couple of van-loads of branches produced from a tree-

Jackie Hyman (far left) on One Night Stand, _nominated for a BAFTA Award in 1994_

felling company working nearby; we've got clamps, stands, and all the bits of wood we need. [. . .]

The morning's shooting is nearly over. [. . .] With very little sleep, such a hard night's work and now a lot of waiting around I suppose I'm a little over-sensitive but I'm really annoyed with the crew. There's simply no respect for other people's property. I have told them time and time again – this is not our stuff, we did not build it or hire it. It is all borrowed. I'm so worried that one of the antique rugs will end up with a cigarette burn in it or that one of the antique tables will get scratched. 99

Filming opera on location is something that defeats even the most skilled of directors (the late Joseph Losey and *Don Giovanni* excepted). Mary Jane Walsh, with a background in films on art, is involved in a production of a new opera, loosely based on a Handel oratorio and entitled *The Triumph of Beauty and Deceit*:

66 June 10th falls well into the second week of a six-week shoot. On this day the scene requires all the cast and six extras. The setting is the Court of Pleasure – the exterior of his pleasure dome – the interiors were filmed earlier in the week at Syon Park in the Great Conservatory. This scene is set at night but we've decided to shoot it 'day for night.'

We only have two days in this location and no weather cover (impossible to arrange on a low-budget project such as this). It's been blisteringly hot for three days but this morning the sky is very overcast and the thunderstorms that have been predicted by the long-range weather forecast look imminent. [. . .]

The new location by the River Thames at Twickenham is in the Water Gardens of York House – it's a strange place with an odd atmosphere which is why we chose it. There is a bizarre fountain with several huge white marble nereids. It should look very effective on film with the strange quality 'day for night' always gives. [. . .]

The cast are extraordinary; very patient and accommodating. They are good-humoured about the delay [in dressing the set] and wait in the makeup bus practising (and perfecting) their skills

Still from The Triumph of Beauty and Deceit, *a new opera film worked on by diarist Mary Jane Walsh*

on video games. They are not experienced film actors but opera trained. They must perform faultlessly once they are called. I admire them enormously. They never hold things up – they always hit their marks and their lip sync[hronisation] is excellent.

I have a personal obsession about bad lip sync. I was determined from the outset that ours will be as accurate and as 'realistic' as possible. The singers sing along with the tape and as well as conductor Diego Masson with a third assistant director assist and record each take. 99

Another view from the production side comes from Kathy Sykes, a production manager on John Sayles's *The Secret of Roan Inish*, photographed by the great Haskell Wexler and shot on location in the northwest of Ireland:

66 The crew were shooting on one of our main locations on a beach called Kate's Strand where we had built four thatched cottages which had been dressed and re-dressed for the periods of 1700, 1830, 1946, and 1949. I started on the set as usual for breakfast and [had] to wait until everything was ready and the crew had

Still from John Sayles's The Secret of Roan Inish, *shot on location in northwest Ireland*

'turned over' on the first shot. As the weather and the tidal conditions are crucial to the story-telling of the film, our call sheet has to take into account every permutation of both, plus the vagaries of filming with children, trained seals and gulls and animatronic seals.

Once the shooting crew were up and running, I went to visit one of our village locations with Mark, our location manager. We are going to take over a very small shop in a village called Mount Charles and dress it with 1949 groceries and general hardware. I wanted to make sure that the very kind and obliging proprietors, Seline and Hugh, were quite aware of the invasion that will hit them next week! [. . .]

[After lunch] we are in the middle of a montage sequence where our two children are clean-ing up the four derelict cottages on the beach. We started on the exteriors and then the weather forced the crew inside, so the afternoon was made up of 'Fiona' and 'Eamon' dusting and scrubbing and sweeping! Our two leading children were cast after a nationwide search and both are first-time actors and doing really well. [. . .]

At 5.30 P.M. Richard Conway, the Special Effects Supervisor on Bertolucci's *Little Buddha*, arrived with two cameraman to shoot a plate shot of stormy seas to complete the end sequence of the film. [. . .] I had organised transport and accommodation for them and sent one of our local location crew out to find a good cliff for the shot. They borrowed a small generator and set off into the rain, prepared to stay for a week until the weather was right for them. **"**

7. Mix and Match: In Post-Production AFTER THE

WRITING AND SHOOTING COMES THE TENSE AND

OFTEN FRUSTRATING TIME OF POST-PRODUCTION,

WITH THE EDITOR COMING INTO HIS OR HER OWN.

Martin Scorsese was in the throes of post-production work on _The Age of Innocence_ in New York, which subsequently opened the Venice Festival to favourable reviews in Europe and the United States:

" Sad news – Alexis Smith died. _The Age of Innocence_ is to be her last film.

In Tele-a-car taxi service car at 10.40. Got the older Yiddish driver again – very sweet – very polite – asks after my parents again. [. . .] The usual horrendous cross town trip – we machete our way through the traffic! Driver gets frustrated

Martin Scorsese discusses scenes for The Age of Innocence _with Daniel Day-Lewis_ (above) _and Michelle Pfeiffer_ (right)

at times – nothing we can do – just inch forward as much as possible. I tell him 'not to rush, to be careful.' Get to new recording studio, 'The Hit Factory,' at 11.10 – ten minutes late!

This is our first day of recording music for _Age_. Elmer Bernstein told me to arrive an hour later so they could work out all the wrinkles in the new studio etc. [In the control room] Elmer has laid down Cue #1 of the day. 'Intro Mrs. Mingott.' Some time, but not an inordinate amount, has been spent on technicalities – the board, mikes, patching, playback etc.

Plays back Cue #1. Rich, full sound. 77 piece orchestra. Quite beautiful. Thelma [Schoonmaker, Scorsese's editor] and Tom Fleischman – Tom's our mixer – arrive. He discusses recording of music with Elmer's engineer Brian, who's in from Ireland.

BDF and I discuss Venice [festival] dates. We try to get the 6th and 7th [September] moved up to 4th and 5th, because I need to be back in time for the _Age_ press junket in NYC – rested. [. . .]

Cue #3. 'The Van der Luyden Dinner.' We play with the synch of the second cymbal crash near end of sequence – three different ways. Some logistical confusion due to placement of monitor in the control room. Some people keep going back and forth in front of it – distracting. Thelma and others work out a system. Frustrating, but after a short while it seems to be OK.

[. . .] Call back Gareth Wigan (Columbia) – Venice situation laid out clearly now re. _Age_ . . . Gareth and I talk about death of Alexis Smith. Watching her talking on the control room monitors, she does so well and looks so elegant in the film. I think she would've liked it.

Above: *Paul Cox directing a scene for* Exile. Right: *Frames from the doorway sequence in* Exile, *described in assistant editor Rochelle Oshlack's diary*

[. . .] Video of *A Stolen Face* (dir. Terence Fisher) – to view for remake. Videotape is very poor quality. Check cassette from Elmer B. of Strauss's op. 117 – Polka Française – also 'Artist's Life' Waltz op. 316. To possibly replace 'Quadrille' in conservatory scene. **"**

Paul Cox, one of Australia's most idiosyncratic and talented directors (*Man of Flowers, Cactus, A Woman's Tale*), relishes editing his film in isolation:

" I usually keep some sort of diary when I am not working on a film. Once the film starts, however, there is no time, no space, for anything that is not directly relevant.

During the editing, I calm down a little, go for walks to the ocean close by to watch the mighty waves, and try hard to repair my personal life (not hard enough, some claim).

Today was very much like every other day in the last two months. Got up at 5.30 A.M., left a note on the staircase for my daughter – just in case she woke up – walked through the dark to the editing room and spent a limited two hours concentrating in the peace and quiet of the early morning. Then it was time to wake up my daughter, make breakfast, and take her to school.

After having dropped her off, I collected my little son from his mother's and took him to kindergarten.

Got back at approximately 9 A.M. and sat behind the Steenbeck for the rest of the day. It's now 7.30 P.M.

I didn't have lunch. I didn't go anywhere. Didn't meet anyone interesting or uninteresting, didn't laugh, didn't cry, didn't accept any phone calls. Come to think of it, I didn't even talk to anyone. To the outsider, an extremely boring day. But I did make some interior journeys. Travelled from face to face, from sea to land, from inner to outer, from outer to inner.

Later this evening, I will go back to look at all the fresh cuts – hopefully, with some objectivity. Then repeat the process early tomorrow morning.

The editing of this film (*Exile*) is more draining and demanding than ever. It was a hard film to make and consequently it has become a hard film to edit. Fortunately, my co-workers, Margot and Rochelle, stand by at all hours. Without them, I would be totally lost in that vast land of celluloid. **"**

Rochelle Oshlack is the assistant editor mentioned in Paul Cox's entry, working on *Exile*:

" Yet another dimension discovered today. Themes and sub-plots are slowly growing into plague proportions. This particular outbreak began when Paul found 'the door' cutting point: when one character exits a doorway, cut to another character entering a doorway, similar frame, different location; new scene. The poetic part of my mind runs amok with the thematic implications. Every doorway in the film now contains a potential metaphysical link to 'the other world.' Ah! But the special doorway; the passage to the character of the Priest Ghost and his spiritual world, exists in nature. When Peter (the mortal exiled) wanders through the forest, under the boughs of the trees, he glides into the spiritual

plane, into the depths of his soul to converse with the only co-habitant of his island who is 300 years old. If you were actually to watch him take this journey, you would probably see him sleeping. But as a privileged film viewer, what you get to see is the journey through the character's mind's-eye – his very hallucination.

Paul referred to the film-making process as 'a beast.' He is wrong. A beast can be caged and sedated. This creative process never ceases. One cathartic journey to the next, all linking and layering theme upon idea upon vision into the next film. The irony of it all is that the privileged film viewer is free from the plague and generally has little understanding of the nature of its existence. **"**

Meanwhile, in Paris, the Polish master, Krzysztof Kieslowski, (*The Decalogue, The Double Life of Veronique*) labours on the first film in a trilogy, a film that would earn him a share of the Golden Lion at Venice three months later:

" 9.45 A.M. Meeting with Marin Karmitz, producer. We talk about photos for the *Blue* film. The choice is fairly limited. Some pictures are missing, not being sent by the production office. Zbyszek Preisner arrives at 10 A.M. We discuss current musical affairs and the projection [of the first mixing of *Three Colours: Blue*] begins. I wonder how the film will function with all the sounds gathered together.

11.50 A.M. End of projection. Producer finds we put in too many side effects. He's right. If we premix this is also to find out the sounds our film doesn't need. We decide to cut the negative during mixing, starting on June 14th in the morning. We also decide to go back to Elzbieta Towarnicka's voice and put it in a concert we use in *Blue*. Two days ago we recorded two other woman singers but the first recording, done a year earlier, seems the best.

1.30 P.M. Last editing corrections with Jacques Witta, the editor. We cut the image and premix; sound editors will have to include the changes in some twenty tapes for each reel. We make about twenty minor cuts, and the film shortens by a minute. I often pass from the *Blue* to the *White*, the second film in the trilogy, as Ursula

Juliette Binoche in a scene from Krzysztof Kieslowski's Three Colours: Blue

Lesiak, editor on *White*, points out certain difficulties. She prepares a second editing version for tomorrow's projection. [. . .]

8 P.M. Going home. In the car we try to imagine Roman's translation tomorrow of some of the coarse dialogue in *White*. The film's action takes place in Poland so the dialogue must be translated for Marin and the French crew. Roman being rather tactful, we suggest that 'Motherfucker Russkoff' (reference to a cheap watch) be replaced by 'Soviet watch, seems to be second hand.' There's more of that, but it's obvious Roman will find the proper words. **99**

Making films in Brazil presents enormous obstacles today. The industry is to all intents and purposes moribund. Maria Cristina Amaral, a film editor, manages to smile through the gloom:

66 I woke up profoundly caught between the laziness brought on by the cloudy day and my previous plan to go to the editing room to check the synchronised rushes of a 16mm documentary I'll edit soon. [. . .] In the midst of my doubts, the telephone rings. It's my great friend and director A.S. Cecilio Neto (I edited his three shorts) inviting me to have lunch with him and a common friend, Luis Crescente, a TV producer. [. . .] We spoke a lot about our projects and mainly about the relationship between the cinema and TV in Brazil, about the ever more remote possibility of their interaction. Brazilian TV continues to set its face against any dialogue with the domestic cinema producers. [. . .]

Well, my projected work at the editing room was delayed until tomorrow.

I used the rest of the day to prepare the cue sheets for the sound editing for the feature I'm working on at present, *Alma Corsária, Alma Gêmea,* by Carlos Reichenbach. It's a wonderful film. I can say I'm privileged because, during a very hard period for Brazilian production, I am working with perhaps the best feature director we have in the country, certainly one of the most creative. In financial terms it is very difficult for all of us. But I'm happy because we managed to prevent the lack of money showing in the quality of imagery on the screen. Now we are finishing the film, by means of digital sound editing (using the Waveframe System, the first Brazilian picture to do so). The result is great so far!

Still from Alma Corsária, Ama Gêmea, *directed by Carlos Rechenbach*

Kim Hyón, from Seoul in South Korea, devotes his life to editing films in what is a lively and developing national industry:

66 Morning. Completed editing a new film, *No! Interruption, Oh, Yes! Love*, directed by Yoo-Jin Kim. Most of the participants including the producer, director and the staff, who previewed the rushes, expressed satisfaction. Anticipate this film will be good entertainment for kids as well as grown-ups.

Afternoon. Called director Kwang-Soo Park who is working on a new film, *To the Starry Island*; discussed casting and shooting schedule. Tentatively agreed to edit the picture during July (I used to team up with Park in cutting his previous films, *Chil-su and Man-su* and *Berlin Report)*.

Evening. Worked on a new screenplay, *Runaway*, until late into the night. Over the past five years I have spent much of my spare time working on this project. It is now entering its final stages. I have devoted the past 22 years to the field of editing, but now I am determined to produce my own film on the brief life of a young man. I would like to produce and direct the film along with most of the other things involved, with the exception of camerawork. In three years, my dream will come true. 99

Christopher Tellefsen edited Whit Stillman's first film, *Metropolitan*. Now he finds himself in Spain, cutting Stillman's *Barcelona*:

66 7.45 A.M. Over coffee, marvelling at my Barcelona cutting suite. In New York, you'd have a closet of an editing room with one window. But state of the art equipment. Here there are two spacious rooms with 20ft ceilings, French windows opening on to a tiled courtyard garden. But the rewinds only go in one direction.

8.30 A.M. Rough cut of second to last scene, all action and dialogue, is working. There was a heavy shooting schedule that day. Four shots not gotten. Mapping out pickups needed to finish the scene. Put aside clips for John Thomas (director of photography) and Whit Stillman to match lighting and actor positions. Also list of second unit shots needed for specific transitions.

10 A.M. Dailies. Tuesday's with sound, and a

first look at yesterday's shooting. Last night's projection of dailies was cancelled. Production went overtime. From Tuesday, viewing key scene between Taylor Nichols and Helena Schmied. Whit breathes a sigh of relief that we got on film what was intended in his script. Actors are very good. The scene will work. [. . .]

2.30 P.M. Rough cut assembly of hospital scenes, shot in sequence. Good to get sense of continuity. Scenes 121 through 150 assembled minus exteriors. These additions help me conceptualise how and where I'll be able to contract time as well as where to place the emphasis within this part of the film as a whole. Finish synching dailies and review them. One full scene which looks good and pickups for three other scenes.

The unit publicist requests a screening of the existing rough cut for Bob Marshak, the new stills photographer. Bob wants to get a feel for John's lighting so that the stills will match the look of the film. 99

Ot Louw edited *Going Home*, the Dutch feature which had its Royal world premiere on June 9th, 1993. His next assignment, *It Will Never Be Spring*, awaits on the editing table:

66 Owing to my absolute lack of assertiveness and my continual but all too rose-tinted predictions, I am forced to work to breaking point in this beautiful weather in order to get everything done on time.

I edit not just features but also documentaries. At present I have two more in the pipeline. Today I am also involved with the documentary *Vanishing People*, by Trix Betlem, which is about the political disappearance of two people. In addition to this, I am busy working on the documentary *Year One* by Joost Seelen. This concerns an Englishman released from prison in August 1992 after serving a thirty-year prison sentence; it follows him during his first year on the outside. Now and then, new material comes from Britain, for example yesterday when we looked through six rolls of 16mm film on the cutting table.

In the case of an editor, all this material must be stored in his head, on his 'hard disk,' so to speak, and the limits to his memory are clearly visible; even an editor, with twenty-five years

Still from director Frouke Fokkema's second feature film, It Will Never Be Spring, *on which editor and diarist Ot Louw worked.*

experience behind him, has his limitations.

Today I am working on *Wild Growth*, director Frouke Fokkema's second baby. [. . .] In this morning's paper it was described as the next *Basic Instinct*. At a temperature of around 30 degrees Centigrade I work heart and soul on the rough cut of this film. [. . .] In general the scenes have been cut as little as possible; in each case the montage simplifies them. Last night I cut two in half and I finished 101 of the 151 scenes. Today, I made 32 cuts so that next Monday I still have 18 to cut. [. . .] Before the film is screened I must also make a scratch mix of the entire picture so that I too will be able to see the rough cut at my leisure and not have to mix in the sync-bands **99** during the projection.

Arguably the most distinguished European film editor of his generation, 63-year-old Ruggero Mastroianni (younger brother of actor Marcello Mastroianni) has worked with most of the great Italian directors:

66 I, Ruggero Mastroianni, reflecting my essential nature as a film editor, will be concise in writing as well. Today, June 10th, 1993, I spent working at Cinecittà in editing suite #29, where I edited some sequences of the film *Giovanni Falcone*, directed by Giuseppe Ferrara, starring Michela Placido and Giancarlo Giannini. 99

Mika and Aki Kaurismäki have established a fervent following both within their native Finland and around the world. Their films brim with a quirky humour and a maverick abruptness worthy of Monte Hellman or Sam Fuller. Mika, the elder brother, supervises post-production on his latest picture:

66 I had to complete the editing of the trailer for *The Last Border*. The film will be released in August so we must get the trailers into cinemas as soon as possible. The trailer is the thing I hate most in this business. And the most difficult one. [. . .] So I did the final changes (for the first and, I hope, the last time I work on a video editing system!), and sent the trailer to the lab for further work. [. . .] The office was very busy on this June 10th. The Finnish-French *Iron Horsemen* was in production and Aki was preparing to shoot the historical concert of the Leningrad Cowboys with the Red Army Chorus of Russia. [. . .]

Jochen Girsch, the sales agent for [my film] *Zombie and the Ghost Train*, called and told me he had seen *Helsinki Napoli* on German television a few days ago (he didn't praise it, so I assume he didn't like it). He informed me that we had won the lawsuit against the owner of the distribution rights of *Zombie* in France, and the rights now reverted to us. Two crazy prospective distributors had already called him. Jochen also said that the German TV deal had reached a favourable stage. *Sehr gut!* My children, impatient, were now sitting

Jolyon Baker and Fanny Bastien in Mika Kaurismäki's
The Last Border

163

Still from Mrinal Sen's The Confined, *in production*

on the office sofa watching a video. I hate videos.

Erkki Astala, our publicity man, wanted me to select the photos for advertising *The Last Border*. We chose eight shots, along with Pia, who had been the stills photographer. Erkki also presented his idea for the poster in Finland. It was accepted.

Klaus Heydemann, our production man, reported on the state of international sales for *The Last Border*. The film has a distribution deal in about twenty countries but several important territories are still unsold. It makes us worried. We must just keep on pushing.

Mrinal Sen has followed in the footsteps of Satyajit Ray as one of India's most distinguished directors (his films include *Bhuvan Shome*, *Interview*, *The Ruins*, and *Genesis*):

I did nothing the whole day. I was waiting for this particular moment – midnight – when one day would be over and another would begin.

To lend the day a very special distinction, I just stopped working. Frankly, I am fantastically active and can as well afford to be fantastically lazy. But right now I am in the middle of produc-

Mrinal Sen (right) directing The Confined *on location in India*

ing a film. I have just finished a substantial part of the shooting in a curious set-up, partly in the beloved ruins that have featured in so many of my films. Now I am on a war footing to get ready for the next stage of filming in a metropolitan high-rise.

[. . .]Throughout the day I have been moving around in my tiny apartment, chatting with my wife about the non-essentials, making and receiving phone calls of not much importance, cutting the callers short which I seldom do.

[Finally] my wife found me at my table scribbling on papers. Looking over my shoulder she asked teasingly, 'Are you writing your diary for the day?' No, I was checking and double-checking my script, a substantial part of which has just been done and the rest to be taken up from June 15th. So, despite my promises to keep myself apart from every conceivable thing, I got into my job. I just could not escape.

Adoor Gopalakrishnan's films (*The Ascent, Rat-Trap, The Walls*) have been well-received at festivals and in his native India. He writes from his home in Trivandrum:

Today I finished the first phase of dialogue dubbing for my film *The Servile*, my seventh feature, at the Chitranjali Studios, Trivandrum, in the 2 P.M. to 9 P.M. shift.

It is sheer coincidence that I happen to be involved in the actual production of a film on this date. There have always been long intervals between my productions. I made my first film after a seven-year struggle. Then it took five years for me to make my second, the problem being lack of finance. For my last five films, the interval seems to have stabilised at three years.

The Servile is based on a short story in Malayalam. The central character is a migrant

Production shot from Adoor Gopalakrishnan's The Servile

labourer from Kerala seeking a living in the neighbouring state. There is a certain universality about the predicament this character faces when his inability to say 'no' to the degenerate and whimsical landlord leads to total submission and the surrender of his essential self.

Today I am in a happier position than when I started twenty years ago. I am no more plagued by problems of finance and sponsorship; the delays now are entirely due to creative difficulties, a sense of responsibility and my answerability to the audiences not only in my home state but all over the world. **99**

Gustavo Graef Marino is directing *Johnny Cien Pesos* in Chile:

66 A holiday in Santiago. It is winter, the start of a long weekend, the city is empty, sleepy and boring as ever. But I have not really noticed all this, and it doesn't bother me. For a long time nothing, or very few things, in the world have interested me except the images which, day in, day out, for several months I have had in front of me on a charming but pretty old-fashioned moviola in this editing room.

I am working with a French editor and a Colombian and Chilean assistant on the cutting of my most recent feature, *Johnny Cien Pesos*. [. . .] These three women obsess me, the Frenchwoman, the Colombian, and the Chilean, the three of them waiting for me in the editing room every evening with a good glass of whisky and images of my protagonist who, frame by frame, day by day, is assuming life. The whisky in

the evening began as a joke, but then became essential for all four of us. Between glasses and various cigarettes we begin to look over the material.

Today was undoubtedly special. After more than two years of research, writing the script, production, filming, and almost three months' editing, we have reached the point of watching the film through in its entirety. The images appear on the small screen, the reference sound 'screeches' through the disgusting speakers, the wax pencil marks on the celluloid flash by, the adhesive between each cut blurs the image. But none of that matters. *Johnny* is moving, speaking, laughing, suffering, he is alive.

All four of us concentrate on every movement on the screen: smoking, with our glasses of whisky clutched tightly, nervous, suffering, and enjoying each cut, feeling as one, friends, loving each other, proud, haughty, arrogant, feeling that we are the best, the invincibles. We've done it! The film exists for the first time. **99**

Canadian actress, writer and director Gale Garnett lends her voice to a film that would receive great acclaim on its appearance during the summer of 1993, *32 Short Films about Glenn Gould*:

66 9 A.M. Standing in a blue-light basement studio, waiting to be kicked into gear by beige, dishwater, takeaway coffee from the polystyrene cup clutched in my paw. The room is, blessedly, air-conditioned (I agree with Katharine Hepburn, who keeps her film and theatre workspaces cold, believing heat deadens the brain). My brain is here to do 'A.D.R.' (Audio-Digital Recording). Used to be called 'looping.' It involves an actor re-recording words spoken when filming. The film in question, *32 Short Films about Glenn Gould* (a docu-drama about Canada's most innovative, gifted, and arguably most eccentric piano virtuoso) was shot last September. And here's me, ten months later, out of costume, out of makeup, having to insert one June sentence into a September characterisation. In heavy New York accent dialect. With perfect timing so that 'the lips match' when the sentence is dropped into the rest of the text. I find my way back to the character (an abrasive tabloid journalist trying to find out, in an interview, if Mr. Gould is gay), and we lay down four takes; two for the control room, two for me. In a fit of masochism, I finish the cold coffee, and head out into the post-cave brilliance of the day. **"**

Editing can be fraught with diplomatic problems, as revealed in the diary of Jim P. Awindor, a director from the National Film and Television Institute in Ghana:

" A client surfaced and demanded a commentary I had promised him that week. He was being pressurised by his client. [. . .] The commentary in question was for a documentary film I had not even finished editing [. . .], about a special programme instituted by the government to mitigate the social cost of adjustment (PAMSCAD). This programme of action is aimed at helping vulnerable groups, to alleviate the economic hardships facing the rural and urban poor. The film was shot three years ago by another director and the rushes were locked in the archives after the director had absconded. The client engaged several film-makers, but none wanted to edit the documentary after viewing the rushes. The simple reason was, as I discovered later, that the shots were not adequate for the purpose for which the film was intended.

So I tried my hand at it, for the sake of the challenge. So the 'technique' I used was editing, writing the commentary alongside, and inserting library shots as I went along. The client did not know about this. So he met me with the preconceived idea that I had finished cutting the film and was now left with only the commentary to do. I told him the week hadn't ended yet and that I would give him the commentary the next day. He reluctantly accepted but insisted on viewing the assembly. I had an 'image' to protect. I did not want to tell him a lie, nor was I ready yet to tell him the facts. I left with him for the studio, hoping that the situation would resolve itself. We startèd running the film (pictures only), and lo and behold after fifteen minutes we had a power cut – which solved the problem! I quickly dashed home, constructed a comprehensive shot list, and wrote the remaining commentary, to be given to the client first thing tomorrow morning. **"**

167 **«**

Gustavo Graef Marino, the Chilean director, at work editing his latest feature Johnny Cien Pesos

8. Marketing the Product LEGIONS OF P.R. PEOPLE, SALES EXECUTIVES, TORRENTS OF FAXES AND PHONE CALLS, ADS IN THE TRADE AND CONSUMER PRESS, PERSONAL APPEARANCES BY STARS AND DIRECTORS — ALL ARE MARSHALLED FOR THE LAUNCH OF A MOTION PICTURE.

Directors themselves constitute an important part of the promotional campaign for any film. Some travel the globe with their creation, others remain obstinately at home, out of reach of the press. Tracey Moffatt, a young Australian Aboriginal, has completed her first feature, *Bedevil*, and blithely enters into the spirit of promotion:

Above: *Tracey Moffatt's* Bedevil. Above right: *Tracey Moffatt caught between marketing and wondering what to wear*

❝ *Bedevil* has been picked up by Ronin Films, one of Australia's great independent film distributors. This morning I went into their office to select images for the promotion of the film. Still photos are so important; luckily I have quite a few good ones. Unfortunately there was one of myself which they wanted to use as the 'director's photograph.' It was taken on the set; you know the kind, sweaty and intense.

I picked it up and scratched it back and forth across a brick wall and said: 'Now that's what I think of this photo!'

Ronin don't want me to do too much publicity for *Bedevil* until its official release in October this year but they did ask me to do a couple of interviews today. The Australian press are quite taken with the new low-budget work being produced here, and we found them to be very supportive.

After the interviews I walked into the city and shopped for clothes. Over the next six months I shall become a 'Film Festival Queen' – Sydney,

Melbourne, Wellington, Auckland, Toronto, and New York. A girl has to look her best. [. . .]

My telephone buddies keep asking me about what I'm going to make next. I tell them, 'I'm thinking.

Promotion for a film begins long before it is completed, and the role of the unit publicist is a crucial one during the shooting phase. Fliss Coombs is at work in London on *Deadly Advice*:

With only one and a half week's shooting left on *Deadly Advice*, there's quite a lot to cram in publicity-wise. I called the *Daily Mail* to find out when they're going to run their location report and to check that they're happy with the pictures I supplied. A good spread now while we're shooting will help to build awareness of the film even though the main thrust of publicity will come with the release early next year.

A writer from *Tatler* magazine was on set today to interview Jane Horrocks during her lunch-break. However, I ascertained that she couldn't arrive in time for our anticipated break and, as Jane was in every scene today, I rearranged the visit for next week. I called *Screen International* to fix a date for their reporter to visit the set next week for an 'in production' story. We need to start thinking about an image for the poster, so I called our distributors, Mayfair Entertainment, to discuss setting up a special stills session. This is quite complicated as the actors it will involve will have finished shooting, their costumes will have been returned to the hire company etc. We have decided to ask our producer, Nigel Stafford-Clark, to come up with a budget for the session and we'll then decide how to proceed.

Tomorrow we have a video crew on set making an Electronic Press Kit which will be used to promote and market the film internationally. I contracted them to give them the call-time and location details and to discuss which interviews they should aim to do tomorrow.

Attending "Cinema Days" at MGM Ocean Village, Southampton, was John Mahony, Chairman of Britain's All Industry Marketing for Cinema Association:

❝ 8 A.M. Arrive at office to deal with last-minute problems on "Cinema Days" which starts at Southampton this evening. Over a hundred regional journalists have registered so far and there will be some 30 to 40 people attending from the industry also. [. . .]

2 P.M. Arrive at Southampton [and go to] MGM's superb Ocean Village multiplex cinema for final preparations. Our first film this evening is *Boxing Helena*, and, as so often happens, the planned press conference with Jennifer Lynch and Sherilyn Fenn has fallen through as they are both still in America. Trevor Green, managing director of Entertainment Film Distributors, has worked miracles. He has managed to get Julian Sands en route from Cambodia to Los Angeles to stop off in London to come along, and also the producer Carl Mazzocone. The ceiling is in pieces because the technical team from MGM is installing a satellite phone link with L.A. so that director Jennifer Lynch can be included in the press conference. [. . .]

7 P.M. Showing of *Boxing Helena*.

9 P.M. *Boxing Helena* press conference takes place. Satellite link, to everyone's relief, works per-fectly. A very successful conference. Much questioning of the producer Carl Mazzocone's successful lawsuit against Kim Basinger. ❞

Christopher Fowler, by his own admission, runs "Britain's largest movie marketing company":

❝ We create trailers, promos, posters, TV and radio campaigns for features as well as 'The Making of . . .' type films. On an average day I work on up to six films in various capacities. Today began with two pages of poster copylines for Alan Rudolph's new film, *Equinox*. I tried to balance the dark/light side theme of the film in poster layouts, and then sent the work off to Metro-Tartan Films.

11 A.M. Meeting with Bernardo Bertolucci and Jeremy Thomas to discuss a short teaser for *Little Buddha*. Bernardo wants simplicity and suggests running a quote from the Dalai Lama, with whom he recently talked about the film. Some Buddhists are having trouble with the title because it juxtaposes the words 'Little' and 'Buddha' – a vague blasphemy. I promise to look into it. We've seen the cut feature, but they are still removing 20 minutes of footage. My worry is, will that footage contain shots I've already used?

Meeting with Julia Kennedy at Cine Electra for *The Baby of Macôn*. Cannes audiences were dis-

Jennifer Lynch's Boxing Helena *was screened at Southampton's "Cinema Days"*

Catherine Deneuve in Indochine, *screened by Christopher Fell at the Bradford Film Theatre*

enchanted with the film; Peter Greenaway may have gone too far. Can the campaign capture an audience that won't be put off by the violent content? We arrange to pull footage from the feature and start work – once our estimate is approved.

In the afternoon I receive back six scripts I wrote for Leslie Nielsen to shoot in Palm Springs for his *Bad Golf Made Easier* tape. [. . .]

There are two screenings today, Michael Winner's *Dirty Weekend* [. . .], and *Undercover Blues*, a pleasant, bland U.S. comedy. Our opinions are asked about the chances of these films in the English marketplace, but the clients don't seem to want to hear anything bad.

In strict contrast to this attitude, Jeremy Thomas calls to ask me what I thought of *Little Buddha*. I tell him I really liked it. He asks if I'll call Bernardo to 'reassure him, as we're working in the dark here,' and I feel privileged to do so.

Day ends with a short Pinewood [Studios] meeting between myself and director Peter Chiang, who has just finished a short 35mm film of one of my short stories (I'm a novelist by night). We're trying to get theatrical distribution, but there's no money in it – story of our lives! [Note: the short did go out on release, with *Red Rock West*.] **"**

At a more local level, Christopher Fell acts as publicity officer for the Bradford Film Theatre in northern England:

❝ We had one person in last night for a film from the BFI's Jazz season. Bad start to my day. I had a thousand labels to correct for *An Actor's*

Stills from Jamón, Jamón (above) *and* Léolo (right), *both of which were screened at the Bradford Film Theatre*

Revenge because the film programmer forgot to tell me he had changed the times. Halfway through, Richard, the persistent editor of a local magazine, suddenly arrived in the office and reminded me I had an appointment with him. I like hard-working editors, so he sold me a £30 ad.

Dreamt I was out of the doldrums of single-figure audiences. The Seventh London Lesbian and Gay Film Festival on Tour could be well attended; plenty of gays in the area, plenty of jazz enthusiasts . . .

July could bring us three-figure heaven. *Indochine*, *Léolo*, *Jamón*, *Jamón*, and *The Story of Qiu Ju*. Lots of leaflets and labels, a classy brochure, mailings to Spanish societies and Chinese restaurants – I'm there!

[. . .] Made a phone call to secure edible underwear for *Jamón, Jamón* competitions. Went home predicting a doubling of the audience tonight for the jazz film and a note of protest from front-of-house the next morning about the ⟩⟩ *Actor's Revenge* cock-up.

Liz Wrenn manages Electric Pictures, one of Britain's foremost distributors of quality films:

❝ Meeting about [Stephen Frears's] *The Snapper*. Majors prefer September after the kiddies' films are out of the way. Art houses only available for August. Cinema dates and demands still incompatible. Politics abound: Ireland can't open after England. Meanwhile, we fly in the face

Left: *Scene from* The Snapper. Above: *Brian Glover and Mark Frankel in* Leon the Pig Farmer

of logic: the first U.K. release *ever* after a BBC television broadcast. [. . .]

11 A.M. Rushed meeting with Black Audio Film Collective. Can we distribute their productions on video? General feeling is that this is a good thing; need to put together costings. [. . .]

Noon. Re-run a tape of *Leon the Pig Farmer.* `

2 P.M. View the last hour of CiBy 2000's *L'ombre du doubt*. Very accomplished movie. Lori, Steve, Andy, Michael all like it. None of us thinks it is big box-office, but the quality of film-making is unmistakable. I'll increase my offer. No word yet if my offer on the Almodóvar [*Kika*] has been accepted.

3 P.M. Flurry of phone calls. Lynda Myles in Prague; Mark Shivas at BBC, about *Snapper*. Sponsorship of *Leon* still up in air. Era Film sends fax from Hongkong, wanting to know if we are still seriously interested in the Zhang Yimou [*Farewell My Concubine*]. 99

Where personal publicity is concerned, few in Britain can rival Michael Winner, director of the *Death Wish* movies, whose new film, *Dirty Weekend*, is almost ready for release as he writes his diary:

66 Attended publicity meeting with United International Pictures to go over British release of *Dirty Weekend* on October 1st. Saw excellent poster and congratulated them! Discussed magazine screening and press screenings to be held shortly, etc. [. . .]

Telephone interview with the *Evening Standard* about the news that Prince Edward is planning to

175 ‹‹

go into documentary film-making. Recommended that he went to film school at the Royal College of Art which is quite near Buckingham Palace, and he could take a number 9 bus.

Meeting with Robert Summer of Sony Music about the album to be released of the pop music soundtrack of *Dirty Weekend*.

Answered various questions from the British press about my film, *The Stone Killer*, due to be shown on British television tomorrow.

Sat for provisional sketches for Royal Academician artist Peter Edwards for an oil painting he is doing of me for the National Portrait Gallery. **"**

Jürgen Schau, general manager of Columbia TriStar in Germany, travels with a star to promote a new release:

" Among the guests present [last night on a cruise along the Rhine] was the Chairman of the German Film Production Fund, and the Chairman of the German Cinema Theatre Association. Naturally we could not help discussing the problems of the domestic film industry and the dominance of American studio product. The current season includes UIP's *Jurassic Park* and Columbia's *Last Action Hero* with Arnold Schwarzenegger. Not to mention the other potential blockbusters. Only one of them will be the big winner at the end of the hot summer. In Europe this battle will not be decided until three months later.

2.30 P.M. I am now on the flight from Düsseldorf to Hamburg. I had invited Christopher Lambert, star of the Columbia film, *Fortress*, to present the picture to the press. Christopher has a lot of fans in Germany, and I expect a lot of attention from his presence.

6 P.M. Christopher lands in Hamburg after a short delay. We greet each other warmly. He is a true professional and is already giving his first interviews at the airport. On the ride to the hotel we catch up with each other. He questions me about the number of release copies, how long the trailers have been running in the cinemas, and discusses the scenes of violence in his film and

Christopher Lambert (right) arrives in Hamburg for promotional duty on Fortress; *Jürgen Schau (centre) looks on*

Christopher Lambert with Jürgen Schau, diarist and general manager of Columbia TriStar, on the promotional trail in Germany

why they have to be there. When we reach the hotel, fans and more journalists are already waiting for him. Some forty interviews **"** have to be given tomorrow.

John Kochman, Director of Foreign Sales at MK2 Diffusion in Paris, deals with a wide variety of overseas clients in selling and promoting films:

" Long conversation with the foreign rights director of the publishers who will release the book on the making of *Mazeppa*, our latest film, when it is released in France in October. We discussed the film's reception in competition in Cannes (mixed), and traded ideas on selling the publishing rights in territories where the film will be released. We agreed that supporting our German distributor, Atlas Film, was a top priority; and that an English subtitled print should be sent to Munich for screenings as soon as possible. This conversation leaves me frustrated once again about how difficult it has been to sell this film.

Yet another call from an Italian TV distribu-

tor who wants to buy a package of films but who won't go near the asking price. I'm a little abrupt, and I don't think I'm very popular with him. I have a feeling he's going to keep trying anyway, without improving his offer. [. . .]

Met with the production secretary to discuss delivery dates of the various printing elements for *Three Colours: Blue* [co-winner of the Golden Lion at Venice later in the summer]. There will be little time, as usual, between approval of the answer print and delivery of release prints.

Researched foreign contracts about to expire. I am working with the legal department to notify foreign rights holders as soon as contracts expire, either to quickly negotiate an extension, or recover the foreign soundtrack or subtitled versions. Our recently installed rights management system, 'Moviebase,' is making this task manageable.

Ended the day discussing *Three Colours: Blue* with Fran Kazui, our Japanese distributor, from Los Angeles. We are now fine-tuning the contract, having already agreed the main points of our deal, and are both looking forward to **"** seeing the finished film.

Selling Hungarian films is now second-nature to Judit Sugár, head of Cine Magyar in Budapest. She is a familiar figure at all the world's major festivals and markets:

❝ I was at my desk as usual at 7.30 A.M. It gives me at least half an hour to read my correspondence quietly, without phones ringing and people dropping in. My first appointment was at 9 A.M., with a Hungarian film-maker whose recently finished film we took to Cannes. I tried to summarise the opinions of people who saw the film, the reactions of those who did not want to see it, and the pending negotiations.

At 10 A.M. I went with my colleagues to see a new film in the studio. After the screening we held a discussion with the producer about the film, about the territories on which we should concentrate our sales effort, and about the publicity materials required etc.

I got back to the office, went through the faxes, and dictated the replies. Today we finalised a contract for the sale of an animated series to Japan, two feature films to Chinese Public Television, and eight films to Polish Television.

At 3 P.M. I received a delegation from Korean TV, who have been screening films for the past two days, and have finally opted for a couple of titles.

Meanwhile I received two very promising scripts from a Hungarian studio, and gave them to the translators, as we feel there is a chance to find German co-producers for the projects. ❞

Harun Yeshayai is an Iranian producer and distributor:

❝ Work in the company progresses at a faster pace nowadays. *The Actor*, a feature film my company is distributing, will go on screen in the coming days. We are busy with promotion work for the film. I checked the ads for the production in the papers, and did some minor corrections. Around noon they brought the film poster from the printer. It has not come out as I had hoped. It seems that we are doomed to do everything at the last minute. I wonder if this is the same in other parts of the world? But I can't stand working in this way any more.

The manager of a movie theatre had promised to let us know before noon today whether he too would show the film. But by 2 P.M. we still had no news from him. [: . .]

All of this is the usual kind of trouble in our business. Basically I am not worried, because I love the job. I have been doing it for the past 25 years and the truth of the matter is that things usually work out. In this country one should not get emotionally involved with a job; in a sense I am pursuing an unwise course. ❞

Still from Mazeppa, *being sold internationally by MK2's John Kochman*

9. Opening Night: The Screening Process THE MOMENT OF TRUTH COMES ON OPENING NIGHTS – OR PERHAPS EVEN EARLIER, IN A SMALL SCREENING ROOM WHERE, SURROUNDED BY EXECUTIVES, DIRECTORS CONFRONT THEIR FATES. AND WHEN THE FILM REACHES THE MAINSTREAM AUDIENCE, THE MANNER OF ITS SCREENING BY THE EXHIBITORS CAN HELP TO DETERMINE ITS SUCCESS OR FAILURE.

Sally Potter, who earned overnight auteur status with *Orlando*, experiences her 29th plane journey in six months, talking about her prize-winning film:

“ I am awake at dawn in Melbourne, Australia, on the second of six press days promoting *Orlando*, staring at a grey skyline and hearing the mournful whistling chime of the trains as they pull into the station on the other side of the river – a sound that induces homesickness for a land I never knew. Somewhere else at the end of a long journey. Or perhaps I am already absorbing the 'tyranny of distance' so palpably present for many Australians.

The morning's interviews include a study guide being prepared for students; the mainstream Sunday paper; a multi-lingual radio station; and a film buffs' show. Among the afternoon's interviews there is a dance magazine, which makes a change. It is good to talk about how the deep structures of dance relate to filmmaking. Not the obvious connections of move-ment, but more an awareness of skeleton – one's own, or the body of the film – and the melancholy quest for an impossible perfection. Plus the sheer pragmatism of dance. As Martha Graham said, either the toe is pointed or it is not.

In the evening I introduce *Orlando* to an apparently eager audience and then go off for a meeting with a dozen or so members of 'Women in Film and Television.' They tell me about the state of play for women in the film industry in Australia.

After the screening, journalist Ramona Koval, who had interviewed me in the afternoon for radio, moderates the Q & A from on-stage. She manages this difficult task with grace, efficiency, and wit, and I find myself more relaxed and open than usual in such situations. I always enjoy the improvisatory nature of these encounters, but there is something about the 'no bullshit' intellectual climate here that encourages both humour and lack of pretence. I feel warmed by the audience's attention and able to savour the sensuality of public speaking. ”

ADVENTURE PICTURES PRESENTS
a film by SALLY POTTER
based on the book by VIRGINIA WOOLF

Orlando PG

SAME PERSON, DIFFERENT SEX

TILDA SWINTON
BILLY ZANE   LOTHAIRE BLUTEAU   JOHN WOOD
CHARLOTTE VALANDREY HEATHCOTE WILLIAMS
AND QUENTIN CRISP AS ELIZABETH I

ADVENTURE PICTURES presents a co-production with LENFILM MIKADO FILM RIO SIGMA FILM PRODUCTIONS with the participation of BRITISH SCREEN developed with the support of the EUROPEAN SCRIPT FUND a film by SALLY POTTER based on the book by VIRGINIA WOOLF ORLANDO TILDA SWINTON BILLY ZANE LOTHAIRE BLUTEAU JOHN WOOD CHARLOTTE VALANDREY HEATHCOTE WILLIAMS and QUENTIN CRISP costume design SANDY POWELL production design BEN VAN OS JAN ROELFS music composed by DAVID MOTION and SALLY POTTER music supervisor BOB LAST editor HERVE SCHNEID director of photography ALEXEI RODIONOV produced by CHRISTOPHER SHEPPARD written and directed by SALLY POTTER distribution supported by EFDO - a project of the MEDIA Programme of the European Community soundtrack available on cds and cassettes

AN ▼ RELEASE

181 ◀◀

For at least one film-maker, the day brought triumph and relief. Peter Freistadt is a director-producer based in Israel.

    It so happened that June 10th, 1993, was a special day, even in the stressful life of a director. June 10th is the birthday of my son Uri (24). Incidentally, we went together to a nearby school and being so instructed by the army, exchanged our old gas masks, from the Gulf War, for new ones. Then I took him to lunch.

    I was very tense and excited all day long, because at 9 PM I had the opening night of my film on Ben Gurion. I am chairman of an organisation called Jews Who Made History, which produces films on famous Jews. And tonight, the result of two years of work was being screened in the Cinematheque in Tel Aviv to many dignitaries and friends. It is a one hour biographical documentary film. It was a total success.

    The price for the glory: at 2 A.M. in the morning I got pains in the chest – delayed reaction to the tensions of the day.

In Holland, director Hans Hylkema reflects on the premiere of his new film 36 hours earlier:

    I wake up surrounded by vases of flowers. The day before yesterday was the premiere of my feature film, *Going Home*, which has taken up all my time during the past two years. It is a film about friendship, set in a colonial past, and the gala opening took place in one of Europe's most beautiful cinemas, the Tuschinski Theatre in Amsterdam, in the presence of Her Majesty, Queen Beatrix.

    Today is not only the day when I can read what the critics have to say in the morning

Dutch director Hans Hylkema (right) with friend at the premiere of his new feature film, Going Home

papers; it is also the first day that the film is being screened to the public in 25 cinemas throughout the Netherlands. I have been dreading the arrival of this first day. We are being plagued by a tropical heatwave and the public searches for a cool place on the cafe terraces rather than in the cinemas.

I go down to the tobacconist on the corner to collect the small pile of morning papers. I cannot imagine anyone not wanting to know what has been written about his or her work; by the same token I could not imagine something negative having been written. [. . .] A quick glance at the negative reviews tells me what I need to know. The reviews that praise the film to the hilt – 'an emotional and violent drama set in the East' – can be interpreted in many ways. I note that entirely contrary opinions are given on the same point and I come to the conclusion that, as a director, this is the best you can hope for. **99**

Budiati Abiyoga, a producer in Indonesia, helped to finance Hylkema's film, and she flew to Amsterdam for the premiere:

66 I just arrived in Indonesia after a short visit to attend the premiere of a film entitled *Going Home*, a joint production of our company PT Prasidi Teta Film/PT Mutiara Eranusa Film, with producers from the Netherlands, Belgium, and Germany. [. . .]

Watching the film at the Tuschinski Theatre, a stately conservative building, attended by the four countries involved, with the opening scene of the tearing down of the Dutch flag, gave me some kind of vibration within my heart. Almost all the shooting of the film took place in Indonesia, and the scene involving the flag was photographed on the first day of shooting at Cirebon, by blockading the main road with five junctions of the city for the whole day. This was only the start of location work involving four nations, four languages, four cultures, four team-working systems which at the beginning were totally different but that finally had to accommodate one another.

[. . .]Queen Beatrix and Prime Minister Ruud Lubbers, the author of the novel, Hellas S. Haasse, as well as the Ambassadors of Indonesia and Belgium, and officials from the German Embassy, all attended the premiere. [. . .] Hans

Russell Crowe in the infamous Romper Stomper

Hylkema, the director of the film, looked tired because he had been involved in preparations for the gala, but the day before he had still made time to accompany us on one of the canal tours of Amsterdam. **99**

The Film Forum in New York has established a reputation with aspiring film-makers around the world as a welcome haven in the United States as well as a source of product for U.S. distributors. Karen Cooper is the lively co-ordinator of this project:

66 Checked the gross book to confirm that *Romper Stomper*, an Australian film, earned $2,910 yesterday, its opening night. This hard-hitting look at neo-Nazi skinheads in Melbourne is a visceral journey into a brutal, racist sub-culture. While it shows the skinheads to be utterly warped and ultimately pathetic, the director, Geoffrey Wright, successfully recreates the excitement of travelling with the pack, the kinetic energy of these brutes.

The theatre manager was alarmed by the

appearance of some forty noisy skinheads at the 10 P.M. show last night. While there were no incidents, the skinheads cheered for 'their people' during the film's opening sequence in which three young Asian women are viciously beaten. Our theatre staff, and undoubtedly the rest of the audience, were horrified. [. . .]

At 3 P.M. I travel uptown with two colleagues to meet with Amelia Antonucci at the Italian Cultural Institute, our liaison to Cinecittà, to plan a comprehensive Fellini Festival for next October. Entitled 'Tutto Fellini,' it is spearheaded by Bruce Goldstein who has already laid the groundwork for an eight-week retrospective that will include everything Fellini has made, even his commercials for Campari. [. . .]

At 5 P.M. I attend a meeting of Film Forum's board of directors. The most interesting discussion centres around our plans for a special event in the spring of 1994: the opening night of a month-long festival honouring the great director-dancer-choreographer, Bob Fosse. We intend to invite 300 people to the opening, raising $300,000 – enough to name our third theatre for Fosse, and wipe out the remaining debt we owe on construction loans taken to build the new Film Forum in 1990.

99

Anne G. Mungai, a documentarist from Kenya, finds herself in New York, at the United Nations Headquarters, preparing for the opening night of her film *Saikati* at the African Film Festival:

66 I was at UNICEF headquarters in New York as an official guest of the 'Day of the African Child', commemorated globally in memory of the uprising and massacre of the children of Soweto, South Africa, on June 16, 1976.

My film *Saikati* was being used as the film from Africa to officially launch the African Film Festival at the Dag Hammarskjold Auditorium at UN headquarters. I therefore spent the day preparing press files, photos and flyers to be given to the public and diplomatic corps who were coming to the screening. [. . .]

The late Federico Fellini, subject of a career tribute at New York's Film Forum

In the afternoon, I received phone calls from Los Angeles and New Jersey from members of the public interested in attending the screening.

[That evening] after brief introductions, the 'Day of the African Child' co-ordinator Mr. Djibril Diallo welcomed the chairman of the African group of Ambassadors to address the audience. Ambassador Ibrahim Sy also spoke, then Mr. Diallo and lastly myself. [. . .]

My film was screened, and those who attended seemed to enjoy it. At the end, I signed autographs, and greeted those who I did not have a chance to talk to before the screening. It was simply great, and difficult to believe, that as an African woman film-maker I received some recognition at the UN. As an African woman film-maker, I struggled through cultures and attitudes that discriminate against women wanting to produce and direct films. [. . .]

I therefore decided that 'Forward ever, backward never' would govern my career in film-making. I would continue the dialogue on Africa, to make films and videos that show my continent from an African perspective, for we indeed have our own dramas and humour that are unique, our own laughter and tears to be interpreted and communicated from our own standpoints. I also resolved henceforth to continue to make films that promote the rights of children. So for me from now on the situation of children and of women will be the central theme of my film-making. **99**

Long before the flashlights and flowers of a gala opening occur, there are the various hidden screenings, involving the film crew, the financiers, distributors, exhibitors, and eventually the critics. Salah Abouseif, an Egyptian director, describes his feelings prior to the very first unveiling of a new feature, *Mr. D:*

66 There is no doubt that June 10th, 1993 was one of the most difficult days in my professional life. On that day, it was decided to screen the first standard copy of my latest film, *Mr. D.*

Although I am a well-known Arab film director, reputable and famous and have made up to

Anne G. Mungai, the Kenyan film-maker, at her editing table

Still from Salah Abousief's latest feature, Mr. D., *screened for crew and technicians on June 10th 1993*

now some forty features, some of which won local and international awards, an overwhelming feeling of fear and panic strikes me whenever I finish a film and it is ready for screening. If this was for the public, I wouldn't panic as I do when one of my films is viewed at the laboratory. For with the public, I can feel and sense the degree of the film's credibility and the audience's liking or rejection of it.

But viewing the first standard copy in the lab, with the rest of the technicians who have contributed to the work, I cannot detect the level of success or failure of my work. For each technician watches the print to judge his own work and how it could be corrected or changed. The Director of Photography watches the copy to gauge its quality and the extent of the lab's success in the development and printing process. The same goes for the Sound Engineer and the Editor; neither is

interested in what the film has to say, how successful it is in reaching the audience, or the audience's understanding and admiration of it. Only the Director and the Screenwriter are concerned with the content of the film and what it has to say, with its ideas and the success of the actors and technicians – especially if the subject is worthy of screening and has no precedents to guarantee its success and contains new views and fresh ideas unfamiliar to the audience.

Not only was I tired, exhausted, and unable to sleep on June 10th, I was also unable to sleep peacefully. I was restless and my brain kept working and working and I was visited by fear and panic. Will they like the film and speak of it with admiration and satisfaction? Will the film be shown at an international festival, and will it receive an award?

This is what I hope and wish for . . . **99**

Janusz Majewski, the Polish screenwriter and director (*Sublokator, System,* etc.), uses the Corpus Christi holiday to visit the movies for once:

66 These days I rarely go to the cinema, and it's not because of the repertoire. The half-full houses, where 90% of the audience are noisy youngsters who react strangely and make it difficult to watch the film, depress me. They obviously transpose the habits of watching television to the cinemas: they talk, go out, come back in . . . And the film which we are watching with them is particularly interesting, *Barton Fink*. I'd heard a lot about it, and had not managed to see it until now. And indeed my wife and I enjoy the intelligent ideas of the Coen brothers and their formal skill, balancing on the edge of parody while maintaining a poker-faced expression. But some woman keeps annoying us. She laughs loudly, constantly proving that she understands the allusions and recognises all the film's 'quotations.' But maybe it's not like that at all? Maybe she's just mad? As we leave the cinema I try to push from my mind the thought that the era of cinema, the film screening, its secret magic, is vanishing forever. It's difficult to come to terms with this when you've given the cinema nearly forty years of your life, making several feature films which have been watched by several million people. Just six years ago, in this same theatre, my comedy *C.K. Deserters* ran on two screens for several weeks with sold-out audiences. Seven million people saw it in Poland alone. And now 100,000 people is a rare 99 triumph. What has actually happened?

In many countries, video offers the only available alternative to seeing a film in the cinema. Asem Tawfik, an Egyptian screenwriter (*An Eye and Three Noses, The Caller, Supermarket,* etc.), laments the fact:

66 Today I saw *The Cook, The Thief, His Wife and Her Lover*, directed by the talented British film-maker Peter Greenaway. That is to say I watched a smuggled video copy, naturally, because it would be impossible for such a superb film to be screened publicly in Egypt. Firstly, because of our respectable censorship, which would undoubtedly consider such a film 'disreputable!' Secondly, because of the degenerating taste of cinemagoers who are gripped in the vice of commercial American films on the one hand and the Egyptian commercial cinema on the other. As a result, our audience would only accept a certain type of film, which any self-respecting film artist will refuse to imitate at any price. Film artists in Egypt do not differ greatly from the martyrs of early Christianity in Roman times. The only difference is that the martyrs were thrown into the arenas to be devoured by lions and hyenas whereas the martyrs of serious Egyptian cinema are thrown into the empty movie theatres to be devoured 99 by the hyenas of inferior cinema 'art.'

Peter Friedman's film about Aids, *Silverlake Life: The View from Here*, has been screened or broadcast in various countries. Here he describes how the New York theatrical opening, a $75-a-ticket benefit for AIDS education, became a nightmare:

66 People I haven't seen in years [attend the pre-screening reception at 6 P.M.], new people, political activists, and rich sympathisers. Speeches came and went. I stumbled my way through five minutes and felt like a fool, as usual.

8 P.M. My dear friend Jeff Lunger, who programmes the Gay and Lesbian Festival with

Peter Friedman, whose June 10th became a nightmare

Sande Zeig, introduced me at the theatre (The Cinema Village). Small theatre, but at least it's full. They did start on time, so maybe there'll be time for me to speak briefly afterwards. But the image keeps jumping! What's wrong with the projector? Everyone is tense – the audience paid a small fortune for their tickets, since it's a charity event; the organisers worked for months to put it together, it's the first public screening in New York, the house is packed – and the projector won't work! Forty-five tortuous minutes later, they start again. They have two projectionists holding the film with their fingers as it runs through the projector, but it still jumps. It's out of focus, out of sync and jumping in the gate. What a disaster! Do we cancel the screening, disappoint everyone and beg the audience not to make the Aids charity refund their money? Do we just bear with it and continue the showing, under these terrible conditions? Being in the room is sheer torture. And what do we do about the second show? Endless discussions in the lobby with the benefit organisers, the festival programmer Jeff Lunger, with the festival board members, with the theatre manager. What a disaster!

10 P.M. They decided to continue, and to give the people lining up for the next show a choice of suffering through it or coming for another screening, which will have to be arranged elsewhere. [. . .] Of course, with the delays, I can't be around for the discussion at all, since I accepted to appear on [the] Charlie Rose [show]. I'm dragged out of the theatre and into a cab to take me to the studio. I feel terrible – I've already worked seventeen hours, I'm jet-lagged, the theatrical opening was a catastrophe, and now I must try to be coherent on television! **99**

Screenings frequently take place for one or two people only. Bonnie Symansky selects films for the Boston Jewish Film Festival and reflects on two shows the previous evening:

66 A hot, steamy day. Riding the commuter train from Salem to my office in downtown Boston. Heads buried in the morning newspaper

Still from Peter Friedman's film about AIDS, Silverlake Life: The View from Here

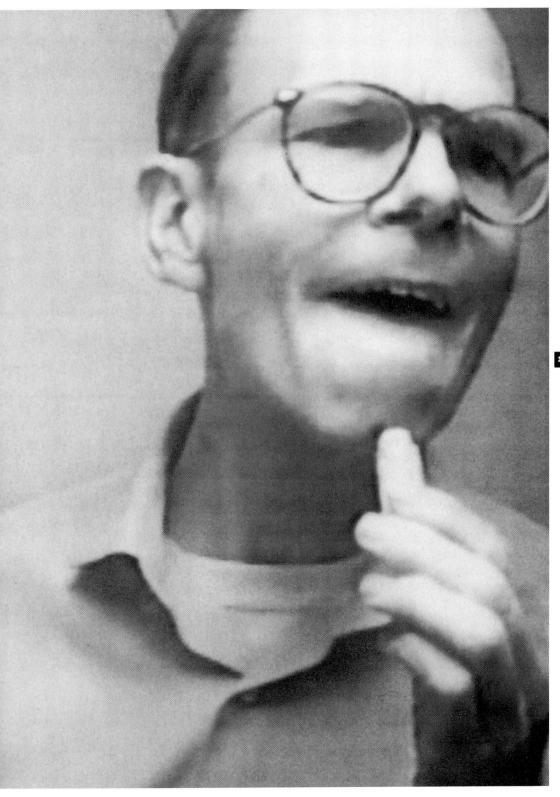

while I gaze out the window as we pass the wetlands, yellow cat-tails and swamps dotting the landscape before we reach the urban congestion. [. . .] I think about the two films I screened last night for inclusion in the Boston Jewish Film Festival. *Birthplace*, a one-hour documentary about a Jewish man who returns to Poland (his birthplace) to find out what happened to his father and brother, who disappeared during the war. The neighbours remember him as a young boy of five, reminisce about how beautiful his mother was and how the whole village danced through the streets at his parents' wedding. But there was a difference: 'There were the Poles and there were the Jews.' 'We gave them food,' they proudly said, but his family was forced to live in the woods, in a pit underground. No one trusted anyone and they feared exposure if they helped the Jews. They did not take responsibility for their indifference – they should have been in opposition. There were no heroes here. Just indifference.

The other film, *His People*, was delightful. Made in the 1920s by Edward Sloman, *His People* was one of the last silent films before the coming of sound. The shots were amazing, the story and scenes complex. I laughed, I cried. Perhaps we should show his last two remaining films as a tribute. So many films but hardly any that celebrate being Jewish – films that make us proud of our history and identity. **99**

For many years Stan Fishman has shouldered the responsibility for selecting films for the Odeon circuit and, despite the commercial demands of the Rank Organisation, he is renowned for his commercial savvy and his enthusiasm for fine craftsmanship on screen:

66 Arrived office, switched on deskside PC, and analysed yesterday's business. Film admissions affected by hot and humid weather. Across Odeon chain we are playing such films as *Groundhog Day*, *Indecent Proposal*, *Jack the Bear*, *Bad Behaviour*, *Three Ninja Kids*, and *The Jungle Book*.

[. . .]Met with my executive assistant, Mike Archibald, to discuss a number of elements regarding matters raised at last evening's 'Cinema 100' Executive Committee meeting in respect of Odeon's involvement with this event. Outline

plans for film premieres and a Film Day in early 1996 were discussed. [. . .]

Talked with George King, Sales Director of Guild, re. a number of business matters and sought his agreement to move *Cliffhanger* from Odeon Leicester Square to Odeon West End on last day of its run (July 8th), so as to accommodate Entertainment Film Distribution's *Super Mario Bros.* premiere and possible BBC coverage on that day at Odeon Leicester Square. [. . .]

Joined our Odeon managers for a marketing meeting and lunch at Planet Hollywood following Entertainment's screening to them of *Super Mario Bros.* Entertainment's marketing plans for the film were outlined and were very favourably received by all our managers.

Guild Film Distributors are screening *Cliffhanger* to our managers this afternoon at Planet Hollywood and I was pleased to meet with Paul Brett, Guild's publicity director, and Thomas Hedman, its managing director, who attended. **99**

Prospects, even in the prosperous film summer of 1993, are not always bright for the cinema manager, as Kelvin Nel, who looks after the long-established Plaza at London's Piccadilly Circus, explains:

66 When I'm faced, after stepping out of Piccadilly Circus underground station, with the view of the Plaza's imposing readagraph, towering above the tourists and the traffic, I always feel a twinge of excitement. After all, though not quite Leicester Square, this is still in the heart of London's West End, and the special atmosphere is identical. However, once inside the Plaza, you swiftly realise that you are just part of an illusion, the illusion being the expectation that the public will turn up in their droves today. [. . .]

My day always begins at 10 A.M. I unlock the numerous doors, check the money in the safes, put out the tills on the concession stands and the floats in the box-office, and check the previous day's figures (if I was not on duty the night before). Recently I've needed a strong cup of tea to help me go over the figures, for they make dismal reading. Out of a seating capacity of 1,447 seats we have only had 1,846 admissions this week. To put that in context, it is like filling up all

192

our regular four theatres, plus an imaginary one, for the first performance of the week only and then not having anybody in for the rest of the week, or the next 26 performances. An atrocious situation and a depressing one.

Although we belong to the multiplex chain of UCI cinemas we, together with the Empire Leicester Square, have our films determined by the distributors, UIP. Unfortunately since the opening of the Trocadero Centre, UIP prefer to put their major releases in there and the Empire. [. . .] Currently, all that keeps us in profit are our sales of popcorn, drinks and ice-cream. ”

In the north of England, Karl Woods manages the Regal Cinema in Northwich, Cheshire, and does virtually everything apart from making the films:

“ 10.20 A.M. Arrived at work. Talked to the projectionist to see if there are any problems – only little things like a torn seat and an arm. [. . .] Got through to the publicity depart-

Cinema manager Karl Woods enters the Jurassic era

ment at UIP. Explained what I'm doing to publicise *Jurassic Park* and asked if they have anything I can use, other than the standee. So they will send me some mini-posters and mobiles – I must remember to contact the local papers, also some fancy dress shops. (I intend to dress up as a dinosaur and walk around town to advertise the film; my wife thinks I'm nuts!) [. . .]

Continued with publicity stunt for *Jurassic Park*. I'm building a seven-foot high Tyrannosaurus Rex out of cardboard and papiermâché. It's actually built now, and all that's left to do is to give it a skin and paint it. Once that's done the T-Rex will go into the foyer surrounded by shrubbery. [. . .]

Did my walkaround. Checked both auditoria for cleanliness, tidiness, warmth and presentabilty. Checked all toilets – clean, tidy, pleasant smell, enough soaps, towels, and loo rolls! And finally checked all exits are clear of any locks and obstructions, and opened easily. ”

193 ◀◀

David Scott works as a projectionist at the Glasgow Film Theatre in Scotland:

“ June 10th started badly. The moment I walked into the Glasgow Film Theatre, Charlie, the senior projectionist, moaned about some film I'd forgotten to spool off and send away! 'Due at friggin' Oxford an' it's still sittin' here!'

Then there was a broken leader at the beginning of *Entertaining Mr. Sloane.*

To cap it all one of my colleagues had phoned in sick and I was faced with the prospect of working his shift the next day. I had envisaged a relaxing and peaceful day with my girlfriend. I've learnt that you can never plan very far ahead if you have the good fortune to be a projectionist.

8.55 P.M. I've just finished showing *Alpine Fire*, the film course show. There was a discussion and included were excerpts via my video projection equipment. This looked like a beautiful film; haunting imagery and crisp cinematography . . . the lot. Unfortunately I seem to be so distracted spooling off reels and checking film transport information that I miss large tracts of the movie.

If I were not a projectionist I think I'd probably choose a career in phrenology. Looking out of the box just now I see so many heads. More pre-

cisely, I see the backs of heads. Such shapes, sizes, degrees of baldness and hair fashion. You only see the faces, peering and gloating, when misfortune strikes and the film snaps. Let's hope that *Knife in the Water* will run smoothly tonight! **"**

Ronald Gow does a variety of tasks at the Clapham Picture House in south London:

" Working in a cinema with three screens and showing four films – all of which have been playing for some time – lends a kind of sameness to the day, the only difference being whether you're doing the box-office, bar, kiosk, or ushering. [. . .] All have in common the insistent ringing of the phone. And it is here that multi-million dollar concepts and years of creative agony get reduced to: 'That's the one where Michael Douglas is having a bad day and blows everyone away.' Worse still, you're asked, 'Is it funny? Will I like it?' [. . .]

Working behind the kiosk is a revelation in terms of human psychology both in what and how choices are made and the large number of people who are unable to enjoy themselves, who remain uptight, aggressive and lacking in humour. [. . .]

The weather being hot meant that we were not that busy and I was given the task of distributing leaflets the length of the high streets. Clapham's more 'smart' bars were invited to partake of our programme. So too was 'Jackets,' a baked potato shop with which the cinema has a special relationship. Celluloid and spuds? Bit strange but I guess that J. Arthur Rank's flour mills and films was a bit odd. **"**

Robert MacMillan owns a cinema he inherited from his father in Kingston, Jamaica:

" This was a typical Thursday at the State Theatre. We had two shows, at 5 P.M. and 8 P.M. – a karate feature, the kind of film our patrons never seem to tire of, entitled *Little Kick Boxer*. It's amazing how these martial arts films have retained their popularity among the 'grass roots' public. The dubbing is so bad that it's almost an art film in itself, but the action keeps

Ronald Gow serving popcorn at the Clapham Picture House

the crowds coming. The only thing is that the prints here get in pretty bad condition sometimes as they have been all over the Caribbean. That means every once in a while it literally snaps – a signal for our clientele to turn their seats upwards and hammer the underside. The first time you hear that, your hair stands on end – but you get used to it. The projectionist just brings up the house lights and that settles them down somewhat. We had one of those unforgettable experiences (or performances) during the second show. Apart from that, all went smoothly. The audience really enjoyed the film, to judge by the frequent outbursts of laughter and shouting. "

Designing a cinema in Singapore has provided a challenge for Geoffrey Malone, founder of the Singapore Film Festival:

" There has been a minor cinemagoing revolution in Singapore with the opening of the Yishun 10 complex I designed for Golden Village Entertainment – the first venture between Golden Harvest from Hongkong and Village Roadshow from Australia. It has had its 2,000,000th patron in less than a year's operation – not bad for the first of its kind in Asia.

I am now working on projects for 6 to14 screen multiplexes in Malaysia, Taiwan, Thailand,

Today, the Morris was screening a film called *Puthia mugam* (in its 13th day) in 70mm on screen #1. Screen #2 was showing *Aranmanaikkili* (55th day). Screen #3 offered *Vedan* (36th day). Screens #4 and 5 were both screening *Ponnumany* (55th day).

There was a queue of people for all five screens. The administrator, Mr. M. Ramathas, took me to meet the owner, Mr. Nanthakumar, who welcomed me very warmly. I asked him to explain why he is involved in the film world as there were plenty of other opportunities open to him. He replied that they have a tea estate in Neelagiri, and a five-star Morris Hotel in Madras, but his father had wanted to create something special in his native Thiruchi, and opened the first three screens in 1981. The other two followed five years later.

'How many people can be here at any one time?' I asked. 'Morris #1 can house 1,270 customers; Morris #2 can have 666, Morris #3 464, #4 some 302, and #5, 300. Altogether some 3,000 people can see the films on all five screens.'

'We are the first people [in India] to introduce the system of showing films on four screens and also we introduced advanced booking. Every day we have an average of 1,200 filmgoers in the complex. [. . .] We identify our audience as consisting of three types. One group is the daily wage-earning labourers, the peasants from the villages. Teachers, civil servants and rich people make up a second group. And the third group is the ladies' audience.' **99**

Yishun 10, the Singapore multiplex designed by Singapore Film Festival founder Geoffrey Malone

Hongkong, and also China. There will be a huge change in cinemagoing in Asia with these complexes coming on stream in the next few years. **99**

R. Regupathy, a Tamil lecturer in southern India, interviews the "administrator" of a multiplex in Thiruchi:

66 I went to visit the Morris Theatre in Thiruchi, and interviewed the administrator, because this is the only theatre in Asia with five screens.

Far from the world of circuits and majors, Amir Hushang Kaveh sends a depressing diary from Tehran:

66 The heavy traffic which is allowed to enter the central part of Tehran on Thursdays (the first day of the weekend) made it impossible for me to reach my office in time for several appointments. I arrived at the dubbing studio at 11 A.M. and asked about the box-office receipts at Asr-e Jadid Cinema, of which I am the manager. Attendances are low, as they have been these past few days. This is the period of the students' exams, and box-office receipts are poor. I called the cinema again at 4 P.M., and there was a slight improvement. There is nothing much to be done

Interior of Cinema City, an independent theatre in Norwich which screened Woody Allen's Shadows and Fog *on June 10th*

at the studio, and we sit and chat for hours.

At about 5 P.M. a cinema manager called to complain about the box-office situation. He has to keep his current film on for another three weeks. Most cinemas are in a similar predicament, and unless something is done, they could go broke. I left the studio at 7 P.M., and went to the cinema. I spent two more futile hours there, worrying about our takings. I left instructions for a taped message to be set on the cinema's phone line for inquiries about the programme schedule for the next day, and then went home. **99**

>> 198

Stefan Kamp, a Dutch film editor, pulls up a chair to watch his latest film on TV, only to discover:

66 Today's unusual, a day off! Finishing a film after eight months of editing two weeks ago, and yet looking forward to another project.

I watched the film tonight on television. The company decided to screen *The Act in Question* in three parts. Quite harmful for a film which runs for 112 minutes – take the knife or splicer and cut three times – here's an entirely different 'film' like I never saw it. A bit frustrating. Enough good memories, anyway. Next project, please. **99**

Pamela Mason of Norwich captures the atmosphere of weekday movie-going in provincial Britain as she tracks down Woody Allen's *Shadows and Fog*:

66 The cinema I went to is called Cinema City, and it's Norwich's independent theatre. Norwich also has a Cannon and an Odeon, but I can't afford them; unemployed, I get free tickets to Cinema City. I practically ran into the theatre, and asked the woman behind the counter if the film had already started. She said no. I had

six minutes to go. So I got my ticket and bought a Diet Coke, and went to the toilet, where the lights were off. I put them on. The seats in the women's toilets in Cinema City are often wet, so it pays to be able to see them clearly.

I didn't recognise the usher (all ushers are volunteers here). He tore my ticket in half and gave me a handout about the film. The cinema does this for all the films it screens. [. . .]. The usher didn't show me to a seat, but there were so few people inside that I didn't need any help. It was so hot that I took my shoes and socks off. The bus driver had done me a favour in making me late: I missed the awful commercials. However, I saw one commercial asking people to contribute to a Tibet charity, which told me things I didn't know about the situation there. I didn't, for instance, realise how large Tibet is, nor did I know about the scale of the Chinese atrocities there. Then the trailers came on: *Mon Père, Ce Héros*, which I saw a while back, and which is terrible, one of the worst films I've seen. Also one for the director's cut of *Blade Runner*. I've never seen the other one, but this looks interesting.

Then the film began. **99**

Wolfgang Borgfeld, from Oberursel, near Frankfurt in Germany, also details a visit to the movies on June 10th:

66 I had made a date with Volker, a friend of mine and connoisseur of action films, to go to the movies in Frankfurt. When I and my fiancée Maria met him in front of the Frankfurt 'Kino-Center,' it was still very hot, 25 degrees or more with high humidity. We wondered for a moment whether it was a smart idea to see a film when the weather was like this, but then decided to go for it. After all, none of us had seen a film for three days or so. We had elected to see *Falling*

Down. Frankfurt has about 42 screens. One film from Germany, two from France, two from England, the rest from America. Three or four were screened in their original version. Films like *Falling Down* or *Indecent Proposal* occupied three screens each, and both these titles could be seen either dubbed or in English.

We wanted to see Michael Douglas with a short haircut and a big temper, got our tickets, bought a cold beer, refused the popcorn that has been invading German cinemas for about two years, and went to our screen. [. . .] But when we entered, we were struck almost literally over the head by the atmosphere, which equalled that of a sauna. None of us wanted to try to see how long we could 'enjoy' a film, even if it was in the original version, without falling asleep or suffocating. 'Sorry, no air-conditioning.' 'Has it broken down?' 'No, we don't have air-conditioning, just ventilation.' So we changed our tickets, opted for the largest screen, and went to see Michael Douglas argue his way through L.A. in German.

But before we had this pleasure, we had to sit through thirty minutes of blunt German advertising. No stories, just mood, images of young, nice, white people apparently living in a style we all want to emulate. [. . .] Then the trailers. [. . .] Then the traditional intermission, during which ice-cream is sold. Despite the heat, we did not feel like buying an ice, and were pretty much fed up. Our shirts were already wet with sweat. Yet it appeared to be precisely the atmosphere we needed to feel what made Michael Douglas crack in L.A. Had there been a fly buzzing around my head in that cinema I guess I too would have gone berserk. **"**

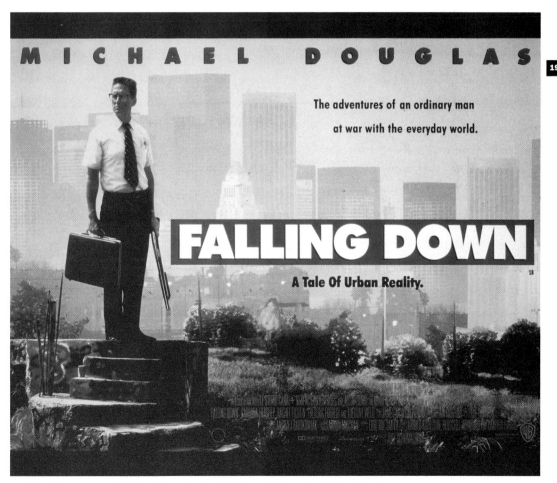

A stiflingly-hot screening of Falling Down *in Frankfurt drove Wolfgang Borgfeld to distraction*

10. The Festival Circuit ALTHOUGH THE WORLD'S FIRST FILM FESTIVAL TOOK PLACE MORE THAN SIXTY YEARS AGO, WHEN VENICE HELD ITS "MOSTRA" IN 1932, THE TRUE IMPORTANCE OF SUCH EVENTS DATES FROM THE 1980S. AT A TIME WHEN SPECIALISED CINEMAS WERE CLOSING THE FESTIVALS PROLIFERATED. TODAY, MANY A BRAVE AND INTERESTING FILM WILL TREK FROM FESTIVAL TO FESTIVAL, WITHOUT BEING PURCHASED FOR THEATRICAL RELEASE ANYWHERE BUT ON ITS HOME TURF. THOSE WHO ORGANISE SUCH GATHERINGS HELP TO SUSTAIN THE BUSINESS AROUND THE WORLD.

>> 200

Edinburgh is one of the world's most tenacious film festivals, having run annually without interruption for 45 years. Penny Thomson, the director, finds herself only two months away from the 1993 event:

❝ 8.45 A.M. [. . .]We are in the final stages of programming 250+ films screened over 16 days. Deal with mail, memos and yesterday's left-over chores.

9.30 - 10 A.M. Staff meeting, About twenty people present. Quick round-up of developments.

The publications people remind everyone that the deadline for copy for the Free Programme brochure is less than a week away. [. . .]

11.30 A.M. Meeting with Hans Rissman, Chief Executive of the Edinburgh International Conference Centre. The Centre is under construction all round our cinema and we are seeking permission to position our hospitality tent on part of the site next door to Filmhouse. Hans readily agrees and asks what more he can do for the Film Festival. He's also a film fan and asks to be put on our mailing list.

Lunchtime. Fly to London, drop bags at The Groucho Club, and then go to Channel Four to discuss festival programming with Rod Stoneman in the Independent Film & Video Department, and also a member of the festival board. He makes a number of suggestions and we discuss the possibility of showing video tape material at the festival. I'm happy to do it but it has to be the best possible, i.e. a Beta SP player with a big screen projector. This means a lot of expensive gear specially hired for the festival. We'll have to find a sponsor as we don't have a big enough equipment budget. The alternative is not to show any V/T material at all, which would be a pity.

Meet with Peter Buckingham from Oasis, who owns the Cameo Cinema in Edinburgh which is once again being used as a festival venue. [. . .] We discuss London film politics and in particular why there's a hold-up on some distributors giving us a Yes for Edinburgh when others are so enthusiastic. We then talk about computerised box-office systems and lines of communication between our two companies. There are a lot of problems but we think we're aware of most and there's a good feeling that both organisations will gain from such close co-operation. **99**

Festival director Hülya Uçansu (right) with Gillo Pontecorvo

Raising money has become an increasing priority for festivals in the 'privatised' era of the 1990s. Phoebe Felen heads a fund-raising company in the Netherlands, and works for the Rotterdam Film Festival:

66 This morning I have an appointment at the Dutch Film Museum in Amsterdam with the director of the Rotterdam International Film Festival, Emile Fallaux. Two years ago, the festival asked me to co-ordinate the sponsoring for them. [. . .] Today we evaluated the results of the sponsoring of the 22nd festival in January-February 1993. In general every sponsor was satisfied with the results and so was the festival.

I could tell Emile something nice about another project we started up for the festival. Last year I made contact on his behalf with PMSvW/Y&R, the most award-laden and controversial advertising agency in Holland at present. As a result, five 'teasers' were made free for the festival. They were shown in fifty cinemas, and it transpired that the most shocking one (I myself still don't dare to watch) was short-listed for the Advertising Festival in Cannes this year. After the text: 'Warning. This film contains shocking images,' you see close-ups of an eye operation with the sound effects of an alarm bell, a drill and factory noises, and a voice over saying, 'Prepare yourself for something new: Go see the International Film Festival in Rotterdam.[. . .]'

The end of my day is good. In the afternoon I hear that a bank is willing to sponsor Cinekid, a children's and youth film festival, one of my other fund-raising projects. **99**

Hülya Uçansu has campaigned tirelessly to put the Istanbul Film Festival on the world map – and has succeeded:

66 10 A.M. First meeting of the day. Briefing the PR department of the festival for preparing a press bulletin about the foreign press coverage of the last festival (it was really great this year!).

11 A.M. Already started working on next year's programme. I have to initiate our correspondence with the French Ministry of Foreign Affairs, as we intend to present a Truffaut retrospective in 1994. [. . .]

I must not forget to inform the Moscow Festival of my arrival date.

I'm going to have lunch with our graphic designer. We're working on the new festival poster for 1994.

3 P.M. There's going to be a meeting about the promotion of Turkish cinema abroad. There will be representatives of various associations involved in the film sector. Hope it will be an efficient get-together.

6 P.M. I have to rush back home and get ready. There is going to be a concert on the Kempinski Terrace. The Vienna Mozart Players will perform Mozart and Vivaldi. After the concert the day might conclude with a little drink on the Bosphorus. **"**

The British screenwriter Michael Eaton was instrumental in establishing "Shots in the Dark," a crime and mystery film festival in his home town of Nottingham:

" The first day of 'Shots in the Dark,' which I helped set up three years ago and which is still Britain's only genre festival. As midnight

Steve James, Quentin Tarantino and John McNaughton at the "Shots in the Dark" Festival, organised by diarist Michael Eaton

struck I was sitting in a restaurant with the festival director, my friend Adrian Wootton, and Quentin Tarantino, the enthusiastic and friendly director of *Reservoir Dogs*, a movie which is idolised by the youth of our town. Quentin has an encyclopedic knowledge of movies and I could sit here all night but I'm holding myself back as I am opening a live show on Friday which I am writing, directing, and performing in.

As someone whose living comes predominantly from TV screenwriting and, when I'm lucky, film scripts, I naturally spend most of my life alone staring at a screen which I try to fill with words that one day someone else will turn into actions. So I try to do one live show a year for the buzz of getting out of the house and in front of a public – a decision which I always start to regret the day before opening. [. . .]

Today will be our first chance to play the show on site in the courthouse and gaol which date back to the Middle Ages. Four actors and three musicians are damp and depressed at the long-range weather forecast, convinced we've got

Crowds arriving for the San Francisco International Lesbian and Gay Festival

a show if only the heavens will let us play it, so every known ritual tradition is plundered for weather magic.

When the hour of the festival launch looms I find myself covered in plaster with half an hour to cut from the show and no prospect of attending the opening gala which we have been planning for the past year. I race across to the venue where bedecked guests are arriving and allow myself two glasses of champagne, and skulk in the corner as they all disappear chortling into the auditorium. **99**

Nancy Fishman plays a major role in producing the San Francisco International Lesbian and Gay Film Festival:

66 There was a hectic atmosphere in the office [of Frameline Distribution] because there were so many volunteers working on the festival.

Left: *Still from* Mala noche. Above: *Festival organiser Ahmad Al Hadari (right) with Egyptian minister Farouk Hosny*

In between answering calls and booking inquiries from around the country about our collection of more than 100 titles, I worked on three projects.

The first was getting a 35mm print of *Mala noche* by Gus van Sant in time for our opening night on June 18th. We are the distributor of the film, which is Gus's first feature. He had been working on getting it blown up to 35mm for release at our festival. It was touch and go whether or not he would get it on time. [. . .]

The second project was *Boys' Shorts: The New Queer Cinema*, a feature-length programme of six short films that we are releasing in July in New York. [. . .]

The third project was a theatrical opening at the Film Forum in New York of Marlon Riggs's new film, *No Regrets (Non, je ne regrette rien)*. It will open on June 23rd with *A Question of Color* by Kathe Sandler. [. . .]

I also tracked Frameline Distribution prints that were coming in for the festival, and talked with my colleague Desi del Valle about distribution prints and about our girlfriends.

I am eager to release a lesbian feature and wonder at moments why I've been working on so many men's films. Not that I don't like them . . .

but I wish there was a million dollar fund for women film-makers in the U.S., and I wish Frameline had more money to fund lesbian film. **"**

Ahmad Al Hadari serves as Chairman of the Alexandria International Film Festival:

" I was anxious to hear if Michelangelo Antonioni, the well-known Italian director, would accept to be head of the jury for the competition that will take place among films chosen from Mediterranean countries. The festival is in its ninth year now, but this is the first time we have arranged an international competition.

I found a message by fax waiting for me at my office, sent by our representative in Rome, to inform me that Mr. Antonioni had agreed to be our guest of honour at the festival next September, but declined to be president of the jury, due to his age. I looked quickly through one of our reference books and realised that he is 81 years old now.

I replied directly that he is more than welcome to be our guest of honour, and that we shall do all we can to make his stay with us during the

Actor and director Barry Primus spends much of his spare time visiting film festivals

festival comfortable and enjoyable for him. We plan to choose an Egyptian lady interpreter, who speaks Italian fluently, to accompany him during his stay in Egypt, to look after him, and to plan his meetings with Egyptian film-makers. It will be an important occasion for us.

Now I have to face the problem of looking for another major figure to be head of the jury. I better wait until I meet members of the organising committee during our meeting tomorrow morning. **"**

Visiting film festivals has become part of the regular landscape of the movie world. Barry Primus, the actor and director (*Mistress*), spends his June 10th in Portugal, at the Troia International Film Festival:

" Had breakfast with members of my committee, which is awarding a prize to the best independent American film at this festival. We went over the exact wording we wanted to include in the award certificates. After some discussion, which I led as president of the committee, we unanimously agreed to give the prize to *Laws of Gravity* and its director Nick Gomez, with *American Heart* receiving an honourable mention.

At 11.30 A.M. I went to the main theatre where the awards would be given. Before I walked in, Salvato Teles de Meneses, the Director of Programming, told me that I should sit down front and that I might be in for a surprise – which I was. After several other awards had been announced, my film *Mistress* was given the prize for the best feature. In taking the award, a lovely ceramic made by a Portuguese artist, I thanked the festival for having me. I also thanked Robert De Niro for supporting, and starring in, the film.

A long lunch followed the award ceremonies, where I had a chance to say goodbye to many of the film-makers and festival people I'd been with in the last ten days. That afternoon Julie Arenal the choreographer and I took a ride to several villages near the festival. We arrived back at the hotel late that night and I spent an hour and a half on *Peppermint Lounge*, a script that is in development and on which I have been working for the last six months. **99**

Nagisa Oshima, at once notorious and admired for such films as *The Empire of the Senses*, *The Ceremony*, and *Diary of a Shinjuku Thief*, visits Switzerland to attend the International Electronic Cinema Festival, but soon finds that the world is pursuing him:

66 I wake up at 7 A.M. in a room in the Montreux Palace Hotel where I arrived last night. I came to Montreux as a member of the international jury at the International Electronic Cinema Festival, which was launched in 1987. I have served on the jury since 1989.

At 11.30 P.M. there was a briefing lunch at the restaurant of the Hôtel Eden au Lac. [. . .] At 3 P.M. the Opening Ceremony took place at the Cité-Centre. I was given a pioneer award by the festival along with Massimo Fichera of Italy. First screening session started at 3.30 P.M. We saw five documentaries until 5.30 P.M. I found *Paco Rabanne, Master*, from NTA, Spain, pretty good, and the others were not so interesting.

Received two faxes. One is from Serge Silberman in Paris which was forwarded from my office in Tokyo. He wanted me to send his condolences to Madame Kawakita for her daughter Kazuko [Shibata]'s sudden death. Another one was from Judy Tossell of Regina Ziegler Filmproduktion in Berlin. They are coming to Montreux to see me. Also, Jeremy Irons will come here by the end of the festival. **99**

The Kobe International Independent Short Film Festival in Japan is being held for the first time, and two of our contributors are in attendance. Liam O'Neill is the Irish director of *The Barber Shop*:

66 I've been here in Kobe since Sunday. There are twenty film-makers from all over the world here with their short films. [The festival has] chosen our films from over 630 entries and flown us all here from our different home countries.

This is just about the last stop for *The Barber Shop*, my first film. It is almost exactly a year since we first screened it to the cast and here it is and here am I in Japan. It has been a great year going to festivals seeing lots of films and meeting other film-makers who are just getting going. How many of us, I wonder, will survive? [. . .]

The scale of this festival is rather nice as there are only twenty films in competition. So we all get to know each other to some extent and there is enough time to make a couple of friends.

Today Chris Gerolmo, Marco Williams and I went to see a Japanese baseball game. We had a great sense of accomplishment in finding out where and when a ball game would be on. Even more accomplishment in arriving there without getting lost. I still like baseball even though I've lived in Ireland for twenty years. It was a different experience to an American ball game; the loyalty of the fans to their team was extraordinary. They cheered, chanted, and clapped in unison with little plastic bats, non-stop despite the fact that their team lost badly. [. . .]

Now that we have all seen each other's films you can begin to decide where each one fits in the pecking order. Competitive festivals have the downside of the competition itself. There is something unpleasant about this prize and money stuff. It's good to meet film-makers at such events but the prize, especially here, where the top award is $50,000, is, I believe, at the back of everyone's mind.

I think about it myself. $50,000. That would certainly make a difference in getting the next project off the ground – because the important thing is always getting another film made. In Ireland it takes a long time and undoubtedly I could go straight into pre-production on another short if I won. **99**

Eva Lopez-Sanchez, a director from Mexico, also attended the Kobe meeting:

66 Films are made out of a loving process. Like a child, a film is conceived, nourished, cared for, and above all loved. It consumes our sleep and gives us dreams as well as nightmares. Finally one day the child is born and we must let it learn to walk on its own two feet.

[My short film] *Lost Objects* has walked a long

Mexican director Eva Lopez-Sanchez (top left) with guests at the Kobe Short Film Festival in Japan

way and has brought us both a long way from Mexico to Japan on the other side of the planet to participate in the Kobe International Independent Film Festival.

Twenty out of 633 films from all over the world were selected to participate in this festival. Representatives of all twenty films in competition are here (directors or producers). It has been not only a rewarding experience to come to Japan and to the festival itself, but we have been given a unique opportunity to encounter twenty very interesting people and to talk about cinema in all sorts of 'broken language.' Kobe is also proud to be the first city in Japan to have projected a film. It has raised a stone monument to commemorate this event.

Lauri Rose Tanner, a consultant in arts administration from San Francisco, prepares to write a definitive manual for would-be festival organisers:

Another crazy day in this long and truly challenging process of writing a book on 'How to Start and Operate Film and Video Festivals.' It's been about six months now that I've been interviewing the people involved in running the twenty or so film and video festivals here in Northern California, and I've got another six months to go until I expect to have a first draft of a manuscript ready to go to the publisher. As the days and weeks of research and transcribing rush by, tapes and papers piling higher and higher on my desk, on the floor. [. . .]

It's been a few days since I returned from the annual conference of NAMAC – the National Alliance for Media Arts and Culture – in Chicago, and I still haven't unpacked the box of hundreds of different pieces of paper which I collected from the different groups that showed up and who put on festivals as part of their activity. I [gave a talk] about the NEA's Media Arts Fund denying funding for all festivals as a smokescreen for not wanting to fund the gay and lesbian events. The crazy contradiction [. . .] is that the NEA [National Endowment for the Arts] may actually give some money to publish my book, and therefore on one hand be supportive of making new and better festivals, while on the other hand clamping down on the sort of festival funding which they believe upsets right-wing fundamentalist legislators.

I do hope this book will end up in the hands of all sorts of communities of people who may be disenfranchised in some way or other, and who by using the film/video festival format will empower themselves, as so many before them have done.[. . .] Maybe this way I'm playing my own little part in helping to continue the tradition of bringing people together in small rooms with large screens to watch the art of film and video unfold before them, and to meet the makers and talk together about what they've seen and how it made them feel.

Heat and mosquitoes in Belize's jungle afflict cast and crew of Nicolas Roeg's Heart of Darkness *(Patrick Ryecart, Chapter 13)*

I

Top: *No crane, no rain machine for Shyam Benegal working on* Sweet Basil *(see Chapter 6).*
Above: *Gavin Millar shivers in Newcastle-upon-Tyne (see Chapter 4).*
Right: *The Australian bush is the setting for Tracey Moffat's* Bedevil *(see Chapter 8)*

Left: *Kenji Takama discusses the pee wee dolly with the director and dolly grip of* Here Comes a Duck's Song *(see Chapter 14).*

Top and above: *Geoffrey Malone designs futuristic multiplexes in Singapore (see Chapter 9)*

VI

Left: *The indefatigable producer-director Roger Corman directs actors on set (see Chapter 11).*
Top: *Mexican director Guita Schyffer has just finished her first feature,* To See You a Bride *(see Chapter 22).*
Above: *Regina Ziegler produces twelve erotic tales – one of them Melvin van Peebles's* Vroom *(see Chapter 11)*

Previous pages: *Adoor Gopalakrishnan on location for*
Vidheyan (The Servile) *(see Chapter 7).*
Top: *Joshua Lucas plays the part of a cowboy in Australia.*
Above: *Harry Hook recces Monument Valley (see*
Chapter 25).
Right: *Director confers with Park Ranger Alice Allen on the*
Paramount Ranch (see Chapter 5)

XI

Top: *Trainer watches Kuwait producer-director Khaled Siddik handle a falcon (see Chapter 24).* Above: *Logistics and locations prove a nightmare for producer Simon Relph (see Chapter 6).* Right: *Filming is never far from the thoughts of Chilean director Silvio Caiozzi Garcia (see Chapter 25)*

XIII

Left: Menace II Society *has more impact than* Jurassic Park *on Indian star Shabana Azmi (see Chapter 22)*.
Above: *Stefan Jarl travels to the land of the midnight sun to film reindeer herds (see Chapter 18)*

Top: *Catalan Lluis Ferrando puts finishing touches to the satirical comedy* Don Jaume el Conquistador *(see Chapter 11)*.
Above: *Wang Bin assists director Zhang Yimou on* To Live

11. Shuttle Diplomacy: The Producers IN THE LEAN, FIT 1990S, PRODUCERS COME IN ALL SHAPES AND SIZES – AND NATIONALITIES. MORE AND MORE WORK INDEPENDENTLY OF THE MAJOR STUDIOS, ALTHOUGH MANY HAVE "FIRST-LOOK" DEALS THAT PROVIDE SPIRITUAL FREEDOM WITHOUT BEARING THE RISK FOR FAILURE. THE DURABLE PRODUCERS WILL HAVE SEVERAL PROJECTS SIMMERING ON THEIR STOVES, SOME FOR YEARS. THE PROFESSION CALLS NOT JUST FOR DURABILITY, BUT FOR THE SKILLS OF AN AGENT, THE INGENUITY OF A FINANCIER, THE PATIENCE OF A PARENT, AND THE HIDE OF AN IGUANA.

Jeremy Thomas, son of British director Ralph Thomas, has demonstrated a flair for surviving as an independent producer of cosmopolitan projects (Oshima's *Merry Christmas, Mr. Lawrence*, Bertolucci's *The Last Emperor* and now *Little Buddha*):

❝ 8.30 A.M. Swim 1,000 metres at Kensington swimming pool – part of my daily routine. I do it to keep my stamina up, but after a few lengths I find all the questions and (of course) the problems of the previous day settling into some kind of order. [. . .]

9.30 A.M. I start to read the papers on an upcoming British Film Institute sub-committee. Having taken on the chairmanship of the Institute I now find myself reading huge volumes of administrative paper, which I am urging them to keep to a minimum. The battles we are fighting at the Institute really come down in the end to one thing – persuading the press, and government, that film and television really *matter*. [. . .]

Alex Wiesendanger and Ying Ruocheng in Jeremy Thomas's production, Little Buddha

11 A.M. Meeting with my lawyers to discuss a film financing proposal from a French investor, which was put to me verbally in Cannes. For once, thank God, the concept is simple and doesn't feature the usual mind-numbing jigsaw. But I do think it's a shame that it can't be a U.K. company making the offer. Of course we still do not have the kind of support for the industry here that the French have enjoyed for forty years, although we're all pressing the government for some kind of tax incentive for production. [. . .]

2.30 P.M. Meet Bernardo Bertolucci at the cutting room in Dean Street for coffee and to discuss the many aspects of *Little Buddha* – the progress of the fine cut, which is now down to the last painful trims; the special effects, titles, and music (which Ryuichi Sakamoto is composing in London at present). We speak in a sort of shorthand developed after many years of collaboration. [. . .]

6 P.M. I start my calls to the States – first calling Anjelica Huston, who is going to direct her first film for me, next year I hope. She's a remarkable woman – witty, highly intelligent, and amazingly straightforward despite all her years in the American media spotlight. Then it's on to the agents, and distributors. The time difference with L.A. is the British producer's blessing and his curse – a blessing because we can at least speak to the States easily each day; and a curse because it makes the London working day so long.

7 P.M. Bernardo and I meet up again and drive home. We only live a few minutes from each other, and when we're making a film together our lives are entwined day and night for months at a time. 🙶

David Puttnam, producer of *Chariots of Fire*, *The Killing Fields* and *The Mission*, and a former head of Columbia Pictures, continues from England to set up adventurous and imaginative projects:

🙶 Drive to Pinewood [Studios] early. Do some letters in the office and then spend the rest of the morning in the cutting room with [Scottish director] Bill Forsyth, reviewing the latest cuts and trims to *Being Human* (our new film starring Robin Williams) in preparation for its

Producers on location: Jeremy Thomas in Nepal (top) *and David Puttnam in Britain* (above)

Roger Corman, godfather to the American independent cinema

American previews later in the month. [. . .]

3 P.M. Meeting of the Bradford Film Advisory Council, which I chair. The Council plans screenings, lectures and film-tours as part of the activities of the National Museum of Photography, Film and Television and the Bradford Film Theatre. [. . .]

5 P.M. Meeting with Steve Norris (Chief Executive of my company, Enigma) and our legal counsel to consider the High Court presentation

of a case against Goldcrest on the division of revenue from a number of profitable films we made in the early 1980s: *Local Hero*, *P'tang Yang Kipperbang*, *Secrets*, and others. The case is important for us but we are fighting it on behalf of a great number of other profit participants.

7 P.M. Mid-morning in Los Angeles so this is the best time of day to make a whole series of phone calls relating to the forthcoming preview of *Being Human*, and to discuss aspects of pre-produc-

tion for our new film, *The War of the Buttons*, which we start shooting in Ireland next month 🙶 [see SCOUTING LOCATIONS].

A host of directors owe their first break to Roger Corman (Coppola, Scorsese, Bogdanovich, Demme, Golan, etc.). An efficient, economic director himself during the 1950s and 1960s, Corman remains active in Hollywood:

🙷 9 A.M. [. . .] Concorde Pictures, my company, has been getting a lot of press due to the release of our dinosaur thriller, *Carnosaur*. With the opening of Spielberg's *Jurassic Park* only days away, it's important to track the competition to make sure they're not stealing my ideas! After all, not many people are aware that Adam Simon's novel, *Carnosaur*, preceded Michael Crichton's *Jurassic Park* by more than five years.

9.30 A.M. The TV crew from "Entertainment Tonight" has just arrived to film a segment on *Carnosaur*, and my assistant has taken the liberty of rearranging my office for the occasion. An 8-foot promotional dinosaur from the film has been installed behind my desk, and it looms precariously over my shoulder as I prepare myself for the usual questions ('Is your dinosaur bigger and better than theirs?' 'Is your movie bloodier and more intense?' . . . 'Of course!' I reply).

The interview finishes just in time for my appointment with Talia Shire, a gifted actress who has appeared in several great films ranging from the *Rocky* pictures to *The Godfather* series. She is preparing to direct an erotic thriller for Concorde, and casting decisions need to be made. We discuss the popular actresses of the day, and decide upon Ally Sheedy for the lead. Tally is happy, and the meeting's a success. She begins shooting in two weeks (around here there is no time to be wasted). Tally is the second in her family to direct a first film for me. The first was her brother, Francis Ford Coppola [*Dementia 13*].

11.30 A.M. I have barely enough time to straighten out my collar before heading out the door to meet Jeff Berg, president of ICM [International Creative Management], for a lunch appointment. I've never been enamoured of the power-lunch subculture of the business – it is frequently a waste of time when one could be making movies. [. . .] We discuss the possibility of expanding operations at Concorde, and working out a few deals between our respective businesses.

[. . .] 5 P.M. I discuss a project with Barbet Schroeder (director of *Reversal of Fortune* and *Single White Female*), and then get caught up with Diane Ladd, an old friend and wonderful actress who made her debut in my film, *The Wild Angels*. We are both delighted that the critics have given her positive reviews for her role as the deranged scientist in *Carnosaur*. A few other calls, and then I return home to change for an awards show 🙶 this evening.

Nik Powell has, with partner Steve Woolley, survived some turbulent moments over the past ten years, during which time his credits as producer include *Mona Lisa*, *Company of Wolves*, *Scandal*, and *The Crying Game*:

🙷 [After commuting by rail to London and making various calls on the train to Japan] I arrive in our new offices in Brewer Street, Soho, for my favourite kind of day – a completely clear one – no meetings, nowhere to go, and no-one to meet. [. . .] At the moment I'm busting a gut to put the finishing touches to the financing of our new film, *Dark Blood*, to be directed by George (*The Vanishing*) Sluizer. I broke the back of this at Cannes a few weeks ago when I raised $6 million of the $7 million I needed in one deal with New Line. The cast is set – Judy Davis, River Phoenix [who died on October 31st, 1993, an event that led to the film being shut down by the producers] and Jonathan Pryce. Only Pryce is still not approved by New Line – today I will try to persuade them by phone to approve him (I do). I also have to call George about various additional conditions they want if they are to accept (which they have) that George is to have final cut. [. . .]

I look at my 'call list' and I see '2 o'clock, call Steve' (Stephen Woolley, my partner in Scala) [see next entry] 'about everything.' Because we are so often in different parts of the globe, this means frequent calls at the dead of night or at 6 A.M. – and frequently waking each other up. [. . .] I go through the usual things with him – *Backbeat* finances; a new development deal we're negotiating; the closing of the Scala Cinema; the settling of various guarantees; the payment of

Stephen Woolley (left) on a recce in the swamps of Louisiana, with Neil Jordan (centre) and Dante Fenetti

negotiating; the closing of the Scala Cinema; the settling of various guarantees; the payment of 'deferrals' on *The Crying Game*; and update on both George Sluizer's *Dark Blood* and Julien Temple's *Galatea*, with Val Kilmer; and has he read the book *Buffalo Soldiers*, about which I'm very excited – he has.

The peripatetic Stephen Woolley awakes in New Orleans at 7.30 A.M. to take a call from partner Nik Powell (see previous entry):

For the past ten days Neil Jordan and I have been shuttling across the States – London to Los Angeles, staying two days, San Francisco, one day, New York, four days, and now New Orleans for five days. It's been a productive time, meeting with David Geffen who is producing the movie with me, and Warner Bros. (the financiers), location scouting with Redmond Morris (co-producer), and Dante Ferretti (designer), and casting with Juliet Taylor for the role of Claudia to co-star in Neil's adapted version of the novel, *Interview with the Vampire*. Claudia is a nine-year-old vampire in Neil's script and we have met some incredible children in L.A. Now we are trying to arrange tests with New Orleans children – the better kids will try out with Brad Pitt, who is already cast in one of the lead roles. [. . .]

We are heading off to find a swamp location and having had a hugely successful previous location search, I am confident we will find a bayou that Neil will like. Yesterday, we had a good day and confirmed seven locations. Despite the oppressive June heat and humidity, it's a pleasure to be guided through these most beautiful swamps. Infested with wild life like alligators, turtles, owls and huge bugs, but most worrying when we occasionally alight from our flat-bottomed speed boat – snakes.

After lunch, we head back to New Orleans to see more streets and cemeteries. Anne Rice, author of *Interview,* is a highly regarded New Orleans citizen and we have been given an enormous amount of access and shown great hospitality. With a little bit of dressing, we hope to transfer the French Quarter back to its original Nineteenth Century state.

The British producer Iain Smith pictured on location

Iain Smith, like many producers by no means a household name, still opens the doors and makes the calls that enable feature films to be made:

❝ I arrived at [our] offices at Shepperton Studios around 8.45 A.M. and spent the best part of the day completing a script breakdown of Christopher Hampton's screenplay of *Mary Reilly* for TriStar Pictures. In the afternoon, I began the complicated process of scheduling the picture.

During the day I spoke with a variety of people including Ron Lynch, Norma Heyman, Ned Tanen, Roland Joffé and John Williams. I also spoke with the managements of Pinewood Studios, Bray Studios, Ardmore Studios in Dublin and the Barrandov Studios in Prague.

I received approximately eighteen calls from people and companies looking for work; three of the individuals were near desperation. I opened four unsolicited projects that arrived in the mail and I placed them on the heap of other scripts and treatments I haven't yet got round to reading. [. . .]

I had a phone conversation with Roland Joffé, who told me he was intrigued by the latest draft of *Seven Years in Tibet* which I am developing in partnership with Vanguard Films in New York.

After I had grabbed something to eat in Ladbroke Grove I joined Stephen Frears and the production designer Stuart Craig at 9 P.M. We discussed the sets, costumes and schedule for *Mary Reilly*, which Stephen will direct. ❞

Working Title Films remains one of the most active and resolute British production companies. Tim Bevan, a young producer at Working Title, spends a typically phone-ridden day:

❝ 10 A.M. Pinewood Studios. I visit the offices of *The Borrowers*, one of our TV shows currently shooting a second series. I meet with Walt de Faria, the executive producer (Walt brought us the rights in the first place). We discuss the success of the first series and then finalise our deal for developing a feature film of *The Borrowers*.

I then go to the set of *U.F.O.*, to seek out Simon Wright, our comedy producer. Simon and

I discuss a number of upcoming comedy projects that we are aiming to put together later this year and next. [. . .]

Eric [Fellner, my partner] and I tend to split our time between L.A. and London. In order to run an effective production business, even making European films, one must have a constant L.A. presence – it is the business centre of the film industry.

I grab a sandwich for lunch and watch the *Four Weddings and a Funeral* rushes on video. Hugh Grant, who plays the lead in the movie, is terrific. The film has been really well cast with excellent actors even in the small roles – it makes such a difference, England has so much talent. Mike Newell [the director] is doing a great job.

Eric and I [. . .] are both concerned about this year's production slate – here we are in June and not one (of three) of our bigger films is going. We discuss directors for *Moonlight and Valentino* – probably the next movie – I'm keen on Gillian Armstrong. [. . .]

4.45 P.M. Phone calls to L.A. Always speak to Michael Kuhn, President of PolyGram Filmed Entertainment, to give him an update. [Then] we speak to Mario Van Peebles' lawyer. Mario directed *Posse* for us last year – he is a great talent, full of energy and ideas. We are closing a deal with Mario and his father Melvin to make a movie about the Black Panther movement. **99**

Mark Shivas began his career as a film critic at Oxford, and for many years has been associated with some of the best "TV movies" to emerge from the BBC. As Head of Films, he spent his day touching on numerous projects and issues:

66 Many phone calls, but first meeting of the day is with Norma Acland, our Head of Business Affairs, where she brings me up to date on the winding up in Spain of Verity Lambert's serial *Eldorado*. Norma has been negotiating with the Spanish company which leased the site from the township of Coin, and tempers have run high. She's also been writing letters back and forth on a feature film we hope to make with Nic Roeg, produced by his son Luc, called (for the moment) *Two Deaths*. That's been a long business too.

Julie Walters and Jeanne Moreau in The Summer House, *produced by Norma Heyman for Mark Shivas at the BBC*

Ruth Caleb, producer, comes to discuss the possibility of a film of Evelyn Waugh's *Put Out More Flags*. She wants to do it via BBC Wales, but I already have a proposal for the same book from an independent producer, Moira Williams, to star Stephen Fry, and that's the proposal I prefer. I made a not very successful version of the novel for television around twenty years ago. Am I destined to be involved in the remake of things I've done before? Is that how old I've become?

Lunch at Clarke's with Norma Heyman who produced for my last run of Screen 2, *Clothes in the Wardrobe* with Jeanne Moreau, Joan Plowright, and Julie Walters. One of the excuses for the lunch is to discuss the American title for *Clothes* because Samuel Goldwyn has picked up the film for theatrical distribution in North America, and they don't have 'wardrobes' over there. The word 'closet' has other connotations. [The final title was *The Summer House*.] This is the fifth of our films that started as TV movies in Britain that Americans have taken for theatrical distribution there, and more are in the pipeline. What is the message here? **99**

For many producers, setting up a project can take months, even years. Roger Garcia, born in Hongkong and now resident in New York, likes to keep his options open:

66 As on many days, I'm preoccupied with a number of projects, [notably] *Makapili (The Collaborator)*, a low-budget feature about peasant collaborators during the Japanese occupation of the Philippines in the second World War. The Filipino director, Raymond Red, and I have been working on the film for a couple of years now but the impetus has really become serious since we received the Hubert Bals Award for the project at the Rotterdam Film Festival in 1993.

I've known Raymond for quite a few years now and produced some of his earlier Super-8 films and his first 16mm film. I believe in long-term collaborations with film-makers because producing films for me is not just an exercise in logistics but also a question of aesthetics – thinking about the type of cinema you want to make. [...]

Today [during a short visit to Hongkong] I am in the process of commissioning the script for

Makapili. We will use Ian Victoriano, a young Filipino who wrote many of Raymond's Super-8 films. At the same time, I am still debating the final format of the film – should we go with Super 16 for TV and then a 35mm release, or should we shoot on Super-8, release on one-inch video for TV, and then use the one-inch for a video-to-film transfer? It strikes me that many different production and post-production options exist today for low budget independents. It's getting more interesting since I would like to expand the limits of self-sufficiency in production, and the cost advantages of new technologies. **99**

Hans de Weers is a Dutch producer whose plans this year included no less than four projects for TV, as well as a feature for 1994:

66 After some phone calls I have a meeting at 10 A.M. with Marleen Gorris (*Christine M.*, *Broken Mirrors*, and *The Last Island*) about her new film *Antonia*, which we hope to shoot next year. It will have to be a co-production with Belgium and/or Germany and/or Britain. *Antonia* is one of the most beautiful scripts I have read and I sincerely hope we can start production in 1994. However, the financing of this film is, for various reasons, still quite difficult. With Marleen and her first assistant we once again go through a very provisional pre-production schedule and discuss location scouting. We agree that our latest plan should work, and by November this year it should be clear whether or not we have a green light for next summer. **99**

Many producers thrive on so-called "first-look" deals with major Hollywood companies, enabling them to develop projects in reasonably balanced circumstances. Antony Ginnane is an expatriate Australian now living in Hollywood:

66 At 9.30 A.M. I breakfast at the Four Seasons Hotel, Beverly Hills, with Ted Kotcheff to discuss the possibility of his directing my production, *The Outpost*, by Casey Jones, based on the short story by Joseph Conrad. Kotcheff and I reminisce over *Wake in Fright* [also known as *Outback*, 1971] – still a powerful analysis of the 'Ugly Australian' – and discuss approaches to the screenplay, leaving it set in Australia, or resetting it in the Philippines at the turn of the century. Ted agrees to read the Philippines version and we will hook up again in a week or so.

At 11.30 A.M. I reach my office at Fries Entertainment in Hollywood where I have a first-look housekeeping deal. I participate in my weekly development status meeting with Chuck Fries re. the various projects I am working on. Our project *Screamers*, a science fiction thriller from the short story by Philip K. Dick with a script by Dan O'Bannon, is almost packaged. We are looking for a Canadian tax deal to add to our foreign pre-sales. Christian Duguay or Stuart Gillard will direct.

I drive over to Century City and lunch with Jerry Offsay, who is #2 at ABC Productions. Jerry used to be my attorney when he was at Loeb and Loeb. We discuss the state of the business.

After lunch I field calls from Australia and New Zealand on two Canadian/New Zealand co-productions, both of which are moving along encouragingly, and review a sheaf of faxes and calls.

Naonori Kawamura, a Japanese producer for both cinema and television, feels geographically removed from the main stream of world film-making:

In the morning, I check the fax at the office as usual. Working in Japan means we share our business hours with neither European nor American offices. Whenever I see a fax machine, so indispensable in our business, it never fails to make me feel as if I'm some kind of stranger, cut off from the whole world.

This morning I found a fax from Peter Kosminsky in England. It was about our plan – which has been a long time developing – to make [Kazuo Ishiguro's novel] *A Pale View of Hills* into a movie. I wish we could make the world understand the Japanese soul through films – though this has always proved quite difficult. The thing is that a film with a Japanese cast, intended for the world market, would hardly attract any funding. (Even Japanese enterprises have seldom given support for such undertakings!)

A treatment of a new work called *Victory Joe!*

arrived on fax from Mike de Leon in the Philippines. A unique comedy with a Japanese cast. Interesting material, but Asian films are no easier to show in Japan than are Japanese ones in Europe or the States.

Kawamura's countryman, Yasuyoshi Tokuma, President of the long-established Daiei, thrives on domestically-oriented productions:

10 A.M. I attended a meeting to discuss *Gamera*. Gamera is a deformed monster turtle, similar to Godzilla, and created by our company, Daiei. This monster was a popular character, and the *Gamera* series attracted a big audience for many years. A few days ago we decided to set up a new project to revive *Gamera* after twenty years' absence. I read through the first draft of the script, but I think we need to rewrite certain parts. I asked our staff to come up with more ideas for making home computer software and promotional tie-ups with other companies in areas unconnected with film. Then I announced that this film would be released in the spring of 1995. [. . .]

At 1.30 P.M. I was informed that Kurosawa's *Medadayo* would be starting its second run. That's not so bad. Last month it finished a six-week run at 128 cinemas across the country. Anyhow, Kurosawa's works have great longevity. I ordered my staff to try to keep his film on release. [. . .]

At 3.30 P.M. I arrived at Studio Jiburi, a production company owned by two directors, Hayao Miyazaki and Isao Takahata, who have had a run of success with animation films and last year they built their own company building. The main purpose of my visit is to check on the progress of their new movie, *Heisei, Tanuki Gassen Bonboko*. [. . .] I was told that production was a little delayed, as usual, but that approximately half the storyboard was completed. They said that soon after the original animation drawings were finished, they would begin to shoot them. To create high-quality production involves greater risk. Ticket sales for their earlier film, *Beni No Buta/Porco Rosso*, reached about $45 million, and was #1 at the box-office in Japan. I'm really hoping for better results this time. The theme of the new film is the timely one of environmental destruction.

Also in the Far East, Kwon Young Rak believes in boosting audiences for domestic Korean films:

" Spent a busy day discussing with Woo-Suk Kang the casting for a new film, *Two Cops*.

Korean film-makers' morale is plunging further as the Hollywood-made film distributors in Korea are launching a publicity campaign for their new films, ahead of summer release.

The activities of young directors and producers are getting more vigorous, along with a recent announcement by the director, Kwang-Soo Park, in which he declared that in future he would try to produce all his films independently.

Two Cops has also been launched on director Woo-Suk Kang's independent initiative. I believe that my responsibility is to recapture our audience, once taken away by Hollywood films.

Today is a special day because we have chosen at lightning speed two top Korean stars, Sung-Kee An and Min-Soo Choi, as main actors for *Two Cops*. "

Top: *Yasuyoshi Tokuma*. Below: *Scene from* Two Cops, *starring two actors chosen by Korean producer Kwon Young Rak*

More and more producers in Europe are extending their network of contacts and partners, as Regina Ziegler's diary indicates:

" Arrived in office with *Erotic Tales* on my mind – twelve films by twelve directors. Tried to call Nagisa Oshima in Montreux [see FESTIVALS] about our meeting next Monday. We'll be discussing *The Chrysanthemum Vow*, his contribution to our erotic project. Sent a fax to his hotel and spent an hour going through his budget. [. . .]

The office [in Berlin] is quieter than usual today – it's Corpus Christi, a holiday in the rest of Germany, which gives me more time to mull over a couple of new scripts that came in this week.

I've hardly managed more than a few pages when the phone rings. Most people in New York are still asleep or contemplating their breakfast – not Melvin van Peebles. He finished shooting his erotic tale, *Vroom*, and needs someone to see the rough cut right away . . . otherwise we may not be ready in time for Venice. Can't be in three places at once. Luckily our co-producer, Herbert Kloiber, is in NY and so a couple of phone calls later, that's fixed. [. . .]

New York again . . . this time a fax from [producer] Ben Barenholtz with notes from a screenwriter on relocating a promising story in Berlin. It's my first collaboration with Ben, as we spent a lot of time looking for the right project. Now we're working with an extremely talented screeenwriter, Olga Humphrey, and I'm very excited to see what she comes up with. "

Above and right: *stills from Melvin van Peebles's* Vroom

Lluis Ferrando, among many tasks, functions as a producer in Barcelona:

❝ When I got to the office, the first thing I did was something I had been meaning to get down to for several days, when I could find a few hours' peace – reading the script of a proposed co-production between Mexico, France and Spain. The film will be called *Garden of Eden*, and is written by Beatriz and Maria Novaro; I had

very much enjoyed their earlier film, *Danzón*. I spent several wonderful hours reading their magnificent new screenplay. I hope that (with or without our participation) it can be filmed soon.

After lunch I had a meeting with the director and writer of a feature that our production company is going to make in August. The provisional title is *El rel en Jaume*. It is a satirical comedy which will be filmed in Catalan, without any subsidy (something that's becoming increasingly rare in

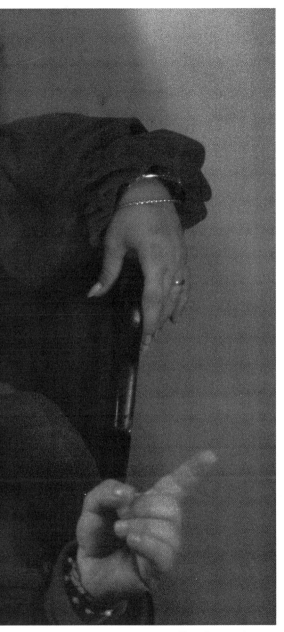

Still from Lluis Ferrando's production of Don Jaume el Conquistador

our cinema, I should mention). We talked about some characters and situations, of ways of giving the story more dramatic force. Then I had to make some phone calls and deal with the day to day running of a production office.

In the evening I went to see a film that has been running for several weeks and which, for a

Spanish film, is extraordinary: *The Bird of Happiness*, directed by Pilar Miró. I liked it a lot and came out thinking this was a good way to end June 10th, 1993. **99**

John O'Shea, the veteran New Zealand producer, continues to cast around for all manner of unusual (and often literary) projects:

66 Rory [O'Shea] in New York, Stuart, and George have acquired all rights to Mervyn Peake's *Gormenghast*, including interactive. Trouble is I've always been unexcited by the musty atmosphere (as in 'Dungeons & Dragons') of the few pages I've read of *Titus Groan*. Hardly struck me as a movie, even on today's menus – maybe an interactive board game! Should read it though. Oh how I wish someone with their connections would ask me to work on an adaptation (and production) of L.H. Myer's *The Near and the Far*.

[. . .] Isidor Saslav, in Wellington, will continue with Bill [Sheat] and me the exchange of research and ideas when he gets back to Texas. He has matched some of the dramatic flurries I've devised for Solomon Scarecrow: a woman who had admired George Bernard Shaw for years wanted and offered to live with and care for 'the genius' after Mrs. Shaw died. (Must remember to contact Simon about Peter O'Toole's availability for GBS.) Send Isidor a clipping from this week's *Variety*, an obituary of Wendy Hiller's husband, Ronald Gow, who wrote *Love on the Dole*, a play that so impressed GBS that he became their lifelong friend. [. . .]

Find time to draft proposal for co-production of *Horse Opera*. Richard [Phelps] has rewritten the start. Will be a lively mix of action, mystery, adventure and parody. A bit like the early Coen Bros, look at contemporary mid-West fables except it'll have the trappings – Injuns, Custer, family – that Richard loves about the traditional Western.

Could suit New Zealand Film Commission now that the new Chairman seeks profit more than Palmes d'Or. Might be better to seek co-production in London. The Brits are sure to relish the chance to divert moviegoers' money from Hollywood pockets. What fun to have New Zealand Maoris playing Injuns and the **99** Taupo Plains doubling for Montana.

Anthony Hopkins, Richard Attenborough and others write in this book about their work on *Shadowlands*. Here Terry Clegg, the executive producer, on the picture, talks about the less glamorous side of the business day:

❝ 8.20 A.M. Walk to 'D' Stage [in the studios] where we are in our fourth scheduled day on 'Hospital Interiors'. Line-up already completed as I arrive. We are using a special piece of camera apparatus today, affectionately called 'The Hello Dolly' because it was made for Barbra Streisand on *Yentl*. [. . .]

Visit the floor. Technical problems with ancient X-ray equipment are causing some delay. Debra Winger announces that she is to visit Scotland for a couple of days. Tell her we built a wall to keep the buggers out but she thinks it's a joke! [. . .]

Talk with Art Director about weekend working for Art dept. staff. Approve purchase of costumes for extras playing football circa 1954 . . . Sign Equity contracts for additional day players in Oxford. Sign purchase orders for Editorial Dept. Read treatment for upcoming project. Read update on Pressure Group document. 6.20 P.M. Wrap. ❞

Studio chiefs and heads of production work in an environment peopled by producers and those who bankroll movies. Václav Marhoul is managing director of the world-famous Barrandov Studios in Prague and these extracts from his diary offer a glimpse into his frenetic profession:

❝ Received a call from a Slovak producer, Rudolf Biermann, inviting me to attend the premiere of his new film, *A Fountain for Suzanne II* in Bratislava. The invitation's accepted. I start to schedule a meeting of graduates of the film school [FAMU]. This get-together will be sponsored by our studio. [. . .]

Contact a composer to arrange a meeting to discuss the modernisation of recording facilities in the film studio complex.

At last managed to see the trade union boss. We

The Academy Award-winning Closely Observed Trains, *filmed at Barrandov Studios*

Still from Milos Forman's The Firemen's Ball, *made at Barrandov Studios, Prague*

settle terms and conditions for our new collective agreement and the date for the annual trade union conference which will take place at the studio.

Wendy Schwarz, an American producer of commercials, calls to confirm our meeting for next week.

A call from Roy Bair, an English producer, who is preparing a feature film, Ben Kingsley's directorial debut. The script will be sent over and a date for a visit to the studio is to be agreed. [. . .]

A call to our London lawyer Lyndsey Posner from Simon and Olswang. I want to discuss how to obtain a loan from the European Bank. The film studio needs money for investment. That's our most urgent task.

The head of the pyrotechnics department rings to discuss a private matter – a fireworks display on June 26th when I am getting married for the first time. Afterwards a call to the director of technology to discuss lighting for the wedding ceremony. [. . .]

A call to Milos Forman, one of our shareholders, preparing for his trip to Prague at the beginning of July.

A call to our New York agent Bobby Lantz. [. . .] With the help of him, Forman and Bruce Ramer (who is one of the best Hollywood lawyers working for Steven Spielberg among others), we are trying to find the right person to represent Barrandov Studios in Los Angeles. **"**

Volker Schlöndorff, the distinguished German director (*Young Törless, The Tin Drum, The Voyager*, etc.), has the daunting task of resuscitating the near-defunct Babelsberg Studios in Berlin:

" At Berlin airport I meet the crew from *Delicatessen*: directors J. Jeunet and M. Caro, as well as their producer Claudie Ossard. A colourful group, coming to visit the studios and to discuss a possible co-production arrangement for their *La Cité des enfants perdus*, a grotesque sci-fi project in a run-down European city (such as Berlin?), a set they would like to create entirely on stage.

10 A.M. While they visit our workshops, carpentry, plaster studio, costumes, lab and post-production, I run for an appointment at the Ministry

of Finance in Potsdam to discuss final details and the possible fiscal implications of our joint venture with John Heyman's Island World entity. After six months of talks, they promise me this morning the required ruling within ten days.

Back at the office, some real bad news. A project we have been preparing for six months (Roger Spottiswoode's *Mesmer*) has been refused the DM 950,000 promised us by ZDF (the second German TV channel). [. . .] The same committee granted DM 400,000 to *The Cannibal*, a low-budget horror film we are producing also. Wieland Schulz-Keil, *Mesmer*'s main producer, is expected for lunch. What shall we do with a shooting start in eight weeks? Definitely too many committees in European film-making. [. . .]

Pierre Couveinhes, my French co-manager, has discussed finances with the *Delicatessen* crew. Their budget is 70 million French francs and they expect us to come in with 30%. As for their use of the studio, I suggest instead of conventional budgeting, to let them use the place, the people, and the equipment for three months, for a flat fee.

2 P.M. While they start working with the pro-duction design department, I pay a short visit to Manfred Krug on the new West Stage, where he is shooting *Der Blaue*, the story of an Eastern secret agent (Stasi) who becomes an M.P. in Bonn. Looking at their set of a suburban interior, I wonder why they don't shoot it on location. It's good business for us, but it doesn't make much sense.

3 P.M. Alberto Grimaldi calls from London. Eoghan Harris's second draft of *The Siege of Stalingrad* is ready. I hope this will be my next work as a director, getting away from management while providing activity in Babelsberg. [. . .]

5 P.M. I meet Wolf Bauer at UFA's Berlin office. We discuss the latest casting on the TV series, *Catherine the Great*. Production may have to be delayed to spring 1994, instead of this summer. Quite a blow for our business plans. On the other hand the BBC seems interested in the *Kindergarten* project and Stanley Donen (no less) has called with a *Marlene* script written by Steven Bach. Of course, all this means a lot of activity for 1994, less this year. How much longer can we wait? How much longer will our best personnel wait? [. . .]

227 «

Post-production facilities at Babelsberg Studios, headed by distinguished German director Volker Schlöndorff

12. Help Me If You Can: Funding and Administration

OUTSIDE THE UNITED STATES, A VITAL PART IN THE SURVIVAL OF CINEMA IS PLAYED BY THE CHIEF EXECUTIVES OF STUDIOS, FILM INSTITUTIONS, FUNDING BODIES, AND EVEN TV BROADCASTERS.

Christian Routh has the deceptively titled role of Selection Coordinator for a media initiative called the European Script Fund, based in London; in fact, he must say yea or nay to literally thousands of applications for script funding:

❝ I have to sign about 250 rejection letters today. It's not my favourite part of the job. We're a development agency funded through the Media Programme, and every year we receive about 1,500 proposals for film and television ideas. About 10% eventually get funded, and the rest . . . Well, they usually get angry.

To explain, or not to explain, that is the question. It's a no-win situation really, for when we try to give 'constructive criticism' in the rejection letters, it invariably rebounds back on us, as indignant writers, producers, and the dreaded pseudo-auteurs snap back with accusations about our collective lack of understanding of their extraordinary cinematic visions. After every funding session we receive several vindictive hate letters from unsuccessful applicants, along with the regular 'your letter is with my lawyers and I'll see you in court' bluffs. Personal attacks and conspiracy theories abound, usually along the lines of 'You feeble pen-pushing Eurocrats couldn't possibly understand what I'm trying to do. . .', or else 'Who do I have to bribe or sleep with to get money out of you? How can I break into the inner sanctum of your favoured few?' [. . .]

Sometimes it feels, especially on Rejection Days like today, that there are no new films left to make. But come Funding Day, I know spirits will soar again in eager anticipation of projects strange and wonderful, as the promise of a Good Story weaves its spell once again. Until then . . . 'I'm sorry to have to inform you that your application for . . . ❞

In Britain, Channel Four has performed an invaluable service to independent, ambitious film-making, by advancing money against TV rights, and commissioning new fiction for the small screen. David Aukin is Head of Drama for the Broadcaster:

❝ 10 A.M. Meeting with Brian Eastman. Discussed *Galahad*, Hugh Laurie's screenplay. Rank are prepared to come in with much of the finance. It's welcome news that they are prepared to back a British film. [. . .]

12.15 P.M. Off to Covent Garden to go on location briefly with *Four Weddings and a Funeral*. It's going well. Meet Andie MacDowell and Hugh Grant but they are too deep in concentration to make small talk. It's a long scene being shot outdoors in soaring temperatures. [. . .] Although we are in the middle of restaurant land, I go off with Mike Newell, the director, to the location catering bus parked off Kingsway where we eat liver and onions. Delicious. Mike is wonderfully relaxed and on top of everything. He'd like a few days extra for the shoot and it's true that the schedule, as with all British films, is unbelievably tight. [. . .]

5 P.M. Return to the Channel and deal with messages. Norma Heyman has shown the script of *My Sister in This House* to Kees Kasander [Dutch producer] who reckons it would cost approximately £1.2 million to produce this film in Holland. This is £500,000 cheaper than in the U.K. This is wonderful news but also appalling. It's wonderful because it means that the film can get made; it's appalling that this can only be achieved by making the film abroad.

In 1990 the five Nordic nations (Denmark, Finland, Iceland, Norway, and Sweden) set up the Nordic Film & TV Fund to provide a subsidy source for quality films made in the region. Bengt Forslund, himself an Oscar-nominated producer and screenwriter, works as Managing Director of the Fund:

A script a day keeps laziness away. I read this morning a Norwegian script. A Swedish producer wants to make a Swedish version parallel to the Norwegian one, with Swedish actors, and now they look to support from our Fund.

I am sceptical for several reasons. I am not especially attracted to the story though it has a good twist at the end, but it's a film about a twelve-year-old boy, neither a children's film, nor a family film, nor for an adult audience. Certainly not for teenagers looking for more forbidden subjects. The target group is too small. [. . .]

At the office at 9 A.M. I write down my comments to the producer. One of the sadder aspects of my work is to make many people disappointed, but it happens now and then that they can be grateful even for 'no.' Behind each applicant stand many people: co-producers, writers, directors. A film is never a one-man-show.

The Media Programme, the European Community's initiative for stimulating – and saving – audiovisual activity in Europe, has numerous projects. EFDO (European Film Distribution Office) is one of these; Ute Schneider is its Secretary General:

As I spend so much of my time travelling around Europe, I'm always happy to spend a few days at the EFDO offices in Hamburg-Altona. [. . .]

No lunch today due to an afternoon appointment with the City of Hamburg's cultural office,

Andie MacDowell and Hugh Grant on location for the hugely successful Four Weddings and a Funeral

which jointly finances our administration costs with the Media Programme of the European Commission. This year we've made an additional application for funds to put on a small festival of EFDO films in Hamburg. This will take place in October with the motto, 'Five Years of EFDO – Looking Back and Forward.' After long discussions, the Office's cultural and budget experts grant us an additional DM 200,000 for our autumn event. We are delighted; it will mean a lot more work, but we'll have the chance to show the people of Hamburg what EFDO has managed to achieve in the past five years.

Zsolt Kézdi-Kovács is General Director of Magyar Filmúnió (which deals with all international activities of the Hungarian cinema):

66 At 10 A.M., nervousness. We have been trying to enroll Hungary in the Media Programme. We have negotiated for a year, and now, a couple of days ago, they accepted our application. I have a small part in it, but that was a good feeling. Suddenly I learn that in our Ministry of Culture some low-ranking bureaucrats are posing fresh questions about the treaty. In a letter I received this morning they ask more and more details about the EC regulations etc. I don't even understand what they are asking. Do they want to change the system of the Common Market or what? 99

Funding comes not just from the major studios, banks, and subsidy institutions, but also from private business. Richard Eu, a company director in Singapore, gives a cautious welcome to the idea:

66 I have been asked to participate in a media and entertainment holding company which plans to be headquartered in Singapore. I am meeting the principal tomorrow, so I have been reviewing the business plan. I think the opportunity is timely, and I should like to move ahead in this deal.

I shall be having another meeting tomorrow with someone who wants to put together a film fund. He's representing the creative team and wants my ideas for the financial structure.

Perhaps I can dovetail this into the proposed holding company.

A proposal came in two days ago to fund a film project called *A Voice Cries Out*, about a group of women who were interned as prisoners of war by the Japanese during WWII. The story is touching and apparently HBO is willing to finance half of it. Still the budget looks high (around $10 million). 99

Ignacio Durán is Director General at the Mexican Institute of Cinematography. As his entry illustrates, he covers several bases:

66 The day begins with a breakfast with the Minister of Culture and the Mexican Ambassador to Germany to discuss a proposal for a season of recent Mexican films to be shown in Germany. At 10 A.M., in the Institute's offices, I meet the Mexican producer, Gonzalo Infante, to talk about the movie, *Broken English*, a co-production with a *chicano* group.

At 10.30 A.M. Francisco Gómez, the director of distribution at the Institute, tells me about the premiere of the film, *The Cronos Device*, at the Cinema Ermita. Then Rebeca Martinez, the deputy director of national distribution, tells me that for the opening of the film *Conjugal Life*, the exhibition chain COTSA has withdrawn two important theatres. She asks me to talk to the head of the chain as soon as possible.

Noon. I agree with Diego Lopez, the director of the Churubusco Studios, a plan to modernise and re-structure the studios. The work must be completed before the end of next year. [. . .]

5.30 P.M. Projection of the film, *In the Middle of Nothing*, for the publicity and distribution departments, so that they can begin to map out their promotional strategy.

6 P.M. Meeting with Antonio Villegas, the next Ambassador of Mexico to Norway concerning programming Mexican cinema in Oslo and Reykjavík (Iceland) next autumn.

6.30 P.M. Working session with the Mexican producer Jorge Sánchez to finalise the shooting schedule and the distribution agreement for *The Garden of Eden*, which will be directed by María Novaro.

7 P.M. Francisco Gómez talks to me about distribution figures. 99

Lineo Tsolo in Souleymane Cissé's Waati, *a Senegalese-South African co-production*

Brendan S. Shehu, like many African film administrators, doubles as both director/producer and General Manager of the Nigerian Film Corporation in Jos:

I previewed a documentary programme, produced by the Nigerian Film Corporation and processed in our new colour film laboratory, the first of its kind in the West African sub-region. The documentary concerned the Transition to Civil Rule Programme in Nigeria and as the producer of the film, I was so happy and overwhelmed with the quality of the production and the completed work that I heaved a thunderous sigh of relief that sent members of my staff into peals of laughter as never before.

With the successful completion of the film and an auspicious test run of the film lab, I knew that I was ready for the commissioning of the facility by President Ibrahim Babangida sometime next month.

However, my day was slightly spoilt later when I got a fax message from Lagos telling me that the Dubbing Studio Manager who we employed from abroad to take care of our new Sound Dubbing Studio, was facing a serious problem in his efforts to acquire a visa for his trip to Nigeria. I immediately decided to send one of my officials to Abuja (Nigeria's new federal capital) to put pressure on the Director of Immigration to expedite the formalities.

Claude Maria Le Gallou is Head of Programming at ATRIA in Paris, an association devoted to the cause of the emerging African cinema:

Today starts with a working session with Souleymane Cissé and his English-speaking assistants, during which we need to finalise the budget and the working schedule for his film

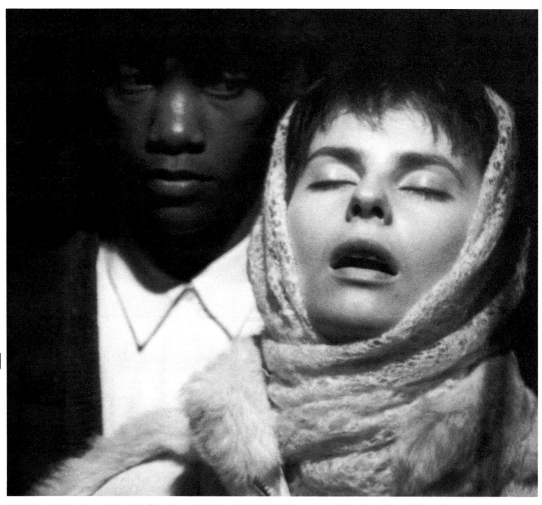

Still from Abderrahmane Sissako's Octobre, *funded by ATRIA in Paris, an association devoted to African cinema*

Waati. The second shooting period is about to begin (after Western Africa, Southern Africa will be the theatre of operations), and the setting up of that part of the shooting is long and difficult. The director is due to leave for Johannesburg, together with a small team, before the end of the month to finish the locating, the casting, the authorisations, etc. After we have concluded and finalised the meeting, we split up and I join the young Gabonese director, Paul Mouketa, whose docufiction film *Boston Tea Party* is in post-production and now being edited in one of the rooms at our Association. Together, we sum up his past three weeks of editing, and study his provisional budget for post-production so that we can write a new application for funds in order to complete the film. Then Paul goes back to his editor and editing room. Time is running out and, on June 18th, he has to go back to Gabon.

Lunchtime is a gathering of several directors and technicians in a small local Turkish restaurant. A lively and friendly break.

The afternoon takes place on the other side of River Seine, in a producer's studio. This time, we have to work on the setting up of a project on which we are co-producers; it is a series of nine African tales, *Yaa Tata*, by the Burkinese director Moustapha Dao. The project will be offered at first to TV channels, and we came here to talk about it with the producer. We also spent some of the afternoon discussing the animal characters with the person who will make the masks. The discussion is animated and one can feel that the project is taking shape.

Back in our offices, I check on the forthcoming festivals where several African films are due to be shown : Edinburgh, Turin, Locarno . . . I need to read the latest mail, confirm the conditions of screening, transport, provide the documentation.

This Festival sector takes much of our time at ATRIA, because all over the world, as in Europe, more and more of them wish to bring African cinema onto the screen.

To close the day, I concentrate more particularly on the two films, *Octobre* by Abderrahmane Sissako (Cannes 1993 *Un Certain Regard*) and *Rabi* by Gaston Kaboré, for which I am in charge of the circulation in very many festivals. These two very beautiful films are requested all over the place. Both already have a commercial distributor, but we are responsible for their presentation at festivals. [. . .]

I arrived at 10 A.M. in the morning and left at 9 P.M. at night. I enjoyed this day, contacts were just right, discussions went deeper, and I had the feeling that each of the productions was going ahead, with well-invested efforts.

A frustrated film-maker, Hashem El Nahas serves as Advisor to the Minister of Culture on Cinema Affairs in Egypt:

A car takes me to my new office at the Cultural Development Fund Office, opposite the Opera House [in Cairo]. A month ago, I was Chairman of the National Film Centre. After about three years of administrative work, I suffered from a severe migraine which required a month and a half of treatment, after which I moved to my new post.

Before I was Chairman of the Centre, I used to work as a documentary director (and made about thirty films). Over the past two years I have shot and edited two films, one on the ceramic artist Mohamed Mandour, and the other on the religious monuments of Cairo (Islamic, Coptic, and Jewish) worst hit by the earthquake last October. [. . .]

Now I am busy working on the arrangements for the Third International Documentary Film Festival and the Sixteenth Documentary and Short Films Festival in Ismailia, which will take place from July 15th to 19th. [During today] I called various people regarding the follow-up and confirmation of participation with films in the festival. [. . .] Contacted Dr. Mamdouh Al Biltagi, Chairman of the Public Information Office [. . .] for his approval of the printing of new copies of some old reels to show at the festival, in commemoration of the pioneer and founder of the *Egyptian Cinema Gazette*, Hasan Murad.

Called Andrea Morini, a friend and the official responsible for the archives in Bologna (Italy), to confirm his acceptance to attend the event as a member of the International Jury. [. . .]

Called the Chief Censor, Hamdi Sourour, to send representatives today to view the nominated films, together with the selection committeee, at Cinema Palace.

Wrote a memo to the Minister of Culture and requested his approval for the nomination of the National Jury and our final recommendations for the International Jury.

233 ◀◀

Dr. S.G. Samarasinghe is Chairman of the National Film Corporation of Sri Lanka, based in Colombo:

9.30 A.M. First day in office since my visit to Washington, Los Angeles and Hollywood. Summoned my fourteen executives in the National Film Corporation of Sri Lanka and explained my mission abroad and the experience gained. [. . .]

11 A.M. I was called to the Parliament to meet the Hon. Prime Minister and the Hon. Minister of Cultural Affairs and Information, to discuss the sale of the NFC's headquarters building to the Iranian Embassy. I explained that in the event the sale goes through, I should be given sufficient time to build a new office to provide accommodation for my officers. [. . .]

4 P.M. Met the Hon. Minister of Cultural Affairs and Information and briefed him about my trip abroad. He was happy that I was successful in giving publicity to the first-ever Film Location project initiated in Sri Lanka with the involvement of the NFC. He further added that there are a few outstanding issues concerning the NFC which should be settled soon, and he asked me to prepare a Cabinet Paper.

13. From Stars to Stand-Ins: The Actors

FROM STARS TO STAND-INS, THE ACTORS ENDOW
THE WRITER'S AND DIRECTOR'S CHARACTERS WITH
FLESH AND BLOOD. OFTEN THEY DO NOT ENTER A
PROJECT UNTIL JUST BEFORE SHOOTING BEGINS.
SOME WILL REFUSE PROPOSALS FOR MONTHS IN
ORDER TO WORK WITH A FAVOURED DIRECTOR,
OR TO LAND A HOLLYWOOD ROLE. FOR MANY,
HOWEVER, A SUITABLE EPITAPH MIGHT READ:
"THEY ALSO SERVE, WHO ONLY STAND AND WAIT."

Sir Anthony Hopkins, winner of the Academy Award for Best Actor on *The Silence of the Lambs*, quickly followed *Howards End* and *The Remains of the Day* with *Shadowlands*:

It is the middle of the 7th week of shooting on *Shadowlands*, with Richard Attenborough directing and Debra Winger as my co-star.

Picked up from home at 7 A.M. and driven to Shepperton Studios. I am not needed on the set until around midday but I must have my hair re-coloured for continuity. Went on set at noon to catch the end of a hospital X-ray scene that Debra was doing and to say goodbye to her as she left for a long weekend in Scotland.

Lined up and rehearsed a scene in which the doctor (Peter Firth) tells Jack Lewis (me) that my wife (Debra Winger) is in remission from cancer.

We broke for lunch and I went to see rushes to see the previous day's scene involving Debra and me in which Jack Lewis talks about God and marriage. I had played the scene as if I were slightly drunk. Richard Attenborough had agreed to do this and it seemed to work. [. . .]

After lunch Richard said that we might have to re-shoot the scene as Brian Eastman (producer) felt it was wrong. He has a point and we plan to re-shoot, although Richard says he will keep the two versions available in case the film gets bogged down. So, we must re-shoot – no big deal.

We got down to the afternoon's shooting. Hospital scenes with Peter Firth – two scenes, two takes per scene. All seemed to go well and we had a relaxed and jokey afternoon finishing at 7 P.M.

I am home by 7.45 P.M. for a light supper (the weather is still very hot) and a quiet evening at home playing the piano. I watched the news on television at 10 o'clock, then went straight to bed for another early call tomorrow. **99**

Meanwhile another distinguished British director, Nicolas Roeg, is filming Joseph Conrad's *Heart of Darkness* in Belize. Patrick Ryecart features in the film, and sends a final day's diary from the location:

66 Supposed to be flying home today. However, another early call followed by a trek through the Belizian bush in the actors' van, having still after five weeks not conquered the problem of whether it is better to have a bite of breakfast before leaving at 6 A.M. and risk regurgitating it over the driver's neck as a result of the local road maintenance, or to risk the caterer's 'bum' on arrival between 7 and 8 A.M., and an essential hundred-yard sprint through the snake and jaguar infested jungle leaving a bemused director – Nic Roeg – wondering what happened during the middle of the first rehearsal.

235 «

Top right: *John Malkovich in* Heart of Darkness. Above: *Tim Roth in the same film*

A quick glance at the morning sun is a reminder that by 11 A.M. we'll be up in the 90's. A quick glance at the daily 'sides' or sheets of script to be shot today is a reminder that one should no longer refer to the original screenplay, and a quick glance at the call sheet is a reminder that one's trailer is stacked with bits of paper that could serve a far more useful purpose than that intended.

The only solution, then, is to have another cup of Guatamalan coffee, which one knows is the cause of these discomforts, and to do major battle with one's costume, or frock, as we English like to call it, which by now is standing up on its own in the corner looking at me stiff with sweat and filth, having remained unwashed for a month due to 'continuity' reasons. This, I gather, is termed 'method' costuming in the U.S., and is a shortcut to destroying any friendly associations one may have made with the crew. A one-inch coating of 'jungle jelly' anti-bite cream follows and the glamorous side of the day is over until tomorrow. Replaced by a hardworking bonhomie, a tough day, and a director for whom we would fall in the river (and frequently do) – if only for the sake of that frock. 99

Also on remote location, if somewhat closer to home, Mick Lally reports from the northwest of Ireland:

66 I am in County Donegal working on *The Secret of Roan Inish* by the American writer and director John Sayles. The film is being made in a place called Rosbeg, a beautiful, wild, mountainous area, full of bays, inlets, and white sandy beaches with clean unpolluted seas. I won't describe how to get here as it is too complicated and in any case they get plenty of tourists as it is. One area, Narin, has quite an eyesore of chalets, mobile homes, and caravans already; abandoned, as it were, in the dunes along the broad, winding, sandy beach. [. . .]

In any case it is wonderful working here, in particular to be working with John Sayles. He has

Sean Penn starred with Al Pacino in Carlito's Way, *directed by Brian De Palma*

a very fine knowledge of, and feel for, the social context of the film – coastal life on the western seaboard in the 1940s and periods prior to that. He seems to have read widely on the matter. He is especially conversant with those classics of Irish folk literature, *The Islandman*, *Peig Sayers*, *Twenty Years a-Growing*; the writings of Liam O. Flaherty, and that wonderful book by David Thompson, *The People and the Sea*. The fruits of this reading is evident in the accuracy of the dialogue he gives to his characters, unlike the nonsense put into our mouths by some other overseas writers and directors from time to time. **,,**

Roger Moore with the late Audrey Hepburn

Taylor Nichols, an American actor involved in Whit Stillman's *Barcelona*, writes from Spain:

,, For the past few days I've been acting with a 'coma patient.' I've never seen Chris so quiet; it's rather pleasant really. Actually, it will be good to move out of the hospital scenes; the set is cramped and a bit depressing.

Working on *Barcelona*, a politically charged story in a foreign country, with a cast and crew from all over the world, has been an eye-opener. Many people really do dislike Americans, or maybe it's just me. One of the most interesting aspects of being in Spain is reading and hearing about the U.S., *not filtered through* the American press.

Today I spoke four different languages, although none very well. I'm getting pretty good at communicating my needs to the crew with my hands. The language barriers have slowed us a little, but with Carlos learning such 'excellent' English slang, we should be up to speed soon.

The days have been long. Some day I'd like to return to Barcelona when there is time to see some sights. **,,**

Sean Penn, actor (*Colors*, *Casualties of War*) and neophyte director (*The Indian Runner*), describes himself as having "deep wrinkles in eyes, good bounce in feet":

,, Got to work. Put on the clothes. The boys put on my face and [makeup]. Walked on to the set [of *Carlito's Way*], heard 'Action!', said and heard etc. Back to trailer. By the way: are Yugoslavian babies allowed to be killed while

we're rolling? If so, does that diminish what we do? Enhance what we do? Just a thought, to which my best answer on this tenth day of June is – we'd better give it our best.

Cut, wrap, adios amigos. **,,**

Roger Moore, forever linked in the minds of successive generations with The Saint and James Bond, awakes in his home in St. Paul de Vence, on the French Riviera:

,, The usual early start to the day – 45 minutes of exercise. No tennis today. I spoke with Lewis Gilbert regarding *Annie and the Castle of Terror* that Bill Nestel had sent me from Rastar Productions. I told him I liked it and would be happy to play Daddy Warbucks. I said I would be speaking later in the day with my agent.

I flew to London on BA 343. Contacted Gene Feldman of Wombat Productions at the St. James's Court Hotel. Will be shooting in the hotel on Friday morning; I am hosting a special about Audrey Hepburn & UNICEF for PBS (did the interviews in New York six weeks ago).

David Wardlow, my agent, called. I talked to Sherry Lansing at Paramount – no writer set yet for *The Saint*. The situation should be resolved in ten days – she said.

Called UNICEF to finalise plans for the concert at Drury Lane Theatre on July 4th with Sir Peter Ustinov. [. . .] Spoke with Bob Baker, my partner in TRI Productions, and told him of my

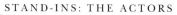

conversation with Sherry and Bill MacDonald. Bill thought we could have Sharon Stone as Simon E. Templar! Leslie Charteris had said it could be a son or daughter!

Tatsuya Nakadai, along with Toshiro Mifune, represents the finest traditions of acting in the Japanese cinema. Memorable in films such as *The Seven Samurai*, *The Human Condition*, *Harakiri*, and *Kwaidan*, he continues to appear before the cameras:

I have just finished shooting the fourteenth episode of a drama series for NHK TV. I haven't appeared in many TV dramas, so I was really relieved. They require a toughness from you which is quite different from what's needed in a film by Kurosawa or Kobayashi. For movies you need your sensitivity, energy and vitality to make one film. For TV dramas you have to be strong enough to keep up with their pace. As I have been brought up in the world of film, I'm used to the sensitive ruggedness they demand.

In this TV drama series my role was the main character of an elderly retired man. He observes his life and the people around him in the golden sunset of his life. We had a wonderful reaction from many viewers and I felt it was an invaluable part. In the cinema, my new film *Moonlight Summer*

238

Above: *Tatsuya Nakadai.*
Right: *Roger Moore working for UNICEF in Guatemala*

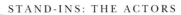

Above: *The sun rises in* Last Song, *featuring Hidetaka Yoshioka (seen also* right*)*

will be released tomorrow. I was interviewed by newspapers and other media. This is a sad war story based on the true episode of two young pilots who visited a primary school in a small town to play their last piano performance of Beethoven's Moonlight Sonata one day before they flew to their deaths as Kamikaze pilots in the summer of 1945. [. . .] I think we have to make such a picture in order to tell the story of a tragic war to the younger generation who have never known real war in Japan. [. . .]

For the first time in 19 years I will play the part of Shakespeare's Richard III [from the end of August]. The older I get the harder it becomes for me to memorise the lines. I spent almost half a day reading through the script and the directions in preparation for the performance.

Hidetaka Yoshioka, at 22, belongs to a new generation of Japanese screen actors:

5.04 A.M. Sunrise. With about sixty crew members I have been waiting for the sunrise since 2.30 A.M. It was the sixth morning since I came to Hakata in Kyushu for shooting [on *Last Song*]. This scene was originally planned to be shot in the morning five days earlier, but no sun was visible at sunrise due to cloud cover. I returned to the hotel, took breakfast early, and went back to sleep. On location we respect the day's weather most of all. We look up at the sky as if we were worshipping God. Today we are worried about a slightly overcast sky but we are preparing to shoot in bright conditions because the stars are shining. I am picked out by several huge lights. Many people's voices echo quietly on the shore. They carefully run through the numerous camera tests while it gradually grows brighter. Preparations are complete. Around 4.30 A.M. the atmosphere is perfect for a sunrise. We wait for the sun to appear. It becomes still again on the shore, with only the echo of the waves to be heard. At 5.04 A.M. the sun emerges. I hear the order, 'Start!' The sun is really monstrous at sunrise, and it fascinates me. The director says, 'OK.' I light my cigarette and look at the sun for a while on my own. Then I make a prayer: 'I would like to dedicate my film *Last Song* to my friend, who is like the sunrise to me. I hope the sunrise today will be the sunrise for my film!'

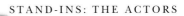

Japanese actor Masaya Kato finds himself ready to appear in a new film in Australia:

❝ I have come to Australia to star in a feature film entitled *Seventh Floor*, a co-production between Japan, Australia, and the U.K.

10.30 A.M. Rice. One hour training at the gym.

1.30 P.M. A lunch meeting with the director Ian Barry. We discuss my character in the film, in particular the fact that my character lived in Australia from the age of ten for many years before returning to Japan and again coming back to Australia. Therefore, to establish this scenario we must also establish my character's English accent.

6.30 P.M. I saw the American film, *Sliver*. Although totally coincidental, there are surprising similarities with *Seventh Floor*.

10.30 P.M. I called the producer to talk about *Sliver*. He had also seen it; however, he pointed out that the basic concept is totally different, so there was nothing to worry about. Instead, we agreed to make a great film despite the fact that *Sliver*'s budget was so much higher. ❞

» 242

Li Baotian won China's Hundred Flowers Award for Best Actor in 1992 (in *New Year*), and sends this ruminative diary on the film-maker's craft:

❝ The greater part of [*The Phoenix's Harp*] has already been shot. Frankly, much of it is unsatisfactory. This film can never be an exemplary work truly reflecting rural life. Vivid, realistic details have been turned into trivial, common objects of ridicule, passionate and imaginatively written scenes have become vague and insipid through affectation. This is all very different to my expectations of the film when I first read the script.

I admit there is always a discrepancy between expectation and reality. As far as this film is concerned, I am deeply disappointed because I feel certain mistakes could have been avoided. Although they are not of my making, they still fill me with dismay and regret.

A perfect film can be likened to a pail of clear water – a rarity in itself. As Goethe said,

Li Baotian directing children on The Phoenix's Harp

Jiang Wen (left) on the set of In the Heat of the Sun

'Perfection is the yardstick of the gods. Attempting to achieve perfection is the yardstick of man.' Film-making is like the act of pouring water into the pail. It's an inspiration of the moment, a fleeting subtlety of feeling. When you translate it into form or shape, it's difficult to portray incisively or vividly, without distortion. What we've left out are like the most precious, most beautiful droplets that trickle down your fingers as you pour the water into the pail. That's why our film has become a 'regrettable art.' [. . .]

The difference between a pail of clear water and one that is forever difficult to fill with clear water is like the difference between idealism and reality. But it is precisely this unattainable perfection that lures me into my unending pursuit of splendour and inspiration, to surpass mediocrity and blandness.

This is the beauty of film, the beauty of art, the beauty of life itself.

Jiang Wen surged to the fore as an actor in Zhang Yimou's *Red Sorghum* in 1987, for which he received the Best Actor prize at the Hundred Flowers Awards. Now he applies his experience to casting, for his first film behind the camera:

Casting actors, still casting actors. This will be my first attempt at directing. The story's about the love between five boys and two girls. The main character has to be portrayed at three different ages between 1969 and 1993 – 12, 17, and 37 years of age. When I was still writing the script I felt elated. But now the headaches are beginning. Where will I find all these people with the same faces? Each male role needs three actors. Then there are the two actresses. I have to find ten actors altogether.

My God! I am actually facing two boys who look exactly like me (I'll be acting the part of the

37-year-old man). Am I looking into two different-sized mirrors? They even blink rapidly like I do. It's the same with the other two groups of actors. All of a sudden, I'm overcome with joy, because we've got the right people for the film. But we're only halfway there. Finding them means that my script is no longer black ink on white paper, but has come to life and is **99** bubbling with energy.

Renay Dantzler – actress, dancer, voice-over artiste – prefers being on a movie or TV set than any other form of work:

66 As I woke up this morning I reflected on last weekend. Working on the film *Twilight of the Dogs*. This is my second on-screen performance. I'm a dancer on a local show which I thoroughly enjoy. But acting is my first love.

This film is directed by John Ellis, the man behind *Invaders*. I'm just an extra, playing a cult member. As a black actress, there are only a few parts you can play. This movie is a white cult film so I had to play a part that was more suitable for someone of my skin colour. But I don't really mind at all. This film gave me an opportunity to learn a lot. My role is a small one but the joy of just participating in the art is one I love immensely.

I will be back on the set in two days. We will film at a sand and gravel area. We will do scenes where some people will get killed and shot at. Also in this part of the film the 'Alien-Woman' will offer us milk from a cow to save us. I think this is wild and crazy but I'm not a writer, just an aspiring actress. My feelings about this business vary. We need more black films, or more films in **99** which black people can easily be cast.

Ezzatollah Entezami has been an actor and stage director in Iran for more than half a century. His diary conveys the physical pressures an actor must so often undergo:

66 I am playing the role of a ghost in a film [*Day of the Angel*] which is now shooting. In one scene I enter an operating theatre in a hospital where my own body is being given electric shock treatment. To shoot that scene I had to sit on a spider crane and bend so that I could touch

my toes. The camera was trained on my head only so that I would be shown 'hovering' in space. My old backache began again, and when I reached home later I couldn't move at all. I can barely walk, and moving even a few yards is an extremely painful exercise for me. I try to bear the pain and finish the film. But I totter and bend in agony in the middle of shooting. I get wet with perspiration and my makeup has to be renewed.

The director had to halt shooting, although he was clearly not satisfied with the final take. When I reached home I wept in solitude. June 10th was unfortunately a bad day for me. After a 52-year career in stage and cinema this was a crashing blow to my pride. **99**

Alireza Khamseh, at 40, belongs to the middle generation of Iranian actors:

66 After two days of rest at home, I set out today for the ancient and beautiful city of Isfahan where shooting began ten days ago on *The Eye of the Devil*. Having experienced centuries of attacks by barbarians, and having survived many bloody wars, Isfahan stands proudly ready to receive all lovers of art and beauty. [. . .]

I am acting the role of a man who came to this city about a hundred years ago in search of a diamond called 'The Eye of the Devil.'

Time hastens its furtive step through our midst while we, having listened to the footsteps of life through the rough passage of history, cast away the dusty mantle of the years and try to effect a **99** revival in Isfahan with the magic of cinema.

Chin Su-Mei, the Taiwanese actress, created a superb impression in *The Wedding Banquet*, which shared the Golden Bear at the Berlin Film Festival in 1993:

66 When I got up this morning I found four pimples on my face, which made me a little vexed. But every single day has been so busy. It's no surprise I'm getting pimples. I only pray there won't be any close-ups.

The location for *Mei-chen* is in Chi Hsiang Camp. To avoid traffic jams, I and my assistant start out early. We happen to bump into the director, Lin Chia-chang, on the way. He tells me

Chin Su-Mei, the Taiwanese actress (left and above), in scenes from May Jane

his assistant is a fast and steady driver, so I jump into his car when the lights turn red. As soon as I get in, he starts describing all the shots he's worked out with great animation and how he's going to execute each one. The experience and energy he demonstrates have an overwhelming effect on me. I quickly flick through my four pages, then close my eyes and try to relax in the hope that after a bit of thought I'll be able to act my part better.

It's been raining heavily all night and all day. Over a hundred costumes have been soaked through, and water can still be wrung out of them. The wooden bridge behind the house has collapsed. The scene at the location is like a bad omen. Because it's still early and not many actors have arrived, we cannot start filming. The director thinks we may as well get some practice, so he teaches us how to put expression into our voices and tells us about synchronised filming. He speaks excitedly, and we all respond with enthusiasm. The atmosphere starts to liven up. I know we have to start work.

The first scene is of my watching my husband being carried away after he's been blown up by a bomb. I stand alone in the square in a fixed position. The workers busy themselves with their own things and nobody takes any notice of me. I can-

not hold back my emotions. I remember the pain of my husband's death in yesterday's scene, of my father abandoning me the day before and, worst of all, of my mother dying and leaving me. But I have no more tears. But then, what does crying prove? As the director says, real sadness has no tears. Tears appear only at the most worthwhile moment when a task has been completed. I'm exhausted. I stand there with the camera directed at my husband lying dead in the middle of the square. All the weight of the pain is on me. After this scene is finished, I'm absolutely worn out. But I know that this kind of emotion must last for the rest of the day, because Mei-chen lived through her life in perpetual sorrow. **99**

Carolyn Walker, like many professional actors and actresses, takes extra work between assignments. When the film involved is directed by John Waters, the drudge may be worthwhile:

66 This is the third day of jury duty on John Waters' new film, *Serial Mom*. What a great day! I'm in Baltimore staying with a friend. I'm from Philadelphia. [. . .]

We're first on camera so I've got to get to wardrobe and makeup right away. With the heat

247 ◀◀

and the third day of wearing the same outfit, our clothes could run to the nearest wash. Kathleen Turner and Sam Waterston are playing husband and wife in this film, and Riki Lake and Matthew Lilliard are their children. The word is that Suzanne Sommers will be in tomorrow. This scene is to shoot our reactions to Kathleen's cross-examination of the witness, Mink Stole. During the scene she turns to her husband for his reaction.

The courtroom is filled with producers, crew, John Waters, and Pat Moran, the casting director.

John is pleased with what he sees, so we move on to the next set-up – Kathleen's reaction to the juror wearing the white shoes, Patty Hearst. I'm sitting behind Patty.

I didn't get a contract for this film so I took extra work. It helps that John says 'there are no extras on my films, only actors.' By the way he directs you, and gets close-ups on camera, you feel like a featured player.

It's great to be busy in the business. My beeper goes off. Yes, it's my agent. I return the call, and learn that she's submitting me for a part. A sitcom . . . how I'd love to do a sitcom. [. . .]

With this new camera angle, the jury will be going in last to get all our reactions to the 'crazy witnesses.' I'm beginning to wonder where the prosecutor hangs out. It's a wrap at 9.30 P.M. What a long day!

Karl Otter, an extra on the same film on the same day, remains less enthusiastic:

66 Extra work can be frequently degrading, depending on the subject. It is the lowest level of the caste system that exists in the American film industry. Hollywood liberalism amounts to lip service in this limited universe called a film set. There is a coldness here today. I am a piece of furniture that moves. I spend a lot of time computing my earnings for the day, convinced that I am only here for the money. Why work as an extra? This isn't acting. This isn't work. But you earn every penny, cooped up in a waiting area, without control, subjugated, losing track of time and place. But this is what I do. This is where I want to be. It is my contribution to film on this day. Am I crazy for being here? Yes. 99

Leah Foley, British actress, model, and former dancer, works as a stand-in for Andie MacDowell on *Four Weddings and a Funeral*:

66 Today the location is the Dôme Café, Covent Garden, so along with the London sights I guess we will be the highlight of the day for many a tourist and passer-by. I arrived at the location at 7 A.M. to find a young, fairly well-dressed yuppy type sitting in a doorway, drinking a bottle of Moët & Chandon from a proper champagne flute! This was quite a contrast with the numerous homeless people asleep in their doorways along the Strand. I felt quite sad before the day had even begun.

My two male colleagues, John and Steve, are old pros at this work – wear light, wear dark, hat on, hat off, glasses on, glasses off. [. . .]

Westminster City Council won't allow rain machines today but somehow with hoses the director, Mike Newell, achieves the right effect. I'm quite happy today as we finished at a reasonable hour and as we're all on a deal it can get a bit tense! When the recession lifts will the deals still stay? I wonder. [. . .] Tomorrow we are in Greenwich. It's a wrap and Mike's last words are, 'Tomorrow you will all wish you had never been born.' I just can't wait! 99

Self-confidence is vital to an actor, but many performers will envy the degree of assurance exuded by Sabiha Khanum, the veteran Pakistani actress:

66 Exactly 44 years ago I started my career, on the stage in June 1949, in an historical play. Film offers started pouring in and my film career was launched. It is still in progress, and I cannot remember a single film in which I played a lead role that was not a hit at the box-office. I won my first Best Actress award in *Promise* in 1955. This was the first Pakistani film to be screened in London, in 1958; the British press gave me glowing tributes and I and my late husband, the famous star Santosh Kumar, were taken to see Pinewood Studios to watch the shoot-

Sabiha Khanum, the veteran Pakistani screen actress who started her career exacly 44 years ago

Anoja Weerasinghe (left) discussing the music score with her composer

ing of *The Captain's Table*. Our interview with the local press and TV made headlines when we were asked about the depiction of love scenes in Pakistani films and responded that love scenes and kisses take place not on the screen but off it.

I won the Best Actress award almost every year. The feather in my cap is the Best Actress prize I won at the Moscow Film Festival of 1977 in the film *One More Sin*. [. . .] I have appeared in more than 200 films, and can easily claim to have remained the most popular and well-known actress in Pakistan. **"**

Anoja Weerasinghe is a an actress from Sri Lanka who has appeared in Paul Cox's film, *Island*:

" At the moment I am producing a film and at the same time appearing as the main actress. I have to be very thin, so am starving to death. Had my tea in bed at 5.30 A.M. Haven't heard from my husband for days. His phone (up country) is not working. Good to start the day by writing a letter to Paul Cox about this diary. He is an honorary patron of the project. Dear Paul, one of the most beautiful men I have ever met. [. . .]

By 10.30 A.M. I had a meeting with Mr. Khemadasa (one of the great music composers) and Mr. Anthony Jackson, director of my film. We had a long discussion about music in our film *The Character of Juliet*. It's a wonderful part to play. It is also a big challenge, and I'm getting frightened. In this film I am acting as a romantic, mentally unbalanced, sophisticated film actress whose life ends in tragedy just like Juliet's in Shakespeare's play. I have to prepare myself a lot. By birth I am a villager; I still speak and behave like one, so I have a lot to do and learn.

In the evening I went to dancing class – two hours non-stop preparation for the part. After the class I went home. So tired. Read my fan mail. Felt so good under the shower. **"**

Anoja Weerasinghe leading a class in acting in Sri Lanka

In Melbourne, Australia, American actor Joshua Lucas describes with tongue in cheek the joys of shooting a Western Down Under – *The Man from Snowy River*.

❝ It began like any other day. I woke up groggy with one eye hurting. The clock read 5.30 A.M. Little did I know that I would be forgotten about by an absent-minded assistant director and could have slept an extra hour. [. . .] Finally I was whisked to set by an angry production runner who was supposed to be asleep. Arriving on set I found myself on top of a small mountain overlooking the flatlands of 1890s Australia (with a simple adjustment of the camera to hide the buildings and power lines). It was cold. It was windy. It was magnificent. Huge rolling clouds swept across the tops of the gum trees as the tall grass whistled with the anticipation of being inevitably destroyed by a movie crew.

A horse laughed in the distance as I stepped into my trailer and began to put on the layers of suede that made my character, 'Luke.' Stepping out, I completed the transformation by strapping on my six-gun and crowning my head with more suede. My spurs jingled as I hit the ground in search of some food, when suddenly the apologetic A.D. handed me a steaming plate of eggs. My next challenge was to eat while mounting a horse made insane by the wind. [. . .]

After much discussion with the director and script supervisor, it was decided that I would only make a cameo appearance in the scene and my lines were dealt out to other characters. And off I was to wait for my cue. It was a simple gallop, nod of the head, and gallop off. However, the horse wanted to practise standing on two legs. After numerous takes interrupted by quick discipline lessons for the horse, the scene was finished and we were on to the next set-up. ❞

251 ◀◀

14. Behind the Cameras As technology and special effects become more complex, so the credit roll at the end of a film takes longer and longer to unfurl. Yet since the earliest days of the cinema, the technicians have out-numbered their other colleagues on a movie set or location, and once shooting is com-plete, they essentially assume responsibility for the production's success. These entries cover a huge diversity of skills.

»252

Vittorio Storaro has enriched the work of Francis Ford Coppola (*Apocalypse Now, One from the Heart*), Warren Beatty (*Reds, Dick Tracy*), and all the recent films by Bertolucci. His eloquent diary, abridged here only for space reasons, reveals the questing mind behind the camera:

❝ The first image that appears in my precon-sciousness at 4.15 in the morning (as usual-ly happens to me the first day of a new experi-ence) is a painting of an Orientalist of the last cen-tury about a camel caravan near the ancient Roman ruins of Palmyra. It was during my pho-tographic research for *The Sheltering Sky* that I was looking at the art of some travelling painters, and I didn't know at that time that one day I would be able to enter into one of those painted images.

A few hours later, at 7 o'clock exactly, the alarm clock goes off. My dream is still echoing in my head while I dress for the day's work. At this particular time in the morning, like I have done in many other hotel rooms, it is very important for me to transfer images that I was dreaming into some figurative ideas of the present assignment. The last movements before going out are usually the choice of my scarf's colour in relation to the mood of the sequence – this morning red – and the unconscious move of my right hand, that automat-ically signs myself before turning the door's lock.

The arrival on set is bathed by the very warm colour of the eastern sun, by the warm 'good morning' and the usual smile from the crew (my grips, electricians and camera crew have been almost the same for over 35 films), by the embrace with director Luigi Bazzoni, the shaking hands with

Vittorio Storaro (centre) on location in the Syrian ruins of Palmyra

producer Giacomo Pezzali, on set for the first day of shooting, by the usual 'vestizione:' the dressing up of the light meter, radio, and viewfinder. I don't remember how many light meters I changed in my life; recently each project has had its own. During the walk towards the first possible camera position, a little smile appears on my face as I imagine which title will be written on the last light meter of my career as a cinematographer.

The present one is *Roma: Imago Urbis*, a multimedia project about the history of Roman culture. The two episodes we are facing now are:

Vittorio Storaro on location for Roma: Imago Urbis

Le Opere and *Le Vie*. They are taking us in exploration of testimonies of Rome all around Europe, the Middle East and North Africa, like the ancient archaeologists. Now we are at Palmyra, Syria, one of the most spectacular places of the ancient world. A desert city of vast columnated streets, lavishly decorated tombs, carving stones and imposing temples, which combines late Hellenist, Parthian and Roman traditions on a scale unmatched in the classical era.

We start filming a portion of the 12th episode [*Le Opere*] from the Arch of Hadrian and dolly after dolly the movie shows its face. Only the sound of the steps of the camera grip can be heard between rolls and cuts. Shoot after shoot, with the sun turning above our heads, I continue my journey with it as usual. Finally we arrive at the main event of the day: the huge Roman theatre, situated very close to the mountain with the Valley of the Tombs behind; it is waiting its own actors to play the spectacle of the day.

My main photographic concept for this episode is inspired by the journey of the sun, from its different moments of: aurore-dawn-morning-day-afternoon-sunset-dusk. The sun was the symbol of Rome – the conquest of cultural light over the barbarian darkness. It emerged from the black night to start a parallel life with the city itself. With its own edification, Rome puts itself in the history of an ancient splendour, building in the solar light its own story on what was, at that time, the known world. I'm continuously checking the position of the sun in the sky, measuring its intensity with the light meter; the main idea is to leave only the stage illuminated by the last beams of the sun's rays. While the sun is lowering on the horizon, while the colour of its beams is changing in front of my eyes, the ancient fear of the loss of the father figure – the sun – takes me once again, like in any sunset moment. A feeling of loneliness is surrounding me when suddenly I scream 'Ready.' The area of the camera position, where everybody is waiting, starts to animate itself. The director says 'Roll,' and very gently the camera enters

the cavea of the theatre, revealing the beautiful scenery built in two different orders of columns. The words cut, check cameras, wrap, follow.

More than usual, after any wrap of my life, I feel the tension of the day going in a moment through my entire body. I sit on a step of the theatre looking at the last beam of conscious sunlight, waiting for another, different, unconscious light that I'm sure will come on the stage from the mother figure: the moon. Like every dusk, I'm assisting at the magic moment of an impossible marriage, right there in front of my eyes, in the sky, between two eternal lovers – the sun and the moon – always together, eternally apart. But in the continuous run behind each other, they are giving us their own energy – natural and artificial, direct and reflected, warm and cold, conscious and unconscious – that gives us the balance that we need. Recently I have come to wish, more and more in a conscious way, for the possible union of these two different energies, these two different parts of ourselves, for a possible conclusion to this love story between sun and moon. I'm still waiting for it.

Few directors of photography have a more illustrious list of credits than the Italian, Giuseppe Rotunno. Since 1954, when he shot certain scenes on *Senso* after the death of G.R. Aldo, he has enhanced the work of Visconti, Fellini, Altman, and others:

Early in the morning I went to a location recce at Tapia Park at the 884 Las Virgenes Calabas, 49 minutes north of Los Angeles. There I met with Mike Nichols, director of *Wolf*, together with some members of the crew in order to make some decisions about scenes involving Jack

255

Giuseppe Rotunno (left) on the set of Wolf, *with Jack Nicholson*

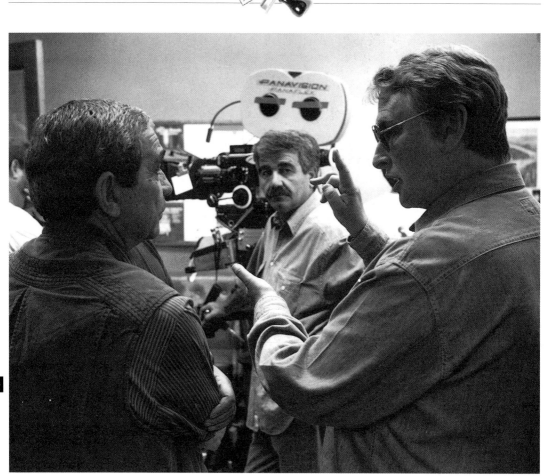

Giuseppe Rotunno (left) with Mike Nichols during the shooting of Wolf

Nicholson and a deer, to be shot day for night.

Immediately after the scouting, I went back to the Columbia lot to view the process dailies shot on stage: interiors, different cars just to simulate movement. Most of the results were good except for a night shot taken in the mountains day for night with a back and two side plates. There was an excess of colour – too much blue and purple together, but visible to the naked eye before the final process. I was upset that due to the lack of time and pressure on the production, we did not have the chance to test the technical instruments needed for this kind of shooting. The tests could have assisted us in the printing of those special plates in the best way possible.

After the screening of the dailies we went to stage #15 to continue shooting [. . .] scenes with Kate Nelligan, Michelle Pfeiffer, and Jack Nicholson. Everything has been going according to plan, and we can say that I really spent this Thursday, June 10th, immersed in the movie world. **99**

Felix Monti is one of the finest cinematographers at work in Latin America. An Argentinian, he has shot films for Luis Puenzo (*The Official Version*), Fernando Solanas, and María Luisa Bemberg:

66 The alarm clock goes off. It's 5 A.M. Autumn is ending and it is cold. From the window I can see a great blanket of mist covering everything. Today is not just one more day in my life as a photographer, for I have to go to the opening of one of my favourite films, *A Wall of Silence* – the first feature by a great friend, Lita Stantic.

Forty km outside the city, we are filming *Living Together*, directed by Carlos Galletini. [. . .] On the

Still from Lita Stantic's Wall of Silence

set I meet up with my gaffer, Jorge Fernández. It is a complicated scene. The action takes place in a big living room, in a real house. It is not a comfortable place for us to work in. The ceilings are low and the sound technician decided to put in isolating panels which will lower the ceiling still more. We have two windows, through which, supposedly, light should filter. Behind us the FX team is working, spreading hoses and fans around the house. The scene must have wind and rain. The film deals with two men locked up together, alone with their memories, during a fierce storm. [. . .]

The assistant director asks how much longer we need. I talk to him about the cramped space, the depth of field, the movement of the camera. He goes off depressed. Jorge and I continue to get an '8' diaphragm. It is a good exposure but even then Soledad has to control the space between the

actors. We have brought the Light. Soledad and Albertina, the assistant camera operators, work on the cart. The director, a friend of many years' standing, and the actors, begin to take over the ground that up to then had been our terrain alone. [. . .]

It is almost nightfall. The last takes of the day. Luckily the wide-angle shots have been completed and with them our major worries are over. The director shouts the final 'Cut!' The hoses that faked the rain are turned off. Our lights are slowly lowered. Everything becomes dark and cold again. Someone turns on another light so that the team can pack up their equipment. Then everyone retires to his or her own reality. We set off for the city for the opening [of Lita's film]. The projection booth seems to be a magician's workroom. Two old projectors and a projectionist as old as the equipment, who dreams of the cinema in the days of the great actors, when the theatres

were full. With Jorge, I correct and adjust everything that it is possible to correct and we stay up
there checking the lights. [. . .] In the distance,
amid the noise and the people, I see Lita, alongside some actors from the film. We're in the cabin.
The theatre lights go down. The noise stops suddenly; from here I can see the titles come up.

I think today we have brought together those
two unique moments – when, out of the darkness,
our lights begin to define the space of a scene and
when, in the darkness of the theatre, the **99**
light of the projector begins to tell a story.

**Peter Suschitzky's diary ruminates on
the uneven life of a cinematographer, from
the major films to the minor commercials,
and the risks involved in selecting each
new assignment:**

66 Today a movie which I shot last year
opened in London with reviews as bad as it
got in Los Angeles. *The Vanishing* probably set
itself up to be shot down, being a remake of a
much-praised Dutch film. Well, I hope that my
latest picture, *M. Butterfly*, directed by David
Cronenberg, will turn out really well.

I am packing my bags, for tomorrow I will
leave for Australia for ten days, in order to shoot
a commercial. At least shooting the occasional
commercial permits me to wait for a film that
might be worth shooting; the ones that are so rare
nowadays, and finding the right context for my
work is all important to me.

I have to 'grade,' or 'time' two projects in the
next month or so – *M. Butterfly*, and two half-hour
films which I shot recently with first-time directors Tom Cruise and Tom Hanks, so one of the
things that I must do before leaving is to contact
the production offices of these projects.

As I prepare for a journey of over 24 hours I
am going to have to decide whether or not to
accept a film which is being offered to me, to
shoot in Los Angeles. I think I will have to say no,
for I feel very uneasy about the quality of the
ingredients and I know from bitter experience
how unhappy one can be if one starts a film the

»258

Luis Brandoni and Jose Sacristan in Living Together,
directed by Carlos Gallentini (see Felix Monti diary)

context of which is not conducive to good work. So I will take a risk and say no, without having any other film in sight, but at least I will be available and not tied up on the wrong project. Weeks and perhaps months of uncertainty lie ahead – the usual fate of the film-maker! **"**

Jaromír Sofr, longtime colleague of Academy Award-winning director Jiří Menzel, prepares for their new film, *The Life and Extraordinary Adventures of Private Ivan Chonkin:*

" Above all I was concerned with the preparations for photographic tests the following day, when we would conduct exposure tests both interior and exterior. Most of the filming will be done on sets, featuring a Russian village at the beginning of the Second World War, which has been specially constructed for this film, about thirty miles northeast of Prague on the now abandoned base where the Soviet army had been stationed after the 1968 invasion.

The tests take place in wooden country buildings in different situations – at sunset, in a room lit by a paraffin lamp etc. We have already done some tests with actors in Moscow ten days ago, because most of the actors are Russian.

The precise atmospheric tests are necessary because the final colouring of the film material is going to be done in the lab. It is a technique which has the full support of Jiří Menzel and which I have already used on my two previous films as cinematographer. However, the changes then were made on the Kodak inter-negative; this time we are going to effect changes on the positive. Thus, when deciding the exposure, and the contrast on the negative, these elements must be taken into consideration.

At 9 A.M. I am discussing our technical requirements and the schedule in Synergia, the co-production office in Wenceslas Square. At 10.30 A.M. I have a meeting in the camera department at Barrandov Studios in order to check all the equipment for the following day. On the way to the studio I stop in the film lab to drop off two tests on Kodak professional Ektachrome 64T for development. After many years, just for my private fun, I am returning to still photography, using an

≫ 260

Jaromír Sofr (right) with Jiří Menzel on location for The Life and Extraordinary Adventures of Private Chonkin

Scene from Oliver Stone's Natural Born Killers, *on which diarist Ray Peschke was chief lighting technician*

old wooden camera from the last century. [. . .]

After a light lunch at my flat, at 1 P.M. I left for the location with Jiří Menzel in the studio car. We were going to survey the village set from a height of 60 feet, using a crane in order to establish how to get the best general views for the picture. This went well. Menzel recorded the best views himself with his camcorder. I don't own such a camera. **99**

Ray Peschke is chief lighting technician for Oscar-winning Robert Richardson on Oliver Stone's *Natural Born Killers*:

66 7 A.M. in Albuquerque, New Mexico's 'Old Town' section; and just another bizarre day on this, my fourth Oliver Stone film. We're starting to set up a scene in a famous souvenir store, the 'Covered Wagon,' which specialises in American Indian handicrafts, jewellery etc., and the lady shop-owner is freaking out about the laying of cables and the changing of fluorescents. She obviously has no idea what filmmaking preparation really entails, and we're just as surprised with her reaction as she is with us. If she only knew what was coming up!

After about an hour of setting up, Oliver begins his rehearsal with the actors. Soon he's ready to shoot. The camera used is a video Betamax set up in a far corner under the ceiling, creating the POV [point of view] of a surveillance camera. The lead characters, mass murderers Mickey and Mallory (Juliette Lewis and Woody Harrelson) storm the store armed to the teeth, kill anywhere between five and eight customers, rob the cashier, throw a hand grenade and then yell, 'Have a good day!' The shop is a mess with overthrown shelves, explosions, rounds of full loads and plenty of smoke. We wonder if the elderly shop-owner has keeled over somewhere after witnessing this spectacle – she's nowhere in sight.

After only a couple of takes, Oliver is satisfied to skip any coverage with 35mm. He and Bob Richardson have been known on this film to flip a coin as to what format to use to shoot a scene, so that every scene has a different, interesting look. We wrap the location around noon and move to the opposite side of town for another offbeat scene in this film which has been described in the local newspapers only as a $30 million 'satire.' **99**

A sheet creates a soft, bouncing light for cinematographer Kenji Takama (also right) on location for Here Comes a Duck's Song

» 262

The 'scope format has enjoyed a revival throughout the world in the past two years. Kenji Takama, a Japanese director of photography, writes from his mountain location:

❝ Today it is exactly one month since we began the location shooting on *Here Comes a Duck's Song*, the third film by Makoto Shiina, and the pale green of flowers and tree buds now covers the mountains of Oku Aizu in a bright green mantle. As the seasons change, the three baby ducks which escaped from Tokyo with the main character in this film have grown into adult birds. This is the first time I've worked in 'scope and I'm using a brand new type of lens called an Ariscope which is imported from Germany.

At the moment 'scope in Japan has only been used in the *Otoko Wa Tsuraiyo* series, and other related films, so that lens development stopped fifteen years ago. The Ariscope lens from Arriflex has excellent functions: sharpness of focus, contrast, easy reduction of distortion, but its size and weight are a big problem which will hopefully be resolved in the future. Today we shot in an empty house in a village that we converted into a restaurant as part of the set; I only used fluorescent lighting, including the ceiling lights which were already installed. I always try to use lighting in as simple a way as possible, and for the bonfire scenes I used the fire itself as a light source. I was very glad to know that Mr. Shiina was impressed with the rushes.

In the restaurant scene we needed it to rain outside, so our special effects team created artificial rain using fire hoses. But then it really started to rain outside. And two weeks ago while we were shooting scenes in the rain, it also began to rain. God up in heaven is helping our filming. We've got three more days of shooting left, and on the final day we're going to recreate the Ryujin Festival in this village, with the help of 700 extras. ❞

Peter Pilatian, a self-employed director/cameraman, underlines the need for assembling precisely the right equipment for a specific job:

❝ Woke up early with a plane to catch and too much to do before leaving for Milwaukee, Wisconsin, where I will film a documentary special for Showtime Television on the 90th anniversary of the Harley-Davidson Motorcycle Co. We expect the attendance of over 200,000 almost fanatical devotees, worshippers, and owners of America's only homemade motorcycle, virtually a sub-culture unto itself. [. . .]

Suddenly I am late for a last-minute camera preparation meeting at the production facility's office, but as I am about to leave the house a call comes in from an ad regarding a used Hi-8 video camera. (Dilemma: I just paid retail for a new one, specifically to use for insert shots in Milwaukee. I am leaving in three hours. Buying the used one instead will save me $600.00. What to do?)

Never mind. I race over to help extract a Sony Betacam 400 from its little overstuffed storage room in a badly-lit underground parking structure at the production company's office building. (Dilemma: My matte box doesn't work with the wide angle lens. What to do?) [. . .]

In the blink of an eye and squiggle of a pen I am in Milwaukee, being met at the airport by a van, talent co-ordinator etc. Once we wrangled all the camera equipment, things started slowing down. The Midwest is still the Midwest, and life moves along at a very reasonable pace.

Bikes (Harleys only) and Bikers are everywhere. Lined up side by side, they look like dominoes, ready to topple. Gleaming chrome, posturing tattooed, heavy-set, bearded all-American bikers, big-bosomed babes, bandanna-wrapped heads – these are the elements from which our crew will create a comedy special for the Showtime cable audience. I try to go to sleep by

midnight knowing that the next three days will be spent shooting with a hand-held Betacam that's heavier than my little 16mm Aaton. **"**

Allen Guilford, a New Zealand cameraman, spends the day waiting . . . and waiting:

" Yesterday I arrived here [in northern Japan] from Auckland, New Zealand, my home and base. I'm here to film Peter Bird as he rows his 29 foot boat through the Tsugaru Straits on his six-month trip, rowing alone from Russia to America. [. . .] He's due to pass through the Straits any day now, but won't stop. He'll keep on rowing towards California, about five months away. The French Argos satellite plots, faxed by Remy in Tokyo, show Peter about twenty miles away, as we make our way over from the hotel to the Hakodate City Hall for a pre-arranged press meeting and two fishing-boat captains. [. . .]

The two skippers are going out to fish and are happy to take us along as they'll be going right past Peter's latest position. I'll be able to film him, then we'll be put ashore nearby and hitchhike back or something. [. . .]

We spend the rest of the day zipping between floors [at the Maritime Safety Agency], drinking endless cups of tea, checking with Immigration,

Lone rower Peter Bird negotiates the Tsugaru Straits (see Allen Guilford's entry on this page)

Customs, Quarantine and Maritime Safety who are reasonably hopeful but all slightly bemused at this dodgey operation. [. . .]

The final satellite plot of the day is faxed to us late afternoon. Peter is still a day away from the Tsugaru Straits. With just a hint of frustration with our not speaking Japanese and some jet-lag on my part, we head back to the Fitness Hotel in downtown Hakodate. I leave the camera in my room with batteries on charge and we go out for an evening meal. 99

Suminda Weerasinghe, a Sri Lankan director of photography, records the details of a long day's shooting on _Shocked_:

66 Today we shot the cart sequence during daylight and the kidnapping sequence up to 11 P.M. (We are shooting this feature film, _Shocked_, at Tissamaharamaya, a small town 268 km from Colombo.) For the night sequence I used very low light level, 8 f.c. key. I planned to push the XT-320 stock used for this particular sequence.

Directed by Chandraratha Mapitigara, _Shocked_ is a low-budget movie even by local standards. We planned to complete shooting in three weeks. Today is our twelfth day, and we are still on schedule. Our stock is limited to 30 x 400 cans of Agfa XT-125 and 20 x 400 cans of Agfa XT-320. At the end of the shoot we will send our exposed stock to India for processing and rush printing. It will take at least another three weeks to come back. Only then can we view the rushes.

I have very limited facilities as D.O.P. on this film. My usual crew is one camera assistant (focus puller and loader), one gaffer, and four grips. But I think we must help and encourage low-budget film-makers for the sake of the industry. 99

Elmer Bernstein's film scores are legendary, from _The Man with the Golden Arm_ to _The Magnificent Seven_:

66 Today was the first day of recording the music for _The Age of Innocence_ which I composed. The recording took place in a very new studio in New York. The studio and orchestra were quite wonderful. As there are ninety minutes of music in this film, this was only the first of

seven days of recording. My crew consisted of my orchestrator, Emilie Bernstein, and recording engineer Brian Masterson from Dublin.

The director, Martin Scorsese [see IN POST PRODUCTION], film editor Thelma Schoonmaker, and producer Barbara Da Fina attended.

First days, especially in a new studio, are generally tense, but in the event all went well and I would say we were all satisfied.

I was first involved with Scorsese when I wrote the score for _The Grifters_. Since then our work together has included _Mad Dog & Glory_, _Cape Fear_, and now _The Age of Innocence_. 99

Kambiz Roshan-Ravan, whose 44th birthday fell on June 10th 1993, devotes his life to writing and performing "music for the movies":

66 For months I have been composing music and designing the overall structure for the musical score accompanying the [Iranian] film, _Symphony of the Roads_. For this film the music must be prepared before shooting begins.

I had many meetings with the director, the production manager, and the director of photography, until I was able to hand in the first sketch for rehearsal. On June 10th, I was busy with the orchestration of the music and putting in the finishing touches. In the afternoon I called the director and the production manager and told them of the progress I had made.

Also I was able to add a few pages to the book I am writing, entitled _Technique of Performing Film Music and Musical Scores in Iran_. 99

As the end of shooting approaches on _Deadly Advice_, C.J. Hobbs, the production designer, still faces the odd challenge to his ingenuity:

66 There was a long lighting session in the kitchen (a set built in the location house) involving a cat and a pair of scissors. Keith, the dressing propsman, erected a swing in the overgrown garden. [. . .] Someone dropped oil in the front hall. Various unsuccessful attempts made to remove it end in frustration.

Near the close of the film I find less and less to do. All the design is done, and the art department

crew deal very well with the day-to-day work, but for the occasional flurry of panic.

Mixed up some blood for the knife of Jack the Ripper (Sir John Mills) using food dye, evostick, French Enamel Varnish and hair-spray. Despite the odd mixture it is unpleasantly realistic.

Between shots I had earlier accosted Mandy Fletcher, the director:

'Do you want your blood fresh or crusty, madam?'

'Crusty,' she said, and galloped past.

[Later.] Meeting at Teddington Studios for the special effect of an actress going through a car windscreen. Ideas range from gutting the product placement car to rigging a minimal structure involving only the dashboard and windscreen. The problem is that the shot is next Wednesday and no preparation has been organised. [. . .]

Returned to set later to work on some complications with Jack the Ripper's knife, while pondering the car problem. The solution is simple enough, but the money and time are not there. Doubtless we shall manage. **"**

Emma Porteous had designed the costumes for a series of TV commercials directed by Mandy Fletcher. Now the pair are reunited on Fletcher's *Deadly Advice*:

" My first job of the day is to go and buy tights for [actress] Imelda Staunton – this is quite usual as tights seem to ladder by themselves! Come back to our wardrobe bus, and check once again the call sheet for today's shoot – everything fine. In the afternoon, am called to set because what was once (in the story) the night of the same day, has now been changed to another evening! Consequently, both artists involved in the scene must have changes of costume. Luckily, this is a modern film, so there is no problem – only some fast thinking, and very little time to do it in.

Later in the day, a discussion occurs over a knife which Jack the Ripper has to produce from his apron. We measure the length and height of the pocket and the prop master arrives in our bus at 6.45 P.M. to look at the apron. We have been worried that if the knife is covered in blood we should have 'repeat' aprons, but as it turns out the knife has dried blood on it. Just as a precaution Cynthea, the costume supervisor, is lining

the pocket with plastic!

We go through tomorrow's filming, listing scene numbers and changes the artists will have for the day – it's surprising how often one checks and double checks! Cynthea labels the garments, and puts them on a rail – it is easier than having to face it first thing in the morning! **"**

Mark Holding, a sound mixer attached to *Deadly Advice*, underlines the need for patience and speed during a typical day at the studio outside London:

" Having a cat on set for a lengthy dialogue scene created problems and a fair amount of anxiety. Matters weren't helped by the director's walking into the boom pole (always very embarrassing for a boom operator). Tempers seemed a bit shorter than usual at times, myself included. We shoot at a very fast pace on this film and as a result you have to be extremely quick to get your views heard. For instance, as soon as the cameraman has lit the set we rehearse – but sometimes the sound crew needs a few minutes to place mikes etc., and you have to raise your voice above the mêlée of activity in order to be heard! Sound technicians prefer to slip around the set creating the minimum of fuss. **"**

Simon Kaye had already recorded and mixed sound for Richard Attenborough on five films prior to *Shadowlands*. Here he reports from the studios at Shepperton:

" The first two sequences of the day were shot on a set of an X-ray room, circa 1951-1953, Debra Winger being the patient. The machine was hand operated, which will require the soundtrack of a period machine to be synchronised with the action. Having discussed with the technical advisors the need for an actual sound effect, I was informed that at a clinic in Dorking in Surrey, such a machine is available. So during post-production I will record a set of effects.

The rest of the day's shooting involved short scenes in a doctor's office set, also at the studio. These sequences didn't present any particular difficulties or requirements. [. . .]

The day ended with a call from my agent in

Los Angeles to confirm that she had closed a deal on my next production, *Black Beauty*, for Warner Bros., to be shot in England in August 1993 for eleven weeks. A happy end to a happy day. **99**

John J. Rodda is mixing sound on *U.F.O.* at Pinewood Studios, where the temperature touches the high 80's Farenheit, and the lighting is all-important:

66 It's a very complicated sequence to shoot – a courtroom scene in a spaceship, so to lay out positions for actors and camera moves which will be matched later in the day must all be carefully considered. The sound department of two [people] is at the mercy of a cameraman. Where we can position microphones depends on lighting, but we are still expected to be able to record clean and natural sound. An entire scene may have to be post-synched due to a lighting plot that gives the boom

no path around the actors. Enough of that! [. . .]

Back on set at 2 P.M. this afternoon and the long haul in the heat of well over 300 Kwatts of lighting. Now we'll shoot the close-ups to match the scene we covered this morning in the wide establishing shots. A visit from the dubbing assistant confirms that they're all happy with the last three and a half weeks' filming, and that post-sync, if needed, will be for performance or to add lines to fill pauses in the action, or back to camera lines. **99**

Recording sound on location presents a challenge to the experienced Japanese sound designer, Kenichi Benitani, as he works on Toho's *Last Song*:

66 3 A.M. I got into a car with the main crew and left the hotel. Nobody talked because of the shortage of sleep. In thirty minutes we were at the seaside location. The generator was already

Sound designer Kenichi Benitani dons his headphones as he works on location in Japan

making a noise and throwing up its lights to guide our footsteps. As there were stars in the sky, I thought no cloud would cross the sun today. We had plenty of time to prepare. Cameras, lights and microphones had been set up in their proper positions. At 5.10 A.M. the sun appeared above a small mountain. The director's voice, 'Ready? Action!' echoed around. We began our battle with the limitations of time. Three cameras followed three naked young men who jumped into the sea. As one of the cameras was in a long-shot position, it was difficult to find the right microphone setting. The sound of the waves blanketed their voices. We shot twelve takes, including their script lines and different camera positions. The balance between their weak speaking voices and the sound of the waves was poor and I wasn't satisfied with the quality of the recorded sound. I would like to partially over-dub their voices later. At 9 A.M. we went back to the hotel. [. . .]

At 4 P.M. we began work at a night location on the wharf, which we couldn't shoot the other day. In this scene a young couple talk against the background of a large young crowd. We worked hard to be ready to record their normal speaking voices by reducing the noise of the crowd. We partly used wireless mikes and recorded the sound of the crowd separately. The sea breeze grew colder. Shooting finished at 11.40 P.M. My long day was over.

Tu Tu-Chih's diary from Taiwan gently emphasises the detachment that comes inevitably to even the busiest of technicians when the weather intervenes:

❝ It's still raining. We've had to stop filming. Our sound team's taken shelter in a prison cell. Outside our window two groups of actors – one of them Kuomintang army officers, the other Communist Party members – are sheltering under the eaves of a building. A very interesting picture.

If it weren't raining, they would be acting a scene in which they would be arguing or fighting. But because of the downpour, the two armies have called a temporary halt and are chatting among themselves. If the rain doesn't stop, the two sides will have to hold a peace conference until we wrap. Then we in our prison cell can

pack up our gear and go back. Sadly, this is only a dream. It's stopped raining.

The two sides resume arguing. I, too, carry on recording their voices. ❞

Once shooting is over, and a film reaches the editing stage, the role of the re-recording mixer becomes significant. Hartanto reports from Jakarta in Indonesia:

❝ I am laying a track for a film called *A Letter for an Angel*. There were two colleagues working with me today: Icang Zaini, a sound effects director, and Indurawh, an assistant re-recording mixer. We concentrated on a scene of fighting on horseback between two tribes. Since the soundtrack collected by the sound recordist was complete, the track laying went smoothly.

Garin Nugroho, the director of the film, was also in the studio. During our work we did encounter some problems. We used Multi-Track Recorder, but the synchronisation system with the image was manual. If a foreign visitor had been watching, he would have laughed at us. But this is the only way to use Multi-Track to finish a film in this country. (For your information, no one in Indonesia uses a Multi-Track system to finalise a film except us!) ❞

Rubik Mansuri, a sound recording engineer in Tehran, laments the fact that most new-comers to the film industry want to be directors or writers:

❝ 8.30 A.M. I come down from my home which happens to be on the top storey of the sound recording studio. I have to work (dub dialogue and sound effects) on the last two reels of the film. I set out for the dubbing studio together with the director of the film. On the way I am told that old Arkady has come to repair the moviola. I explain to the director that I must supervise the repair work. This moviola has been working for more than thirty years. We have grown old together. It makes so much noise that you can scarcely hear the soundtrack. It does have one advantage over me – it has the right to go on the blink now and then. The trouble is that all the newcomers want to be either a director or a screenwriter. Nobody wants to be merely a technician. Arkady finished the repair by 11 A.M. and left. The film director and I go to the dubbing room. But before we have begun work, a producer hurries in and explains that one line of dialogue in a film of his which is due to go on screen next week absolutely must be changed. The director recognises the urgency of the case and we make plans to start work on his film at 4 P.M. After the change of dialogue I leave for lunch and a rest. At 4.30 I returned to the dubbing room. The director was there. We started work, but again we were interrupted, this time by someone who needs a change in a trailer. The poor director agrees to leave and return at 9.30 P.M.

It is 9 P.M. I am tired, and praying to God that the director may not come back.

Igor Vigdorgik brings intense patience and application to his sound recording in the Lenfilm Studios, St. Petersburg:

“ A few days ago I finished laying down the dialogues [for *A Jail Romance*] and now I need quickly to select the background noises and to prepare for recording the music and the synchronised sounds. Today I rose at 8 A.M. and at ten I was already in the sound library. I spent more than two hours searching for the sound of a dog breathing. I listened to a great number of recordings but none was quite what I was looking for. The dog was either too young or breathed too often. [. . .] It’s amazing how you always get stuck on the simplest of things.

At 1 P.M. I went to a viewing theatre to watch

Igor Vigdorgik at work at the sound console in Lenfilm Studios, St. Petersburg

Jim Clark, one of the world's most respected film editors

what had already been done. The film's German backer was there along with the studio director, the composer and of course the director and the editor. [. . .] Afterwards we excitedly discussed what we had seen for about an hour and a half. [. . .] I stayed talking to the composer. Over a coffee we discussed the mood of the music, the number and type of instruments, and an approximate recording schedule. **"**

Jim Clark enjoys a reputation second to none among film editors. Although he has worked for many major directors around the world, he enjoys life in London:

" I took public transport to Twickenham Studios this morning, fearing the roadworks on the M4 would again snarl up traffic. The walk from Richmond station is always a pleasure in the early morning. I was in the cutting room by 8.30 A.M., and got stuck into the work directly. We've been cutting [Bruce Beresford's] *A Good Man in Africa* for the past three days, and

have already reached reel 8 (out of 13), which means we are making excellent time. The picture has to be ready for preview in America on July 13th, so we now have just less than a month to refine the cut and make a temp mix. Working with Bruce Beresford is a most agreeable experience because he is a director who knows very clearly what he wants to see on the screen and is quick on decisions. He also turns up on time and attends to the film.

This morning we reviewed reels, 2, 3 and 4 which I had recut yesterday. Bruce came up with a few changes in each, but generally seems happy with the results. As my assistant is also making changes we whizz through the reels at speed. The picture, which was running long at last Monday's rough-cut screening, is beginning to take on better momentum as we hack away – line cutting and trimming off the fat. This is always the most rewarding period for the editor. Now I can discuss the cuts with the director instead of working in a vacuum, and be certain we are making the best choices – also we are without pressure from the producers who will keep off our backs until

Still from U.F.O., *designed by David McHenry*

the director's cut is ready for them to see. Having transferred all the rushes to videotapes gives us instant access to the material, and is very much quicker than dragging the film from its boxes, lacing it up and running on the moviola.

Bruce left me after lunch and I was able to start making changes, working through reels 2, 3 and 4 until 7 P.M., when I once again crossed Richmond Bridge and returned home. A productive sort of day – routine, perhaps, but that's the nature of film editing.

David McHenry celebrates his first film, U.F.O. , as a production designer, after working only in television:

[U.F.O.]'s budget is low by anyone's standards – £1 million – and my budget is even more ridiculous: £35,000 to build a futuristic space ship complex, and £20,000 to dress it. One week to go after only four weeks' shooting and I know

I've made it within budget. I made it because of three people: Martyn John, my art director; Judi Farr, my production buyer/set decorator; and John Maher, my construction manager. [. . .]

It's a bizarre film, way beyond anything that British cinema has ever attempted. It will be damned by the highbrow critics, but it is populist cinema and of very high quality. I showed some taped rushes of the 'bridge' set to John Maher today, and he couldn't believe how great it looked. 'It makes *Aliens* look like a pile of shit' (to quote him!)

I get stuck in heavy optical meetings, very long, and absolute concentration required. I called in Rob Dickenson to deal with extra optical effects because the production office was not happy with existing ones. [. . .]

We've got a packed final week of shooting still to go. A new set every day and big turn-rounds of sets within that. I'm understaffed with my construction crew and will have to call in more labour to cope with an ever-changing schedule.

Toni Lüdi uses The Bear *to illustrate his Film Academy classes*

Toni Lüdi, a German production designer, devotes much of his time to training newcomers in the craft of art direction:

❝ We had a hot and sunny day in Munich. In the morning I worked on the construction for an advertising spot. A very technical construction. This commercial will be shot in a studio in Düsseldorf. [. . .]

In the afternoon I revised a lecture on the subject, 'Designing Nature – The Example of *The Bear*' [the film by Jean-Jacques Annaud, 1988]. I will give the lecture at the Baden-Württemberg Film Academy. Since I have been running the new course on Production Design at the Rosenheim Vocational High School I am often invited to give lectures. The need to build up a study system demands an intensive analysis of production design. It forces me to set my ideas in order. In doing so I learn a lot myself. [. . .]

Perhaps training good production designers will help our films. Everyone on a film crew, and especially those who contribute some creative input, need to work at the same professionally high level to serve the project.

I particularly value the lecture on *The Bear*, because with a project that takes place entirely in natural surroundings it is not obvious even to many professionals in the trade what role a production designer can play. The atmospheric designing of Nature is an exceptional challenge that must be met without the work being obvious to an audience. A valley has to look bright, a rockface dangerous and threatening, and everything must be subordinate to the atmosphere of each scene in a way that is credible and not pretentious.

The difference between this and the careless and unconsidered images, the visual pollution that we see in many TV productions, lies in a careful and professional production design. By production design I mean the selection of the locations, the design of the sets and furnishings, the decisions about the colour tones and the arrangement of the properties, and not the photography by the cameraman. ❞

Still from Carl – My Childhood Symphony, *which has costumes designed by diarist Manon Rasmussen*

In the summer of 1993, the Danish director Erik Clausen was shooting a biographical film about the childhood of composer Carl Nielsen. Manon Rasmussen writes about her work as a costume designer on the film:

66 I have been working on [the film about Carl Nielsen's childhood, 1872-1883] for five months. We are spending today at the studio in Risby, a farm outside Copenhagen, making a scene in an inn in 1879 in which Nielsen, aged thirteen,

is musically inspired by a resident pianist and sensually so by the feminine charms of the waitress.

My assistant and I start with the ten male extras. They are ordinary men of a certain type, labourers whose role is to sit at length over their ale. I give them local colour, with fat and sweat etc., so it looks as if they've kept their clothes on for several days.

The actors arrive. The young Carl Nielsen is in uniform – he was a trumpeter in the army. The pianist is a hunchback who sits bent over; he has to wear an artificial hump – phew, he'll be hot – the forecast is for 28 degrees today and there's no air-conditioning on the set. The waitress is young and beautiful and her femininity must be emphasised, so she's pulled in at the waist and filled out in the bosom. Ready to shoot. We've finished on time. We begin with Carl Nielsen; he plays the violin for the pianist. It's a difficult and important scene. It takes time. **"**

Norma Webb serves as makeup artist on Richard Attenborough's *Shadowlands*, and her day begins at 7 A.M.:

" First customer – fairly straightforward: makeup to look like no makeup, period 1953. [. . .] Interestingly the lady in question is a genuine radiographer, playing the same role. Very depressing subject, cancer, especially as it's so personal to me. In fact during the past three weeks there have been many occasions on set that have reduced the crew to tears.

9.25 A.M. We're ready to shoot. Uncomfortable scene: Debra Winger submerged in an X-ray machine. There are lighter moments in the film, but on the whole it's fairly emotional. **"**

Casting and makeup are all part of the day's work for Wang Xizhong on a cool summer's day in Beijing:

" I got to the makeup room quite early to prepare plastic moulds and wigs for the trial makeup for *Deng Xiaoping*. This film is directed by Ding Yinnan. I've worked with him several times before. The crew for this film hasn't yet been formally set up, but I've already started taking part in casting and doing a trial makeup on actors. A few days ago, we found an opera singer from Sichuan. The shape of his face is very similar to Deng's, but he's too short. Recently, I met an actor who could be made up to look very much like Deng, but he was too tall! It's really difficult. Still, I'd like to make both of them up as possible reserves. Casting actors requires a lot of effort. Particularly for the roles of important figures such as Deng, one needs to find people who resemble them in appearance as well as manner. Soon I'll have to accompany the assistant director to Sichuan, where Deng

Xiaoping comes from, to see if there's anyone more suitable to be found there.

The Chinese film industry is not doing very well at present. Audiences are dwindling, many films have made a loss. But there's a continuous stream of Hongkong films being made here on the mainland. Today at the Beijing Film Studio lot, three Hongkong productions – *Xinfang Shiyu*, *Legend of an Assassin*, and *Shadow Boxing* (all kung fu movies) – were being shot simultaneously on the studio's 'Ming and Qing Dynasty street.' The site was streaming with traffic and packed with people. At nightfall, crackers were set off, sparks flew everywhere. Lights suspended high on cranes gave the effect of daylight. It was a busy, thriving scene. The atmosphere they'd created was like a dream. In fact, there's a saying in Hongkong film circles that 'films are dreams,' in other words detached from reality. **"**

Mostafa Rastgar serves as a special effects technician in Iran:

" Through a friend I was asked to do special effects for a TV war film. In the morning I planted the materials for a bullet effect on the bodies of actors as well as in the ground, and exploded them after a few minutes.

Around noon and under scorching sunlight, the director asked me to prepare a series of explosions. While doing that, I wondered if I have a viable position in the world of cinema. True, my work may be rewarded with festival prizes, but after working on over forty projects, would anybody care about my future if I was crippled during work? The answer is of course negative.

I prepared the scene while simultaneously fighting the mosquitoes. Shooting began, but soon had to be stopped because the actors had walked beyond the security zone towards the explosives. Shooting was resumed and with each explosion the actors threw themselves to the ground.

After the scene was shot, the dust-covered faces of the actors caused laughter. Many other scenes – some with artificial smoke – were shot during the day. Working in a temperature of 45 degrees Celsius was hard, but the results were satisfactory, and our return to the hotel was mixed with jokes and laughter. **"**

A stuntman, dressed in Draculan regalia, braves the flames for the watching cameras

Another Iranian technician, the cinematographer Abdolkarim Farhad Saba, recalls an incident during shooting:

❝ Today my mind is preoccupied by the argument that occurred between me and Abbas Kiarostami, director of *Beneath the Olive Trees*, and that led to a halt in the shooting programme. Kiarostami is an old friend, and the incident could have been avoided if either of us had been more considerate.

The two of us had spent long days together, and like two wanton boys had looked for something precious among the olive tree groves with a video camera. Several years ago Kiarostami and I, accompanied by the child actor of *Where Is My Friend's Home?*, had walked through the narrow, dark, and winding alleys of the nearby village, in search of a lost friend, and this year we were searching for a friend whose traces we had lost.

Maybe I have not grown up yet, and I wonder where this naughty child will lead me. Perhaps in a hundred years, the film, *Friendship with an Olive Branch*, will unfurl on world screens. ❞

The life of the professional stuntman is not only dangerous but also anonymous in the eyes of the filmgoing public. Jörg Pohl spends June 10th flirting with flames and car crashes:

❝ We start the first stunt after careful preparation and safety measures. My partner, dressed as Count Dracula, runs, pulling a fire-roller behind him, through a graveyard. The fire on his back develops an incredible temperature. We made it up with a mixture of petrol, combustible material, and smoke powder, so that the audience will have the feeling that the devil himself has appeared in the graveyard. Our little team stands there rooted to the spot and watches the supernatural scene with delight. Seconds

seem like minutes. Then he is there. The trained extinguishing team knows every move, and everyone knows that every second counts. Everything runs like clockwork and before you can think, my partner has been extinguished. [. . .]

We are in our workshop and are going over our test vehicle one more time. It is the one which I am going to do the overturn in, which in a few days' time is going to be shot for a German thriller. The problem is to turn the car on to its roof and then to hit a container on the other side of the street in the centre with the rear of the car.

We arrive at our fenced-off and secured training area and prepare for our rehearsal. We are very anxious to see whether our calculations about the speed, the angle of the ramp, and the distance to the container will work out exactly this time too.

[Now] I am sitting in my test car, waiting for the signal to start. The last seconds before the start seem like an eternity. I go once more in my mind through all the safety measures and calculations. But then I get the signal and everything goes very quickly. I race the 185 hp car up to the calculated speed, turn into the bend and simultaneously have the right wheels of the car on the ramp. A split second later I spin the wheel, overturn and slide on the car's roof towards the container. I can feel the hard slam against the rear of the car and know that our calculations have not let us down. There is nothing now that will interfere with the hundredth performance of this stunt in the next couple of days. **99**

James Swanson's company organised the remarkable aerial stunts on the Sylvester Stallone hit, *Cliffhanger*. He is based in Chobham, in Surrey, England:

66 The day revolves around generating publicity for our company. To show our prowess to the U.K. film industry we are having a private showing of [*Cliffhanger*]. [. . .]

Empire magazine has featured *Cliffhanger* in this month's issue, with a special section on our air-to-air transfer, which we're rather proud of. Let's hope it impresses the right people. Simon Crane,

On top of the world: On Deadly Ground, *with aerial stunts by James Swanson's company*

277 **«**

和乘車婦女（清末）
拉洋車夫
北京
93.
6.
10.
靖刚记于

选自邵瑞刚《第100本电影 资料本》）

the stuntman who actually went across, rings up to explain that they used the shot of the test dummy, yet said it was him! Yes, we know, but it was our best still – and it was obvious that he'd spot it!

The feature we are working on at the moment is *On Deadly Ground*, Steven Seagal's actioner set in Alaska. We've got two crew on it – an aerial co-ordinator and a safety engineer. Nobody's called, so I guess it's going smoothly. **99**

Research occupies the talents of Chinese art director Shao Ruigang:

66 Early today, I went to Beijing Library's archive section to do some design work prior to the shooting of *Saijinha*. Each time before filming begins, I have to fill bookloads of drawings, compiled from various sources, recording with my own words and pictures numerous objects, buildings, costumes and jewellery worn by the characters, the general atmosphere of the scene and each minute prop that might appear in the film. Then I start my production design labours. How time has passed since I began working in film some twenty years ago and my stacks of books have increased all the while. Each is numbered chronologically and kept in my storeroom so that I can refer to them at any time. [. . .]

Saijinhua takes place precisely during the late Qing Dynasty. It's about Zhao Caiyun, a benevolent prostitute of great repute who lived at the end of the Qing period and describes her life of frustration and misfortune. [. . .] The artistic design is going to be a major project. It'll take me the next two years to do the preparatory work. [. . .]

As I look at the splendid photographs [of old Beijing], a series of blueprints for the film's artistic design emerges in my mind's eye. Bada Lane in Qianmen, which was frequented by Saijinjua, her own residence, the mansions of high-ranking officials who visited her, the homes of wealthy merchants, sumptuous ceremonial banquets, resplendent halls with their life of luxury and dissipation, teeming crowds of spectators at the execution ground in Caishikou where patriotic heroes were slaughtered, the sorry episode of the Empress

Sketch of old Beijing, found by Shao Ruigang in the Beijing Library

279 ◀◀

Left *and* above: *Watercolours of Old Beijing used by Chinese art director Shao Ruigang as background material*

Dowager fleeing west, and so on. [. . .] I greedily leaf through the pages, recording, sketching, forgetful of everything else. I work without interruption, until I fill my entire notebook. When at last I pause, it's four o'clock in the afternoon and I remember that I haven't even had my lunch. But I feel no hunger. Perhaps all this rich material has already filled me to capacity. **99**

Subtitling has become technically more sophisticated with the years but as Israel Ouval points out, pitfalls still await the professional movie translator:

66 'A translation is like a woman,' said Lea Goldberg, a famous Israeli poetess and translator. 'It's either beautiful or faithful.' This is probably the universal conflict of all translators, to strive for beauty or fidelity.

In Israel films are not dubbed (except for cartoons for kids). In the past 25 years I have translated a few thousand films but today I have to proof-read one of the most difficult tasks I have ever had: Shakespeare's (and Kenneth Branagh's) *Much Ado about Nothing*. The film is due to open the Jerusalem Film Festival on a huge screen in the open air opposite the walls of the Old City before an expected audience of 4,000 spectators.

This is not the first time I have had to deal with Branagh and Shakespeare. I have also translated *Henry V*, but *Much Ado*, being a comedy, is even harder. The Hebrew language presents its difficulties too. On the one hand Shakespeare's idiomatic English tends to be translated into ancient Hebrew; yet the film, being modern, destined to be watched by a modern audience, demands a modern language – but can we accept Shakespeare in up-to-date Hebrew? Maybe a certain synthesis is required. I will have to reconsider these points while proof-reading the subtitles. Then, of course, a translation meant to be read should be different from that which must be heard. Moreover, the span of time of a fleeting subtitle is so brief that it has to be concise enough to deliver the message. No one can stop the **99** screening to re-read a subtitle.

And in many large countries (France, Italy, Germany, Spain) dubbing remains the preferred form of translation. Osman Raghebis is an actor/director much in demand by top directors:

66 After a ten-day holiday in the south of France, following three months in Poland as dialogue and dialect supervisor on Steven Spielberg's *Schindler's List*, I started sorting out the text changes and corrections required for the post-production work due next month in London.

10 A.M. Contacted Ilse Schwarzwald, Dieter Meyer's secretary at Constantin Film who called me during my absence as they would like me to direct the German dubbing of Bille August's latest film, *The House of the Spirits*, with Meryl Streep, Glenn Close, and Jeremy Irons. We'll start recording most probably at the end of August.

10.30 A.M. Called Korinna Heimburger at the Bavarian State Radio to discuss the casting of

two radio plays that I will be directing for them next week.

3.30 P.M. Quick visit to ARRI Studios to dub a part in a television series for Matias von Stegmann.

Finally I dropped in on FSM Studios to pick up a VHS copy for my files of the German version of Youssef Chahine's film *Alexandria Again and Again*, which I had directed before leaving 🙶 for Poland.

Directors are frequently closet technicians. Go Riju, a young Japanese film-maker, explains his dreams for the future:

🙶 When I woke this morning it was a very bright day. I decided to go to the nearby park [in Tokyo], taking some beer with me. I drank the beer while watching some carp in the pool. Delicious. A film director who doesn't make any films is like an unemployed man lost in a world of fantasies. But that's an enjoyable thing and I became much happier. [. . .]

I would like to produce a new series of films in Cineco – transferring video to film format – and of course I plan to direct one of them. I have always liked the feeling of a good quality video screen, which I've adapted into my films in many ways. I once shot all the scenes with a video camera and created a fake documentary-style film, and so I sometimes go to see tests of Cineco. I'm amazed by the development of technology compared to the past. There are no lines [on the image]; on the contrary they will be more difficult to make when I need them. There's almost no problem in showing an obvious 'edge' when it's moving fast. When we change it to 'Bistasize' and show it on the screen, the visual image is unique and strange.

I've recently been assured that I can create a completely new image, totally different from the former Cineco images. Nobody tries to make such experimental things. But I want to try the idea and it's worth making several series. I can shoot very lively images by using several Hi-8 cameras at the same time. [. . .] Making a black-and-white image seems to be very interest- 🙶 ing; there are a thousand ways of doing it.

Japanese director Go Riju

Jem Cohen, based in New York, works in all formats – Super 8, video, 35mm film etc. – and makes TV commercials to support his own experimental films:

🙶 I am at a shopping mall in New Jersey. [. . .] The crew mills around. We pull fake walls off the truck, a rented phone-booth, tools . . . The commercial is shot in black-and-white and 16mm. It is 'reality based,' and will have a grainy look, appearing to have been shot hand-held, off the cuff, guerrilla-style. Real people, mixed in with hired actors, face the camera and talk about the product. They stand in front of a wall of product. Their devotion seems total. The product is relatively innocuous. It used to be something simple that you wore, but now it is something dazzling, that you inflate, that lights up, that adjusts to specifics of activity that you didn't know existed.

Practically every shot is at an angle so extremely cocked that if looked at objectively, each frame would suggest a calmly frozen earthquake – people at 45 degrees, desktops everything should be rolling off of, perilously tilting displays of the product. But no one runs to catch these tilted things before they hit the ground. No one is surprised at the odd tilt of the cameras. This once-radical language has become such common currency, in fact, both cameras are mounted on special tripod heads designed solely to 'dutch' the shots with maximum ease.

I imagine the ghosts of Dziga Vertov, Orson Welles, and the pioneers of *cinéma vérité* peering through the plate glass windows of the mall, watching the ease with which their stolen language is spoken.

I don't think about it for long. On the job, I don't think about anything for long. We move through a large number of set-ups efficiently. We move like plumbers, bricklayers, window washers . . . (Of course, the head plumber – the director – is probably making between $5,000 and $10,000 a day.) Luckily, I have a boss who knows that I am working to support my own films, and respects that. Usually, it is something that I keep to myself in this business. Occasionally during the day I find myself converting hourly wages 🙶 into rolls of raw stock that I'll buy.

15. At the Cutting Edge? The Censors THE

DEBATE ON CENSORSHIP OF FILMS HAS SWELLED

WITH THE ARRIVAL OF VIDEO, LASER-DISCS, AND

SATELLITE AND CABLE TV. THE RATING SYSTEMS IN

THE UNITED STATES, BRITAIN AND OTHER COUN-

TRIES CAN MATERIALLY AFFECT THE BOX-OFFICE

SUCCESS AND NOTORIETY OF A PRODUCTION, WHILE

284 CENSORSHIP OF A MORE ABSTRACT KIND CONTINUES

TO UNDERMINE THE FILM ARTIST IN MANY WAYS.

The Administration Commission of the Motion Picture Code of Ethics examines all films likely to offend the public taste in Japan, and Oeda Shigeki works there:

66 I joined the final check screening of one disputed scene in *The Crying Game* to be shown at Cine Switch in Ginza at 11 A.M. In this scene Jody's girlfriend, Dill, shows Fergus her naked body and the audience discover she is a man. Japanese customs have already requested a re-touch of this scene because the genitals can clearly be seen. We can allow it if the offending part is indistinct but [not] if it's seen too obviously. Herald Ace, the distributor of the film, insisted on making it much brighter because it is a key factor in the story. [. . .] After discussion, our foreign film examiners decided to [. . .] give this film Classification R – prohibited to audiences under 15 years old – and accepted Herald Ace's request to make the scene much brighter. 99

Jaye Davidson in a scene from The Crying Game

Still from Evil Dead III – Army of Darkness, *seen by the Swedish censor Gunnel Arrback*

The Swedish National Board of Film Censors has often hit the headlines, due to its firm rejection of violence on screen. Gunnel Arrback is the current Director of the Board:

❝ As June 10th happened to be a Thursday, all six film censors (including myself) were present along with the four administrative employees and our film technician. As usual on Thursdays, we all discussed what had happened in the past week: what films had been screened, what decisions on age limits had been taken, and what discussions we had had with distributors and with the general public. [. . .]

We spent some time over the film *Cliffhanger*, starring Sylvester Stallone. The Board had earlier decided to cut one scene of a fairly drawn-out assault to pass it with the age limit of 15. The distributor had made an appeal against this to the courts, and we were expecting their decision.

We also planned the work of the day.

One of the interesting things about being a film censor is that when you come to work, you never really know how you are going to spend the day. Some films are pre-advised to us long beforehand, others come as a surprise – and in many cases the distributors are in a hurry and want the screening and the decision at once. Usually we are able to oblige.

After coffee, I and a colleague had a look at a trailer for *Evil Dead III – Army of Darkness*, which was a curious combination of violent action, science fiction, and comedy. We passed it with a 15 age limit, the argument being the amount of violence that was actually shown.

Having had this trailer as an appetiser, I went on to screen an American movie called *The Crush*, about an erotically precocious girl of fourteen, who tries to seduce a journalist twice her age and who, when he doesn't comply with her wishes,

BRITISH BOARD OF FILM CENSORS

75-77. SHAFTESBURY AVENUE, W.

This picture *"The Dublin Rebellion"*

has been passed for Universal Exhibition

G.A. Redford

Examiner..*BZJ* President

..*Uett*..

tries to murder him and to harm his adult girlfriend. The distributor wanted an age limit of 11. Two of my colleagues had already seen the film and arrived at different conclusions about this age limit. So I was to decide. I found myself on the side of a 15 age limit, my argument being the whole theme of the film as well as some rather violent sequences at the end of the movie. **99**

Cliffhanger also appeared on the menu of the Netherlands Film Examining Board on June 10th, as Cornelius Crans, the Director of the Board, describes:

66 Today, there are two films on the programme [for classification]: a reissue of the classic Disney film, *Bambi*, and *Cliffhanger*. A distributor is under no obligation to submit a film to the Netherlands Film Examining Board. The result is that, if a film isn't submitted, it automatically gets

the label: 16 years. The company which will release *Cliffhanger* is uncertain whether the film will get a 12 or a 16 and is therefore letting us see it today.

Five of forty members of the Board gather to watch the films. In the meantime the results of the Swedish (15 years and a few cuts) and the Belgian (all ages) Boards have become known. The five Dutch members decide unanimously – in consultation with me – not to admit youngsters under the age of 16. 'The film is characterised by an unbearable tension, combined with ruthless, sadistic violence,' says one member. Others talk of an 'overkill of extreme, rude, and **99** repulsive violence.'

In London, Margaret Ford, Deputy Director of the British Board of Film Classification, approaches the end of her day's work:

66 My secretary interrupts with the *Jurassic Park* report. As we hoped, the children appear to have loved it, rating it Good and Scary rather than Too Frightening for Me – and 98% thought it the best film they'd seen recently. Set

---

Left: Cliffhanger *seized the attention of various censors around the world. Still shows Sylvester Stallone and Janine Turner.* Above: *Early British censor's certificate*

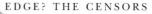

about changing a screening for the President and Vice-Presidents of the Board, but drop a hint to UIP [the distributors] that the PG [Parental Guidance rating] is a strong possibility if a **99** warning is attached.

Censors do not always agree, as John Dickie, the Chief Censor at the Office of Film and Literature Classification in Sydney, Australia, explains:

66 Today I was part of a panel scheduled to review *Red Rock West*. The film is an offbeat black comedy with Dennis Hopper adding another flamboyant character to his already formidable list. While there is a slightly madcap element about the film for the first hour, the action and the violence heighten considerably in the final thirty minutes. For the classification panel the issues are the violence and the language. A choice has to be made, whether the film will be classified M, which is a recommended category for those aged 15 years and over, or an MA Film, which will make it legally restricted. [. . .]

My colleagues and I are unable to agree. There is concern whether the depictions are sufficiently strong to restrict the film from those aged under 15. There are several incidents, including an execution by a hit-man, the impaling of a hit-man on a statue in a graveyard, and a barrage of shots into the chest.

The other matter of concern is the level of the fuck language. The observation is made that Dennis Hopper has turned the use of fuck language into an art form.

My view is that the violence has sufficient strength in the last half-hour to take the film into the MA category. My colleagues indicate they would like further time to consider the issues before reaching a final decision.

As with all classification decisions, if the initial panel does not reach an unanimous decision, the film is referred back to the Senior Censor to arrange another screening by another panel. Once the second panel has viewed the film it **99** will be debated at the weekly Board meeting.

Dennis Hopper in Red Rock West, *scrutinised on June 10th by the Australian censor*

Still from Francisco Athie's Lolo, *mysteriously not shown in Mexico*

Jaime Humberto Hermosillo, one of Mexico's major screenwriters and directors (*La tarea prohibida* etc.), goes to the movies and encounters a sinister form of censorship:

“ This evening, in the company of my friend and occasional co-screenwriter, Arturo Villaseñor, I went to a cinema in the centre of [Guadalajara] to see a Mexican film, *Lolo*, by Francisco Athie, which won the opera prima prize at the Latin American Film Festival in Havana last December. [. . .]

Without prior warning, instead of *Lolo* they showed another film. It seems part of a plot – and one has to call it that – against good quality national films, because except in unusual circumstances (which only prove the rule), they are screened in the worst theatres and without publicity.

Objectively, bad exhibition is a disguised form of censorship and in my case it's the last straw. I have suffered this censorship myself with nearly all my films and, in particular, with the two most recent, *Encuentro inesperado* and *La tarea prohibida*. ”

Censorship can mark a film industry in subtle and insidious ways. Gul Anand, a Hindu film-maker from Bombay, touches upon one such manifestation:

“ Spoke on the phone with Mrs. Rafia Amin, in Hyderabad, about the possibility of turning the script of my next film, *Chori Chupke* (which she is writing), featuring Muslim characters to one with Hindu characters. She was upset, and so was I, to make such drastic changes. But I explained to her that in the present climate in the country (the Ayodhya incident when Hindus brought down the Babri Mosque, and the subsequent riots and killings), the distributors were fighting shy of dealing with Muslim subjects.

Otherwise, it is to the credit of the Indian film industry that, while making a film, cast and credits are finalised purely on merit. In fact Hindi mythological themes have often been treated by Muslim writers and Muslim religious themes have been filmed by Hindu directors. For me personally it is traumatic to be dragged into a situation which is not of my making or belief. **"**

On the same topic, K.G. George writes from his sojourn in the hill station of Ponmudi, 60 km from Trivandrum in India:

" After a cold breakfast settled down to continue with my work. I am here to complete the re-writing of a screenplay on which I started more than a year ago. The increasing communal divide in this country inspired the subject, and indeed a draft was completed before the demolition of the mosque at Ayodhya, which substantiated its validity.

Nirmala, a Hindu woman, nearing thirty, employed with a small salary, remains unmarried due to her father's inability to raise enough money for her dowry. She falls in love with a tele-

phone operator, who happens to be a Muslim. They decide to get married. But the woman's brother, member of a Hindu revivalist group, intervenes and foils their wedding plans. Undaunted, the couple start to live together. A few days later, the man dies in a road accident, apparently murdered. The incident provokes communal riots, death, and destruction. Back at home, Nirmala realises that she is going to bear the dead lover's child. Her family compels her to destroy the embryo. But she wants to have the child. Her angry father threatens to kill her. Aritha, a sympathetic journalist, comes to the rescue. Normala is taken to a remote village, where Aritha's parents live. By the time the determined brother pursues Nirmala to the village, the **"** entire village is waiting to punish him.

Barbara Hammer has just screened her first feature, *Nitrate Kisses*, at the Gay and Lesbian Festival in Boston:

" I have a lot to think about today as I rent a bicycle for a day ride to the outer lighthouse and beaches [of Nantucket Island], such as what

Frances Lorraine and Sally Binford in Barbara Hammer's Nitrate Kisses

it meant for a member of the National Endowment for the Arts to tell me, 'We aren't supposed to talk to you,' when I asked if the final report on *Nitrate Kisses* had been signed off yet. My film, the theme of which is the censorship of the history of lesbians and gays, contains explicit love-making scenes and although the film was finished according to the grant deadline and with all the monies provided, it has not received the signature on my final report that will close the file and enable me to apply for another film grant. **99**

Above left and bottom right: *Film certificates.* Above: Barbara Hammer. Right: *Scene from* Nitrate Kisses

Not all countries screen advertisements during cinema programmes, but in those that do, censorship plays its role. Bob Wittenbach is a director of the Cinema Advertising Association in Britain:

66 The Cinema Advertising Association is a trade body representing the cinema advertising contractors operating in the U.K. and Eire. Our primary function is to promote, monitor, and maintain standards of cinema advertising exhibition and also to commission and conduct research into the cinema itself as an advertising medium.

9.30 A.M. In the Rank Preview Theatre to view this week's 'newcomers.' This is a screening for the benefit of the CAA's Copy Panel of all the new ads due to be shown in cinemas over the next week or so. Ten advertisements is slightly more than usual in one week, but five of these are ten-second vignettes for Tizer (a fizzy soft drink) which are being booked three at a time, interspersed throughout the ad reels. The new 'Guinness' ad looks especially good on the screen! No problems with any of these. [. . .]

4 P.M. *Jurassic Park* opens tomorrow in the States, but the U.K. film distributors, UIP, cannot yet tell me what certificate it will get. I will need to recommend whether alcohol ads can be allowed to be run with this film. **99**

Bashir El Deek, a professional screenwriter in Egypt, finds himself on the receiving end of pre-production censorship:

66 Today I had to start work as early as possible. My daily thought and dream is to write early in the morning like Hemingway. This, unfortunately, has not happened once in all my years, as far as I can remember. I am writing a script for a serial based on a book by Dr. Taha Hussein, called *Adeeb*. [. . .] I agreed over the phone to do the work when I was abroad, and I had not read this particular book. When I studied the story, I found that there were only three characters! You can imagine what it's like to try to turn this into a 13-hour serial!

Soon after I started my work, I received a letter from the censors refusing one of my scripts without explanation save to say that it was 'contrary to the public order and morally offensive.' Such a term is so elastic; it stretches to include

everything as it depends purely on personal interpretation and vision, as the decision is made by a number of officials at the Censorship Department. Anything could be contrary to the public order of the State, from the point of view of the censor, and any sentence in any dialogue can be termed morally offensive.

Lately a new and stupid fad has emerged at the Censorship Department, called the preservation of 'Egypt's image abroad.' This sentence is also meaningless. I pose an important question: What kind of art can escape the grip of such people and such an atmosphere? **99**

BRITISH BOARD OF FILM CLASSIFICATION

SOHO SQUARE LONDON W1

This is to certify that

has been classified for cinema exhibition

PRESIDENT   U   DIRECTOR

UNIVERSAL
Suitable for all

16. Reading Between the Lines: Journalists and Critics

WHILE CERTAIN STAR-VEHICLES AND HOLLYWOOD BLOCKBUSTERS WILL ENJOY ENORMOUS POPULARITY DESPITE A CRITICAL DRUBBING, A MAJORITY OF FILMS DEPENDS ON THE JOURNALISTS AND CRITICS FOR WIDESPREAD APPRECIATION. CRITICS ARE OFTEN LOATHED AND FEARED BY THE INDUSTRY; AT THE SAME TIME, THEY ARE COURTED, WINED AND DINED, AND GENERALLY FLATTERED BY THE PRESS DEPARTMENTS OF MAJOR DISTRIBUTORS.

>> 294

Monitoring the pulse of Hollywood is a responsibility borne with daily pleasure and, perhaps, apprehension by industry expert and author Peter Bart, Vice President and Editorial Director of Variety Inc.:

" An editor is doing his job right when he's pondering issues and events other people aren't even aware of as yet. There were two such items on my agenda this morning. The first concerned MGM and its long-dormant sister company, United Artists. For the last twenty-four hours sources have been phoning me with reports and rumours about an impending change. UA was about to be spun off and reactivated with a $150 million infusion from Credit Lyonnais – that seemed to be the emerging consensus. What was unclear, however, was the identity of the individ-

Left: *Peter Bart.* Above: *Rob Reiner and Tom Hanks on the set of* Sleepless in Seattle

uals who would be involved in this caper. One group believed Frank Mancuso [former President of Paramount Pictures] would be tapped to spearhead the operation. Another suggests it will be Ted Turner and his organization. Other names are also being bandied about.

The questions always facing an editor are these: Do you go with the story now, even though you can't verify the details, or do you hold it and risk being scooped by a competitor? Who do you call to augment the facts?

The second item was equally thorny. Last night I attended the initial screening of *The Last Action Hero*, the clangorous and extremely expensive Arnold Schwarzenegger epic that represents Sony's big entry for the summer. The only other people at the screening were agents representing the star and director along with assorted producers and studio personnel. Their response was euphoric. I left them congratulating one another and slipped outside into the cool night air to gather my thoughts.

Despite the exuberant responses inside, the film was clearly a problem not only for Sony, but for me as well. I would envision the chain of events: Our critic would blast it. Sony would be irate. The studio would predict blockbuster business. My paper would forecast disappointing results. The fur would fly.

All of that is simply part of the job. Our task is to call them as we see them. The studio's role is to defend its product. Nonetheless, the morning after the screening, I felt a keen sense of empathy for the studio execs and film-makers alike. Here was a project with an intriguing basic premise, but somehow it went awry. Having been in the business for twenty years, I was acutely aware of that narrow line between success and failure. Why did this film fall on the wrong side of the line? All day long execs from other studios and top agents called in with their analyses and predictions – the film is too long, Schwarzenegger shouldn't do broad comedy, etc. There are even rumours that Sony may delay the opening and

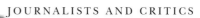

Still from The Cronos Device, *written about by Steven Gaydos*

we play a tape from another new film, *Sleepless in Seattle*. What a brilliant idea to revive that old Jimmy Durante rendition of 'As Time Goes By' – 'Da woild will always welcome lovers, as time goes by,' sings Jimmy, and my wife turns to me and smiles, 'Da woild will always miss Jimmy Durante.' What a glorious form of immortality show biz extends to its chosen ones, I reflect. It almost justifies the tremors and turmoil that mar one's path day-to-day. "

Steven Gaydos has his ear to the ground as a trade journalist in Los Angeles, first with *The Hollywood Reporter* and then with *Variety*. He is also involved in film-making himself:

" 9.30 A.M. At work on the 'Independent Producers' special issue for *The Hollywood Reporter*. I'm especially gratified because our publisher, Bob Dowling, took me to lunch last week and told me that after spending time with Neil Jordan in Ireland, and seeing film communities in Australia, he wants the issue to reflect 'the spirit and passion' of the indie film-makers. [. . .]

12.30 P.M. Spoke to director Ate de Jong [see Chapter 5]. He says our film, *All Men Are Mortal*, will start shooting in Budapest on September 15th. This is sixteen years after I first wrote to Simone de Beauvoir about obtaining the rights.

1 P.M. Lunch with Trimark's David Bowers. Trimark's stock soared on rumour of Sony buyout!

3.30 P.M. Monte Hellman calls to tell me [see Chapter 1] that our film *Iguana* is invited for competition at the Dunkerque Film Festival in October.

4 P.M. Producer Arthur Gorson called. We're talking about a variety of subjects, from October Films' interest in his picture, *The Cronos Device*, which just won the Grand Prix at the Critics' Week in Cannes, to showing my Simone de Beauvoir script to American Playhouse. [. . .]

5 P.M. Met with Morgan Mason at the William Morris Agency. Absolutely one of the coolest people I've met in this business. Unlike my former agent, Bill Block at ICM [. . .], Mason talks only about indie projects. [. . .]

7.30 P.M. Dinner at 'El Cholo' with Monte Hellman. We continue our long-running argument about who's a bigger or more dangerous liar: Ross Perot or Bill Clinton. He thinks I'm

hone the cut. The studio ardently denies this, however. The film would ultimately be released on schedule.

The day also offered other encounters. I go out to Disney to lunch with Joe Roth, the former production chief at Fox who has set up an independent company at Disney. Fifteen years earlier when I was production chief at Lorimar I'd given Joe his first producing job. Now, years later, he is wizened and greying but still has that spark of humour and perspective. And despite the creative freedom granted him at Disney, he understands full well how carefully he must marshall his projects. With Disney releasing as many as sixty features a year, Roth knows that his films must command urgent attention with their storylines and creative elements.

The day ends with another screening, at the Malibu home of Ron Meyer, who always seems relaxed and good-natured despite the pressures of his job as second-in-command of the giant CAA agency. After an enjoyable dinner of pizza, salad and pasta, we see a biofilm of Tina Turner, *What's Love Got to Do with It*. This is a Hollywood crowd and everyone there is fit and trim and eats sparingly – David Geffen, Demi Moore and her husband, Bruce Willis, director Irwin Winkler and his wife Margo, among others.

It is midnight when we start the drive from Malibu back to Beverly Hills. The roads are virtually empty. Everyone already in bed, girding for the rigours that lie ahead. As my wife and I drive,

River Phoenix and Keanu Reeves in Gus Van Sant's My Own Private Idaho

crazy for wanting a third party to bust up the corruption, and I think he's crazy for trusting a third-rate, blow-dried tele-evangelist. **"**

David Stratton, a familiar reviewer in *Variety*, and also respected for his weekly film presentations on SBS television in Australia, has written several books on the cinema:

" Read *Sydney Morning Herald* film critic Lynden Barber's reviews of new films opening today. He likes Phil Noyce's *Sliver* more than I do, pretty much dismisses *Super Mario Bros.* and *Made in America*, and likes *Hangin' with the Homeboys*, which I haven't seen.

Other films on in Sydney today, as advertised in the Herald include: *Aladdin, Hellraiser III, Deep Cover, The Vanishing* [Hollywood version], *Groundhog Day, Indecent Proposal, CB4, School Ties, Bob Roberts, Blade Runner [Director's Cut], Falling Down, The Crying Game, Sommersby, Singles, Cop and a Half, Rich in Love, Enchanted April, Bad Lieutenant,*

Passion Fish, and a revival of *Mean Streets*.

Unusually, there are no Australian films playing first run at the moment, but the NZ film, *Crush*, is on, and there are several foreign language films: *Mediterraneo, Man Bites Dog, Jamón Jamón, La Tarea, Les amants de Pont-Neuf, Lovers.* There are some documentaries getting first run releases: *The Joys of the Women, Blast 'Em, Carving the White*, and *Manufacturing Consent*. In repertory there are some ads for *A Clockwork Orange* (never out of release in Australia), *High Heels*, and *My Own Private Idaho*. There's also an ad for the 40th Sydney Film Festival, which opens tomorrow.

[Like many diarists, Stratton comments on the untimely death of Kazuko Shibata: 'Devastating news. I'd seen her in Cannes and she was fine. What a loss!' See also Chapter 22.]

My task today is to write the scripts for films I've programmed on SBS TV over the next couple of weeks. I use a system called Q-Word: the disk on which I programme the scripts fits into the auto-cue system at the studio, so it doesn't

Still from Fire in the Sky, *with James Garner (right) which diarist Barry Norman writes about*

have to be retyped. This takes most of the day. I have to write in the manner of my own speech – this is to be spoken, not read. 🙶

For twenty years, Barry Norman has hosted Britain's most popular TV programme about the cinema. Son of director Leslie Norman, he has written several books about Hollywood and its films:

🙸 A change of plan means that I'm in London [today] instead of Hollywood. My producer, Bruce Thompson, and I had intended to prerecord next Monday's programme (the last in the series) and go to L.A. to stockpile material for the autumn and winter run. Specifically, we had in mind interviews with Clint Eastwood and Tom Cruise that would provide us with 'special' programmes when their films, *In the Line of Fire* and *The Firm*, open in Britain. But Eastwood is filming in Texas with Kevin Costner [on *A Perfect World*] and Cruise has taken his wife Nicole Kidman to Australia to spend the summer with his in-laws.

So everything is postponed, at least until August when Bruce and I will think again. It's important for a programme like *Film 93*, even with its tight budget, to go to America at least once a year, not only to gather material but to talk and listen and keep in touch with what's going on. Hollywood, after all, is the capital of mainstream cinema. For the moment, however, I remain in London, revising my script for next week's programme, which includes the ludicrous and awful *Boxing Helena* and the equally preposterous *Fire in the Sky*. Happily, rotten films often make for a lively and amusing programme and I think that will be the case this time. Script seems okay but I'll revise it again, as I always do, before I go to the studio on Monday. 🙶

Philip French plays an important role in British film criticism. His weekly column in the *Observer* is often quoted and exerts considerable influence on the intelligentsia. His books, such as *Westerns*, *The Movie Moguls*, and *Malle on Malle*, underline his commitment to good cinema:

🙸 5 A.M. If this were London I'd start the day by polishing my weekly column and faxing it to the *Observer*. But I'm vacationing at my rural retreat in Sweden a mile from a metalled road,

Still from Nicholas Ray's Party Girl, *seen on TV by Philip French*

five miles from the nearest shop, twelve miles from Karlstad, provincial capital of Värmland. The sun glints on the lake across the field outside; two deer graze at the edge of the forest; the light recalls the establishing montage of *Cries and Whispers*.

Before breakfast I sit on the verandah reading a biography of Michael Curtiz, one of a batch of books I'm reviewing. Yesterday on Swedish TV I saw for the first time William Powell as private eye Philo Vance in Curtiz's 65-minute whodunit, *The Kennel Murder Case*, made in August 1933, the month I was born. By constant camera movement, dynamic editing and dramatic lighting, Curtiz turns a talkative, almost actionless script into an essentially cinematic experience. [. . .]

At noon my wife and I drive into Karlstad to pick up newspapers. At the excellent local library

I photocopy an entry from Volume 28 of the Swedish Academy's dictionary explaining the literal and figurative meaning of *Smultronställe* (wild strawberry place/patch). This is to be reproduced in the BFI monograph my wife and I are writing on Bergman's *Smultronstället* (inaccurately rendered in English as *Wild Strawberries*). [. . .]

Put in a couple of hours on my new book of reflections on the cinema, provisionally called *Across the River and Up the Odessa Steps*. Am writing on sport in the movies at the moment and draft the sections on cricket, boxing, and fishing. After dinner read the chapter on *Wild Strawberries* in Ingmar Bergman's *Bilder*, with the assistance of my wife – this remarkable book is much better than his autobiography, *The Magic Lantern*. Eventually put it aside to end the day watching

On location for Wild Strawberries*: Ingmar Bergman (left) with Bibi Andersson and Victor Sjöström*

Nicholas Ray's *Party Girl* on TV. Rightly it is shown in letterbox format as all widescreen movies are on Swedish TV.

Pieter van Lierop has devoted the past twenty years to writing about film in the Dutch press, and mentions one of the most disturbing trends in current journalism:

I always regard the appearance of my film review page [on Thursdays] as the height of the working week, and feel I have earned the right to go riding for an hour. I am not particularly good at it but get a lot of enjoyment from the exercise. Today I am unlucky; I get a horse called 'Diabolical' – the name speaks for itself, it is a beast from hell!

There are no press screenings today. The afternoon is a depressing one. [. . .] My paper, *Utrechts Nieuwsblad*, is going to merge with another one. [. . .] It is obvious that my colleagues want the paper to follow the general trend, i.e. shorter articles, larger pictures – in colour – a greater response to what the readers want, and more human interest. They expect to fight off competition with the help of an electronic media. I know for certain they are making a mistake. Within ten years, papers will still be read by people who prefer reading, who want to know more details, and who want to reflect. [. . .] I fear that sooner or later even I will be told that film reviews are of secondary importance and that I must concentrate more on interviews, not with the likes of Zhang Yimou or Chen Kaige or Abbas Kiarostami, but with Jack Nicholson, Al Pacino, and Woody Allen

Still from The Scent of Green Papaya, *directed by Tran Anh Hung, which Michel Boujut watched on June 10th*

Corriere della Sera is regarded as possibly the most influential paper in Italy. Tullio Kezich is its film critic:

" 9 A.M. Busy correcting the proofs of *Under the Stars of '44*, an unpublished journal by the director Steno, which I am editing for publication. Make useless phone calls to people who can talk about that period. Not one to be found: all dead or on holiday?

10.30 A.M. I take my wife, Alessandra Levantesi (who is a member of the selection committee of the Venice Film Festival), to the projection room where she has to screen a couple of films. I buy the newspapers and learn that ex-premier Giulio Andreotti is accused of being behind the murder of a blackmailing journalist. Just like in the movies. The charge puzzles me, even if I have not liked this politician since the days of *Umberto D.*, when he wrote an article saying that [the director] Vittorio De Sica did not honour his country. I decide to quote this sentence as an epigraph to the biography of De Sica

that I'm writing with Callisto Cosulich. [. . .]

Noon. I'm working on a presentation for Volker Schlöndorff's interview with Billy Wilder, which will be aired by the RAI at an impossible hour, after midnight. [. . .]

[During the evening] I call Ermanno Olmi, who is at home on the range in Asiago and dining with mutual friend the producer Roberto Cicutto. Olmi is still working on the editing of *Il segreto del Bosco Vecchio*, featuring Paolo Villaggio; the editing is finished and now the master is reducing the film to a standard length. Ermanno tells me he'll have completed it in a month, in order to go to Morocco for *Genesis*, the beautiful script of which I have read. "

Michel Boujut writes for magazines such as Télérama in France, and also produces TV programmes on the cinema:

" I am viewing archive documents on Michel Simon and his son François for the TV-film that I am preparing. Two people full of fire that everything opposes and that everything brings together. They loved and served their art in uncompromising fashion. It will be an evocation of crossed destinies, through a montage of interviews of the father and the son, of extracts from their films and from their work on the stage. [. . .]

Saw again *The Scent of Green Papaya*, one month after Cannes. The first long-feature by the young Franco-Vietnamese Tran Anh Hung is a real Zen film, sensuality blended with spirituality, in this house-garden, like an oasis in the midst of the war. Our barbarism, we who have wrecked this Vietnamese civilisation so serene and so delicate (in spite of the servitude of the rituals), appears in the background, barely suggested by the sirens of the curfew . . . Tran Anh Hung, whom I meet, explains to me that his film is also a response to the exotic insignificance of *The Lover* and *Indochine*. [. . .]

I complete my article for *Télérama* about Anthony Mann, because a Parisian cinema is presenting a retrospective of his Western films starring James Stewart: *Winchester 73*, *Bend of the River*, *The Naked Spur*, and *The Man from Laramie* . . . My admiration is undiminished when re-discovering the films. Rigorous narrative and clarity of direction, in splendid landscapes amid which a wounded hero knows no respite, no soothing. Fortunately, at the end of the path, a beautiful blonde and a brunette are awaiting the tall and lanky Jimmy.

A film critic's work often extends to areas beyond the mere columns in a newspaper or magazine. Wanda Wertenstein is the doyenne of Polish critics:

66 June 10th, being this year the great Roman Catholic Corpus Christi holiday (falling on the Thursday after Trinity Sunday), was not a workday. I went to Mass and the traditional procession, and then visited [the director] Andrzej Wajda and his wife Krystyna, where we discussed some ideas for a new system of teaching film directors and scriptwriters, as well as screen and stage actors. At home I corrected proofs of the Polish edition of David Robinson's *Chaplin: His Life and Art*, which I translated. This job took up the rest of my time today. 99

Tomoe Kogo has written books in Japanese about the silent era, and a biography of D.W. Griffith, and she has done much of her research in the west:

66 On a typically hot and humid summer day in a suburb of Tokyo, this muggy rabbit hutch of mine is more pleasant than the freezing, air-conditioned library of the British Film Institute.

After a short nap, I switched on my word processor. It murmured for 1.05 seconds. A smooth, greenish-grey monitor surface sparkled and outlined some familiar names . . . ALICE GUY, LOIS WEBER, DOROTHY ARZNER. Thirteen years have passed since I encountered them, women directors vanished from film history just after the coming of sound. These days I'm writing an article to try to solve their mysterious disappearance.

As I faced the monitor, a fax machine started to scream and roll out some thin paper. On its matte surface, I saw Claire Hunt's familiar handwriting, asking me to translate some Japanese sentences. Claire and her partner, Kim Longinotto, are making a documentary film on Japanese women. Their production company, Twentieth Century Vixen, has made two films on Japanese women already, and their latest documentary is due to be finished this autumn.

I hope that as you come across this entry, some time in 1994, you will already know about our work . . . 99

Chen Pao-Hsu covers cinema for newspapers in Taipei:

66 The public premiere of a number of Mainland Chinese films was held in Taipei yesterday at the First Mainland China-Taiwan Film Forum. This is the first occasion of its kind in 45 years since Taiwan and Mainland China were separated. Altogether, eight films which had won international awards were screened.

Having covered several film festivals abroad, I'd already seen five of the films. So today, while still on holiday, I took the opportunity of going to the cinema and seeing Chen Kaige's *King of the Children*. The astonishing thing was that this artistic work, which apparently only went out in three

Still from Chen Kaige's King of the Children, *watched by Chen Pao-Hsu in Taipei*

prints on the Mainland, drew a 70% audience in the 1,500-seat cinema in Taipei, and its reception was quite favourable. This may have something to do with the fact that the number of screenings will be limited and that the audience came along with prior knowledge of what to expect.

With the steady increase in contact between Taiwan and the Mainland, in addition to the gradual rise in reputation of Chinese films in the international arena, the coming together of the film industries and creative talents of Taiwan, Hongkong, and Mainland China will undoubtedly be the trend of the future. This is a news topic I shall continue to pay attention to. **99**

The Indonesian Marselli Sumarno, like most good critics, readily admits that he is a film addict and has been fascinated by the cinema since his childhood:

66 People say that the happy man is he who does whatever he likes and can live from what he has done.

[I am a member] of the Film Committee of the Jakarta Art Board. Our duty, among other things, is to organise each month a national or foreign film week. With the co-operation of the Goethe Institut, we will be screening films this June by the German director, Frank Beyer. [. . .]

Top: *An army general takes the first shot of* General Sudirman. Below: *Reels are rushed from one screen to another in Indonesia*

Srimati Runki Banerjee in Satyajit Ray's legendary Pather Panchali

The thing that impresses me about Beyer is the fact that even in the days when he was politically repressed by the East German government, he had a brilliant sense of cinema. [. . .]

After I grew up, I studied in [Indonesia's only] film school, in Jakarta. Then I began to write articles on film for the largest newspaper in the country. I just wanted to earn some money to buy tickets to the movies, but soon became a serious writer on the subject. **99**

The journalist Swapan Kumar Ghosh laments the superficial treatment accorded to good films in India:

66 [During the past 15 years] I have observed, as a film critic, that our country is loath to treat film as a serious subject, even in newspapers and periodicals. At best, the cinema is considered as a crass medium of cheap entertainment. This is despite the fact that long ago, Satyajit Ray's *Pather Panchali* was seen and acclaimed nationally and internationally. Before Ray, it was unthinkable that India could produce 'CINEMA.' [. . .]

On June 10th, I met Mrinal Sen [see Chapter 7] in the evening. After a silent period of about three years, Sen has begun shooting his new film, *The Detained*. His seventy years belie his enthusiasm for film and work. Even when he is not making films, he is forever talking about, and wondering about films. Mrinal almost smells of film. He is at present making a screen version of a story by Saadat Hasan Manto. But, as usual, Sen is concerned only with the essence of the story, not the fat content. He declares that he always treats all material, published or unpublished, as a take-off point. 'The story grows with me every day,' he says. **99**

A.R. Slote, a "showbiz journalist" from Karachi in Pakistan, learns on June 10th that he has been appointed a member of the Central Board of Film Censors:

66 At about 10.45 A.M. I settled down busily to produce the Showbiz Page of the Star Daily. I have been doing this for the last 23 years, and in 1989 I won the National Film Award for Best Film Journalist.

In the afternoon I visited Mr. Muzaffar

A.R. Slote (right), nominated to the Pakistani board of censors

Husain, three-times Chairman of the Pakistan Film Producers' Association (PFPA), ex-Managing Director of the National Film Development Corporation (NAFDEC), and an active film-maker cum distributor, for an exchange of views about current censorship policy and the future of the domestic film industry. He seemed rather worried by the huge increase in the cost of production (which has gone up to Rs. 4 million for an average film) and the closure of theatres in big cities like Karachi (32 demolished during the past dozen years) and Lahore. He didn't sound very happy about the policy of the censors either.

I also happened to meet Mr. Haroon Rashid, owner of two of Karachi's leading cinemas and founder-president of the Pakistan Motion Picture Investors' Association (PMPIA). He was very pleased with the change in public viewing trends – from terrorist themes to comedies. 'I think our film-makers should pay more attention to quality rather than quantity, if they want angry filmgoers to return to the cinema,' he said. [. . .]

As I have been listening, writing, and commenting on the so-called crisis in the Pakistan film industry during more than three decades, I came to the conclusion before going to bed tonight that films will continue to be made with outside finance and that filmgoers will go on patronising them for many years to come, despite competition from TV, video, and satellite, because the cinema has its own charm and appeal. **"**

Medhat Mahfouz works as a film critic in Cairo, Egypt, and admits that he watches *2001* and *Terminator 2* on his VCR at least once a month:

" 8-11 A.M. I wrote an article for my newspaper, *El Alam El-Yom*, a financial daily. The article is based on some preliminary data from a survey being made by the Cultural Development Fund. It shows that there are only 150 cinemas in the whole of Egypt, and that attendances are running at a rate of only 10% of what they were 25 years ago. The average Egyptian visits the cinema once every three years!

Noon. I signed a contract to translate a new book about the history of world cinema into Arabic. [. . .]

1-4 P.M. I made some improvements to my first effort at screenwriting. It is called *Silence of the Dreams*, about Aids, but could also apply to the plague of religious fundamentalism.

4-6 P.M. I received the assistant editor of my film guide, *Films on Videotape, TV and in Cinemas*. We discussed some new films and reviewed some entries on the computer. **"**

Rafik Al Atassi prefers television to the printed word in order to present his critical opinions to his Syrian public:

" Today I supervised a press and media review of *Dances with Wolves*, and ran a public discussion.

I also prepared an episode for my weekly TV programme, *Sound and Vision*, which deals with aspects of the domestic and international cinema through meetings with Syrian film personalities.

I have, for the first time, embarked on a production for the small screen. I am supervising the filming of a new TV series in north-western Syria entitled *The Stranger and the River*. Today I also appeared on national TV to explain to viewers the British Film Institute's idea of choosing June 10th as a day in the life of world cinema. **"**

Top: *Egyptian film critic Medhat Mahfouz watched Kubrick's* 2001: A Space Odyssey, *starring Keir Dullea and Gary Lockwood.* Above: *Kevin Costner in* Dances with Wolves, *discussed on June 10th by Rafik Al Atassi*

17. The Animators GRAPHICS, PAINTING, MODELLING, AND FILM MERGE AND OVERLAP IN THE REALM OF ANIMATION. SOME OF THE MOST INVENTIVE ARTISTS IN THE CINEMA HAVE WORKED IN THIS MEDIUM: WALT DISNEY, NORMAN MCLAREN, WALERIAN BOROWCZYK, RICHARD WILLIAMS . . . ANIMATORS TEND TO BE SOLITARY CREATURES, NURSING THEIR TALENT AND HUMOUR THROUGH LONG PERIODS OF GESTATION IN THE STUDIO.

308

Paul Driessen, a flying Dutchman who has found support and congenial colleagues at the National Film Board of Canada, has won a host of awards for his adventurous and outspoken work:

66 Now after a trip back to Holland, and then to the animation festival at Annecy in France it's back to the National Film Board of Canada in Montreal to animate the last season of my *End of All Seasons*, or whatever the title will be – a multi-screen handmade short, which the big NFB computers will colour in, position, and shoot, either on 35mm or 70mm.

Animating snow in June will feel kind of strange, particularly after our more than usual share of that stuff this winter. But it's an exciting film to work on. A lot of funny little spring, summer, fall and winter stories. I ended up with visual storytelling as opposed to my family's verbal talents. The animation goes fast and well but the

multi-screen editing will be complicated. It's the kind of film I could only do at the NFB with its sophisticated equipment and its interest in going beyond the ordinary. My Dutch films usually are much more primitive technically but, interestingly, don't seem to suffer from it. It proves that it's the idea that counts, not the polish. 99

One of Driessen's mentors, the Dutch producer and documentarist Nico Crama, regrets that not more "is done in [the Netherlands] to retain talented film-makers who could strengthen our film culture":

66 My first job of the day is to gather information about the TV mini-series, *Uncles and Aunts*, and write a promotional entry for an international catalogue. For a film-maker, I seem to be spending a lot of time behind the word processor

A day in the life of Dutch animator Gerrit van Dijk

Uncles and Aunts, *conceived and animated by Paul Driessen, and produced by Nico Crama*

these days. *Uncles and Aunts* is an animated spoof on the traditional family album. It was conceived and animated by my friend Paul Driessen. A few years ago we made this three-minute film between our other activities, and we were agreeably surprised when it received an award for the best short TV-series at the Annecy Animation festival in 1991. This encouraged us to continue with this series, of which three sequels have been completed now. As usual the revenues from these animated shorts hardly cover the production costs, but we do have a lot of fun doing these finger exercises. Animation has always been one of the best products of Dutch cinema, and we aim to keep it that way.

Among today's mail is yet another invitation to enter a film for a festival. Every year I have to write more 'Thanks, but no thanks' notes to festi-val organisers all over the world. Entering a film involves time, effort and money, and there are not many festivals that can give a short film the kind of publicity that leads to commercial distrib-ution or television screenings. There comes a time in a film-maker's life when rewards are at least as important as awards. **99**

Riitta Nelimarkka is a Finnish artist whose talents comprise textiles, book illustration and collage, as well as animation, for which she has won many prizes:

66 A visual metaphor from the book [by André Bazin which I am translating] sur-faces in my mind: light descending through a win-dow-pane and forming a threatening shadow in

the form of a cross on something . . . Only I do not remember what. Annoying, because a good memory is precisely what I need for my work with the animation movie, *La Valse*. It seems that someone in this family [three sons, one husband] is making it his business to mislay my sketches for it.

All the desks in my studio have been taken over by *La Valse* and so, for that matter, have all the horizontal planes in the rest of the house. [. . .]

Summer has come to Finland and the light never fails. In a way this is a rather unsuitable season in which to animate – in the dark in artificial light. What is animation? It is fun as long as it lasts, just like the Finnish summer, which is beautiful, short, and unnecessarily green. [. . .]

I animate, draw and listen to music. At times I would like to see someone with a sense of humour and then again I would not. I go to the greenhouse to pick some mint for my tea, beat a tattoo, do sums with a pencil and paper. I work in an old-fashioned way, I am my own virtual contact. I say to myself, 'Don't animate that,' and then animate it anyway, only to realise later on that it is the linchpin of the entire scene. I smile. **"**

In Brisbane, Australia, Catherine Sinnamon ponders the nature of animation, the loneliest of all the film arts:

" It has become a habit to commence each working day in a café, where I take time to draw. These sketches have come to record my thoughts, dreams, emotions, and sometimes predicaments, as I do not keep a written diary. [. . .]

Worked alone in the studio as usual, setting up the lights, operating the camera, and manipulating the puppet. I was working on a close-up of the puppet with emphasis on texture. I found difficulty in framing the next shot, where I had to pull back from a close-up to a medium shot; from the innocent reverie of texture to the objectivity of line. [. . .] Shooting went well so there were no

Animation cel from Riitta Nelimarkka's La Valse

retakes. Not by choice, but for geographical reasons, I work in isolation. I do not encounter other film-makers. I have taught myself everything I know about film technique, and must find my own solutions to technical problems and the recurring advent of unplanned disasters. I have no professional assistance. [. . .]

I ordered too much film stock from Kodak in Melbourne. Fool! Now what am I going to live on for the rest of the month? My film is unfunded, due to the belief here that puppet animation is a dinosaur in the technology race. [. . .]

Some of the preoccupations I had in architecture school have merged in the film with new elements in the storyboard. There has been little need to make any major deviations from this. As I alone manipulate the puppet, I have come to realise how my emotional state is reflected in its movements. I have to keep remembering to 'be the character' on set, between running back and forth to the camera, or the gestures become meaningless. I notice also that I need to take care what background music I listen to, when animating, because the puppet, the camera and the lighting resonate immediately with the music. [. . .]

The idea was to create a film that set up a dialogue between the eye of the camera and the world that exists on the film set. I hope the camera is not simply recording the plot of the film. Animation is a flexible medium. One can explore so many aspects of film that live action would not permit, while still retaining some semblance of realism. **99**

Hollywood has regained the lead in animation technology that it had held for so long under Walt Disney. Steven Paul Leiva is a writer and producer in Los Angeles:

66 On June 10th I was in the middle of the sixth week of production on the animated feature, *Betty Boop*. I am producing the film with my partner in Rees/Leiva Productions, Jerry Rees. We had spent the previous year developing the script, which Jerry wrote, for Richard Zanuck, Lili Fini Zanuck and Richard Fleischer, the executive producers, and for MGM, the studio backing the project.

It had been a busy six weeks as we were setting up an animation studio from scratch, while starting work on character design and storyboards. About twenty staff people were hired and were working on both the creative and the production end, with many more to come. [. . .]

I have a strong interest in theatre and will be having a play of mine produced in 1994 at The Friends and Artists Theater Ensemble in L.A. Theatre and animation – no matter how it may seem on the surface – are not so far apart. I have

313 «

always maintained that animators should turn to the theatre far more often than to live action film for inspiration.

Why? Because in both forms a major task is to suspend the disbelief of the audience. [. . .] For animation is an art form that is quite obvious in its artifice. It is, after all, drawings on the screen, or dimensional models, which are moving, and few are gullible enough to believe that they moved themselves and someone just had to 'doc-

Steven Paul Leiva (left) and Jerry Rees with Betty Boop artwork on the wall in the background

ument' it on camera. Animation is nowhere near reality. Yet animation must make the audience believe in the world and characters it is presenting, which is, simply stated, unbelievable. Animation, like the theatre, is a performance art. The audience must believe that which is being performed, or the creators have failed. **"**

Ivan Stoyanovich, one of Bulgaria's leading film commentators, serves now as head of an animation studio in Sofia:

I took the bus to the Studio for Animation Films 'Sofia,' where I have recently been appointed director. I have always been interested in animation, have written some scripts, and have sat on committees and juries. I think that the slight respect gained by Bulgarian cinema in recent decades should be credited to its animators. But, as a result of an impotent Bolshevik regime, this excellent studio has been in a cul-de-sac, and I am trying my best to regain its prestige.

June 10th was a happy day, when we managed to get some funds and settle overdue bills for water, electricity, and telephone, all of which had been cut off, and even to start production on a couple of talented scripts. [. . .]

The evening ended with a boring report on administrative problems about the budget for new animation projects, but, at home at last, I indulged myself in watching the TV series of Bergman's *Fanny and Alexander.*

315

Left: *Ivan Stoyanovich, long-established expert from Bulgaria.*
Above: *Still from* Fanny and Alexander

18. The Documentarists THERE IS A HANDFUL OF

FILM FESTIVALS DEVOTED TO THE DOCUMENTARY,

BUT MOST DOCUMENTARY FILM-MAKERS WILL BE

CONFINED TO THE SMALL SCREEN. A NOTABLE

MINORITY OF THEM PERSIST IN RESEARCHING

AND SHOOTING DOCUMENTARIES WITH BOTH AN

AESTHETIC AND A SOCIOLOGICAL RING.

▶▶ 316

The work of Stefan Jarl (*They Call Us Misfits, Nature's Revenge, The Threat* etc.) has travelled the world, startling festival and TV audiences with its piercing, uncompromising view of contemporary social problems, and illuminated by an unerring visual flair and rapport with the Nordic landscape. In 1993 he won the European Film Award for Best Documentary:

❝ In a few hours I'll be standing in Jokkmokk far up in the north of Sweden, north of the polar circle. There is a film festival [there]. I've been invited to participate in a debate and attend the screening of five of my films. I take a cab to the airport and fly to Stockholm; there I must change to another flight to Luleå. The only connection from there to Jokkmokk is by car for two hours on bad roads.

Finally there, I'm met by a cold wind that sweeps down from the still snow-covered mountains in the north. I was prepared for the cold. I've been up here before and shot two films with Lappish subjects: *The Threat and Jarna, Reindeer Herdsman in the Year 2000.* [. . .]

Thinking of my short film, which I'm going to finish up here, is really the reason why I have travelled to Jokkmokk. I don't have any money, true, but through participating in the film festival I at least get the trip paid. My two colleagues are on their way by car. They have 1,100 km to drive from Stockholm and don't arrive until this evening.

The film will depict the intrusion of the Swedish big cities on the world of the Sames [Lapps]. Control of the streams, logging of large areas and tourism: this threatens the Sames' chances of surviving as a minority with their reindeer and their culture. Most of the film is already shot. We're supplementing the beginning and end.

We need help finding the right locations. I don't have to say much before the map's on the table: 'Here, you must go there!' The forestry company has transformed the forest into a moonscape. Our contact becomes our friend and offers to come with us. It transpires that Lars Anders was once a beast-of-prey tracker for the Department of the Environment. He knows how many bears there are and where they usually can be found. Will we be able to film bears, I wonder?

Eager and excited, we return to the hotel. The midnight sun makes it as light as day, even though it's 1 A.M. in the morning. It's hard to sleep and we toss down a few whiskies. [. . .] Why do I throw myself again and again into these

*Stefan Jarl (*top, *on left) on location for his documentary on the Lapps,* Reindeer Herdsman in the Year 2000 *(above)*

>> 318

unfinanced projects that only threaten to give me ulcers? Where is the audience today in the cinema for this short film recorded on 35mm with stereo sound, about the Sames' situation?

Thank heavens my co-workers, cinematographer Per Källberg, who has shot ten of my films, and the technician, Stefan Hencz, are so patient about their wages . . . **99**

Another Swede, Christina Olofson, who has directed and co-directed fictional feature films, also enjoys the challenge of making documentaries:

66 [My] film's working title is *Nina*. A documentary that describes a not so unusual woman in Sweden today. In the words of Lars Noren: what moment of your childhood deprived you of a future? I'm going to look through the material and synchronise it during the day.

[While I'm running along the beach in the early morning] I think about how we should proceed. What kind of film is it? How well do we portray Nina's story? Doubt! The shooting covers different periods. Good, but also difficult. Good because it gives me the chance to see what needs to be dealt with more deeply. Difficult because it's hard to start again every time, mentally. The producer within me also says that it will be more expensive, more film is needed, the trips back and forth from *Nina* through mid-Sweden are long, and petrol costs money, also TIME! [. . .]

After the run I bike to my studio, about ten minutes from where I live. It's a minute studio where I find concentration. When I shut the door behind me I leave the world outside. Beyond the window there are enormous rhododendron bushes. The caretaker and his wife are dedicated people who keep the building in excellent repair and spend a lot of time in the garden outside my window.

I sit down at the cutting table and study the images. I synchronise the sound. I visualise the journey (by car) to Nina's childhood home. I see how Nina's eyebrows grow deeper. In the end her face cracks and the tears come. I turn down the sound. The room grows quiet. The film comes out of the camera, I turn up the sound. [. . .]

I realise that the editing will be difficult. It's all about finding a structure, a rhythm. To make the

Left: *Nina Sundberg in Christina Olofson's* Darling Nina.
Above: *Christina Olofson*

difficulties bearable I call my editor, Annette, and tell her about the material to hand. Decide what we're going to talk about later in the summer, and how to handle the editing. The phone rings – contracts! Yeah, that's the producer in me talking! The artist and economist go hand in hand! The last of my money has been decided upon, but no agreement has been made yet. It's dragging on. Me, nervous? I never count my chickens before the signatures are in place. A bitter lesson: everyone is nice and obliging until the **99** contracts are due.

Her fellow countryman, Ulf von Strauss, prepares to shoot the final scene of a new documentary:

66 I leave for Södertälje, a small town south of Stockholm. My team is already on site. Since November last year we have been shooting a documentary for Swedish television on anabolic steroids. It has been a troublesome production.

The trade in steroids runs to a turnover almost matching that of the narcotics trade. During the research and the filming we have come up against a lot of obstacles and a lot of silence. And, as usual when you're working on a documentary, you often find only more questions when you're looking for answers.

At the cemetery in Södertälje we'll shoot a rather complicated scene with the camera up in a crane rolling on a rail. The film is a documentary reconstruction of my own research into the subject of steroids. The starting point is the death of a young athlete as a consequence of misuse of steroids. I ask myself: Who killed Patrik? – which is also the title of the film. [. . .]

In the final scene I light a candle for Patrik on his grave and, with more knowledge and more disenchantment than when I began my investigation at the same spot in the beginning of the film, leave the location. **99**

▶▶ 320

Oladipupo Ladebo, who has made children's films for CBS, also focuses on a medical issue in his documentary, made in his native Nigeria:

66 I am working on a documentary drama on the affliction and prevalence of Vesico Vagina Fistula among African teenage girls. Obstetric Fistula, the collective medical term for VVF, is claimed by many medical experts to be 'one social calamity too many' in several developing countries where maternity services are sparse or mistrusted, or both. The victims are mostly poor, uneducated, very young girls who customarily marry early and practise sexual intercourse. Because the growth of the pelvis is still incomplete, they suffer obstructed labour which invariably leads to bladder injuries. The resultant urinary incontinence has been described as one of the most frightful of all human afflictions. The incontinence is sometimes confused with venereal disease and the affected family feels a sense of shame. [. . .]

The present documentary, for which I drafted the screenplay in November 1991, will run for 90 minutes and its worldwide distribution should raise money for the establishment of a VVF Trust Fund for Africa. **99**

Jaan Ruus, a film critic and journalist in Estonia, notes the difficulties that his compatriots have in adapting to their newly-won liberty:

66 The duty of the magazine [for which I write], *Theatre, Music, Cinema*, is to give a digest of the annual film reviews – one of the few traditions which has remained unchanged since the old times. In 1992, 24 films were made in Estonia, ten of them full-length. Estonian documentarists have been very cautious during the past year. They cannot adapt themselves to the new times, they cannot grasp the processes, and they observe reality as though from a distance. Only Mark Soosaar has succeeded in following the election campaigns of two Estonian presidential candidates from the inside and in confronting the candidates in accordance with the rules of dramatisation. One acts like a yokel, and the other is pictured as a dandy. [. . .] But Soosaar is clearly on the side of the country fellow. Thus it turns out to be not so much a reliable documentary of that time but an agit-prop poster for the peasant. Although containing some acute observations and nice documents of the period (for instance an interview with a dutiful old black person who hoists the flag of Estonia in front of the UN building in New York for the first time, knowing nothing about Estonia). **99**

Nature documentaries constitute a significant portion of world television programming. Alex de Verteuil, a specialist in this area, enters the wetlands of Trinidad to film a rare species:

66 We are shooting material for our documentary on the Nariva Swamp, Trinidad's largest wetland, now under severe threat through illegal rice cultivation. Our main objective today is to record the white-fronted capuchin, a beautiful little monkey that occurs sparsely in the Nariva, but is said to be abundant in the Trinity Hills. [. . .]

7.30 A.M. We have found them, a troop of about a dozen white-fronted capuchins. They are feeding on the fruit of the wild tobacco plant fringing the road. They peep out shyly from between the leaves and every now and then one

The rarely-glimpsed capuchin monkey, photographed by Robert Lee on location in Trinidad

of them sallies forth to the end of the branch to grab a handful of berries before scooting back to the safety of the high-wood. Robert Lee, our cameraman, has shouldered camera and tripod and advances, somehow stooping with his awkward load, trying to appear inconspicuous but looking like some huge lumbering beetle, to within 100 ft of the monkeys.

8.30 A.M. The sun broke through a short while ago and everything is flooded in the most wonderful light. Some vestiges of early morning mist are still rising through the trees. The capuchins are now about 60 ft from us and we have switched from the 12 x 120 zoom to the 400mm Nikon which we are using with an adaptor. We can fill the frame with the faces of these lovely little creatures. The light is perfect and we are shooting at f8. [. . .]

10 A.M. We used 1,200 ft on the capuchins. Robert is very excited as are we all – confident we have some excellent footage. The audio is wonderful. 99

19. Surviving Against the Odds THIS SECTION IS COMPOSED OF DIARIES FROM FILM-MAKERS IN THE DEVELOPING COUNTRIES AS WELL AS THOSE WHO SURVIVE ON THE OUTER FRONTIERS OF INDEPENDENT CINEMA. THEIR WORK PROVIDES HOPE FOR DISCOVERY AT FILM FESTIVALS AROUND THE WORLD. THESE ARE MAVERICKS WHO REFUSE TO GIVE UP IN THE FACE OF ECONOMIC AND POLITICAL OBSTACLES.

Financing pictures is difficult anywhere, but Egyptian producer-director Mohamed Khan describes how he was obliged to make a second feature simply to pay off his bank loan:

❝ I am putting the final touches to the rewrites on the script for *A Very Hot Day*, which is what I call my 'bank film.' Why 'bank film?' Well, after producing a feature a couple of years ago, entitled *Knight of the City*, with a bank loan – which is a rarity in the local industry – I ended up owing more money than what I had borrowed, due to the foreign distribution problems and a delayed release. Release was held up for eighteen months, causing the bank interest to multiply. The distributors did not like the idea of banks funding film producers because then they, the distributors, would no longer be in control. So my bank was very understanding in the circumstances, and decided to waive any further interest on the debt for one year to give the whole idea a better chance of survival. That's when the idea of *A Very Hot Day* struck me – to make a low-budget movie quickly with the main actors, director of

Publicity still from Mohamed Khan's A Very Hot Day

Production pictures from Arnold Antonin's latest Haitian film

photography, screenwriter, editor, composer, and myself as director/producer all working for free, with the aim of pre-selling the picture and settling the bank debt, thus showing the bank how serious we are and how we want to work on future projects in partnership. **"**

Arnold Antonin communicates the exasperation and dogged perseverence born of the struggle to keep filming in contemporary Haiti:

" 7 A.M. Interior daylight. I wake up. The sunbeams filter through the shutters. Today will be a typical summer day in Port-au-Prince: dazzling and stifling. The anguished voice of a radio announcer reminds us that we are under an emb-

argo and that the cost of living is increasing by the day, that there have been shots during the night in several working class suburbs of the capital.

I check my timetable for the day ahead. 10 A.M.: a screening (followed by a debate) of two shorts that I directed for Unicef. One about Children's Rights, the other about drugs among children of the street. Noon: meeting with one of my ex-film students at the National School of Arts. He completed his studies four years ago but has not found a job since. He wants to become a 'boat person' and leave for the promised land of Florida. 2 P.M.: meeting with foreign friends making a short stay here to discuss the violation of human rights in Haiti; we might make a film on the subject. [. . .]

But the day docs not go according to plan. The screening did not take place because of an

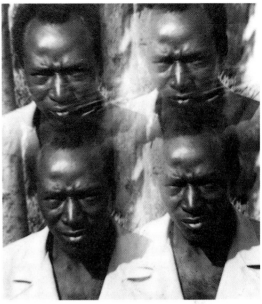

Left: *From the UNICEF film,* Accord sur les droits des enfants. Above: *Experimental images from Antonin Artaud*

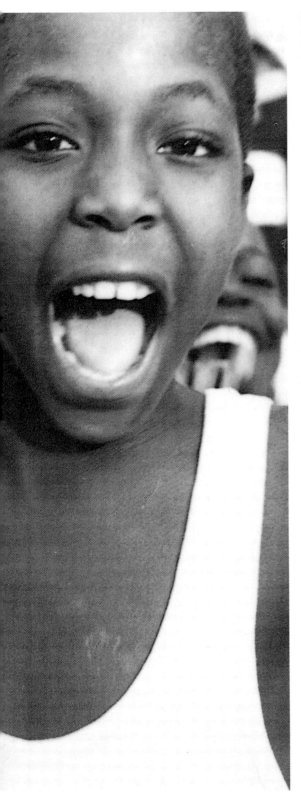

electricity cut, a black-out as we say in Haiti, that went on for twelve hours. The student rang to tell me that he is ill, probably with the typho-malaria epidemic that has devastated the country for some weeks now. [. . .]

At 10 P.M. I begin work on my script. The story is based on a true life event that occurred a few weeks ago: at the corner of a street here, a few currency dealers offer the passers-by their piles of green banknotes. A man, armed with a machete, approaches one of them and severs his head in a single sharp movement, worthy of one of Akira Kurosawa's samourais. He has barely the time to pick up a few notes. He is arrested. From that point, in flashbacks, I will reconstruct the story of an affable and gentle young man. **"**

Kofi Middleton-Mends directs films and lectures in Accra (Ghana):

" I was a resource person [today] at a workshop organised by the Commission on Culture [in Accra] on the subject of 'Video Feature Production – The Professional Approach.'

Feature film production on celluloid has been an expensive business over the past several years with very few being made in Ghana. With the advent of video equipment, features in that medium have been inundating our screens for some eight years. This is simply because the equipment is comparatively less expensive to use. But the quality of the production, a hundred years after the invention of motion picture photography, is most disappointing. [. . .]

The aim of the workshop was to create an awareness of the possibility of doing things the professional way. There is only one film school in this country, and it is unthinkable that every director will pass through its doors. [. . .]

Audiences seem to have abandoned kung-fu and other films of that kind, and are eager to identify with familiar faces, stories, themes, and locations. They feel at home with these video productions but soon, if we are not careful, lack of professionalism will signal the death of what is a worthwhile **99** substitute for expensive celluloid.

Mozambique, in southern Africa on the coast of the Indian Ocean, became independent from Portugal in 1975, but democracy and stability have remained elusive, as the director José A.R. Cardoso observes:

66 In my country, there was once a film institute, sponsored by the State, which produced films and nurtured professionals in all aspects of cinematography. Today, this institute no longer exists and the staff that worked there has been taking on whatever comes up in order to survive. A few are still connected with the production thanks to video – by working either for the local TV network, or, like me, for the recently created private production and advertising film companies.

At 63 years of age, I have dozens of documentaries on film and video, as well as medium-length fictional films, to my credit. I now concentrate on commercials. Although this kind of work is not what I would like to do, I continue with it just in order to make ends meet and as a means of financing cultural projects and documentaries, as well as films. Right now I am completing the screenplay for a fictional film, which I intend to make this year, and which is adapted from two short stories by the Mozambican writer, **99** Calano da Silva.

Even securing quality film stock with which to shoot looms as a major hurdle for film-makers in developing countries. Shaji N. Karun is a director and cinematographer from Trivandrum in Kerala, in southern India:

66 A friend had taken away the 16mm rolls I was planning to use [for my documentary on the Marxist Communist leader, E.M. Sankaran Namboodiripad, who turns 84 in three days' time]. I spoke to this friend over the telephone yesterday and told him I would be stuck if he didn't return it. I have a feeling that he will not live up to his promise. If so, I need at least three days to buy new stock from Madras, because I have to send someone with cash to Kodak there. I have already spent a lot in acquiring stock and I don't want to invest even more money for this purpose. Time is running out. I must make a decision. What should I do about the stock?

Should I switch to video? As a film-maker I do not really want to get involved with video. I know it has great potential and the video language on MTV is almost worthy of art. [. . .] But it is always the 'small' details that I have wanted. So I hope I will retrieve the film stock and avoid having to shoot on video.

6 P.M. Still no news from my friend. I hope he will return the stock . . .

8 P.M. I phoned my assistant to arrange **99** two tapes of Sony Sp for June 13th.

"Getting the backing" remains a common obstacle for independent film-makers throughout the world. B. Chintu Mohapatra, an assistant director (to, among others, Shyam Benegal), writes from Bombay, India:

66 How to start? What to start? Where to get the funds? These questions have been in my mind around the clock for the past few months. I want to start an independent venture, but the biggest problem is funding.

Today I am away from my headquarters (Bombay) and staying with my eldest brother Sabyasachi Mohapatra, who himself is an eminent film-maker in Orissa. It is a great chance for me to discuss with him the various aspects of film-making – especially for me, without resources and

On location in Bolivia for Jorge Sanjinés' Para recibir el canto de los pajaros

without prior experience of independent projects, although I have worked with Shyam Benegal, Kalpane Lazmi, A.K. Bir and my brother.

I came upon an interesting book recently, the official catalogue of the Swiss Film Centre, in which I found many short feature films made in 16mm and lasting between 5 and 45 minutes. I discuss this with my brother, so that I can start with a short feature of this kind, which would be within our reach finance-wise. **99**

Muhammad Ahmad Khan also comes from Bombay, but now lives in London as a producer-director – and has discovered that life is by no means easy for Asian film-makers:

66 The phone rang. It was my friend Zia from Southend-on-Sea. 'Ahmad, I just heard that Kamaal Sahib passed away – is it true?' That is how the day began for me. I called Bombay and Tajdar Amrohi, Kamaal Sahib's son, confirmed that his father had died and was already buried.

Amir Hyder Kamaal Amrohi – the last of the Indian movie moghuls – *was* dead. I rang Zia back to confirm the rumours, and we both felt sad as we remembered how, many years ago, we had studied at the Kamaal Amrohi Film Institute in Bombay under Kamaal Sahib. [. . .] Not many people in the U.K. know of him, but to Urdu and Hindi speaking people he was India's answer to Cecil B.

DeMille, and all his films were epic in scope.

Kamaal Sahib gave me my first break as a writer-director of a documentary entitled *Smoking or Health*, which he produced for the Films Division.

Life in England is not 'cushy' for ethnic film-makers like myself and the British film industry languishes in the doldrums anyway. Added to this there is discrimination, and I haven't worked since April 1992 when I directed the National Asthma Campaign's video for ethnic minorities in English, Bengali, Hindi, Urdu, Punjabi, and Gujarathi dialects, and that was done in a mere two weeks.

India has a vast number of talented film-makers but after coming to settle down in Britain I realise that the BBC and ITV do not encourage ethnic talent. I have been applying for jobs to the BBC and the independent broadcasters and have not even been shortlisted. [. . .] So today I have decided that I shall no longer apply for work here but return to India to make films. **99**

La nacion clandestina **has established Jorge Sanjinés as the outstanding Bolivian director of his generation, but without any kind of firm legislation, the cinema struggles to survive there:**

327 ◀◀

66 Three days ago we finished shooting our most recent film, *To Receive the Song of the Birds*. We began in October last year. We filmed the bulk of the movie in six weeks, then had to wait through several months of rain before we could complete the remaining scenes. Today I feel greatly relieved that we have finished that beautiful, but dramatic, period of filming, but I am also very concerned to see the quality of our negative. In Bolivia there are no film laboratories, so we cannot develop the stock immediately. It is extremely risky to send part of the material to labs abroad. We have suffered mishaps in the past which have taught us the hard way that we should develop everything at the same time.

Fortunately, in the cold, dry climate of La Paz we can keep the exposed negative for some while without risk. However, so many things can happen during shooting, and we cannot find out what has occurred straight away, something that's taken for granted in countries with labs. So this is

Scene from Para recibir el canto de los pajaros (*To Receive the Song of the Birds*), *set in Bolivia*

a time of uncertainty and we are anxious. Will everything be fine? Did the camera always work perfectly? Will the plane arrive safely when it takes all our material to be developed? We have a parallel video control, but this only allows us to monitor the movements and general performance of the actors. It isn't the same!

Today I am going to ring Geraldine Chaplin to tell her that we have finally finished the shooting. She has an important role in the film and it was marvellous to have her with us in December 1992, not only because we benefited from her talent, but also because we were touched by her warmth as a person and by her natural humility and agreeable nature.

In neighbouring Brazil, Suzana Amaral, who has made several TV movies and also *The Hour of the Star* for theatrical release, reflects sadly on her struggle for survival:

I am in my country house just a few kilometres from the city [São Paulo] where I live. Like all Brazilian film-makers, I am going through moments of depression. Since the economic situation of the country collapsed a few years ago, our prospects for making films have shrunk to a minimum.

The film institute [Embrafilme] supported by the government, which subsidised our cinema, was closed for good in 1991, and since then

each of us has tried to survive within our special areas.

In the last few years I have written three screenplays. I have believed in many projects, but nothing came of them. I have directed films for TV, in Portugal and Brazil, for institutions, for private companies, and I have also made TV commercials.

Today, when I think about the cinema, I feel a kind of melancholy, a great sadness; there is a big question in the air and I cannot find any answers . . .In order to survive, we make use of our profession just to make ends meet, but the work we do is a far cry from what we had dreamed of when we first started . . .

But even so, we persevere. I still believe that some of my projects will materialise this year. [. . .]

Today, in particular, because it is Corpus Christi Day and a holiday, I am not doing anything . . . just resting, thinking, writing about one's vocation which is still to be a film-maker at the end of the century, during a period when the cinema, along with the Western world as a whole, is passing through a serious economic crisis. I look through the window and see the cold insistent rain pouring down. I wipe away a stubborn tear. I make an effort to understand that we need to have hope. 99

Marcelia Cartaxo and Jose Dumont in Brazilian director Suzana Amaral's The Hour of the Star

Fellow Brazilian Ana Carolina T. Soares, based in Rio de Janeiro, strikes a similar chord:

" This is a curious date for me to be writing about the cinema sector in my country. Our film industry has been paralysed since March 15, 1990, when ex-President Collor destroyed all means of production, distribution, supervision and exhibition of Brazilian films, which then enjoyed an audience of some 7 to 8 million. We are stuck in a rut, afraid, impoverished, and searching for ideas that might offer a solution for MP's, ministers, and even our President. In three years, only two features have been made, with a budget of just $100,000 each. [. . .]

I have had a project since 1990 called *The Death of Desire*. It is about the actress Sarah Bernhardt's tour to Rio de Janeiro in 1905 when the actress is caught in a major professional and personal crisis. She accepts an offer to go on tour in Buenos Aires, Rio, and New York, and when she arrives in Argentina, she loses her dresser who dies of typhoid fever. This mishap deepens her grief. When she reaches Rio, she is totally stressed out and falls victim to the envy, cruelty, and revenge of three new dressers imposed on her in Brazil. This culminates in an accident during her final performance in *Tosca*. She falls at the back of the stage and suffers a compound fracture in her right leg. She goes to New York, eventually has the leg amputated – and carries on working with a wooden leg . . .

In order for the project to see the light of day, I had a tense discussion with the Vice-President of the São Paulo State Bank (BANESPA) on June 10th, when I presented it for assessment and applied for $500,000 in funding. Unfortunately, the bank is unwilling to accept my three previous features as a real guarantee for such an advance. It wants real assets, such as property. On the other hand, according to federal law I am entitled to an 80% tax benefit on the total budget of a film. My rights to this benefit expire in June. If the bank doesn't let us know about the results of its film selection by June 30th, I will lose this benefit forever. [. . .]

Also today I took part in a long meeting with a group of producers at the Bank of Espirito Santo. They have been trying to open the way to getting credit for film production. In order to obtain this loan – and the minimum amount is $2 million – you must give as guarantee one and a half times as much as the budget. This makes it impossible for any film-maker to comply. And furthermore, the production must be strictly commercial.

So this is how I ended my day as a film-maker. I have been making my living from cinema since 1967. I am tired and without hope. "

Arabella Hutter lives in London and wants to complete a documentary about the Directors' Fortnight at the Cannes Film Festival:

" All morning [we] work on the budget. We need to bring the figures down to avoid frightening possible investors. It's also fairly complicated because we decided to make several versions of it: one which shows how much our Spanish co-producers have spent, how much they have promised to spend, how much we spent, what the total final budget will be, and last and most important the amount we still need to finish the film. It's a documentary featured called *Celluloid Phoenix*, about the Directors' Fortnight in Cannes, and was initiated by Mr. Young's Preview Theatre in London.

I was brought into the film because my mother tongue is French and I speak Spanish. We started shooting without all the finance necessary for finishing and now we are looking for the completion funds . . . without being paid (on deferral, as it is called). To gain a better understanding of photography I worked as a camera assistant on a short where everybody was on deferrals. "

"Once again, day to day survival had a positive outlook," writes José M. Vergés, a production manager in Barcelona (Spain):

" Today we approached the end of a another gloomy week business-wise. My company, as well as thousands of others struggling with Spain's deep recession, has been struggling on a day by day basis for survival. Restructuring had been going on the previous week, involving the sad loss of certain employees.

So going to work on June 10th was not a happy process. Somehow, the Spanish saying of

'No hay mal que cien años dure' is once more very true. That morning things began to pick up, and a busy day was forthcoming.

By 11 A.M. I met with my employer and friend. By the end of the day I had projects through to almost the end of the year lying on my desk and waiting to be budgeted. Once again, day to day survival had a positive outlook.

Meetings involved two TV series, four commercials, three live music recordings, and a sports event, plus rental of audiovisual equipment for three conventions.

At the moment, I don't know how many of these projects will take shape, but the breath of fresh air after a week of inactivity had a very positive effect on our staff. **99**

The life of an independent producer in the former Yugoslavia is hazardous as well as financially precarious. Damir Teresak is a Croat based in Zagreb:

66 It is difficult to work under the pressure of war, especially in our profession. Even if the war is going on not here but in Bosnia, the frustration for me is intense. It is worse because I recently lost my younger brother Nenad, who was one of the best gaffers in Croatia and who died in a car accident at the end of 1992. [. . .]

I am the first independent producer in Croatia and I have recently produced a full-length feature, *Golden Years*, through my company, Maxima Film. The first screening was in Zagreb

Still from Golden Years, *directed by Croatian Damir Teresak*

332

in April, but although it proved a success I must find a way to sell the picture abroad. Tomorrow I hope I will get an answer from the San Sebastian Film Festival, telling me if the film has been selected. I am worried. It is hard for productions from a small country like Croatia to penetrate the world market. A festival like San Sebastian could help me a lot. [. . .]

I see great potential for shooting co-productions and foreign films in Croatia once the war stops, because we have beautiful landscapes and highly professional film-makers on hand. **"**

Sheer brashness and an irrepressible optimism in the face of penury serve the independent film-maker well in the battle to get recognition, as the story of Tiana [Thi Thanh Nga], a Vietnamese woman director, shows:

" After five years I completed my first nonfiction film, *From Hollywood to Hanoi*, last year. In September we (me, the film, and diehard volunteers) premiered the picture at the Telluride Film Festival in Colorado alongside *The Crying Game*, *Léolo*, *El Mariachi*, and *Strictly Ballroom*. We were picked 'Best of Telluride' by the festival director, Bill Pence. By November I was meeting Emma Thompson, Kenneth Branagh, Sir Dickie [Attenborough], and Lord Lew [Grade] at the gala benefit dinner in London for the opening of the London Film Festival. Not bad for a girl from Saigon who ended up in Hollywood and left it all to go back and find her roots in Vietnam.

I received a congratulatory fax from Emma and Ken. Maybe I'll have it framed.

All this time we have been screening the film with a cheapie, rough sound mix. With the critical acclaim it has been receiving, I was hoping for distribution. As of today, no distribution yet, but we have played in over ten festivals, and have been invited to play in commercial theatres by exhibitors and managers who saw *From Hollywood to Hanoi* at festivals. I have now added another hat to my already overloaded head! I am my own distributor.

Today I woke up after two hours of fitful sleep on the floor in my tiny office at Du Art Film Labs

Scene from Damir Teresak's Golden Years, *produced in the former Yugoslavia*

334

in New York. What am I doing to myself? I am homeless with a film. I ache constantly. I have no personal life. The Vietnamese media in California (all very anti-Communist) are devastating my poor parents with horrendous write-ups. Most of them have not even seen the film.

The phones and faxes are already buzzing. Where are the posters, flyers? The prints didn't arrive in San Francisco on time, press kits were due yesterday at the American Film Institute in Hollywood. Could you send more photos priority mail to AP by noon, and what about a still for the *International Herald Tribune* story in Paris – due yesterday?

I gotta raise some more money fast, I decide. I use a friend's Federal Express account. I'll explain to him later. When I was filming along the Ho Chi Minh Trail in Hanoi two years ago I remember thinking, I'm doin' this guerrilla style. Shoot now, screen later, worry later, pay later. [. . .]

The film lab is now playing tough with me. You haven't paid, so we can't do any more work. I can't blame them. They have been wonderfully supportive. But I'm opening at the Film Forum here in New York on July 21st and the New York Times press screenings are coming up. WE GOTTA GET A REAL SOUND MIX. I go and beg. I thought I would get good at it but people scram when they see me. She wants more free favours. Michael Haussmann, a producer downstairs, said, 'Batten down the hatches! Tiana's intern is going to raid us.' Jennifer Thompson, my most dedicated intern, merely stopped by to ask for film cores and paper clips. [. . .]

It's 4 A.M. now, and I'm at the computer and fax machine. Oliver Stone has offered the services of his publicist to help us open the film in L.A. I haven't got a theatre booking yet. I have no more prints. Right now I have no more steam. I need to sleep. My bed (a Japanese futon) is under the film work bench. Instead I unspool a reel of film. I turn on the Steenbeck [editing table]. I look at the images: a Vietnamese woman driven mad by the war. She is my aunt. A teenage girl who shaved her head in a Thai refugee camp because she was raped repeatedly at sea by Thai pirates and blamed herself . . .

The ebullient Tiana on location in Vietnam for her documentary,
From Hollywood to Hanoi

335

20. Preserving the Legacy: Archives and Memorabilia

FILM ARCHIVES ARE NOW FOR THE MOST PART RECOGNISED AND FUNDED BY NATIONAL GOVERNMENTS, ALTHOUGH IT TOOK MANY YEARS TO REACH THAT HAPPY STATE, AND THERE NEVER SEEMS TO BE SUFFICIENT MONEY AVAILABLE TO PRESERVE AND RESTORE THE THOUSANDS OF FILMS IN NEED OF ATTENTION. THOSE WHO COLLECT MEMORABILIA, STILLS AND ARTEFACTS FROM THE HISTORY OF THE CINEMA, ALSO DESERVE CREDIT IN THIS SECTION.

>> 336

Just as Melina Mercouri believed that the Elgin Marbles should be returned from the British Museum to Athens, so Ray Jiing, Director of the National Film Archive in Taiwan, visits Paris to retrieve a cache of Chinese films:

❝ I'm in Paris to make arrangements for the repatriation of a large collection of Chinese films from decades ago, belonging to a great producer and studio chief, Ms. Tung Yue-chuan. Ms. Tung lives in Hongkong and, years ago, entrusted her private collection to a group of French scholars who were better able to care for the films. The entire batch was shipped to France and now resides in the CNC Archive in Bois d'Arcy. Now that Taiwan has a fully-equipped, modern film archive, Ms. Tung feels the time has come to return her collection to the Chinese people. I agree. The collection is of major cultural significance and will go a long way towards filling the gaps we have in our record of Chinese

Treasures recovered by the Taiwanese film archive. Opposite: Madame Butterfly. Top: *the animated* Princess Iron Fan
Above: Hua Mo-Lan

338

Sterling Hayden (left) in Crime Wave, *mentioned in Jacques Lourcelles' diary*

cinema. Nostalgia is strong among the Chinese, who have been exiled from their history – I seek to honour that nostalgia.

But it is a very sensitive situation too. The French scholars I have been dealing with will have invested a great portion of their lives' work in preserving and studying these films. Although they have been extraordinarily co-opera-tive, I can sense their concern. **99**

Jacques Lourcelles, an avid and passionate French cinephile, underlines the role of the private collection:

66 Telephone Alberto di Fabro, one of the programmers at the French Cinémathèque, to confirm that I can lend him the 16mm print of *Cloak and Dagger* which he needs for his pro-gramme on espionage in film due to be shown at Chaillot during the whole summer. I suggest that

he could add two rare titles by Joseph H. Lewis, *Spy Ring* and *Bombs over Burma* which, to my knowledge have never been shown in France, and of which I have the prints. This reminds me that I promised Thierry Frémaux, of the Lumière Institute in Lyon, to seek for some prints of films by André de Toth for the tribute they will give him in the autumn. Without too much difficulty, I can locate *None Shall Escape* (the best he has done among the ones I have seen) and *Crime Wave* (aka *The City Is Dark*). In the 1960s, I formed, together with my friend Pierre Guinle, a small collection of 16mm prints in order for us to see certain films that were otherwise difficult, almost impossible to find in France and even in Europe. If need be, we can help out, for free, a film archive, a festival, or any other cinema organisations wanting to bring to the public a film or a director that we like. [. . .]

Telephoned Italo Monzi, an Argentinian friend. [. . .] Since 1981, Italo has gathered a

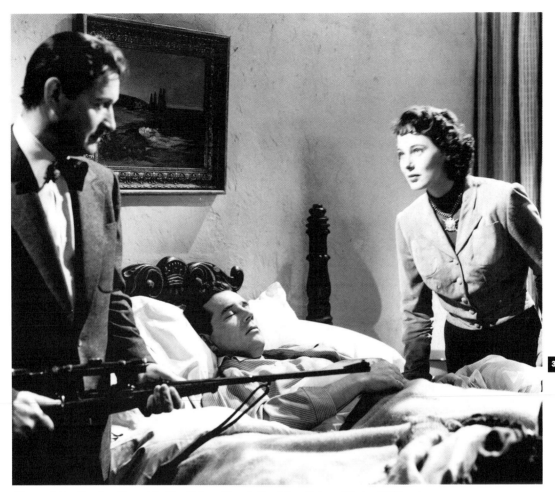

339 ◀◀

Above: *Robert Douglas, Howard Duff and Marta Toren in* Spy Ring. Below: *The late Bill Douglas*

fabulous video collection thanks to a network of faithful relationships around the globe. In the hand-written list he gave me, of the few five thousand titles that form his collection up to now, one can find – say at random – 17 by Jack Conway, 37 by Michael Curtiz, 20 by Roy del Ruth, along with for example, 18 by Juan de Orduna, 11 by Alberto de Zavalia, 10 by Maurice Elvey, 13 by Karl Hartl, 20 by Mario Mattoli, 15 by Francisco Mugica, 17 by Luis Saslavsky, 15 by Gustav Ucicky, 19 by Herbert Wilcox or 18 by Bayon Herrera. The appearance of video has been the single cinephilic revolution (and probably cinematographic as well) during the past thirty years. Even if few people use video to its full capacity, it enables some film buffs, at little expense and within a short period of time, to form a collection

with a variety that equals and sometimes surpasses the catalogue of the largest film archives in the world.

Collectors have preserved film memorabilia in the most secluded of locations, as David Bruce, Director of the Scottish Film Council, discovers during a journey on June 10th:

It is my birthday and I am a long way from home. In fact I am in a village called Sturminster Marshall, about 400 miles south of my normal territory. I am here because it is more or less en route from London and a meeting of the 'Cinema 100' Executive Committee to Barnstaple in Devon and happens to be the home of the sister of my companion on this adventure. [. . .]

The reason for being here is to see again the extraordinary collection of materials relating to cinema and its pre-history which the late [Scottish director] Bill Douglas and Peter Jewell collected voraciously over a period of nearly thirty years. My colleague is Alison Morrison-Low of the National Museums of Scotland who is an expert on scientific instruments, optics, photo-history and related matters. For the past 21 months, since meeting Peter at the 1991 Edinburgh International Film Festival, he and I have been exploring the possibility of finding a home in Scotland for the collection.

Although this is my second visit, I am still astonished by the quantity and variety. [. . .] The books, on every conceivable aspect of cinema, run to many thousands, the artefacts range, as Peter says, from the sublime to the ridiculous – well, never really ridiculous but certainly sometimes fairly trivial. The signed photographs of the Hollywood stars, the Charlie Chaplin dolls and games, the Mickey Mouses in every material from porcelain to plastic, the Victorian optical toys, the letters, postcards, playbills, souvenirs of premieres, the histories, biographies, and catalogues. [. . .]

What we have seen is really an archive for cine and photo historians and scholars, as much as the raw material for public viewing, although there is plenty for that as well. Certainly we would be daft not to explore all the possibilities for finding a safe haven for the collection, not least for the sake of the collectors.

Madeline Matz, Reference Librarian at the Motion Picture, Broadcasting, and Recorded Sound Division of the Library of Congress in Washington, deals with the public from around the world :

Selected 35 films, from 1905 to 1947, that include filmographic image defects, for Eric Rondepierre, a French artist, who will be working [here] from June 21st-July 2nd. His project comprises photographing still images from the viewing screen. [. . .]

Met with Sara Stone from the National Archives Stills Archive, who will be teaching a course in using audiovisual library collections and reading rooms. We discussed preservation, collections access, reading room procedures, cataloguing outtakes, and First World War films. [. . .]

Continued to compile a list of the Library's holdings of the films of Blanche Sweet.

Responded to a letter from the Curator of the Cinémathèque de la Danse in Paris regarding the film works of Carmen Amaya. I consulted several books on Mexican and Spanish cinema, and photocopied *Variety* and the *New York Times* film reviews and a *Variety* obituary.

Risa Shuman produces a series on Canada's TV Ontario entitled *Saturday Night at the Movies*, which is celebrating its twentieth anniversary. Delving into the past makes up an essential portion of her work and passion:

Every year, we have a ten-day shoot in Los Angeles, gathering interview material to be used throughout the season. Today I was staying at the Century Plaza Hotel, which was once part of the Twentieth Century-Fox backlot. My room overlooks the studio and I can see the huge sound stages and the 'New York' street from my balcony.

In the morning I went to the Centre for Motion Picture Study at the Academy of Motion Picture Arts and Sciences. It is a wonderful research library. I got out the files for some of the people we would be interviewing in the next two weeks – Roddy McDowall, Fay Wray, Jane Wyatt, Jane Withers, and director Andrew Stone who, I discover, is probably the last remaining silent film director still alive at the age of 91. The

Still from Martin Ritt's Sounder, *praised by John Wayne in a letter to the director*

files contain original newspaper clippings, studio press releases, and other very valuable items. Around the room are displays from some of the other special collections – in one cabinet were letters from the Cary Grant collection including a fan letter from Woody Allen; in another, the papers of Martin Ritt including a letter from John Wayne praising *Sounder* and a thank-you letter from Sean Connery after completing the filming for *The Molly Maguires.*

21. Opening Eyes and Minds: The Study of Film

FILM SCHOOLS HAVE PROLIFERATED SINCE THE 1960S, AND AT UNIVERSITY LEVEL THE APPRECIATION AND ANALYSIS OF THE CINEMA ARE FINALLY ACCEPTED IN EVEN THE MOST HAUGHTY OF ESTABLISHMENTS. THOSE WHO TEACH, AND THOSE WHO LEARN, ABOUT FILM, HAVE PROVED SOME OF OUR MOST ENGAGING DIARISTS.

>> 342

The National Film & Television School at Beaconsfield, outside London, is one of the most important such establishments in Europe. Bob Portal studies production there:

66 Heard yesterday that our 16mm short, *Eavesdropping*, is to be entered for the Edinburgh Festival shorts section. This will entail not only a change of title, but also a radical recut. [. . .] Adam and Thomas, editor and director respectively of this cute little epic, pick me up on the corner of Marylebone Road and Lissom Grove at 9.30 A.M. Car-sharing is a way of life at the NFTS [. . .] because so few students choose to (or can afford to) run cars. This is one of the most irritating factors when planning a budget shoot at the Film School. Transportation and catering, actually. Perennial problem for the student production team.

We arrive and start to view yesterday's long and very languorous cut of our film. Suggestions are made to shorten the beginning, and we leave Adam to implement the changes. I have an 11.30 A.M. appointment with Soosy Meating, one of

Left: *Still from student film,* Eavesdropping. Above: *Anna Karina and Eddie Constantine in Godard's* Alphaville

the School's full-time production co-ordinators. I want to discuss the budget for post-production, to ensure we can get a print done on the remainder of our allocation. Yes, we can apparently, if we scrimp and save (what's new?). [. . .]

I take a hike to the Animation Department for my second fixed appointment – to see Lianna, who is working on a 35mm short, *The Cannon Woman,* which I have stepped in to oversee and schedule. We talk over the work involved, and she realises that what she hoped to achieve in three weeks is going to take her six. The joy of the NFTS Animation Dept. is that once started on a project, the finishing line can slip away into the nebulous future without anyone really noticing or caring.

Neil Graham, a twenty-year-old student from Liverpool, prepares for his second-year exams in film studies at the University of Warwick:

I still find it strange that I have chosen to lock myself within this dark room [intensively watching films] every day this week while it is 85 degrees outside. Having said that I do not think there is anything else I would rather be doing.

A quick glance at the revision schedule informed me that today's plan was to revise 'Realism in the Cinema.' For today, this was to mean Ken Loach – quite topical seeing that he has scooped an award at Cannes, and a comparison of *The Day After* and *Threads*. As I loaded *Kes* into the VCR I could hear the familiar soundtrack from *Alphaville* booming out from next door. Obviously, a fellow student had elected to tackle 'Jean-Luc Godard and Modernism' today. So I suppose at that precise moment between the two of us we were covering the whole range of the cinema. In one room a socio-political film which attempted to become a fiction film in the style of a documentary; whereas in the next room a film whose concern it was to present itself as the exact opposite – with film being exactly that, just film, pure illusionism. [. . .]

Film Studies is often accused of being a 'Mickey Mouse' course; I think what I sat through today [*Kes*, *The Day After*, and *Threads*] would be beyond the average computer scientist or accountant. Part of the joy of my course is that it encourages you to ask yourself questions about the critical techniques you apply to a film text. **99**

Vincent Kinnaird, also twenty, is an Irishman studying in France:

66 I'm still a plankton in the ocean, as they say, but I've already made two short films and it's only a matter of time before I get the funding and recognition to make a 'real' one, meaning one which will get shown to the public and tour the festivals.

My nationality is Irish but I'm currently in France, forever writing and gaining inspiration while preparing a dissertation on various young Parisian directors who are in the process of making, or who have already made, the transition from short to feature film.

Today I'm in the process of writing up this report, after interviewing Thomas Bardinat, whose short film *Le Jour du bac* won the national prize at the Festival du Court-Métrage at Clermont. I have also interviewed Dominik Moll,

David Bradley, the young hero of Ken Loach's Kes, *watched by student Neil Graham*

Demi Moore and Robert Redford in Indecent Proposal, *mentioned by Vincent Kinnaird*

who has just completed his first feature film, *Intimité*, from the novel by Sartre. [. . .]

On seeing *Indecent Proposal* just yesterday, it seems to me that for the most part the Hollywood movie (except for the likes of Woody Allen or Robert Altman) is becoming ever more like the pop video and TV commercial in style. At a certain level this is good, interesting and certainly brings in the money, but . . .

Like the difference between Mills & Boon and George Orwell in literature, there is also a difference between unanimous distraction or pastime and specific talent, inspiration, sentiment, desire, and the need and power to move people and tell the world a story by means of the magical spectacle that is cinema. **99**

Dariusz Sikora, a student from Poland, faces the climax of his course at FAMU, the Czech Film School in Prague:

 This was a very important day for me. I had been preparing myself for it for five years – five years studying in the Department of Editing for Film and Television at FAMU. Today was my oral exam, defending my diploma which comprises two parts: theory and practical. For my theory submission I have written a full-length feature script about a generation of frustrated young people, a generation which can be blamed and can also be seen as victims, and for which it seems there can be only one solution: death. It is a script about a generation 'on the run,' rushing down a long, dark tunnel in the vain hope of finding even the slightest glimmer of light at the end. [. . .]

In her assessment of the script, the Czech director Drahomira Vihanova writes that my work is of much better quality than many of the professional ones she has seen, and that I take up where Kieslowski leaves off – that's some responsibility.

The practical element of my finals is the editing of a film (singlehandedly). I get top marks for both elements of my work and leave my studies as 'Master of Arts.'

So today was a landmark. The end of an important stage of my life. [. . .] Soon I shall return to Poland, to my wife and daughter. Will I be able to find work in my profession out in the provinces where I live, that will enable me to fulfil my obligations, i.e. to make money? **99**

The Graduate Film Department at New York University has nurtured many outstanding talents. Ian Maitland is Chairman of the Department:

66 Students lined up outside my office. Getting equipment sheets signed to do tests for next year. Getting a signature for a Nagra [machine] to record some sound for the last picture that's booked for mixing the day after tomorrow. 'Can you sign this insurance for me?' 'Do you know where I can get a job for the summer?' 'If you don't let me shoot in August, my father is going to disown me!' [. . .]

Back to work on the curriculum for the 1993-94 school year. You can teach the basics of directing, but there's no way you can teach talent and experience. Therefore part of this new curriculum must be the opportunity for students to see top name directors working with actors, so they can follow first hand how the professional func-

tions, and witness the end result. My plan is to invite Arthur Penn, Martin Scorsese, Lee Grant, and a number of other top names to give Master sessions to our students. Spike Lee (a former student) is willing to teach in the Graduate Department all next year. Thank you, Spike. 99

Dr. Galina Kopaneva, of the Czech Republic, teaches film at Charles University in Prague:

66 My first-year undergraduate oral examinations [today] focused on silent film genres and moral issues as reflected by Polish film in the 1960s. From my experience in previous years, when students were dismissive of everything apart from post-modernism, I was pleasantly surprised with their empathy and how carefully they were reading images and decoded visual poetry of old films by Wajda, Zanussi, Kieslowski, Holland, Kijowski, Falk etc.

Left: *Spike Lee, former student of Ian Maitland, directing* Jungle Fever. Above: *Zbigniew Cybulski as the reluctant assassin in Wajda's classic from 1958,* Ashes and Diamonds

Despite the fact that these films were made during the Communist era, now condemned and denigrated, students understood that through them the film-makers were expressing their opposition to totalitarianism. They considered most of the films as addressing today's issues, articulating their ethical message, identifying the underlying patterns and interpreting them as a comment on the human condition (individual-power-choice). They appreciated how the films used an apparently documentary style of shooting and emotionally charged acting. They did not miss a fast, rock-video style of editing in the twelve films they saw during the term. Granted that the first six undergraduates might not represent a trend for the whole year, it nevertheless seems that even when cinema programmes are totally Americanised, there remains a perceived need for films requiring intellectual commitment and appreciation of individual style. **"**

Zheng Dongtian lectures in film directing at the Beijing Film Academy:

" I run for my life. In the curtain of rain, the Academy's main building seems a long way off. It's now 8.40 A.M. The first film has been on for ten minutes. I've never run with such urgency to watch a film.

Absolutely drenched, I rush into the tiny cinema. In the dark, I grope my way to the first empty seat and sit down. I'm gasping. The character on the screen is also gasping. It's a black-and-white film. A young artist is doing press-ups beneath an easel on which stands a somewhat obscure paint-

ing. I can't tell if he's tired himself out by painting or if he's worried about the fate of his picture.

The film's over. It's title was *Winter and Spring*, the directing debut of my student Wang Xiaoshuai and a friend of his. They made it for $14,000, which they got for a commercial they had shot. (In China, making a film like this would normally cost ten times as much.) Perhaps for precisely this reason, the film may never get a public screening.

I and the other lecturers of the Department of Film Directing ask Wang Xiaoshuai to our office. Wang had brought this, his first film after graduating, to show his teachers. It's been a tradition at

Entrance to the University of Cinema in Buenos Aires

the Academy for many years. He'd not asked any-one else to see it before today. Some lecturers liked it, others didn't. But everyone agreed that the film had been made with genuine feeling. [. . .]

According to our traditional way of classifying students, Wang should belong to the Sixth generation of directors. But as most of them have not yet made any films, they cannot be regarded as a representative group. The Sixth Generation may not yet exist in practice. But Wang's work has created a new context in which films of his generation may exist. In my view, his piece is significant for this fact alone. I'd run through the rain just to watch this film. **99**

Dr. György Kárpáti makes documentaries and also serves as Professor at the Academy of Drama and Film in Budapest, Hungary:

66 9 A.M. Presenting the diploma works for the Board of the third 'non-fiction' post-graduate class of mine. Two videos (one documentary, one scientific report) accepted as correct, professional achievements, but the third, photographed and directed by Tamás Borbás, was a real hit, unprecedented in recent years. A portrait of a 16-year-old sick girl suffering from a rare disease, who edits and draws a magazine for children in hospitals, this will be aired soon by Hungarian TV. **99**

Manuel Antin, a veteran Argentinian film-maker, decided in 1991 to establish a film school in Buenos Aires:

66 The University of Cinema is an institute offering an education in the humanities, with particular reference to the cinema and its technologies. In less than three years we have made good progress. Year by year, the number of students has increased. There are now some 500 and we have had to look for more teachers.

On June 10th something very interesting occurred. I asked a prestigious Argentinian film director to give a course. He told me that it seemed to him illogical that, at the moment when cinema was dying, I should create a space in which to teach film. My reply was, 'If it is true that cinema is dying, initiatives like mine can help

to effect a cure.' My response must have been persuasive because that talented director agreed that same day to join the teaching staff and he is also trying to recreate in young people an interest in this threatened field. **99**

Eitan Green, director of films like *Lena*, *When Night Falls*, and *American Citizen*, is Head of the Screenwriting Department at Tel Aviv University:

66 On Thursday mornings we have a staff meeting for the heads of the film and television department. The meeting opens with two toasts: one for the current department head, who was elected once again for the next two years, and one for a colleague who has returned to Tel Aviv with his PhD from New York University. [. . .] Later we discuss several ongoing matters and one issue of principle: teaching the basics of direction using video or film (I also teach film directing). One of the teachers supports the use of video and this indeed is what is being used in the department as 'the world is going to video.' I believe, as I always have, that video is a tool for experienced directors, and one that corrupts the inexperienced. [. . .]

I still have one more class, the final one of the year and the last class of three terms devoted to writing a feature film screenplay. Usually I discuss one script with all the students but today, due to the year's end and the fact that I want to talk about all of the projects, I conduct separate 15-minute talks with each student to discuss their individual project. What occurs during these two hours is actually what I hope will occur in my next film, the script for which I shall begin to write now that the academic year is over. **99**

Tzvi Tal (Israel) bills himself as "cinema researcher, teacher, and farmer." He is also engaged in taking his MA in film history:

66 At the beginning of June I had to face a major cinematic dilemma: how to convince sixth form pupils, between the ages of 15 and 16, to watch De Sica's *Shoeshine* without their causing trouble?

This was to be the last film they watched with

me as part of their course on 'Films of Childhood, Adolescence and Youth.' How could one manage to convince the youth of today that a black-and-white film without excessive contemporary Hollywoodian effects can have a human content and be very meaningful? By force! – is my answer in this particular case. I sent away the most disruptive student with a mission to write an essay on Italian Neorealism! The others sat calmly and a few minutes later they were all enjoying the film.

All through the academic year I was thinking about how to teach cinema to young people who only want to watch 'action' films, as they understand it. How to expose them to timeless works of art? How to make them interested in a cinema that is different from the one that generally interests them? There are populist teachers: they give the pupils the films they want and then try to analyse their cinematic language. When, then, will they be exposed to Fellini, Godard and others? How will they cope with Hungarian or Peruvian films? The teacher of cinema faces the same problem as the film director – they try to mock, make fun when breaking conventions. The director creates cinematic characters, the **99** teacher tries to open eyes and also minds!

The European Film College in Denmark opened its doors in January 1993. Mark Le Fanu, a former Cambridge don and author of a book on Tarkovsky, teaches at the College:

66 Morning at the European Film College, a large, modern (Finnish-designed) complex in Jutland, constructed campus-style on a hillside looking out across the beautiful bay of Mols. [. . .]

The youngsters in Vittorio De Sica's neo-realist Shoeshine, *discussed by Tzvi Tal*

Forty ambitious young film producers are staying here for a week under the aegis of EAVE (Entrepreneurs de l'Audiovisuel Européen), one of the MEDIA projects designed to support the European film and television industries.

Intensive daily sessions, indoors, on 'pitching,' on finance, on script development, on the numerous other skills that a producer needs to stay afloat in today's competitive environment. [. . .]

At mealtimes there's a babel of different languages (though in the 'formal' sessions everyone without exception speaks English – fluently). [. . .] I'm an outsider at this gathering – I teach film history at the College during term-time – and I'm curious to find out, close-up, what sort of an animal a producer is. At a plenary session later in the afternoon one thing emerges: a surprising hostility to directors – at any event, to directors who would classify themselves as auteurs. It seems to be felt that, too often, the overriding claims of art get in the way of commercial savvy. Particularly galling to some of them is the notion that in a number of European countries it is still directors, rather than producers, who control the final cut. [. . .] Behind these considerations one glimpses the old anxiety, 'Is film culture, or is it business?' It's both, of course, but for me, an outsider and sceptical by disposition, the EAVE producers seem slightly too weighted towards the latter interpretation. Actually, the 'cultivated' film – the film of talk, of *velleité*, of psychology – is what Europe has always done well: better, perhaps, than the Americans. Should we throw out the baby with the bathwater? **99**

The veteran Chilean cinematographer, Héctor Riós, who himself studied at Italy's Centro Sperimentale in the late 1950s, now teaches students in Valparaiso:

66 June 10th is a religious festival in Chile; everyone is on holiday, and there is nothing I can report. Yesterday, on the other hand, was an interesting work day for me. It took place in the Cinema Workshop that I am running under the auspices of the Federico Santa Maria University in Valparaiso. This workshop, which teaches photography and camerawork, has sixteen students, most of whom have graduated, or

are about to graduate from different private audiovisual institutions in the city. [. . .]

The students have divided into two groups of eight. One went out to take still photos of subjects related to the city, such as the activities of the port of Valparaiso. They were accompanied by an assistant teacher. The other group stayed with me in the university practising camerawork. They had to have detailed knowledge of three kinds of camera: a 16mm Bolex Paillard, a 16mm Arriflex St and a 35mm Arriflex II. I explained the way these cameras work, the different reflex systems, the different ways of threading film, etc. Then we loaded and unloaded the camera with blank film and threaded it through.

I saw that these young students were really motivated and enthusiastic about this work since it was the first time that they had had physical contact with cameras and with film. Until today, they only had a theoretical knowledge and their practical experience had been limited to video. In the next few weeks, they will be working on **99** actual film exercises.

Birgit Hein lives in Cologne (Germany) and is Professor for Film and Video at an arts school in Braunschweig:

66 First I went to the graphic arts department to make colour prints from the video that I shot in Jamaica, which will form part of my new film on the sex tourism of older women. I was enthusiastic about the prints. It seems that this printing is a new kind of 'still photography.'

Then I had an appointment with a young woman, to talk about her diploma thesis on lesbian photography. She studies at a university in a nearby town, where they have no female professor who can give her specialist attention. As she insisted on a female advisor, they asked me to help out. This is so typical of the situation at German universities, and also at my school; altogether we have 53 professors and only three are women! I had a long and intense talk with [the student] about the content and the artistic qualities of the series of photographs she had chosen. After she left, I met my assistants to prepare the programme of films and videos to screen at the annual **99** presentation of student works at the school.

Still from Pukar *(1939), preserved by the National Film Archive of India*

P.K. Nair, long the head of India's National Film Archive, continues to teach at the Film and Television Institute in Pune:

     June 10th fell in the midst of our annual Film Appreciation course, organised by the National Film Archive in collaboration with the Film and Television Institute of India. This is a five-week, intensive academic exercise, designed to sensitise the lay viewer to the language of cinema as an effective medium of communication and art. The sixty-odd participants come from different parts of the country and sometimes from nearby nations such as Sri Lanka and Bangladesh, and from various disciplines. They include university teachers, research workers, film critics, film society organisers, practising artists, amateur film-makers and social workers. [. . .]

    I was present in the class from 9.30 A.M., as a keen observer of the first two sessions presented by my colleagues, and participated in the discussions. The first session was on Educational/Instructional films. [. . .] The second session dealt with Film Semiotics – the opening sequence of John Huston's *The Maltese Falcon* was shown and analysed. The afternoon session on Indian Film History was presented by me. The topic covered was the war period – with the rise of nationalist forces, the break-up of the studio system, and the transition to musical escapism.

The Brooks Institute in California concentrates on the teaching of photography, but motion pictures also feature at this professional school. Film-maker and writer Dennis Lanson teaches at Brooks and expresses the frustration often attached to the vocation:

    My job today at Brooks Institute involves directing a student-crewed and scripted project, a nostalgic, heavily voice-overed child's view of a dysfunctional family, called *Laughing*

352

Still from Kismet, *the record-breaking 1943 Indian release*

Dogs and Paper Hats. After three days on location at a country shack in the breathtaking Santa Ynez Valley (outside Santa Barbara) we have moved to the stage. Everyone is tired, work is excruciatingly slow, the actors sit around for hours, the lighting is set for the wrong scene and has to be redone. My co-teacher, who is supervising the photography and the production management, is irritable with the students and myself. I'm becoming bored with a project that is not really mine, not for money, and that will never be as good as it could be under other circumstances.

22. Getting Together JUNE 10TH APPEARED TO BE JUST ANOTHER DAY IN THE LIFE OF WORLD CINEMA. ON A PRIVATE LEVEL, HOWEVER, IT YIELDED BIRTHS AND DEATHS THAT INSPIRED OUR DIARISTS TO RECORD THEIR EMOTIONAL REACTIONS. ON A PUBLIC LEVEL, IT WAS ALSO THE DAY OF CORPUS CHRISTI, ONE OF THE MOST SOLEMN DAYS IN THE CATHOLIC CALENDAR, WHILE IN EASTERN EUROPE AND BEYOND, PEOPLE REMEMBERED THE MASSACRE AT LIDICE, FIFTY YEARS AGO TO THE DAY. IN HOLLYWOOD, *JURASSIC PARK* WAS BEING UNVEILED AT A SERIES OF LATE-NIGHT SCREENINGS; AND IN DENMARK AND THE CZECH REPUBLIC, CONFERENCES ON FILM-MAKING WERE HELD.

354

Across the world, in Bombay, hub of an extraordinarily prolific film industry, the actor-producer-director Shashi Kapoor underlines the family element in film-making (and his elder brother Raj Kapoor was the most popular of all Indian stars):

66 My day started at six in the morning with a glass of orange juice. The monsoon had not arrived so it was extremely hot. By the time I was ready to go to our studio, my fifteen-months-old grandson Zahan Prithviraj Kapoor came to me with his beautiful smile and asked in his very

EPY 5018

Actor-producer-director extraordinaire, Shashi Kapoor belongs to a remarkable movie dynasty

young, newly-learned language for juice. I looked at him and wondered whether he too would carry on the great tradition of the Kapoors with the film and theatre world initiated by his great grandfather Shri Prithviraj Kapoor since 1927. [. . .]

I got to our studio after an hour of very boring, hot and hectic driving. There was a pre-production meeting on during the morning. My production staff and direction staff were there. Without wasting any time in the traditional Indian Greetings we got on with our work. We are in the process of going into production with two movies and two TV serials.

At lunch I went over to my nephew Randhir Kapoor's office in the same studio, which is now being run by him and his young brother Rajiv Kapoor. Both are actors also. Another brother, Rishi Kapoor, is in his early forties and doing a number of films as a leading man. We all had a traditional Peshawari meal (non-spice food from the far north of India and Pakistan). After the meal we go to our various jobs and I am asked by my daughter who manages the Prithvi Theatre to come and confirm the minutes of our last meeting. The studio where we worked is called R.K. Studios, which was started by my elder brother Raj Kapoor, who for over forty years acted in, produced, directed and edited many big successful films. He is a legend not only in our country but also in the world of cinema.

I reached the Prithvi Theatre for our meeting with my daughter, who has also acted·in a few films and is now concentrating on the theatre. We are joined by my two sons Kunal and Karan, who also have done quite a few Indian films. We have a very heated meeting with the hot weather adding fuel to it! [. . .]

I get a call from my second brother Shammi Kapoor, an actor, director of many films over many years, and also a cinema owner in Bombay and Delhi. I am asked to a dinner being hosted by him in honour of the film delegations from Uzbekistan, Kirghistan, and Turkministan. After finishing my meetings I reached home to see my grandson before he goes to sleep. We have a lovely time imitating each other. I think he will be a good actor one day.

After the dinner with the foreign delegates and the Kapoor family (which is quite huge), I go to my residence and in the stillness and quiet of the hot night I go over the happenings of the day – very normal yet very exciting.

I thank the Heavens and my father that I am a part of the film and theatre scene in India **99** and the world. God bless us everyone.

Colin Salmon in Tomorrow Calling

The mother of Chinese composer Zhao Jiping (*Red Sorghum, Ju Dou,* and *Raise the Red Lantern*) dies on June 10th at the age of 87:

66 Today, I find it impossible to concentrate on the score [for Zhang Yimou's new film, *Living*]. My mother's kindly face, and that expression she had in her eyes before she died still appear before me. I suddenly realise that mother's whole life and the piece I'm writing are mysteriously alike in spirit. Mother was born at the beginning of the century and experienced every historical period of our country. As head of our household, she had to bring up seven sons and daughters in the face of countless difficulties. [. . .] I remember mother once telling me how she escaped in the 1930s from the Central Plain of Hebei, which had been occupied by the Japanese, and made her way to Sichuan, travelling for miles in search of my father. I remember how, at the end of 1948, father was suddenly thrown into prison and how, during the course of a single night, white hairs began to appear in mother's black hair. I remember how, during the Cultural revolution, father was harassed to death and how mother sobbed her heart out, as though wanting to die. And she – this good, Chinese woman – quietly accepted all of it. Relying on that tenacity so special to the Chinese, she raised her children and carried on 'living.'

Today's diary is an elegy to my mother. She has departed from us, but has given me inspiration and motivation to create music. Mother, may these strains release your soul from purg- **99** atory. Rest in peace.

Tim Leandro of London rejoices in the birth of a daughter, and then realises he is due to edit a film on the same day, June 10th:

66 It should be a day to remember, a rare day, but already I find my memory of it is fading. I am probably going through something akin to shock, but these are the shocks we live for.

She was born at 5.24 P.M. yesterday, although when she jumped, kicking, blue and crying into my hands I didn't notice her sex. My wife Jan had to tell me that we had made a girl. Our beautiful, curly-haired little Carmen had come to join us.

I arranged yesterday with Andrea Macarthur at the Whitehouse to cut Colin Salmon's voice-overs into *Tomorrow Calling* – a short film for Channel Four and British Screen – this afternoon. We were supposed to do it yesterday but my hands were full, so to speak. [. . .] I felt terrible as I explained the situation to Jan. [But] if anything she was relieved. Still not confident about breastfeeding and nervous with our new child, she felt safest with a midwife on call round the clock. [. . .]

At the edit, concentrating was difficult. I felt euphoric and strangely detached but Andrea and I managed to cut something together. The voice-overs worked, knitting the narrative together in exactly the way I'd imagined. That was very pleasing. However, since I was rather spaced out, it may take a bit more tinkering about with, until that indefinable feel is right.

I'd imagined that having a child would inject such a massive dose of perspective into my life that film-making might suddenly appear mean-

ingless or nothing more than work. That hasn't happened. I find that although the birth of my daughter is the most significant part of my life (by several orders of magnitude) so far, I still get the same charge and maintain that maddening, bloody-minded obsession with getting it right on film that I have always had. The only change is, if anything, a greater urgency, a sense that I am no longer doing it just for me. **"**

Gerald Pratley, an Englishman who emigrated to Canada after the Second World War and became one of his adopted country's most familiar and respected film authorities, founded the Ontario Film Institute in the late 1960s. Like many critics on June 10th, he noted the awesome arrival of *Jurassic Park*:

" Leave early for the 10 A.M. press screening of Spielberg's *Jurassic Park*, probably the most pre-publicised film in history, with *Time*, *Newsweek*, and *Maclean's* all giving over their

357 **«**

Gathering of the stars and the author at the U.S. opening of Steven Spielberg's Jurassic Park

covers after a parade of dinosaurs have poked their heads into all aspects of life for the past year and more. Now a fresh invasion awaits us with $100 million-worth of 'tie-in' merchandise about to flood the world.

The effects in the film, as a change from spectacular car and truck crashes and over-charged explosions, are truly remarkable and it is the hundreds of experts who carried it out who have made the film possible. We have come a long way from *King Kong*, but when the film is over, in spite of Lord Attenborough and Sam Neill, what do we have but another variation of the mad scientist who creates a life which destroys him – although not physically on this occasion; 'Dickie' will live to work again. The film itself has no more brain-power than the dinosaurs roaming **"** around in it.

»» 358

Shabana Azmi, resplendent star of Indian films and also of *Madame Sousatzka, City of Joy*, and *Son of the Pink Panther*, spends June 10th in Chicago, with *Jurassic Park* looming on her horizon also:

"We should have been on a plane back to Bombay. Instead we are still in Chicago. *Jurassic Park*, Spielberg's new film, is opening in the United States tomorrow, and there will be some special previews at 11.30 P.M. tonight. No power on earth can stop my husband, screenwriter Javed Akhtar, an unabashed Spielberg fan, from catching that preview. How our colleagues in Bombay would turn green with envy! So the flight home is abandoned.

I had never seen a Spielberg film – an unforgivable act of omission in Javed's view – and so considerable energy is devoted into initiating me into the world of Spielberg, D.N.A., and dinosaurs. [. . .] I don't want to be a spoilsport, and go along with the spirit of things. However, my heart is in a lesser known film, *Menace II Society*, directed by 21-year-old twins, about what it means to be black in America. To my surprise everyone agrees to see this film as well, and off we go to the 2.30 P.M. show.

Menace II Society moves me deeply. It explores

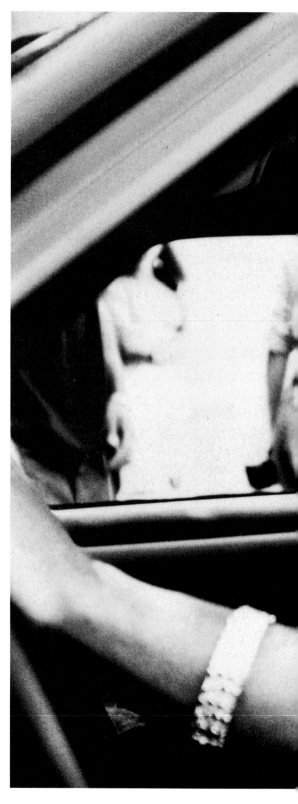

A tense moment from Menace II Society

Top and above: *Two stills from* Menace II Society *(see Shabana Azmi's diary)*

every single stereotypical notion of the black community in America and, without a trace of sentimentality, fills you with a sense of doom – creating a symbiotic bond of empathy with its characters. It is an insider's point of view. **"**

Lynda Myles, former Director of the Edinburgh International Film Festival, head of the Pacific Film Archive, and a European studio executive for Columbia Pictures, now functions as an independent producer (e.g. *The Snapper***) and is one of the prime movers behind the East West Producers' Seminar:**

" Awoke to slight sense of shock at finding myself in a 12th Century castle in the middle of Moravia. Unlikely though this may seem, Castle Trest is the setting for this year's East West Producers' Seminar, which I co-run with a friend and colleague, Katya Krausova. [. . .]

Locate the dining-room and find the first group of the British contingent, who will lead today's workshops: Simon Perry, the head of British Screen, and a strike force of British independent producers – Steve Clark-Hall, a Seminar regular, and two new recruits, Timothy Burrill and Keith Griffiths. We are surrounded by a disparate group of fifty young producers and wannabee producers selected by Katya and me, from Romania, Bulgaria, Poland, the Czech Republic, Slovakia, and Hungary. [. . .]

At 10 A.M., introduce the first session on the role of the creative producer. It feels like the first morning of a shoot: my overwhelming emotion is sheer amazement that we are here at all and that we've managed to get this far. [. . .]

The concept of a producer as we're defining it is quite alien in Eastern Central Europe and Eastern Europe, and we get tied in linguistic knots trying to define and differentiate between their notion of a producer as a production manager and our rather more initiating and collaborative role. Simon is wonderfully magisterial, while Timothy makes an impassioned speech about the producer's role. After lunch, move on to the art of the deal and the art of the pitch which involves much animated and slightly hysteria-inducing role-playing by the panel. **"**

361 «

A gathering in Moravia for the East West Producers' Seminar, with Lynda Myles seated fourth from left

Timothy Burrill, who is based in London and produces for both the cinema and TV, gives his account of the day at Castle Trest:

❝ The breakfast room was full of teams of interpreters as well as the producers, for our deliberations were going to be translated into six different languages. As it was the first day of the [East West Producers'] Seminar there was not much fraternisation. However, I chatted up a Canadian girl who was with the Czechs and who had come from Calgary where I had worked on the original *Superman*. [. . .]

I fear we all droned on a bit during the morning. My rather flamboyant attempts to enliven the discussions were either totally unsuitable or misunderstood by the translator. Lunch came and against all my rules I succumbed to two glasses of white wine. Alas the food was horribly reminiscent of my Welsh prep school during the war.

Despite some unforeseen problems with the translation system that no doubt caused our organisers much mental agony, the afternoon went rather better and at the last session, instead of sitting opposite the producers on our dais, we went into little groups, which proved far more productive. ❞

Even in the remote Moravian countryside, Steve Clark-Hall, another delegate to the East West Producers' Seminar, cannot drag himself away from the many anxieties about his latest project:

❝ The fax machine to London works only spasmodically, and I am trying to keep in touch. There is a major casting problem on *Narrow Rooms*. Derek Jarman wants Keith Collins to play Roy and Channel Four are threatening to pull out. A fax confirms that Derek will refuse to make the film with another actor. I fax Channel Four to fix a meeting. Talk to Simon Perry of British Screen (who's also here at the Seminar); he says he will go with Derek's preference, so the future of the film hangs on Channel Four's backing down or not.

Do an exercise for students showing how a U.K. film gets financed – it all looks so very easy on paper! ❞

Many contributors, in different countries, mourned in their diaries the loss of Kazuko Shibata, who died in Tokyo early on June 8th, 1993. Known to directors, producers, distributors, and festival programmers around the world, she symbolised an uncompromising commitment to all that is most adventurous and imaginative in film-making. Akira Kurosawa, the most celebrated of all living Japanese directors, attended her funeral:

❝ On this day was the funeral of Kazuko Shibata, the vice president of France Eigasha. Kazuko was 53 years old. Her life was still in bloom. I couldn't believe her sudden death because I caught a glimpse of her at the Cannes Film Festival and I heard the news so soon afterwards. I'd known her since she was a little girl. She was once an assistant director on one of my productions. She loved films with all her heart. Her aesthetic judgement was unmistakable. She also made great efforts to introduce many excellent films to Japan. Talking to a friend standing beside me at her funeral, I said: 'She was hardly over fifty when she died, yet we see her work with complete admiration.' There is no greater sorrow than watching the death of people who still have a great future. I never thought we should come upon such a sad day. ❞

Aito Mäkinen, co-founder of the Finnish Film Archive, and a documentarist himself, also recalls the young Kazuko Shibata:

❝ I was shattered yesterday evening. Returning to the studio after an afternoon around the town – trying to work out how to use the statues of Helsinki in a documentary about 'experiencing art' – there was a fax from Tokyo announcing that Kazuko Kawakita-Shibata had died a couple of days earlier.

I still remember, as if it were yesterday, the delightful young girl with her mother in Dubrovnik in 1956. Henri Langlois [founder of La Cinémathèque Française] was lecturing Kashiko Kawakita, the ambassador of Japanese cinema [and mother of Kazuko], and myself about the strategy in founding a film archive: 'The state will never launch it. You will have to

The late Kazuko Shibata (centre), with her distinguished mother, Kashiko Kawakita (left) and Spanish director Victor Erice

begin it privately and prove through your work that it would be an irreparable loss to discontinue the activities for financial reasons.'

Kazuko Shibata, the president of the Japan Film Library her mother founded, and the tireless discoverer of new talent, is going to be buried in Tokyo today. Yet only a few weeks ago, in Cannes, she was so full of life. **99**

The president of Herald Ace, Inc., a production and distribution company (Kurosawa's *Ran*, Oshima's *Merry Christmas Mr. Lawrence* etc.) is Masato Hara. He too laments the passing of a valued colleague:

❝ When I saw [Kazuko Shibata] at Cannes at the end of May, she was full of energy. She was only 53 years old and her sudden death was a real shock to me. A sub-arachnoidal haemorrhage struck her on June 4th. Within three days, she was dead, without regaining consciousness. At her home in Shiba Shirogane, several hundred closely associated film personalities gathered to mourn. It was she who introduced to Japan the work of Angelopoulos, Wenders, and Jarmusch. [. . .] At the funeral I saw Hou Hsiao-hsien and Akira Kurosawa, which also reminded me of her wonderful personality and her large list of personal contacts. [. . .] She was born as an only daughter of the late Nagamasa Kawakita and his wife Kashiko, and devoted her entire life to film. I wanted not only to mourn for her but also to applaud her from my heart. ❞

Takehiro Nakajima, a Japanese writer and director, describes the occasion:

❝ At 1 P.M. I went to Kazuko Kawakita-Shibata's informal funeral. There were many people outside her home in Shirogane. I accompanied her to the Berlin Film Festival in February this year. *Okoge*, which I wrote and directed, was entered in the Panorama section, and Kazuko was handling the world sales of the picture. [. . .] I was at a loss after hearing of her sudden death. As well as her devoted contribution to the release of many wonderful films from the West, she made a positive contribution to the introduction of some unique Japanese films outside this country. Who will follow in her footsteps?

I felt empty. Her husband, Hayao Shibata, the chief mourner, spoke through his tears: 'Please applaud her because she dedicated herself to her job in the film world.' Next to the tall director, Akira Kurosawa, was the film critic Nagaharu Yodokawa, who was tiny, just like a child, and could barely stand, just slouching forward. When the coffin was loaded into the hearse and left her home, Mr. Kurosawa applauded loudly and smiled. Others did so too, while some could not bring themselves to clap. ❞

Claude Sautet has acquired a high reputation outside his native France only late in life – with the success of *Un Cœur en hiver* both in Britain and the United States. Yet his earlier films, many starring Yves Montand and Gerard Depardieu (*César et Rosalie, Vincent, François, Paul et les autres, Garçon!* etc.) are marvels of sage and intelligent direction:

❝ On the plane to Yokohama (for the French Film Festival in Japan). I am thrilled to return to this country, to meet up again with professional friends (we see each other so seldom), and a different audience. Only one problem: finding good red wine, without which life is for me rather tasteless. I have just read an English review of *Un Cœur en Hiver*. As it is favourable, I can't withhold a surge of affectionate gratitude for my old Henry James . . . But cinema is not literature. I always compare its adventure to that of jazz . . . Or rather painting when photography appeared. The emergence of impressionism, fauvism, cubism etc . . . For us, something similar has happened with television. The perspectives soon diminished. And so has the public in the cinemas. It exists, and will endure but its role has changed. And so long as our creations remain ephemeral, it will retain its fragile beauty. ❞

Reza Kianian, set designer, screenwriter, and actor from Iran, manages to create something new and meaningful during the day:

❝ The poisonous monotony of daily life effaces all days and obliterates memories, unless some out of the ordinary event serves as an antidote. I am acting in a film these days and I hoped to be busy today. But I was told I had no shooting programme for Thursday, June 10th. [. . .] Fortunately I had a meeting with a number of screenwriters, directors and producers of films for children, and our meeting ended with a decision to establish a club for all people engaged in making films for children and young adults. The establishment of this club will be announced in a few months. ❞

364

Poster for Claude Sautet's award-winning feature film, Un Cœur en hiver

Govind Nihalani, of Bombay in India, is inspired by this "Day in the Life of World Cinema" to start his next feature film:

❝ I had been working on a feature film for the last year and a half. I was finding it difficult to raise the finance on account of its theme – terrorism and the moral dilemmas faced by those directly involved in the process of tackling it. Terrorism, though very much a disturbing reality in our country today, continues to be avoided as a serious topic for cinema because producers feel it places them in a very vulnerable position. [. . .]

And a few days after I heard about 'June 10th, 1993' from the British Film Institute, I resolved that come what may, I would participate in that historic day by starting production on my new

film. When I took the decision I had no idea where the support for the project would come from. I put together a small amount of money, and got friends, actors, and technicians to promise their support. The credit facilities for processing were extended to me by Adlabs, owned by my friends Manmohan Shetty and Vasant Mamania (who incidentally had helped me with my first feature, *The Cry of the Wounded*, which won the Golden Peacock at the New Delhi International Film Festival in 1981).

On June 10th, at 9.30 A.M., I started shooting my film, *The Times of Betrayal*, at Rajkamal Studios in Bombay. I am aware that completing the picture will not be an easy task, but I also know one thing: beg or borrow, it will be ready within a year. ❞

23. Waiting and Watching: The Next Assignment

SOME CONTRIBUTORS FOUND THEMSELVES IN AN INTERVAL, OR LULL, BETWEEN ONE ASSIGNMENT AND ANOTHER. RELAXING, REMINISCING, HOPING, THEY REFLECT A STATE OF MIND COMMON TO ANYONE INVOLVED IN FILM.

Bob Rafelson has directed few films, but each has been a work of unusual richness: *Five Easy Pieces, The King of Marvin Gardens, Stay Hungry, The Mountains of the Moon* etc. Yet his is a maverick talent that does not endear itself to the average Hollywood studio executive, and between the lines of this most poignant of diaries lurks a frustration at not being able to function as a director:

❝ Last night, well into the morning, I sat with a friend, probably for the final time before she dies. A few of us gathered to love her. About eight people altogether, standing in a kitchen eating take-out sushi.

My friend, who was nearly in one of my early movies – she's now about forty – clutched a machine governing the amount of morphine entering through her spine. Imagine . . . she stood holding this black box, wires leading out, and eating with chopsticks in the other hand.

She had 102 degrees fever. The cancer had made her thin, almost ghostly. Still she's beautiful. And always, even now, funny. I stayed up talking, then thinking, 'til 5 A.M. At dawn I took a walk.

Thank God I didn't think about making a movie (or not making one).

I slept, I got up at 2 P.M. in the afternoon and then sat still, thinking. There were no phone calls.

Nothing to interfere either with the solitude or the unproductivity of the day. At sunset I climbed a hill behind my house.

L.A. is a pointless place to be when you're not working. But maybe I am working. I just don't know it. ❞

John Schlesinger, between assignments in a career that has hardly lost momentum since the heady days of *Darling* and *Midnight Cowboy*, plans a new apartment in London:

❝ Several appreciative phone calls about my first private screening of *The Innocent* two nights ago. It went very well, although some people thought the humour over a dismembered body in two suitcases was unintentional and that I

Left: *Karen Black and Jack Nicholson in* Five Easy Pieces. *Above:* Jon Voight and Dustin Hoffman in Midnight Cowboy

might have been upset by so much laughter from the audience. They were wrong!

To Derek Frost's studio, who is designing our new apartment. We choose colours and tiles for bathrooms and kitchens. Warm white for most of the walls with great splashes of bright colour to jolly up the greyest of London days. [. . .] I am excited by the prospect of a home in London again after so many months as a wandering Ishmael.

In the afternoon I visit Joe Janni – the producer of six of my British films and to whom I really owe the start of my career. Though dreadfully infirm after a stroke during post-production on *Yanks*, he now has his leg in plaster after a recent

fall and cannot move. His extraordinary sense of humour has mercifully not deserted him. We reminisce about the old days and laugh a lot. [. . .]

Back to the office where some appreciative letters about *The Innocent* have arrived. Then it's time for the California calls. One to ICM and Jeff Berg [my agent], another to Alan Greisman of Savoy Pictures who are very probably backing my next film – *Dead Giveaway* – which I am directing and co-producing in the fall. There are some overseas partners interested, but as always they have alternative casting suggestions. All flavour-of-the-month stuff with no real understanding of what the parts call for. **"**

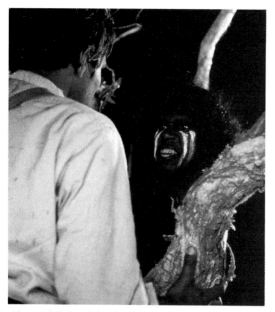

Above: *Still from Schepisi's* The Chant of Jimmy Blacksmith. Right: *Fred Schepisi*

Fred Schepisi, the Australian director who made his breakthrough with *The Devil's Playground* and *The Chant of Jimmie Blacksmith*, finds himself not only between films but also, literally, between days!

❝ June 10th didn't exist for me. I was crossing the International Date Line on a Qantas flight, so I went from June 9th to June 11th. On this non-existent day, I finished my first holiday for six years. A much needed break after having just completed principal photography on *Six Degrees of Separation*, based on John Guare's play of the same name.

I went, with my wife Mary and son Nicholas, from 90 degree tropical splendour (in Maui) to 50 degree winter in the city of Melbourne. I went to work immediately on post-production on *Six Degrees*, which will be completed in Melbourne. On the journey I read three scripts, one by Steve Martin, one by Steve Tesich, and one by Michael Goldenberg. The latter's *Interpretation of Dreams* is a film I'm endeavouring to make my next directing assignment. While reading it I was preparing a casting list, which I believe is the key to having the film produced. I also made preliminary production/budget notes. ❞

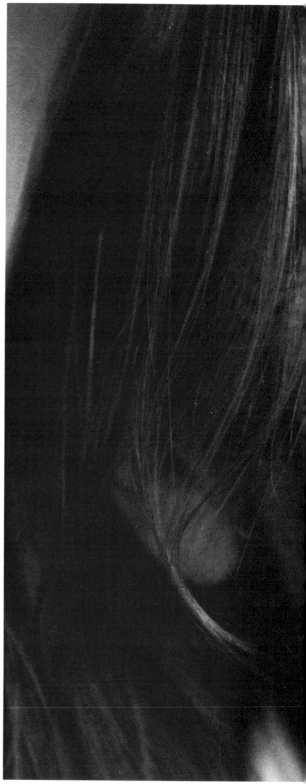

Above: *Suzanne Osten's* The Mozart Brothers.
Opposite: *Still from Christopher Young's production*, Prague

Suzanne Osten enjoys equal celebrity as a stage and film director in Sweden, and some of her films (*The Mozart Brothers, The Guardian Angel*, and *Speak Up! It's So Dark*) have found an audience outside Scandinavia:

❝ 1 P.M. Meeting at Swedish Film Institute with the newly established Film Consultant, B. She wants me to come up with ideas and prepare me for future contacts. We talk about my work in the theatre – my experiences working for children and on drama for children versus film and what I have considered as a conventional and happy childhood genre. My film *Speak Up! It's So Dark* has reached a large youth audience because I have worked so much for youth in the theatre. Do I really have something for children in film? To my surprise, B. invites me for a talk, and *she knows my work*. It is a free talk.

P. works with adult fiction. He praises the first draft of my 'Norwegian' screenplay, encourages me and gives me support. 'Go ahead – it's worth doing.'

Ten years ago we collaborated in creating new written drama for youths and children in Stockholm. We have gone our different ways. I was afraid that our mutual ideas would stand in my way in this new power relationship. Sweden is a small country and everybody knows everybody. It can get pretty messy. How to retain your integri-

ty in the interests of a genuinely good project? [. . .]

I leave the Institute in a state of euphoria and hunger (no lunch, just coffee, coffee, coffee). Nothing is decided; everything remains to be done. But there were no humiliating scenes. Ideas, instead, and respect. ❞

The enterprising young Scottish producer, Christopher Young, has his office in London and has mastered the art of seeking funds in Europe:

❝ The working day begins with my sorting through piles of unanswered mail [after my visit to the Isle of Jura] and listening to eighteen messages on the answering machine. Only one of particular interest – U.S. distributor Miramax have sold the U.S. video rights to *Venus Peter* to Live Entertainment who will release it in autumn . . .

I have lunch with my brother Patrick who is a director of the company. We discuss my application to the European Script Fund Incentive Funding Scheme. I am keen to apply as I have developed and produced both *Venus Peter* and *Prague* and have two strongly European projects currently in development. One is *Silver*, an original script which I have commissioned Vitor Gonçalves to write and direct. Vitor is a Portuguese writer/director whose debut feature *A Girl in Summer* was a critical success in Portugal. We intend to make a contemporary adventure story set in Lisbon and the Highlands and islands of Scotland. He is just about to finish a first draft screenplay, and we are looking for a writer to work with him on the next draft as the dialogue will be mainly in English.

The other [project] is a definitive version of the whole of Proust's *A la recherche du temps perdu* from Harold Pinter's screenplay – he and I are currently looking for a suitable director. [. . .]

After lunch I make a few calls including one to Morton Wax in New York who specialises in releasing pictures at very low cost. He has written to me about *Prague* which has no U.S. distributor and I promise to send him a video-cassette. Also to Claudie Ossard, French producer of *Delicatessen*, who is also applying to the Incentive Funding Scheme. And to Manuel Pedroso de Lima who will be my Portuguese co-producer for

371

Silver – we discuss Vitor's next contract as he arrives in London this evening to continue 🙶 work on the script.

José Luis Borau, when he directed *Poachers* in 1975, appeared likely to become a world-famous name. Instead he has opted for a many-sided role within Spanish cinema:

🙶 From 8 A.M. to noon I worked on the script of what I hope will be my next film – a realist drama which takes place in a small industrial city in the north of Spain. The provisional title is *Father and Son*, and it deals with the difficult relationship between a boy of fourteen, his father and the father's new lover who is an attractive woman, but rather enigmatic, especially for the boy, who is soon fatally attracted to her. Of course, this is only the beginning. After that, as the stories develop, they often end up very different to how they started out. At least, that has always been my experience. [. . .]

>> 372

Last thing in the evening I interviewed Manuel Barbachano, a famous Mexican producer (*Nazarin*, *Torero*, *Pedro Páramo*), whom the Spanish Film Archive was justly honouring this week. I'm preparing a book on Spanish cineastes who went into exile as a result of the Spanish Civil War and Barbachano has worked with many of them: directors (Buñuel, Velo), executive producers (Amérigo), musicians (Hernández, Breton), designers (Fontanals), actors (Ofelia Guilmain, August Benedico) etc. He gave me some very interesting information and we agreed to meet again in Mexico, under more relaxed circumstances.

That was all. As you can see, plans and projects. I don't think that the current situation of cinema, in general or in Spain, can go 🙶 on for much longer.

Shinya Tsukamoto, the young director of *Tetsuo – Body Hammer*, *Hiruko the Goblin*, and *Tetsuo II*, responds with pleasure to the prospects awaiting him now that his work has been acknowledged internationally:

🙶 At the moment, one of the secret film projects which I plan to begin shooting in the autumn is making steady progress. It will be

Above: *José Luis Borau, the Spanish director, also acted in his 1975 feature,* Poachers. Right: *Shinya Tsukamoto, director of* Tetsuo – Body Hammer *and* Tetsuo II

374

Torgny Wickman's The Language of Love *(1969) swept round the world in the pre-video era*

different from conventional sci-fi movies. Now I am waiting for my scriptwriter to have a free schedule. This is the first time that I've asked someone else to write a script for me. So far I've been tied up working on consecutive film projects, but now I've got time to work on several films. I've had two offers from Hollywood. As one of my aims is to make American films, I would like to consider these offers carefully. As part of a small project, I am making a video logo for MTV. They gave me complete artistic freedom, so I am going to make it entirely in 'Tetsuo' style. In addition, the foreign sales of *Tetsuo* and *Tetsuo II* have been wonderful. Recently I have received more acting offers, and I'm currently playing the role of a murderer in Kaizo Hayashi's new film, and after the summer I'll have quite a good part in Naoto Takenaka's next picture.

Torgny Wickman is in his early eighties, and still intent on making films. A veteran of the Swedish commercial cinema (he made the controversial *Language of Love* in 1969), he writes in a positive tone, and in fact won a grant for his project one week after this diary was logged:

" In my editing room lie two short films unfinished due to lack of money; 1992 was a great loss. One is the second film in a series about Swedish furniture designers [. . .] and the other is called *A Blues About Now* and is the middle picture in a triptych about time. [. . .]

I have written and directed twenty features. In recent years I have written, directed and produced two short films about the Swedish church painter Albertus Pictor who lived in the latter part

Still from Zelda Barron's Secret Places

of the Fifteenth Century [and inspired Bergman for *The Seventh Seal*]. I have written a 24-page synopsis about him. Every summer he left Stockholm and his old wife. [. . .] His Madonnas were dark one year and blonde the next.

I've sent the synopsis to one of the Swedish Film Institute's two feature film consultants, Per Lysander. His response has been quite favourable. I have also asked for a personal meeting to discuss it further. Certainly I'm old but I believe like Kurosawa that it's only after 80 that you reach your full creative potential. This afternoon I phoned Per Lysander and made an appointment for next Thursday. Then I took out my synopsis and began reading. *Albertus and the Madonnas* will, I hope, be my best film. **99**

Zelda Barron has directed three features (*Secret Places*, *Shag*, and *The Bulldance*), and her screenwriting has been lucrative and respected. Today, however, she finds herself between assignments, and obliged to return to her old stamping ground:

66 Due to the recession and bills to pay, I was returning to a job I hadn't done for eleven years but had in the past been employed to do on major feature films for twenty-five years: continuity. June 10th was the third day of a four-day commercial being shot at Pinewood Studios. [. . .] There were some consolations – old friends, some not seen for twenty years or more. A classy crew

indeed, including Howard Atherton, director of photography (*Indecent Proposal*), a clapper-boy when I last saw him; designer Assheton Gorton (*The French Lieutenant's Woman*); and a delightful actress, Cherie Lunghi. [. . .]

I have spent days, months, and years trying to get a few of my own projects off the ground. Right now, thanks to the success of 'small' British films at the Oscars this year, films which deal with people who talk to each other instead of killing or raping them, all three are moving along rather nicely. Fingers crossed! [. . .]

When I got home there were two messages on my machine, both from the U.S. Warren Beatty is producing a new film later in the year and wants to talk to me about working with him on it. And good news from Susan Gee, a producer with whom I had several meetings in L.A. earlier in 1993 about a project she wishes me to direct, a funny script and, surprisingly, one which might just be a goer. Up go the spirits! **99**

Raafat El-Mihi, a 50-year-old screenwriter and director (*Love Has a Final Story*) in Egypt, looks back on his day with an ironic detachment:

66 Something amusing happened to me. I was surprised to receive a call from a Saudi distributor and producer; I had heard his name mentioned in cinema circles over the past two years but had not met him. All I knew was that he was a very rich 25-year-old. I was optimistic. Maybe I could carry out one of my projects with the help of this young man. I met him at 11.30 A.M. in his office. I was startled by his asking me to write a screenplay with a part for him to appear in. I apologised, trying to prevent myself from laughing, despite my feeling of offence and indignation at such a request.

I left his office and began to walk the streets of Cairo. What a humiliation! Of course if he had sounded in the least bit intelligent or looked hopeful, I might have considered it. Why not? A new face launching himself with his own money. But the catastrophe was that he had nothing encouraging to offer that was remotely connected to the cinema (apart of course from production and distribution). **99**

24. Frustrations, Tensions, and the Whole

Damned Thing UNCERTAINTY CAN STRIKE EVEN THE

MOST ASSURED AND ESTABLISHED OF DIRECTORS,

EITHER JUST BEFORE A FILM IS RELEASED, OR IN THE

TEETH OF ECONOMIC OR POLITICAL HEADWINDS.

Sydney Pollack's *The Firm* became one of the major hits of 1993, grossing over $200 million worldwide. On June 10th, however, the director was by no means sure of its reception:

❝ Day 13 of the final mix of *The Firm*. This is the fastest I've ever had to work – and it's a bit insane. Eight weeks from completion of principal photography until the picture had to be

Sydney Pollack pictured on location for The Firm, *which he screened on June 10th 1993*

locked in order to meet the July 1st date. It's happening more and more.

9.30 A.M. Screening for U.I.P. International in the big screening room at Paramount. We put together a black-track-reject-trial print and a quick and rough sound mix on the last five reels in order to make the screening. It was imperfect but absolutely necessary for them to see it now. Michael Williams-Jones [President of U.I.P.] and Anne Bennett were extremely complimentary about the film. [. . .]

I have big problems with the colour print and some serious sound problems, and not enough time to fix them. I've been on the phone with Phil Hitos, the timer at DeLuxe [laboratories], trying to get him to go back into the negative to make these corrections. The lot is under enormous pressure to get an I.P. made in order to begin printing the 1,800 prints by the end of next week. [. . .]

This afternoon we mixed reels 14 and 15. I've double-checked the end credits to make sure that two new songs are listed. [. . .]

Peggy Segal, the publicist, is urging me to do press work – which I hate – but will have to do to support the film. [. . .]

Dave Grusin, the composer, and I talked about changing two of the piano cues. We'll do it in the morning. The mixers are getting **99** tired now. It's 7 P.M.

Konstantin Lopushansky's diary captures the profound pessimism – and yet also the sense of derision – that lies at the heart of many a contemporary Russian film-maker:

66 I woke up with snatches of a phrase in my mind: '. . . but with a human face.' The grey, unfamiliar street in the dream remained in my memory and I remember pushing through a crowd and somebody next to me uttering these words. I hasten to add that my dream has nothing whatsoever to do with the film I am making, even though the title, *Apocalyptic Dream*, would appear to suggest a connection. It is simply a linguistic coincidence.

So, having awoken, I realised that this extremely vague phrase concerning the 'human face' would hang over the day ahead. [. . .]

Today, I must talk to the head of the studio.

[. . .] The bottom line is that they want to 'close' my film, as we say in my country or, in simpler terms, they want to stop shooting due to lack of funds. There is money but it's impossible to get hold of it. An absolutely surreal situation but for us Russians, alas, it is typical. My film is 'closed' once a week, and I am even getting used to it. However, on this occasion it seems that myself and those involved with the film will remain for an indefinite period without any means to live, and this casts a wholly different light on the situation.

Such was the conversation with the head of the studio . . . I was examining his face and the office while acutely aware of how out of place my behaviour was and yet at the same time I was unable to do anything about it. The reason for my behaviour was that eight years ago I sat in this very same office, opposite the very same man. At that time, he had 'closed' my film because of a discrepancy in ideology and now it is because of a discrepancy in the free market situation in the studio.

In short, the whole scene is being repeated: the discussion, the characters involved, and the sense behind the occasion. Only the dialogue has altered slightly: the word 'ideology' has been replaced pretty much by the term 'free market,' and art, both now and then, is essentially not required by anybody. [. . .]

Leaving the meeting, I suddenly reflect for a moment, is there any metaphor for what has happened in my country? Or rather, is there any explanation as to why the one thing we were all anticipating with such feverish excitement never took place? Why it sunk into a quagmire, and was replaced by a bureaucratic metamorphosis akin to a swamp – a swamp where nobody can venture, and where all those who seek to cross it plunge to the bottom? [. . .]

At 5 P.M., I have a meeting scheduled with the representative of a certain 'commercial structure,' the term we Russians give nowadays to the green shoots of capitalism springing up in our country. The reason for the meeting is simple, in the words of my colleague: this firm intends to invest money into the production. The company itself, so it seems, is in some dirty basement; this, of course, is purely for security reasons. I cannot

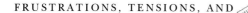

find out precisely what the firm does. It purports to sell women's swimwear and sanitary tampons.

The meeting was as follows: within a short time I had shaken the dusty steps of the basement with a moving speech about spirituality and Russia's historical calling towards post-modernism as being the only possible stylistic solution to the forthcoming film. My call was answered by two mangy cats who stood staring at me in surprise. [. . .] Finally, the boss raised his eyes and said, 'Well,' and then repeated the word, changing the intonation and spreading his hands in a gesture of helplessness. The bodyguard, a clean-shaven thug dressed in a track suit, repeated this gesture and in so doing revealed a hand-pistol under his jacket. I realised that this was not the time to get heavily embroiled in a conversation about the problems of post-modernism. However, instead of doing just that, I continued to stand there examining his face, just like in the

Marla Ingham and Laura Franklin at work on Confessions of a Marriage Junkie

The Hispanic New Yorker, Leon Constantiner, suffers the aggravations and despondency of manya producer:

66 It would have been pleasant to have been able to write this diary for June 10th about the project that I had planned to put into production in the next five days. Unfortunately, today the project fell through. Negotiations broke off between me as producer and the two co-directors of the documentary. Regrettably, we could not agree on the fine tuning. We had the same aims: to work well at producing a great documentary on the value and work of women pilots during the Second World War. But it didn't work out. The work remains in the inkwell, on the editing table, and in the dark room, and I'll have to begin a new project.

It all hurts. It hurts to see how a dream crumbles, how desires are blocked, how an illusion comes to nothing. But despite all this, cinema continues and will continue so long as dreams, desires and illusions exist. Everyone who shares 99 these values can and should make films.

379 ≪

Even when a project seems poised on the cusp of fruition, problems lie in wait, as John M. Landsberg's diary from Santa Barbara, California, makes plain:

66 Can I call it working when the cameras aren't rolling, when I'm not agonising over a costume that doesn't fit my concept of the character, when I'm not wrestling with a dolly that won't roll smoothly, when I'm not struggling to coax an actor to the point of understanding and expression that will bring a fictional person to life – a fictional person, I might add, who has become more real to me than most of the people I know? [. . .]

Then again, am I ever not working, in my head at least, on my film?

Today I had the opportunity to think about resuming the edit of my first feature film, *Confessions of a Marriage Junkie*, which I brought to fruition only through the extraordinary and unique creation of an independent educational workshop in which various professional film-makers and I taught 23 novices how to make a 35mm

bad dream, not having the strength to get up and leave the meeting. These, then, were the 'faces.' I will only say that it was at that moment I suddenly realised that there are some faces that should be hidden away under clothing, like other obscene parts of the body; in other words, they 99 should not be shown in their naked form.

feature, and then guided them through the entire production. The money ran out, of course, after two years of work, but recently I saw more on the horizon, and I am at last going to finish, after this most recent hiatus of about eight months. The waiting is horrible, but all the frustrations will be worth it in the end. [. . .]

Plans, plans, plans. Nobody realises that a film is 90% planning and only 10% doing. And 100% dealing with one disaster after another. If you can solve a couple of dozen major problems every day for a few years, you can make a movie. **99**

Pilar Miró has enjoyed a colourful and controversial career in the Spanish film world – government administrator, festival chief and film director:

66 For Thursday June 10th, the shooting schedule decreed: Location 'Bar.' Interior Night. Sequences 14 and 41. Shooting from 8 A.M. to 7 P.M. Characters: Rafael, Susi, Katy, Juan, Manfulleda, Cordero, Mustela, Leticia, taxi driver. Four special women. Seventy extras. Glasses, drinks. Choreographer. Light effects. Playback 'Vaya con dios,' Celia Cruz. The filming of *High Seduction* had begun on May 17th and I was finishing the fourth week of filming. Everything had gone very well so far, it didn't seem at all like a film [. . .]

[Returning from the Cannes Festival on May 13th, where my previous film, *The Bird of Happiness* had been presented in 'Un Certain Regard'] I intended to begin filming *High Seduction* the following Monday. But then in 24 hours, everything changed. Three days before the start of shooting, the film was suspended indefinitely. And not through lack of budget, casting problems, location difficulties, the odd earthquake, or sudden and unexpected death. No, nothing like that. The author of the original book, after following the development of the project for six months, without expressing any disagreement with the script, the cast, the producer, with me or with any passing stranger, sent a lawyer to our offices, withdrawing his authorisation. We knew nothing more. She doesn't answer.

So, on June 10th, at home, in a state of more advanced schizophrenia than usual, I talked on

Pilar Miró, the talented and controversial Spaniard

the phone with my producer, who is fighting tenaciously to find a script – the same as the aborted one, only completely different. [. . .] It has cheered me up to contribute to this book, and perhaps it would have been an additional luxury to have been able to report on a day's filming in Spain. And I ask myself, but what have I done to deserve this? And I reply – it's strange, but I love CINEMA. **99**

Alain Corneau, the experienced French director of police thrillers (*Police Python 357*, *Série noire*, etc.) spends a a frustrating day during the script stage of his next project:

66 On this very morning of June 10th 1993, there lands on my desk, in typed form, the seventh version of the script on which Pascal Quignard (writer), Jean-Louis Livi (producer) and myself have been working for several months already. After the first impatient re-reading, I feel

380

The late Patrick Dewaere in Alain Corneau's French thriller Série noire

yet again that I do not know how to go further with it. How long will it take, this time, to see in which direction we should go to improve the text?

When will I be able again to read the text as an outsider in order to see the faults?

Answer: never, of course!

The process is much more mysterious than that . . .

This angry need to understand what we are actually doing is omnipresent, when we know very well that it is a complete illusion.

Ah! These editing sessions when, instead of 'seeing' the film, one stupidly looks at the shots and rough assembly passing across the screen . . .

Since we cannot be 'a spectator,' how come we still make it to the end of the editing? I don't know. I have never known. Once, I thought I knew. Today, I know that I will *never* know. **99**

Yvette Biró, a Hungarian who teaches film in the U.S. and has written some much-admired books on film aesthetics, also finds herself frustrated at not being able to move ahead with her own films:

382

66 Early morning [and] I'm waiting for a call, promised by my Hungarian co-producer. He is to arrange my trip to Berlin where I am planning to go in order to find further help for my film project, *Arrivals and Departures*. The call never comes through.

At 10.10 A.M. I call the French partner, Ognon Pictures, hoping to reach M. Balsan, the most charming unavailable man who ever existed. His phone system is perfect: only the answering machine is turned on, so one has the chance of hearing his kind voice, without ever reaching him. Later I manage to get via another number the information that Monsieur is not in, won't be and, moreover, Monsieur is going to fly to St. Petersburg. This is rather far off for a meeting. Fine, will try again!

At noon I cannot wait any longer for the Budapest call. I try it, to no avail. The phone is apparently switched to receive fax messages. [. . .]

I am angry and sorry, thinking of the terrible system of making films. Doubts, bitterness, worries. This is the third (!) year of my relentless effort to bring my film together. Which is longer,

bureaucracy and indifference or my endurance? The musing generates energy. Between despair and nothingness I rather choose despair. [. . .]

My involvement with film was accidental. It started as a forced marriage, after graduation, when I was assigned by the university to take a job at the film studio. Later it became an everlasting love affair with all the necessary hatred and passion. I have worked in many fields within the profession: as dramaturge, critic, essayist, teacher and screenwriter – dealing always with words, writing for and about cinema, words intended to be applied to film. My recent job, as a professor at NYU Graduate Film School, brings together all these activities, turning all my questions and understanding of film into words. **99**

Ömer Kavur, a Turkish producer-director, takes solace from his frustrations in a game of soccer:

66 Just another typical day. Many appointments in the office. Lots of talk and very little accomplished. You're trying to develop a serial for television when you realise how alienated you feel; the electronic media have their own rules which have nothing to do with the cinema . . . Frustration.

The best part of the day for me, however, is playing soccer with friends. The team is composed of three directors, two actors, a cameraman, and a lighting guy. Ever since the crisis in the industry, and the unemployment, you try at least to regain your pride by beating your opponents (businessmen) each week in these soccer games. You feel much better.

Returning home, physically drained, you try to think about the script you have written. You suddenly recognise that three years have gone by and you still don't know from where and how you should secure funding. Anxiety . . .

Still you work on it, you alter a scene, change a bit of dialogue etc.

You go to bed with these thoughts in your head and manipulate the possibilities until the awareness of dreaming comes upon you. It's the same dream you have each night, the dream that brings you hope and joy, the dream in which you feel alive . . . You're actually filming! **99**

Kiran Joneja in Shaheen, *directed by Kaled M. Siddik*

During the 1970s, Kaled M. Siddik won many awards and admirers with his feature film, *The Cruel Sea*, made from his own resources in Kuwait. But now he seems thwarted at every turn by the aftermath of the Gulf War:

❝ It was 9.30 A.M. when I unlocked the door to my office revealing the mountain of meshed, unspooled magnetic soundtracks of the Arabic version of my feature film, *Shaheen*, which I co-produced and directed before the Iraqi invasion of my country. The film is based on a short story by Boccaccio, which I adapted for the screen, about caravan traders of Hijaz in the

Arabian Peninsula and European adventurers along the Silk Road in medieval times.

I arrived last night from London where I re-voiced the English version and where the negative of the film is deposited.

This tedious job of fishing and sorting through the jungle of magnetic tracks, searching for the right takes, and after such a long interval, is so frustrating and boring that it would be easier to reshoot the entire dialogue of the film all over again. This mess was caused by the Iraqi forces, who looted about 95% of my country's assets during their seven-month occupation. [. . .]

All my motion picture production and post-

EPY 5018

25   ▷ 25A

Kaled M. Siddik

production hardware were looted during the course of the occupation, along with each and every item in the office and the studio. Even the promotional stills of the film were looted, except the director's pictures!

To finalise and complete the film in its different versions I prefer to use the technical services of London, where I feel more at home without the communication barrier and where everyone is very supportive and sympathetic to my situation, as they were during the Gulf War – with the exception of the customs staff, who always suspect and distrust any coloured person. Even if one goes through the red channel at Heathrow and declares, there is always another officer who stops you after the declaration channel.

London-based Sindamani Bridglal seems on the verge of completing her film, *A View from the Shore*, but . . . :

❝I sometimes wonder why life in the presumed fast lane of film-making can be so exciting one day and so dreary another.

[. . .] Yesterday was our day to view the answerprint of the film that has taken me more or less two years to co-produce and direct. Now the post-production is lurching along for all sorts of reasons including the fact that my Caribbean financiers, who took a year to opt to make the film and then another to give the money, suddenly decided that after spending a great deal of money on the production they

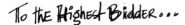

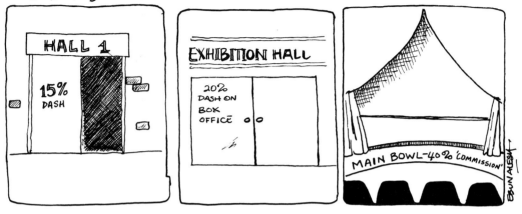

Producers must bargain for their share of box-office in Nigeria

would keep back the final $25,000!

This explains why we saw the answerprint only yesterday (although we finished cutting the film in March), and why I am calling the Caribbean today for the very last instalment of $5,000.

I, the co-producer, and the editor turn up at Metrocolor, the laboratory. Colin, the technician, is getting there but needs to do some more work on a few sequences, especially of the sea. Because of the spray my sparkling Caribbean sea looks very much like the English Channel! He agrees and goes to work on it. Calculated that my phone bill for these Caribbean calls is well over £60 for the past quarter and of course my co-producer says, yes, of course I will get the expenses back. Just like the taxi fare receipt, I counter, that I gave you three weeks back and I haven't seen the cash yet. [. . .]

Whereas yesterday was great because I saw the film for the first time without all the editor's marks, the scratches from the Steenbeck, and the rush print colours, today has been frustrating and disappointing. I couldn't even get through to the Caribbean financiers, they are tied up in meetings all day. [. . .] Still, I did manage to finish the feature film outline that I have been working on for the last few weeks. Posted it too! **99**

Similar anxieties assail Afolabi Adesanya, a Nigerian director whose first feature, *Sango's Wand*, was released in 1988:

66 Was at the National Theatre, Iganmu, Lagos, to collect my production company's share of the box-office earnings of our film, *Sango's Wand*, screened from May 28th to June 1st. It was a fruitless trip. Just like the previous trips, yesterday, and the day before that. Typical of the government establishment in this country! Interminable waiting. Interminable trips. Unjustifiable bargaining over one's hard-earned money. So much for our arts and culture administrators, who always swear they are on the job to protect our interest and not their own pockets. But it is not their fault. Were it not for the connivance of fellow-producers, they would not be so brazen.

To get a screening date, a bargain must be made. To get your share of the box-office, another round of bargaining. But is the country itself not a bargain? Perhaps if fellow film-makers can rationalise why they are in business, and why arts administrators should not be skimming the cream off our hard-earned returns, and that we are indebted to our investors, then we shall be able to run these administrators out of office. But then we don't have a forum, a platform, a guild or union to articulate our stance, on any issue pertaining to us. We meet casually. We are just all floating, drifting. [. . .]

Yet film production is on its death bed. No doctors. No nurses. The Nigerian Film Corporation built a colour lab and a sound studio at Jos. They were due to be opened officially last month. What happened? The President dropped it in favour of a state visit to Edo. Invitation cards had been printed and sent out. Flights and accommodation reserved for guests. The last-minute cancellation is an ominous sign. [. . .]

We [film-makers] need to organise, we need to come together as a common interest group, a pressure group, a team, a union, a guild. We need an efficient distribution and exhibition **99** network. It is imperative.

Guita Schyfter has just finished her first feature, *To See You a Bride*, in Mexico, but a series of setbacks leaves her somewhat

>> 386

disenchanted:

66 [My film] deals with the adaptation, rejection and acceptance of two young Jewish girls, Mexican by birth, and how they shape their lives under the pressures of the early 1960s and their own awareness of conflicting loyalties. [. . .]

Fly back [from Guadalajara] to Mexico City and directly from the airport I go to the Mexican Institute of Cinematography (they are my major producers) to find out if the release prints have finally arrived from New York. They have not, although the Institute has paid for them in full and in advance. Nor has my negative which I need to create the trailer. All this has delayed the theatrical release of *To See You a Bride*, and since I recommended the laboratory, my producers hold me responsible. I call New York and the lab says that I still owe money, which I do not, because the verbal agreement with the head of the lab had stipulated an overall fee. He is not in New York and will not return until June 16th. I will never make a verbal agreement again. I call my brother, who lives in Costa Rica and ask him to lend me the money. [. . .]

While I'm at the Institute they inform me that there has also been a misunderstanding about the

Guita Schyfter and crew on location in Mexico

invitation to the Montreal World Film Festival. The head of festivals at the Mexican Institute says the film had been invited verbally to the Official Competition. Montreal claims that there is a mix-up and in fact the film is invited to the Latin

American section. The Institute is trying to get in touch with Montreal, but I too should send them a fax asking for an explanation. I feel really frustrated and a bit humiliated with all these verbal agreements, and again decide I shall never again commit to one. Everything in writing from now on.

On my way out, someone from the press department hands me a review which he thinks I should read. It is the worst review about the film yet to appear. I call a friend and read it to her over the phone. She says a review that slags off everything is not worth worrying about. It hurts me just the same. **99**

25. Passing Thoughts WE END THE BOOK

WITH SOME OF THE WISEST AND MOST CAREFULLY

CONSIDERED OF ALL THE ENTRIES RECEIVED.

PROMPTED BY FATIGUE, INDOLENCE, NOSTALGIA,

OR A JOURNEY ABROAD, THESE DIARIES ILLUSTRATE

BOTH THE COMMITMENT AND THE VERY PRIVATE

NATURE OF THE FILM-MAKER'S PERSONALITY.

>> 388

Francesco Rosi represents for many cine-philes the antithesis of the "baroque" Italian cinema represented by Fellini, Visconti, and Bertolucci. His angry, astringent studies of corruption (*Salvatore Giuliano, Hands over the City, Exquisite Corpses*) have not diminished his profound humanism:

When he's not shooting, or writing scripts, or dealing with actors or locations to see, a film director always has the feeling that he is wasting time. Or at least that's what happens to me. Thus the desk covered in papers, the telephone, the mail piling up, or people to see, are things that could always be replaced by something better. [. . .]

I spent the morning checking the French translation of my adaptation of Primo Levi's *The Truce*, my next film project. This reminded me of fifty years ago today, June 10th 1943, when Mussolini declared war, and the prophetic value of Levi's title which still reminds us that life is a truce between one war and the next.

I then went to mail the script to Paris. The Post Office is nearby and I like doing these tasks personally whenever I have the time. I popped round to the framemaker's shop. He still has to finish some work for me from last year; I pretended to be annoyed, he pretended to be mortified, and we will carry on like this for another year. I also went to see my favourite fishmonger and chatted with him for a while. He told me that Giulietta [Masina] had called him several times from Los Angeles, where she and [her husband] Federico Fellini went to receive the Oscar, to remind him of the fresh bass for Federico on his return. I too bought a bass and returned home. I chatted with my wife on the phone: I live on the first floor, she on the ground floor and we find that speaking on the phone distils the topics of conversation better. My daughter has called me from Morocco, where she is making a film [*Abraham*] with Richard Harris and Barbara Hershey. She's happy and I'm happy for her.

I went out on the terrace and gave one glance to the flowers, another to Rome; one can see it all and sometimes I have to lower the blinds, otherwise I get distracted and do nothing at all. I read the papers, which puts me in a bad mood. I play some music, but immediately take off the record; I'm not in the right mood.

Francesco Rosi, at home in the big city and ever ready to excoriate its corruption

Still from Edgar Reitz's massive opus on life in Germany Die Zweite Heimat

I avoided answering the telephone, except for just one call: I was asked to decide to go to Naples for the showing of my latest film, *Neapolitan Diary*, a 90 minute blend of autobiography and documentary which I shot last year and has been shown on television. 'When? From July 22nd to 25th?' Oh my God, and what if I have to go and scout a location? How can I make them understand that to decide on such a commitment a month and a half beforehand gives me a feeling of not being master of my own time? **"**

The Cuban director Enrique Pineda Barnet sends a love letter to his muse:

" I should be jealous of all the other declarations of love that have been made to you. I do not understand, however, why I feel a secret pleasure in sharing you. Is it some sort of perversity, a strange habit, an inevitable necessity? I remember when I first saw you; you had still not uttered your first words; I saw you in *The Kiss* and some mechanical piano cried a furtive tear.

In my early years, my mother took me to see you with her sailor boyfriend. I began to confuse the fantasy of the cinema seats with the reality of your romances . . . My undoing and my frenzy . . . to see you and not to see you, to feel you in my life and to decipher you through my astonished eyes. Yes, in truth you changed everything: my way of looking, of feeling, of living.

You disturbed every night of my adolescence, always that same conflict between reality and imagination. I don't know if I saw through your eyes. I often dreamed that you saw through mine. So much shared solitude. All happiness and agony together, juxtaposed, successive, always intense. Until the moment came for me to invade you or for you to invade me, when I began to express myself through you. I have loved you so dearly. You have given me so much life. I feel that in you I survive and live on, I translate myself into a magic carpet of lights, forever moving backwards and forwards. Reality, fantasy. 'How could I not have loved your large, staring eyes?'

You do not grow old. You are already 100 and your body is intact. You leave us in your wake, silent, forever awaiting your miracle. Reality, fantasy.

I cannot be jealous of other admirers if I share with them that delicious pain of possessing you, this shared and solitary promiscuity in your embrace . . . Yours, as always . . . **99**

Edgar Reitz, at 60 years of age, belongs to the generation who first flowered in the 1960s. Only during the 1980s, however, did he find an enduring niche in film history with his extraordinary fresco of everyday life in Germany through the decades: *Heimat*, and then its sequel, *Die zweite Heimat*:

66 This is the evening when the 'Schwabing Riots' began, which started the young people's revolt in 1963. In the fifth episode of *Die zweite Heimat*, I describe the relationship between revolution and the state of the weather, a connection which only the eye of the camera can properly reveal.

Today there is the same weather as in 1963. But there is no revolt in sight. Being young is no longer associated with feelings of hope and belief in the future. [. . .]

After the disappointments I have experienced over recent weeks with German television, I am deeply annoyed and can no longer tell whether my style of film-making has any future in this country, which gets more opposed to culture every day. [. . .]

It is an old problem for the Germans, that they hate their artists and their intellectuals. Films that try to communicate a feeling for the history of the art of the cinema are hated and attacked here. [. . .]

It comforts me that in other European countries there is still a love for their indigenous cinema. In recent months I have given countless interviews, done TV programmes, and been to film festivals and had discussions with the audiences for my film-novel. Since the premiere of *Die zweite Heimat* at the Venice Film Festival in

September 1992, all I have been doing is trying to win new friends for the film. I wanted to make a new genre of narrative film internationally known. My 26-hour film had been meant from the start to be *a single film* and not a television series, which was how it was classified. [. . .]

I have just experienced a little miracle with the work in Italy. Since it could not be sold to television there, Mikado Film has been able to experiment with a cinema run. The results are sensational. They are showing the 13 parts there in ordinary cinemas and have one part running for a week, with four screenings a day, therefore 28 times per week. Then the second part follows for a week, and so on, until thirteen weeks later, that's to say a quarter of a year, the film reaches its conclusion. The performances in Rome and Milan were all sold out, and the Italian press are asking what could have brought on this intoxication. Social habits changed. Members of the audience met one another once a week for months at a film, became friends, went to parties together afterwards, and achieved a level of experience which they could compare to nothing else. More than 150,000 tickets were sold in one cinema alone in Rome for *Die zweite Heimat*. The distributor reports over a million visitors. An isolated case? A portent of new possibilities for the future? **99**

The flying Finn, Jörn Donner, has been a portal figure in Scandinavian cinema for thirty years, as critic, director, and producer. He invested in the first Kaurismäki film, won his country's foremost literary prize, and served as a Member of Parliament for several years:

66 Even today, like any other day, I'm thinking of a film, but I'm not making a film, either short or long. Why?

Directing is an all-consuming task. The obstacles are many in the face of what I really want to do.

The self-inflicted obstacles are that I am an M.P. and I don't have a free run with my time, except for all too brief periods. This will continue until the end of March, 1995.

Self-inflicted is the fact that I also produce a lot. Today I have four films in production, all, regrettably, for TV.

Self-inflicted too is my passion for films, or as Bergman has said, it's my mistress, while writing is an occupation, a wife.

Not self-inflicted is the European film's dilemma – its poor performance at the cinema, its general commercial inferiority.

Not self-inflicted is the fact that I live on the periphery of Europe, which means that the memories and dramas I draw from this environment are strange to most Europeans, which is understandable. After all, I know rather little about Portugal.

I get up early this morning, like all other days, a habit I've picked up at too many film shoots. Instead of erratic work I've got meetings and politics. The dreams I do have remain dreams (or nightmares) at present because they cannot be transformed on to paper, script, plans, or cinematic action.

I also note that there is a distance between my way of thinking about film and what is trendy right now. But I learned early to disregard critics, because I've been a critic myself. Consequently, one day, in the future, I want once again to **99** make the dream into a reality.

Reconciliation, at least on a creative level, between the Chinese Mainland and Taiwan seems to peep through the lines of director Ling Zifeng's diary. Ling is considered one of China's greatest veteran film-makers, and his recent works include *Rickshaw Boy* and *Border Town.*

66 This is my third day in Taiwan. [. . .] Taking my camera, I went downstairs in the lift to take a photo of myself outside the main entrance of the hotel as a souvenir. [. . .] Luckily, the people on the street were all Chinese; they looked and talked like me. I approached a middle-aged man, smiled at him (he didn't look educated, more of a worker type), and asked if he'd take a photo of me. There was no language barrier. If I'd been in another country, it wouldn't have been so easy.

Yesterday, the opening ceremony of the First Film Forum between Mainland China and Taiwan was held at the Rixin Theatre. Four years ago, in 1989, the first Mainland China-Taiwan

Veteran Chinese film-maker, Ling Zifeng

Film Exhibition took place in New York's Chinatown. I was invited, but that was in America. I remember saying to my Taiwanese colleagues that I hoped the next film week would be held in Beijing or Taiwan. Four years later, my wish has been realised.

Taiwan and the Mainland have been severed for over forty years. [. . .] Today, the papers reported the opening of the event in Taipei, and printed a photograph of me with Mee Hsing, Chairman of the Golden Horse Awards. They also mentioned my announcement at the press conference of my plans to make three films before I reached the age of 80 – *Tianqiao*, *Li Bo*, and *The Grand Master* – adding that I spoke cheerfully, with humour, and didn't at all have the bearing of an old man. Actually, I'm already 77 – thank you for the compliment! [. . .]

During a visit today with a group of young directors and actors to the Central Motion Picture Company Studios, we went into the Motion Master Simulation Theatre to watch a film called *Space Travel* in specially-designed seats that move sideways, up and down, and in circles. During this tremendously breathtaking experience, those normally vivacious, lovable actresses uttered shrill squeals. Even the young directors and actors were gasping. They were satisfying their appetite for excitement and turbulence and enjoying the thrill to the full.

When the film was over and the machinery came to a halt, the arena fell silent again. At that moment, what astonished these youngsters even more was that I, whom they usually call 'Old Grandad,' had also come through this extraordinary moment and, moreover, come through unscathed.

I'm very fond of the youngsters who have accompanied me on this trip. [. . .] They've instilled in me a kind of vitality or energy, and are constantly giving me food for thought. Today, as cinema the world over goes through a depression, I ask myself how I can break out from my old mould and create anew, how to clear a new path, and, together with these young directors, **"** strive for a rebirth of film.

A younger (46) Chinese director, from Taiwan, Edward Yang has found an enthusiastic response in the West to films like *A Bright Summer Day* and *The Terroriser*.

" Life goes on even if world cinema does not. What makes cinema interesting is always when it interacts with and relates to life. A century ago we were handed a gift of a creative tool called Motion Pictures. A hundred years later, the greatest film ever made is still recognised as *Citizen Kane*. Has any of us ever wondered that the troubles we face with cinema today are basically a result of our inability to master this art form as it deserves to be? The power of cinema comes from its resemblance to life experience. Twentieth Century men have greatly expanded their experience of reality through film.

Television soon became cinema's arch-rival when it became widely popular, because many film-makers felt threatened by its existence and they were no longer the provider for an expanded reality. Many more advanced tools are being invented every day, since technology never stops progressing. World cinema has long lost its original monopoly of people's dreams and very few of us have the courage to recognise this fact. We sink ever deeper into this hole of complaining and

bitching about people not turning up at the cinema. Even major film festivals dig ever deeper into the developing world to come up with entries to fill the bill, even risking racial motivation by giving them major awards to justify their choice and replace a standard of excellence with ethnic diversity.

From every angle, the motion picture is outdated, and deservedly so, after a hundred years on the road. The bottom line is that we are less and less moved and excited when emerging from the cinema. But, LIFE does not get out of date, poor creativity does!

Without a creative mind, cinema is as lifeless as an empty film can. Too many of us have turned out undeserving work to justify our one day's value as a film-maker. [. . .] The question remains: one hundred years ago we entered this 'school' of cinema; what have we got to show for it, now that we are facing the next century? And, like our forefathers a century ago, what do we have in our hands to face our children with **"** for the next hundred years?

393 **«**

Erland Josephson (Sweden) enhanced many of the films of Ingmar Bergman with his urbane, suave, and often ironic presence (*The Face*, *Scenes from a Marriage*, *Fanny and Alexander* etc.). He has also acted in many European countries:

" At present I have nothing to do with film, except as a spectator. [. . .] There are innumerable descriptions of a film-maker when he's actually filming, but not quite so many about what he does when he's not working. In reality it is probably that a lot of what he does and a majority of his behaviour even this idle day, a day long after he's finished shooting, and long before he starts again, is marked by his passion for the catty world where he was once at ease and still has a feeling of being a temporary guest. [. . .]

The camera must restore order. I have to take shape. Please watch me! I take out some synopses, check some offers, Bulgaria, Finland, Italy, Greece, Sweden. Proposals of realities. Projects in faraway places that people are planning; some plans are realised, others go down the tube.

My name lies there somewhere in the stacks

Left: *Chilean producer-director Silvio Caiozzi García.* Above: *Still from* Julio comienza en Julio

of paper, next to other names as possibilities, proposals, dreams.

I'm preparing a seminar for the day after tomorrow. In Jokkmokk, far up in the Lapp wilderness, there is a festival that defiantly calls itself 'All Sweden Film Festival.' It's an orgy in film, the cinema as a place of culture, cult, a temple for worshipping human destinies. You get a stronger belief in the future of film than in, for example, Cannes where you live in a luxurious hotel and defy the crisis, sloshing drinks and complaining about the missing millions (dollars, of course).

Long live Jokkmokk! Long live cinema! I sit down and flick through old and new film ideas that I've had and adore. I try them on imaginary audiences north of the polar circle.

Suddenly I hear the whole world's film cameras whirring. There's a lot going on. I want to be there. I lie down on the bed, gaze at the ceiling, and let June 10th, 1993, pass by. **99**

Silvio Caiozzi García, a producer-director from Chile, also spends a lazy, relaxing day:

66 Today I got up feeling calm. Today I haven't felt that damned knot in my stomach which often makes me sick. That wrenching caused by questions like: Did I choose the right actor? Will I manage to film all the scenes before sunset? Will I manage to enthuse the crew today with the feeling that we're doing something very good and entertaining? Will I have a mental block when I'm exhausted, which means that I

won't be able to solve even the tiniest problem? etc. etc. etc.

Today I don't feel that damned knot in my stomach that reminds me of exam days at school. I feel happy because today is a holiday [Corpus Christi] in my country. And what's more it is a holiday that I can share with my family, not one of those when I have to tell them that I haven't completed my filming schedule and that we're going to shoot even though it's a holiday.

We went to breathe non-contaminated air at the seaside. Of course I didn't take a camera, so as not to have any contaminating memory. It was a wonderfully tranquil day, without a care in the world. Curiously, when we got back from the coast at night, I felt a slight knot. Of course, I remembered that we start filming tomorrow **99** at 7 A.M.

Bertrand Tavernier began his career as a publicist and film buff, which he remains to this day. Author, critic, polemicist, and a director of several sensitive films (*L'Horloger de Saint-Paul*, *Le Juge et l'assassin*, *Un Dimanche à la campagne*, *La Vie et rien d'autre*), he writes his diary while airborne:

66 Why am I dreaming this morning of the days when I was 13 years old, of the days at boarding school and, most of all, about Tilda Thamar, the sex-symbol of the 1950s who was nicknamed the 'Argentinian sex-bomb'? The fact is that today is the 10th of June and that it is the day of Saint Landry, a particularly strange saint (what did he accomplish to be devoted a whole day?) whose name irresistibly leads me to a long forgotten actor named Gérard Landry. He acted in a few Italian historic films. I remember *Un Chevalier de la révolte* or *La Vengeance* with, according to the poster, '1000 extras' – and after some research, I find his name in *Les Hommes sans peur* by Yvan Noe, also in the film with this mouthwatering title – *Béatrice devant le désir* by Jean de Marguenat. But the film that does trigger all those memories is *La Caraque blonde* by Jaqueline Audry. I can see us all dreaming and discussing in a bed-

Bertrand Tavernier on set, although he reveals in his diary his true calling – that of film buff

room at College Saint-Martin over the stills of the film. Firstly, because this French 'Western' movie was shot in colour, secondly and mostly, because it said that Tilda Thamar, co-starring with Gérard Landry, appeared bathing naked.

Just as I am recollecting the event, I am, as often the case, between two planes, between two journeys. Today, I am on my way back from Heidelberg and on my way to Japan – to introduce *L.627* in Yokohama where Unifrance Film have organised a French film festival. The fact is that a director today finds himself not only busier waiting around and looking for funds than shooting, but also spends much more time introducing previous films than preparing new ones. So, last night, I was in Heidelberg to show *La Guerre sans nom* to students, on the request of my editor Luce Grunenwaldt whose fiancée works at the French Institute. After numerous questions, we have an animated dinner in a Thai restaurant where I meet Nathalie Dessay, sublime Olympia in the *Tales of Hoffmann* produced at the Opéra de Lyon, and after an extremely short night, I find myself on the plane from Frankfurt to Paris. [. . .]

>> 398

[Later, after changing planes] I doze off during the film – a Japanese film, because I am on a Japanese airline and the food and service are excellent – that describes, with a burlesque verve, funny at times though often overdone, the misfortunes of a Japanese group who came to build a bridge in a Far Eastern country torn by civil war.

Stopover in Moscow, in a deserted airport, always desolate. I see fewer stout women, of the garrulous type, or former hammer throwers who, having failed to win a medal at the Olympics, find themselves checking foreign passports of passengers in transit. As a sign of the times, the propaganda literature translated into different languages has been replaced by slot machines . . . Is that a gain? An Irish pub has remained open . . . The duty free shop, as always, is closed, but one can buy Baskin Robbins ice-cream and a shop selling Levi jeans and tee-shirts, still open, offers a few articles on sale. One can find the same at Tulsa or Albuquerque airport. Indeed, one cannot stop progress. A bit further on, one can

"Gritty

"The film succeeds tr

th DIDIER BEZACE · JEAN-PAUL COMART · CHARLOTTE KADY · JEAN-RC
et Design GUY-CLAUDE FRANÇOIS · Costume Design JACQUELINE MOREAU
enplay MICHEL ALEXANDRE and BERTRAND TAVERNIER · Director BERTR

Poster for Bertrand Tavernier's underrated study of French police work, L.627

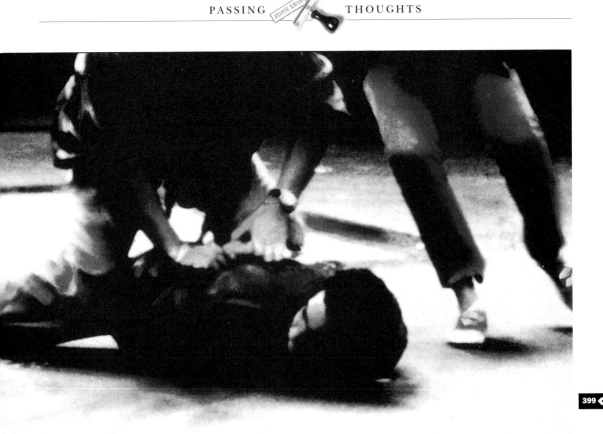

399 **«**

m writ large…a formidable portrait" Derek Malcolm THE GUARDIAN

hantly…one of Tavernier's best and most challenging films" VARIETY

ALAIN SARDE AND FREDERIC BOURBOULON
PRESENT

L.627 (15)

BERTRAND TAVERNIER'S
PROVOCATIVE CRIME THRILLER

ILO · NILS TAVERNIER · PHILIPPE TORRETON · LARA GUIRAO · CÉCILE GARCIA-FOGEL and CLAUDE BROSSET · Photography ALAIN CHOQUAI
ARIANE BOEGLIN · Sound MICHEL DESROIS GÉRARD LAMPS · Director of Production CHRISTINE RASPILLÈRE · Original Music PHILIPPE SARD
AVERNIER · Executive Producer FRÉDÉRIC BOURBOULON · A LITTLE BEAR - LES FILMS ALAIN SARDE Coproduction with the participation of CANA
CAS SOFIARP and INVESTIMAGE 3 · English Subtitles DOLBY STEREO
An Artificial Eye Release

discover on the window of another boutique large posters promoting the new CD by Michael Bolton, of whom I have never heard.

Some Japanese are practising on the slot machines. I think of this taxi driver in Tokyo who had seen *Pépé le Moko* thirty-two times and asked me whether Mireille Balin was still alive. That was a few years ago. There were no slot machines in Moscow airport and Disney had not yet settled in France.

We will soon be called. I can hear the sound of coins falling. It is 11.58 A.M. and indeed we are in 1993.

Many directors have combined film-making with another profession. Nils Malmros, whose films about young people (*The Tree of Knowledge, Beauty and the Beast*) have represented Denmark at festivals everywhere, is a qualified doctor of medicine:

>> 400

❝ My day did not have much to do with films. I was on 24-hour front-line duty at Farsoe Hospital in the casualty ward. In other words, I was the doctor who had to receive all the acutely ill patients and give them first-aid treatment. [. . .]

Towards the end of the afternoon, a sixty-year-old man was brought in who had suffered a sudden collapse because of a blood clot in his heart. There was very little sign of cardiac activity when they brought him in, and it proved impossible to revive him with electric shock treatment or injections of adrenaline.

The evening seemed quiet enough to begin with, but at 9 P.M. an unconscious little girl of three was admitted. She had been looking for sweets in her granny's handbag and had eaten all the little red, green and white pills she had found in a small box. It was the medicine her granny took for her heart condition . . .

How do you sleep at night when you're on duty like this? Have you given them the right treatment? Was there something you overlooked? What's next? At 3 A.M. the little girl started to have convulsions – and, at the same time, they brought in an eighty-year-old man whose left side was paralysed as the result of a cerebral hæmorrhage.

I've never been able to run off films like hot cakes. I've always needed to think them over

again and again, to let my ideas mature gradually through the course of reflection and dreams. Between films I've been studying medicine, and after 22½ years and seven full-length films I have actually become a doctor.

On several occasions I've felt that I was doing my last film, and that afterwards I had nothing more to say. But after some time inspiration has come to me again, in the form of psychological blocks and experiences from my own life that had to be expressed and released.

It is half a year now since the premiere of my latest film, *The Pain of Love* – and once again I felt that it would be my last film. Nor was June 10th exactly the right sort of day to give me time to think about new possibilities. Or was it?

It's happened to me before that just when I was most under pressure, and therefore perhaps had not slept very deeply, images and emotional impressions have surfaced in my dreams. There was a time when I was an assistant surgeon that I woke up in the middle of the night and found myself standing up and holding the curtains as high in the air as I could. I had learnt that if something's bleeding, you must hold it up as high as possible to try to reduce it. My curtains were 'bleeding,' and it was my fault they were bleeding because I hadn't done a proper job stitching up some patient.

I now know that there is another film growing within me. It will concern all those things we try to repress in our subsconscious, but that are always forcing themselves on us. That film grew a little stronger on June 10th, too. ❞

Peter Greenaway also leads a "hybrid" life – painting, and directing films such as *The Draughtsman's Contract, The Belly of an Architect, Drowning by Numbers*, and *Prospero's Books*:

❝ Venice. A festival, but not the Venice Film Festival – the Venice Biennale. The Commune de Venezia has leased me the Palazzo Fortuny for a hundred days, to use for an exhibition-installation. Officially, the event is described as a 'slittamenti' – having no satisfactory English equivalent other than a 'sliding' or a 'gliding.' I don't find the word very illuminating, but the

Director Peter Greenaway, whose career has oscillated between the art gallery and the cinema screen

intention is clear enough. In the pursuit of a cross-over of the cultural disciplines, we should make an event. For me that means a cinema-painting-television-exhibition with architecture – a three-dimensional film that lasts all day for a hundred days with an audience that's not chained to its seats – too good to miss such an opportunity for an essay in mega-cinema. [. . .]

[My] grand schemes have been compromised by circumstances – mainly political – the self-scourging of Venice town councils in the wake of the corruption scandals, the slipperiness of finance that is there and then not there, and a natural Venetian conservatism – hold the extravagances and excesses in check. Probably just as well. In the event we have still done much – and

all exclusively supported by the Commune de Venezia. With Ben van Os, Jan Roelfs and Renier van Brummelen – all of us collaborators on some five feature films – we have hung the interior with blue and silver Carpaccio drapes and crimson Crivelli banners. We have turned the first floor Fortuny museum into a film set that supposes Mariano Fortuny has just left the room. He died in 1947 and his last coffee cup has been kept warm and his last cigar has been kept smoking – for 46 years. The visitors are to be the extras in this hypothetical film – for a start – they can smell the coffee and inhale the smoke.

Five smaller rooms are arranged to show film excerpts that relate to the exhibition's title, *Watching Water*, with texts and paintings, and each room is awash with colour-coded light-reflections. The ground floor is converted into a canal with moving light. Water and electricity do not mix. We have mixed them. [. . .]

[The exhibition opens that night, and Greenaway describes the reactions – mostly positive – of the huge crowds and the art critics.] At midnight the sweating curators bravely face the crowd and offer excuses that we must close. Everyone can come back in the morning. A guard leaves the building to fetch champagne and despite the urgent knocking is not allowed in for nobody believes he is who he says he is. The policemen insist on having their photographs taken, and the champagne-guard laughs and weeps with pleasure at the largest crowd witnessed at the Fortuny in 20 years. Ten minutes later there is a violent thunderstorm and everyone is washed away. It might never have happened. **99**

The film historian Lorenzo Codelli happens to visit Venice on June 10th, and sees not only the Greenaway exhibit:

66 A short visit to Venice to attend the vernissage of the Biennale d'Arte centenary exhibition. The last one, hopefully, under our corrupt *ancien regime*. [At the Giudecca island] Wim Wenders presents a few of his electronic paintings, colourful but not so original. And Bob

Peter Greenaway at the opening of his exhibit in Venice (see his diary)

Wilson offers a wide secluded space peopled by just the head of a statue, and some bizarre echoes; you must leave your shoes outside the door. Somewhere were also artifacts by Pedro Almodóvar, but I couldn't find them. [. . .]

The ancient and decadent Palazzo Fortuny, near San Marco, was respectfully remodeled by Peter Greenaway, to host his 'Watching Water' exhibit. Helped by his usual designers, lighting and sound engineers, he is able to submerge this labyrinthine *Honey Pot* in tricks and visual delights – especially the huge and almost empty *pain- oterra*, flooded by imaginary waves.

Avant-garde film-maker Gerald Saul, a Canadian from Regina, speculates on the everyday curiosity that has animated direc- tors from Bergman to Zanussi:

❝Why do I even load the camera some days, when the majority of the time I am only wasting film stock? The key for me is curiosity. When I expose the film, I cannot help but obsess my thoughts with the curiosity of what the pho- tographed image will look like. When I was in grade school and shooting 8mm film, the waiting period, like any waiting period for a ten-year-old, seemed endless. Regina is an isolated city, with the nearest lab over 300 miles away. The thrill of receiving a developed roll in the mail could only be compared with Christmas. Although I am twenty years older and my patience is longer, when a roll of rushes arrives the first thing I must do is unravel a dozen metres of it on to the floor and squint at those 16mm images, just to make sure they are stuck to the base. I am ever fascinat- ed by the physicality of film, of touching it, smelling it, cutting it and taping it. I have taken to scratching at film, removing and destroying the image with no way of restoring it to its original state. This frightens me. The loss is real but I carry on, always in the hope that the changes I make will improve the film, and not diminish it.

Uncertainty is my mainstay. If I felt complete- ly confident that what I shoot will end up being exactly what I expected it to be, then the thrill of creating would be destroyed. The key to the film experience lies in the beauty of surprise. This must be true for the film-makers as well as the audience. Although many film-makers wish to exert absolute control over their images, I believe the struggle of predictability over chaos can never be won. I am seduced by the chance events ❞ that make a film real.

Lawrence "Lory" Smith, Director of Producer Services at the Utah Film Commission, has worked on over fifty films and TV projects including *Indiana Jones and the Last Crusade, Wind*, and *The Stand*:

❝What is it that causes those of us who find ourselves in this crazy blend of art and com- merce to continue to strive and achieve, to pitch and to perform, to labour and to love? In my mind it is that final act of magic, to sit in a crowded the- atre, in the dark, watching all those marvellous celluloid images moving, breathing, acting, living, and dying, knowing all the human effort that went into accomplishing those little bits of business, knowing full well that movies teach us about our- selves and others, take us to times and places we would never otherwise have a chance to see.

Movies help to build bridges to the lessons of our pasts, presents, and futures, forging new iden- tities, discoveries and possibilities. It is a labour to be consummately devoted to, because when it is done well it has the power to touch people's lives. In the minutiae of daily activity, of stress and hard work, it is sometimes easy to lose sight of the very thing that attracted most of the creative, bright and energetic people to this business in the first place. In the intellectual discourse of the world, movies actually matter. Bearing that in ❞ mind, may we all strive to do our best work.

Garin Nugroho is an Indonesian film director (*Love in a Slice of Bread, Letter to an Angel*:

❝When I woke up in the morning, I read the advertisements in the newspaper. I am so surprised that although our population in Indonesia amounts to 200 million, we can only produce about eight films each year, when not so long ago we were producing a hundred.

And the rest, our dreams, our way of life, our savvy, our sensuality, and our heroism are all only Hollywood's dream. We love Hollywood, we

admire its capacity to become the architect of the world. But we have to love and to talk about ourselves in this multi-cultural century. If we do not do that, and if each nation did not discuss its problems, then even more misunderstandings **99** would arise.

Roger Gnoan M'Bala is 51 years old and has been been directing films for over twenty years in the Republic of the Ivory Coast:

66 Cinema imposed itself on me rather as a desire forges itself to the mind, never to leave it. I was enthusiastic and I wanted to say

Roger Gnoan M'Bala directing actors on his film, Au nom du Christ

things that had tickled my throat for a long time.

The Ivory Coast had just celebrated its eight years of Independence. Everything was left to be said and done. I did not know that I was about to plant my feet on slippery ground. Soon the screen became darker, like the sky during a thunderstorm.

In 1972, *Amanie*, my short film, award-winner at Dinard and Carthage . . . There you are!

Then there was *Ablakon*, *Bouka*, and *Au nom du Christ*.

On the eve of the centenary of cinema: What place is there for African film, born just 34 years ago? Not even half as old as the big brother.

One must keep on fighting in spite of disillusions and lack of understanding. One must exist simply to harmonise the balance in cinema.

The late Peter Cushing became what French critics would term "an axiom" by dint of his powerful appearances in the classic Hammer films of the 1950s and 1960s, when he interpreted Frankenstein (five times), Van Helsing, and Sherlock Holmes among others:

> Fifteen days after my last birthday.
> Have toupee – would travel.
> No offers.
> Slept mostly.

Gregory Neri, a young independent film-maker (*A Weekend with Barbara and Ingrid*, *Meet the Mosaics*) from Venice, California, imagines himself in a horror movie:

> I wake up this morning, blood on my hands. I can't see where the blood has come from, but it's fresh and wet. I get up and wash my hands and notice there is mud and grass on my bare feet. I see a trail of dirty footprints leading out of my room. I follow the trail.

It leads through my kitchen, where my knife collection has been overturned. All the knives are scattered, save one: a butcher's knife, which is missing. I follow the footprints and I am suddenly in my backyard. It is a complete mess: everything has been knocked over and there are drops of blood on the grass. I follow the trail of destruction towards the trash-cans. I hesitate, staring down at

one of the cans. The flies are already in force and it is only 7 A.M. A sickening smell emanates from the can. I put my hand on the lid, my frightened eyes wander downwards, and I left the lid – and wake up.

It was only a dream. It is Thursday, June 10th, 1993. I am in my bed.

I am so upset that I do nothing for the rest of the day.

Harry Hook graduated with flying colours from Britain's National Film and Television School. He has already made features such as *The Kitchen Toto* and *Lord of the Flies*. A recce in Arizona prompts some reflections on myths and movies alike:

 Recently I have finished writing a Western, *Peacemakers*, which is set in southern Arizona during the turbulent 1880s, and I have spent the past week driving along the U.S./Mexican border to the places where my characters lived, walked, laughed and died. I wondered how much had changed in the intervening hundred and ten years. Would the indigenous Apaches or the White trailblazers of the old West recognise this land if they were alive today?

Man's voracious appetite for comfort and progress has created an endless grid of highways, gas stations, motels and mini-malls. A suffocating uniformity has become the norm. But at dusk, while heat still radiated from the walls of the buildings, I looked above the level of Tucson's neon skyline and I saw the last of the sun highlighting a dramatic, cactus-covered hillside. This place may no longer be 'wild,' but it is certainly the West.

As long as there have been movies there have always been Westerns and I'm very happy to see them return to favour in the wake of Clint Eastwood's *Unforgiven*. Tombstone (known as 'the town too tough to die') nowadays is little more than a tourist attraction with the feel of a 1950s movie set. Walking down 'Tough Nut' street it struck me just how alive Western mythology remains today. In reality Tombstone survived and flourished for a very short period: 1879-1891. After that the gold mines stopped producing and virtually everyone packed up and moved on. It

was here that the famous gun fight at the OK Corral took place. [. . .]

The history of the South-West may be revised, retold and distorted by movies but all the while the mythology is kept alive. The distinction between fact and fiction, past and present, seems ever more vague. Today one can visit the fabricated movie town of Old Tucson and act along as director, stuntman, hero or villain in a make-believe movie shootout. It seems that movie-making itself has become the stuff of myth. Go to the most out of the way place and the locals may not be able to tell you who lived there or what of interest happened there, but they'll always recall which movie used the location.

On the way out of town I stopped at the famous Boothill graveyard. My favourite epitaph rests over the grave of Les More, a man killed in a saloon gunfight.

'Here lies Les More,
4 shots from a .44
No Les, no more.'

[. . .] Leaving Arizona behind I head west for Los Angeles. In my current mood it dawns on me that Hollywood is a mining town – it's a latter-day Tombstone, 'the town too tough to die.' Suddenly I see all of us working in the film business as miners, prospectors, entrepreneurs, good-time girls, outlaws, gamblers and lawmen.

That makes me smile and I switch to the country station.

Once again, the deep frustration of hoping that this time it could be perfect – and knowing that it's far from being so.

Once again, the uncertainty of the fate of the work.

Once again, facing the insurmountable problems of working in a depleted film industry.

Once again, trying to make every monumental obstacle work to your advantage.

Once again, the ordeal of coming face to face with the final result of your labours.

Frightening.

But once again, involved in the most joyous work imaginable.

Once again, the exhilaration of cinema.

Once again coming to terrible terms with your life and finding out yet again that you thrive in the best job in the world.

Once again, hoping against hope that this time the movie will be good.

Once again, filming.

He who can live without making a movie, should not be filming.

In Mexico, director Arturo Ripstein, who began as assistant to Buñuel on *The Exterminating Angel* and won his spurs on the festival circuit with films like *Castle of Purity* and *The Holy Office*, speculates on the essence of creative cinema:

Strangely enough, on this date, I'm making a movie. It is very difficult to make films in our Third World countries. We don't earn a living from it.

I'm in the last stages of the final mix of a film called *The Beginning and the End (Principio y fin)*, based on a novel by the Egyptian writer Naguib Mahfouz.

Poor people are similar the world over.

INDEX

411

413

Contributors

The following is a list of people who supplied diaries for the book:

Ian Abbey, Bassem Abdallah, Abdel Latif Abdel Hamid, Ahmed Abdel Wahab, Asghar Abdollahi, Budiati Abiyoga, Salah Abouseif, Eric Peter Abramson, Nan Triveni Achnas, Herbert Achternbusch, Robert van Ackeren, Rafael Acosta de Arriba, Afolabi Adesanya, Percy Adlon, Margit Adorf, Behruz Afkhami, Age (Agenore Incrocci), Javier Aguirre, Jenny Agutter, Nabi Ahmed, Marianne Ahrne, Seno Gumira Ajidarma, Benny Rizal Alferthinus, Mohammad Reza Aligholi, Mary Alleguen, Alice M. Allen, John D. Allen, John Alzapiedi, Maria Christina Amaral, Suzana Amaral, Grace F. Amilbangsa, Ahmad Avand Amini, Willeke van Ammelrooy, Dev Anand, Gul Anand, Satish Anand, Allison Anders, Ivar Andersson, Claire Andrade-Watkins, Angerer der Ältere, Manuel Antin, Arnold Antonin, Michael Apted, Souhel Arafeh, M. Archibald, S.M. Ardan, Chalid Arifin, Viktor Aristov, Ejaz Arman, Matt Arnoldi, Gunnel Arrback, Ray Arthur, Konstantin Artiukhov, Rafik Al Atassi, Bhanu Athaiya, Francisco Athié, Kemala Atmojo, Shantha Attanayaka, Richard Attenborough, Michael Attree, Michelle Aubert, David Aukin, Antonio Avati, Pupi Avati, Ronit Avneri, Jim Awindor, Gabriel Axel, Kianush Ayari, Shabana Azmi, Madelaine Susanne Bååk, Amir Badie, Rakhshan Banietemad, Hasmukh Baradi, Wouter Barendrecht, John Barnett, György Báron, Zelda Barron, Peter Bart, Roman Baskin, Baback Bayat, Mia Bays, Jean Beaudry, Kabir Bedi, Rakesh Bedi, Hans Beerekamp, Dev Benegal, Shyam Benegal, Kenichi Benitani, Brian Benlifer, Jan Bernard, Elmer Bernstein, Claire Best, Shel Howard Beugen, Avril Beukes, Tim Bevan, Bahram Beyzaie, Nigol Bezjian, Dharmesh Bhatt, Alan Birkinshaw, Yvette Biro, Maureen Blackwood, Daniel Blewitt, John Bloomfield, Milena Bochet, Leslie Bohem, Claudio Bonivento, Danny Boon, John Boorman, José Luis Borau, Wolfgang Borgfeld, Martin Botha, Michel Boujut, Tait Brady, Ulf Brantås, Anja Breien, Laurel Bresnahan, Paul Brett, Sindamani Bridglal, Sid Brooks, Fred Brown, Christopher Browne, David Bruce, Nancy Buchanan, Nigel Buchanan, Subagjo Budisantoso, Peter van Bueren, Lew Bukowiecki, David Burbidge, Hugh S. Burns, Timothy Burrill, Ed Delos Santos Cabagnot, Pogus Caesar, Silvio Caiozzi García, Jaime Camino, José A.R. Cardoso, Carlos Caridad Montero, Henning Carlsen, Jay Carlyle, Jenne Casarotto, Suso Cecchi d'Amico, Youssef Chahine, Chang Chang-Yann, Chang Hung-Yi, Pedro Chaskel Benko, Basu Chatterji, Rashid Chaudhri, Khalid Saeed Chawla, Philip Cheah, Peter Chelsom, Chen Kun-Hou, Chen Pao Hsu, Angela Cheyne, Peggy Chiao, Chin Su-Mei, Alex Chomicz, Michael Chomse, Chu Tien Wen, Jim Clark, Brendan Carl Clarke, Steve Clarke-Hall, Jakob Claussen, Terry Clegg, Jennifer Clevers, Lorenzo Codelli, Jem Cohen, John Robert Cohn, Harley Cokliss, Annie Collins, Karen Collins, Leon Constantiner, Thomas Constantinides, Fliss Coombs, Karen Cooper, Roger Corman, Alain Corneau, Alberto Cortes, Judy Counihan, Paul Cox, Edgardo Cozarinsky, Nico Crama, Cornelius Crans, Stella Cranston-Fox, Robin Crichton, Jose Cuerda, Uma da Cunha, Peter Cushing, Mohammad Mehdi Dadgu, Christopher Dando, Renay Dantzler, Puran Darakhshandeh, Gira Daruwalla, Daryl E. Dasch, Buddhadeb Dasgupta, Chidananda Dasgupta, Pradip Datta, Andrée Davanture, Richard Davenport, Paul Davies, Nissim Dayan, Manet Dayrit, Mizwar Deddy, Bashir El-Deek, Margo Roan Del Vecchio, Peter Delpeut, Sylvia Denham, Nick Deocampo, András Dér, Michel Deville, John Dickie, Juan Diego, Gerrit van Dijk, Ross Dimsey, Mursi Saad El-Din, Prem Dissanayake, Dmitri Dolinin, Pino Donaggio, Jörn Donner, Bogdan-Cristian Dragan, Paul Driessen, Georges Dufaux, Peter Dunne, Ignacio Duran, Stéphane Durand, Sara Duvall, Michael Eaton, Shuntaro Emi, Ezzatollah Entezami, Majid Entezami, Abdoullah Eskandari, Roy Esperanza, Richard Eu, Richard Falcon, Gemma Fallon, Phoebe Felen, Christopher Fell, Raimund Felt, Lluis Ferrando, Susie Figgis, Nancy Fishman, Stan Fishman, Helga Fjordholm, Leah Foley, James Di Fonzo, David Forbes, Margaret Ford, Bengt Forslund, Marcia Forsyth-Grant, Christopher Fowler, Freddie Francis, Stuart Francis, Ricardo Franco, Bernhard Frankfurter, Peter Freistadt, Philip French, Peter Friedman, Miriam Gallagher, Annamaria Gallone, Soetomo Gandasoebrata, Spencer Gandley, Amrit Gangar, Adam Ganz, Alon Garbuz, Roger Garcia, José Luis García Agraz, Luis García-Berlanga, Gale Garnett, Norman Garwood, Robert Gaspard, Tatiana Gaviola Artigas, Steven Gaydos, Lisa Gaye, Mushtaq Gazdar, Romain Geib, Hans Geissendörfer, Izza Genini, K G George, Susan George, Arend de Geus, Shubhash Ghai, Faramarz Gharibian, Swapan Kumar Ghosh, Ben Gibson, Tony Giddings, Terry Gilliam, Graeme Gillies, Antony Ginnane, Samantha Glen, Robert Glinski, Kate Glover, Asha Godage, Renee Goddard, K. George Godwin, Iraj Golafshan, Menahem Golan, Shelley Goldstein, Houshang Golmakani, Adoor Gopalakrishnan, Arthur H. Gorson, Heymann Götz, Carol Gould, Ronald Gow, Gustavo Graef Marino, Tim Grafft, Neil Graham, Eitan Green, Kate Green, Peter Greenaway, David Greenberg, Jason De Groote, Val Guest, Allen Guilford, Aijaz Gul, János Gulyás, Aruna Gunarathna, S.A.L. Gunaratne, Neena Gupta, Rosemarie Gwilliam, Kamal Haasan, Ahmad Al Hadari, Petra Haffter, Paul Hainsworth, Haitham Hakki, Elmo Sydney Halliday, Barbara Hammer, Han Lan-Fang, Stephen Hance, Sumiko Haneda, Rosemary Hanes, Marion Hänsel, Kazuo Hara, Masato Hara, Lal Harindranath, Charlie Harris, Mr. Hartanto, Vanessa J. Harte, Ai M. Haryadi, Saleh Hashem, Ebrahim Hatamikia, Dag Vidar Haugen, Kaizo Hayashi, Chris Haywood, Henrik Heckmann, Hassan Hedayat, Birgit Hein, Monte Hellman, Veit Helmer, Don Henderson, Jaime Humberto Hermosillo, Taylor Hewstan, John Heyer, Sally Hibbin, Karen Higgins, Aaron Hill, Kees Hin, R.A. Hipwood, Sheikh Nazir Hissain, C.J. Hobbs, Adrian Hodges, Doug Hodges, Thom Hoffman, John Hogarth, Mark Holding, Agnieszka Holland, Nick Holland, Harry Hook, Sir Anthony Hopkins, Jane Horrocks, Rita Horst, Dr. Adel Hosni, Tom Houghton, Jason C. Hu, King Hu, Hu Yihong, Huang Jianzhong, Jack Huan-Chung Liu, Christoph Hübner, Hugh Hudson, John Hughes, Jacobus François Human, Hung Pei-Ying, Mary Ann Hushlak, Altaf Hussain, Arabella Hutter, Jill Hyem, Hans Hylkema, Jacalyn Hyman, Kim Hyón, Virgilio Iafrate, Arvo Iho, Eirik Ildahl, Kazuo Inoue, Anthony Irving, B.R. Ishara, Nazrul Islam, Steve Jaggs, Anand Jain, Stefan Jarl, Martin Jarvis, Amarnath Jayatilaka, Mahvash Jazayeri, Eric Jenks, Jiang Wen, Ray Jiing, Jaromil Jires, Roland Joffé, Stephen Jones, Ate De Jong, Erland Josephson, Reinhard Jud, Abdel El-Kader Telmissany, Jeremy Kagan, Masood Kalantari, Mahmoud Kalari, Mohamed Kamel El-Kalioubi, Hussein M. Kalla, Stefan Kamp, L. Michel Kane, Shashi Kapoor, Niniek L. Karim, Varuzh Karim-Masihi, Dr. György Kárpáti, Shaji Karun, Donald Karunaratne, Teguh Karya, Masaya Kato, Avtar K. Kaul, Brian Kaulback, Patricio Kaulen Bravo, Mika Kaurismäki, Amir Hushang Kaveh, Ömer Kavur, Naonori Kawamura, Simon Kaye, Boo-Dee Keerthisena, Buddhi Keerthisena, Sebastian Keffert, Bridget Kelly, Paddy Kelly, Hans Kemna, Ian Kerkhof, Peter Kern, Liz Kerry, Kilian Kerwin, Zsolt Kézdi-Kovács, Tullio Kezich, Alireza Khamseh, Mohamed Khan, Muhammad Ahmad Khan, Muhammad Qavi Khan, Sabiha Khanum, Zouheir Al Khiami, George Loutfi Al-Khoury, Reza Kianian, Abbas Kiarostami, Krzysztof Kieslowski, Kaljo Kiisk, Takeo Kimura, Viki King, Vincent Kinnaird, Scott Kirby, Michael Kirkup, Susan Kirr, Yuri Klimov, Matjaz Klopcic, David Kluge, Anna Kristina Knaevelsrud, John Kochman, Tomoe Kogo, Richard Kooris, Galina Kopaneva, Jahangir Kosari, Tsugunobu Kotani, N.D. Kothari, Wasanthe Kotuwella, Jeroen Krabbé, Norma Kraus, Herbert Krill, Julianus Kriswantoro, Grzegorz Krolikeiwicz, Naguib Ktiri-Idrissi, Clemens Kuby, Valentin Kuik, Kei Kumai, Rajeev Kumar, Kazuo Kuroki, Akira Kurosawa, Kwon Young Rak, Erika Laansalu, Oladipupo Ladebo, Nabyl Lahlou, Mick Lally, Ellen Sophie Lande, John Landsberg, Lang Hsiong, Dennis Lanson, Christian Lara, A. Rahim Latif, Ernst Josef Lauscher, Mark Le Fanu, Claude Maria Le Gallou, Malcolm Le Grice, Michael Leader,

Tim Leandro, Jack Lechner, Keith Ross Leckie, Moise Nkao Ze Lecourt, Lee Daw-Ming, Lee Fu-Hsiong, Lee Hsing, Monette Lee, Sang Sup Lee, Lee Tien-Yang, Lee You-Ning, Jean Pierre Lefebvre, Steven Paul Leiva, Karoliina Leon, Lau Kar Leung, Sydney Levine, Li Baotian, Li Shaohong, Pieter van Lierop, Kay Tong Lim, Melanie Lindsell, Richard Lindström, Ling Zi-Feng, Bill Linsman, Renita & Hannes Lintrop, Jan Lipsansky, Mikhail Litviakov, Gyarmathy Livia, Milan Ljubic, John F Llewellyn, Tom Loizeaux, Eva Lopez-Sanchez, Konstantin Lopushansky, Michael T. Louie, Jacques Lourcelles, Ot Louw, Lu Liping, Joshua Lucas, Daniele Luchetti, Lü Yue, Heidi Lüdi, Toni Lüdi, Niamh Lynch, Roger Gnoan M'Bala, Néjia Ben Mabrouk, Jim McBride, Andrew McCarthy, Christopher McGill, David McGillivray, David McHenry, Yvonne Mackay, Robert A. Macmillan, Larry Madden, Medhat Mahfouz, M.D. Mahindapala, John Mahony, Ian Maitland, Prabodh Maitra, Janusz Majewski, Bimal Majumber, Mohammad Malas, Buce Malawau, Mohammed Ali Maleh, Louis Malle, Poul Malmkjaer, Nils Malmros, Geoffrey T. Malone, Sandy Mandelberger, Tooraj Mansoori, Rubik Mansuri, Rein Maran, Steve Marco, Václav Marhoul, Liana Marletta, Alain Marter, Olley Maruma, Ramses Marzouk, Tanete A. Pong Masak, Pamela Mason, Ruggero Mastroianni, Shoji Masui, Richard Christian Matheson, Lawrence Matthews, Madeline Matz, Aito Mäkinen, Daniel Meadows, Ernesto Medina Torres, Dariush Mehrjui, Balan Menon, Jiri Menzel, Carole Meyers, Kofi Middleton-Mends, Raafat El-Mihi, Sergei Mikaeljan, Tahmineh R. Milani, Gavin Millar, Carol Mills, Tome Minami, Oktai Mirgasumov, Pilar Miró, Purshottam Mistri, Tracey Moffatt, Oussama Mohammed, B. Chintu Mohapatra, Sabyasachi Mohapatra, Alfred Molina, Felix Monti, Collin Moore, Cornelius Moore, Roger Moore, Gholamreza Moosavi, Hushang Moradi Kermani, Jacobo Morales, Oswald Morris, Fatemeh Motamed Arya, Lynne Motijoane, Dan Muggia, Richard Muirhead, Alena Müllerová, Anne G. Mungai, Andrew G. Munro, Shinobu Muraki, Yoshihiro Muraki, Pat Murphy, Matthew Myers, Steve Myers, Lynda Myles, Jonas Myrstrand, Masatoshi Nagase, Hashem El-Nahas, P.K. Nair, Tatsuya Nakadai, Shun Nakahara, Takehiro Nakajima, Jamshed Naqvi, Senaka Navaratne, Brian Nefsky, Kelvin Nel, Riitta Nelimarkka, Gregory Neri, Thomas Nestmann, A.S. Cecilio Neto, Jorge Neves Martins, Nicola Newman, Ng Chun Bong, Taylor Nichols, Govind Nihalani, Hideaki Nitani, Jean-Guy Noël, Syed Noor, Barry Norman, Nova Scotia Film Office, Garin Nugroho, Sergio Nunez Martinez, Colin Nutley, Václav N´yvlt, Vincent O'Donnell, Liam O'Neill, John O'Shea, Phil O'Shea, Marcie Oberndorf-Kelso, Shigeaki Oeda, Galina Ogurnaia, Jung-Wan Oh, Dr. Abdul M. Oiunelsoud, Ignacio Oliva, Maggie Ollerenshaw, Christina Olofson, Vladimir Oravsky, Nagisa Oshima, Rochelle Oshlack, Suzanne Osten, Mike Ostler, Herb Otte, Karl Otter, Ervin Ounapuu, Israel Ouval, Talvo Pabut, Volker Pade, Michele Paiva, Fridbert Pálsson, Damien Parer, Kwang-Su Park, Alan Parker, Reza Parsa, Carlos Pasini Hansen, Klára Paszternák, Gothami Pathiraja, Anand Patwardhan, Raoul Peck, Ahmad Pejman, Sean Penn, Reinhart Peschke, Miklós Peternák, Ginette Petit, Gavin Petrie, Tina Petrova, Theodore Phailbus, Gordon Phillips, Peter Pilatian, Enrique Pineda Barnet, Tama Poata, Jörg Pohl, Sydney Pollack, Janno Põldma, Lara Polop, Viliam Poltikovic, Maria Louisa Ponte, Kiumars Poorahmad, Bob Portal, Emma Porteous, Asha Posley, Steven Poster, Sally Potter, Nik Powell, Des Power, Max van Praag, Parghi Prakash, Jujur Prananto, K.L. Prasad, Gerald Pratley, Lee Pressman, Gaylene Preston, Barry Primus, Janine Prins, Peter Przygodda, Pu Cunxin, V. Purushothaman, David Puttnam, Tasheen Al Qawadri, Mustafa Qureshi, Fons Rademakers, Bob Rafelson, Bozorgmehr Rafia, Osman Ragheb, Waha Al Raheb, Laila Rakvaag, M. Ramaswamy, Iraj Raminfar, C. Umamaheswar Rao, Darren Rapier, Lars Rasmussen, Manon Rasmussen, Mostafa Rastgar, Hossein Razavi, Mr. R. Regupathy, Mohd Moinur Rehman, Allon Reich, Edgar Reitz, Simon Relph, François Renaud, Monique Renault, László L. Révész, Olof Rhodin, Arnold Rifkin, Go Riju, Arturo Ripstein, Dino Risi, Héctor Ríos, Edel Robinson, Thomas Robsahm Tognazzi, Eddie Romero, Fred Roos, Lise Roos, Kambiz Roshan-Ravan, Francesco Rosi, Kaspar Rostrup, Giuseppe Rotunno, Philippe Rousselot, Christian Routh, Peter Rowe, Brad Rushing, Homa Rusta, Ago Ruus, Jaan Ruus, Patrick Ryecart, Asis Saati, Abdolkarim Farhad Saba, Rafic Al Sabban, Taher Rahbar Saber, Shirani Sabratnam, Sayed Saeed, Riaz Ur-Rehman Saghar, Amsari Salim, Gabriele Salvatores, Dr.S.G. Samarasinghe, Otto Sander, Jorge Sanjinés, David Saperstein, Kwasi Sasu, Gerald Saul, Elvino Sauro, Claude Sautet, Ferdinando Scarfiotti, Jerry Schatzberg, Jnrgen Schau, Fred Schepisi, John Schlesinger, Volker Schlöndorff, Carl Schmitt, Ute Schneider, Guita Schyfter, Martin Scorsese, Allan Scott, David Scott, Gordon Seaman, Katy Segrove, Aparna Sen, Mrinal Sen, Mrinal Sen, Teymour Serri, R Seshadri Rajan, Islam Shahabi, Mohammed Shaheen, Shao Ruigang, Morteza Shayesteh, Dan Shea, Bill Shearer, Mohamed Shebl, Patrick Sheehan, Brendan Shehu, C. Jay Shih, Jung Won Shin, Mark Shivas, Jnri Shkubel, Ali R. Shoja Noori, Shomari Productions, Risa Shuman, Kaled M. Sidaik, Dariusz Sikora, Guillaume Silberfeld, Kurt Silberschneider, T. Chandana Silva, Malcolm Silver, Pat Silver-Lasky, Peeter Simm, Jacqueline Simons, Mary Simons, Marta Símová, Khosrow Sinai, Ingrid Sinclair, Gail Singer, Anant Singh, Catherine Sinnamon, Vilgot Sjöman, Asa Sjöström, Martin Skyba, Tony Sloman, A.R. Slote, George Sluizer, Milos Smetana, Pieter Jan Smit, Iain Smith, Lawrence "Lory" Smith, Sheamus Smith, Ana Carolina T. Soares, Hatoek Soebroto, Jaromír Sofr, Sergey Sokolov, Adeola Solanke, Giancarlo Soldi, Erpád Sopsits, Türkan Soray, Alexander Sorokin, Augustin Sotto, Ian Soutar, Mike Southon, Mária Sós, John G. Spence, Neville Spence, Penelope Spheeris, Saige Spinney, Ivan Stadtrucker, Nigel Stafford-Clark, Imelda Staunton, Pavel Stingl, Tim Stone, Julia Stoneham, Ian Stonehouse, Rod Stoneman, Vittorio Storaro, Lee Stork, Ivan Stoyanovich, David Stratton, Ulf von Strauss, Charles Sturridge, D. Gonzalo Suárez, Michael Subasinghe, Mr. V.T. Subramaniam, János Sugár, Judit Sugár, Armida Suguion-Reyna, Eva Sukova, Marselli Sumarno, Sun Zhou, Masayuki Suo, Peter Suschitzky, Lasse Svanberg, Jan Svankmajer, Carl Henrik Svenstedt, Zdenek Sverák, Dmitry Svetozarov, Jan Svoboda, James Swanson, Kathy Sykes, Maja Sylvan, Bonnie Symansky, András Szöke, Kidlat Tahimik, Kenji Takama, Tsvi Tal, Lauri Rose Tanner, Amin Tarokh, Petra Tarsanne, Bertrand Tavernier, Dean Tavoularis, Asem Tawfik, Jacqueline Taylor, Stanley T. Taylor, Sue Teddern, Christopher Tellefsen, Damir Teresak, Vishvanath Thenuwara, Jeremy Thomas, R H Thomson, Penny Thomson, Willem Thÿssen, Tiana, Gerard F. Tierney, Kevin Tierney, Syed Kaisar Tirmazi, Harimawan Tjahjadi, Yasuyoshi Tokuma, Michael Tolkin, Carol Topolski, Mark Torrance, Nestor Torre, Helena Trestíková, Christine Tseng, Tsu-Wei Lan, Shinya Tsukamoto, Tu Tu-Chih, Elbert Tuganov, Leah Tunkara, Ann S. Turner, John Kenneth Turner, Simon Fisher Turner, Jonathan Tyrrell, Hulya Uçansu, Chaerul Umam, Sule Umar, Karel Vachek, Mohammad Ebrahim Vahidzadeh, Els Vandervorst, Ben Vanos, Mita Vasishth, Jean van de Velde, Vlastimil Venclík, Pascal Verdosci, Rosa Verges Coma, Jose M. Vergés, Michael Verhoeven, Alex De Verteuil, Caroline Vié, Igor Vigdorgik, Hardi Volmer, Pantelis Voulgaris, Jnrgen Vsych, Louise Wadley, Carolyn L.A. Walker, Golda Walker, Mary Jane Walsh, Esther Walz, Chris Wang, Wei Wang, Wang Bin, Wang Hsiao-Ti, Wang Xi Zhong, Linda Peterson Warren, John Warrington, Maria Fuglevaag Warsinski, Norma Webb, Anoja Weerasinghe, Suminda Weerasinghe, Raja Weeratna, Hans de Weers, Wei Ti, Bill Weir, Wanda Wertenstein, Mike Westgate, Frans Westra, Paul Wheeler, Billie Whitelaw, Wirjo Wibowo, Laurie Wickboldt, Torgny Wickman, Putu Wijaya, Anthony Williams, Neil Wilson, Michael Winner, Bob Wittenbach, Jeanne C. Wolf, Arthur N.T. Wong, Edmond Wong Kin Yip, Karl John Woods, Stephen Woolley, Harry Wordon, Elizabeth Wrenn, Avery Wright, Wu Wen Guang, Wu Ziniu, Xia Gang, Edward Yang, Chung-Fan Yang, Chihyen Yee, Hung-Ya, Harun Yeshayai, Jef Yorsten, Kiju Yoshishige Yoshida, Hidetaka Yoshioka, Michiyo Yoshizaki, Christopher Young, Siraj Zaidi, Krzysztof Zanussi, Bernardino Zapponi, Alireza Zarrindast, Noureddin Zarrinkelk, Sameer Zekra, Mai Zetterling, Zhang Yuan, Zhao Jiping, Zheng Dongtian, Zhou Xiaowen, Regina Ziegler, Nils Zurawski, Erik van Zuylen

PHOTOGRAPHIC ACKNOWLEDGEMENTS

Page 7 Sarah Quill/BFI Stills; 10 K.C. Bailey; 12-13 Deana Newcombe © 20th Century Fox; 14 River Phoenix, BFI Stills, Posters and Designs;15 Joyce Rudolph© New Line Cinema; 16-17 Joyce Rudolph, © New Line Cinema; 19 © Electric Shadow Productions; 20-21 Felix Adlon; 22 *Ride in the Whirlwind*, BFI Stills, Posters and Designs; 24 *A Touch of Zen*, BFI Stills, Posters and Designs; 26-27 *The Cronos Device*, BFI Stills, Posters and Designs, © Ventana Films; 31 *Satyricon*, BFI Stills, Posters and Designs; 34 Josef Rezac, © Portobello Pictures; 37 *Epilogo*, BFI Stills, Posters and Designs; 39 *The Nasty Girl*, BFI Stills, Posters and Designs; 39 © Mainline Pictures; 42 Krzysztof Wellman; 44-45 Marta Sentis; 46 Marta Sentis; 48-49 © Taipei Golden Horse Film Festival; 56 Holly Gilliam; 57 Terry Gilliam; 58 Liam Longman © Samuelson Productions; 60-61 *The Seduction of Joe Tynan*, BFI Stills, Posters and Designs; 61-62 David Bailey, © Warner Bros. Ltd; 63 *Brideshead Revisited*, BFI Stills, Posters and Designs; 64 Miriam Gallagher; 65-66 Paul Gaster; 68 Su Santa De; 71 *I am Curious Yellow*, BFI Stills, Posters and Designs; 75-6 V Egorov; 80 *Wittgenstein*, BFI Stills, Posters and Designs; 82-4 Katalin Volcanszky; 88-89 *Farewell My Concubine*, BFI Stills, Posters and Designs; 96 Moira Conway; 98 Richard Blanshard; 102 © 1993 Cinergi Productions N.V.; 104-5 © Afravision; 111 Mary Ann Camilleri; 116-7 *Apocalypse Now*, BFI Stills, Posters and Designs; 120-1 Parallax Pictures; 122-3 *Frenzy*, BFI Stills, Posters and Designs; 126-7 Fabrizio Marchesi, © PhotoMovie; 129 Bertrand La Foret; 129 Keith Hamshere, © Shadowlands Productions; 134 © Mayfair Entertainment International; 138 Ben Glass; 146 Kerry Hayes; © Skreba/Creon Films Ltd; 147-8 © Film Barcelona Inc; 150-1 Simon Annand; 153 David Appleby; 154-5 © Columbia Pictures 1993; 157 © Illumination Films; 156-7 © Illumination Films; 158 *Three Colours: Blue*, BFI Stills, Posters and Designs; 160 Pief Weyman; 165-6 Subhash Nandy for both; 169 Gil Hanley; 170-1 © Electric Pictures; 172-3 © Metro Tartan; 174-5 *Leon the Pig Farmer*, BFI Stills, Posters and Designs; *The Snapper*, © BBC; 177-8 © Columbia Tristar Films Sellschaft MbH; 178 MK II Diffusion; 181 *Orlando*, BFI Stills, Posters and Designs; 182 © Jacques Happe; 183-5 © Academy Entertainment Inc; 186-7 © Nation Newspapers Ltd; 189-90 © Elena Seibert; 193 © The Chronicle; 196-7 © Geoffrey Malone; 198 © Cinema City; 199 *Falling Down*, BFI Stills, Posters and Designs; 200 Smura Davidson; 201-202 © Frameline (for Mala Noche), © Haruko 1993 (for cinema print); 205 Alexandria International Film Festival; 208 Eva Lopez-Sanchez; ref; 211 Angelo Novi; 211 David Appleby; 212 © Concord New Horizon's Corporation; 214 Redmond Morris, © Warner Bros. Productions Ltd; 216 © BBC; 219 © Daici Co. Ltd; 219 © Kang Woo Suk Productions; 220-1 © Regina Ziegler Film Produktion; 222-3 © Figaro Films S.A.; 224-5 *Closely Observed Trains*, BFI Stills, Posters and Designs; 227 © Babelsburg Studios; 229 *Four Weddings and a Funeral*, BFI Stills, Posters and Designs; 231-2 © Atria; 235 Erik Heinila, © 1993 Turner Pictures Incorporated; 236 *Carlito's Way*, BFI Stills, Posters and Designs, © Universal Pictures 1993; 237-9 © UNICEF 1992, Horst Cerni, © UNICEF; 244 Fu Jia; 250-1 Vishvanath Thenuwara; 253-4 Marco Carosi; 255-6 Françoise Duhamel, © Columbia Studios 1993; 257 *Wall of Silence* , BFI Stills, Posters and Designs; 261 *Natural Born Killers*, BFI Stills, Posters and Designs; 262-3 Kengo Tarumi; 264 Allen Guilford; © Allen Guilford; 270 Jeremy Gibbs; 273 John Johansen; 275 Jörg Pohl, © Jörg Pohl; 276-7 © Flying Pictures; 278-281 Shao Ruigang, © Beijing Library; *Crying Game*, BFI Stills, Posters and Designs; 285 *Evil Dead III – Army of Darkness*, BFI Stills, Posters and Designs, © Guild Film Distribution Ltd; 286 *Cliffhanger*, BFI Stills, Posters and Designs; 287 1916 Censor Certificate, BFI Stills, Posters and Designs ; 288-9 *Red Rock West*, BFI Stills, Posters and Designs; Barbara Hammer; 290 *Lolo*, BFI Stills, Posters and Designs; 292 Geoffrey Nelson [portrait]; Barbara Hammer [two actors]; 293 British Board of Film Certification; 294 © Variety; 295 *Sleepless in Seattle*, BFI Stills, Posters and Designs; 296 *The Cronos Device*, BFI Stills, Posters and Designs; 297 *My Own Private Idaho*, BFI Stills, Posters and Designs; 298 *Fire in the Sky*, BFI Stills, Posters and Designs; 299 *Wild Strawberries*, BFI Stills, Posters and Designs; *Party Girl*, BFI Stills, Posters and Designs; 301 *Scent of the Green Papaya*, BFI Stills, Posters and Designs; 303 *King of the Children*, BFI Stills, Posters and Designs; 304 Puspen Abri, Dian Handoyo, © Jakarta-Jakarta; 305 *Pather Panchali*, BFI Stills, Posters and Designs; 307 *2001*, BFI Stills, Posters and Designs; 307 *Dances with Wolves*, BFI Stills, Posters and Designs; 309 Gerrit Van Dijk; 310 © Paul Driessen and Nico Crama; 311 © Riita Nelimarkka; 312/3 Rebecca Rees, © Rees/Leiva Productions, © Betty Boop Art Copyright 1993, King Features/Fleischer Studios [artwork behind]; 314-5 *Fanny and Alexander*, BFI Stills, Posters and Designs; 314-5 'Sofia' Animated Film Studio; 317 Stefan Jarl; 318-9 © Co Film 1994; 321 Roger Neckles, © Pearl and Dean (Caribbean); 322 Khan Film 1994; 322 Arnold Antonin (for all); 327-8 Jorge Sanjinés, © Grupo Ukaman; 329 *Hour of the Star*, BFI Stills, Posters and Designs; 331-3 © Maxima Film; 334-5 *Hollywood to Hanoi*, BFI Stills, Posters and Designs; 336 National Film Archive of Taiwan, © Xin Hua Company; 337 National Film Archive of Taiwan, © United China Motion Picture Corporation [top], National Film Archive of Taiwan, © Hua Tsun Film company; 338 *Crime Wave*, BFI Stills, Posters and Designs, *Spy Ring*, BFI Stills, Posters and Designs; 339 BFI Stills, Posters and Designs; 341 *Sounder*, BFI Stills, Posters and Designs; 342 Bob Portal; 343 *Alphaville*, BFI Stills, Posters and Designs; 344 *Kes*, BFI Stills, Posters and Designs; 345 *Indecent Proposal*, BFI Stills, Posters and Designs; 346 *Jungle Fever*, BFI Stills, Posters and Designs; 347 *Ashes and Diamonds*, BFI Stills, Posters and Designs; 348 © Universidad del Cine; 350 *Shoeshine*, BFI Stills, Posters and Designs; 352 National Film Archive of India; 353 National Film Archive of India; 353 Peter Smith; 356 Michael Birt, © Channel Four Television; 357 Alex Bailey, © UIP; 358-9 D Stevens, © New Line Cinema Corporation; 361 © Lynda Myles; 363 © Mr Kawakita; 365 *Un Coeur en Hiver*, BFI Stills, Posters and Designs; 366 *Five Easy Pieces*, BFI Stills, Posters and Designs; 367 *Midnight Cowboy*, BFI Stills, Posters and Designs; 368 *The Chant of Jimmy Blacksmith*, BFI Stills, Posters and Designs; 368-9 David Geraghty, courtesy of Heald and Weekly Times; 370 *Mozart Brothers*, BFI Stills, Posters and Designs; 371 *Prague*, BFI Stills, Posters and Designs; 372 *Poachers*, BFI Stills, Posters and Designs; 373 © F2 Co. Ltd; 374 *Language of Love*, BFI Stills, Posters and Designs; 375 *Secret Places*, BFI Stills, Posters and Designs; 376 *The Firm*, BFI Stills, Posters and Designs; 380 © Pilar Miro; 381 *Serie Noire*, BFI Stills, Posters and Designs; 383 © Siddik Productions; 384 © Siddik Productions; 385 © Ebun Alesh; 386-7 © Producciones Arte Nuevo S.A. Mexico; 389 © Agenzia Fotogiornalistica; 390 *Die Zweite Heimat*, BFI Stills, Posters and Designs; 394 © Andrea Films; 395 © Andrea Films; 396-7 © Jacques Prayer, Little Bear; 398-9 *L.627*, BFI Stills, Posters and Designs; 401 © Allarts

Colour section: pageI E Heinta; © Turner Pictures International; II Moira Conway; IV Kengo Tarumi; V © Geoffrey Malone; VI © Concord New Horizon's Corp; XII © Producciones Arte Nuevo SA. Mexico; VII © Regina Ziegler Film Production; X Harry Hook; XI J Stiver; © US National Park Service, Sanat Monica Mountains National Recreation Area; XII © Siddik Productions; XII Kerry Hayes; ©Skreba/Creon Films; XIII © Andrea Films; XIV Darren Michaels; © 1993 New Line Cinema; XV Stefan Jarl; XVI © Figaro Films; Angelo Novi, © Buena Vista International

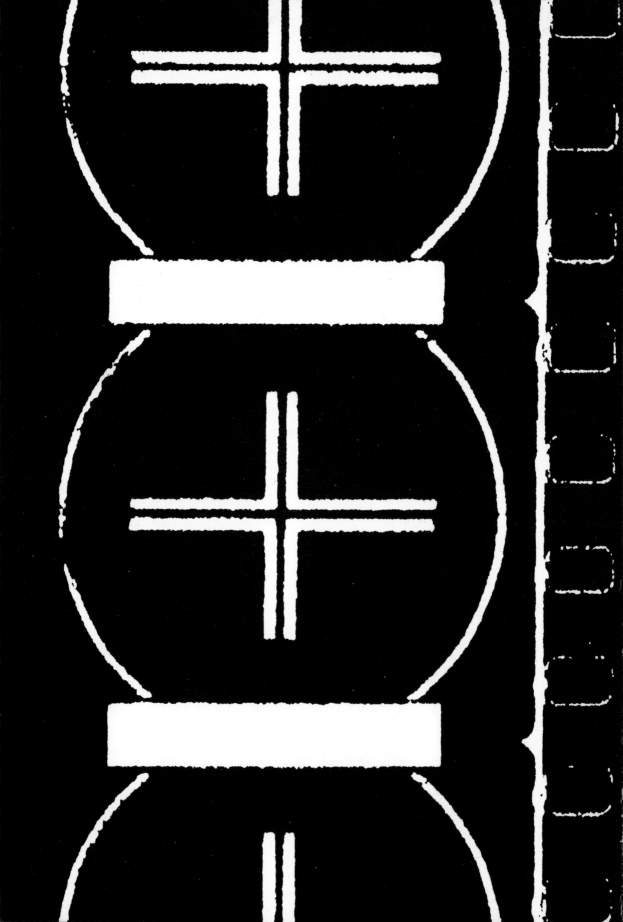